# An American Musical Dynasty

# *An American Musical Dynasty*

A Biography of the Wolle Family
of Bethlehem, Pennsylvania

by

Paul S. Larson

Bethlehem: Lehigh University Press
London: Associated University Presses

© 2002 by Rosemont Publishing & Printing Corp.

All rights reserved. Authorization to photocopy items for internal or personal use, or the internal or personal use of specific clients, is granted by the copyright owner, provided that a base fee of $10.00, plus eight cents per page, per copy, is paid directly to the Clearance Center, 222 Rosewood Drive, Danvers, Massachusetts 01923. [0-934223-68-8/02 $10.00 + 8¢ pp, pc.]

Associated University Presses
440 Forsgate Drive
Cranbury, New Jersey 08512

Associated University Presses
16 Barter Street
London WC1A 2AH, England

Associated University Presses
P.O. Box 338, Port Credit
Mississauga, Ontario
Canada L5G 4L8

The paper used in this publication meets the requirements of the American National Standards for Permanence of Paper for Printed Library Materials Z39.48–1984.

**Library of Congress Cataloging-in-Publication Data**

Larson, Paul, 1932-
   An American musical dynasty : a biography of the Wolle family / by Paul S. Larson.
      p. cm.
   Includes bibliographical references (p.  ) and index.
   ISBN 0–934223–68–8 (alk. paper)
   1. Wolle family. 2. Musicians–Pennsylvania–Bethlehem–Biography. 3. Music–Pennsylvania–Bethlehem–History and criticism. 4. Church music–Moravian Church in America. Church music–Pennsylvania–Bethlehem. I. Title.
ML385.L365 2002
780'.92'273--dc21                                           00-069162
[B]                                                                             CIP

Set in 11 on 13 pt. Galliard at the Lehigh University Press.
Designed by Philip A. Metzger.

PRINTED IN THE UNITED STATES OF AMERICA

To Barbara,
who asked me to tell this story,

And to Jan, my wife,
who helped me tell it correctly.

# Contents

List of Illustrations     9

Acknowledgments     11

Introduction     13

## Section I. Peter Wolle: Founder of a Dynasty

1. A Moravian Novice     21
2. Serving as a Teacher     47
3. Serving as a Musician and a Composer     59
4. Service Completed     94

## Section II. Theodore Wolle: Continuing the Legacy in the Midst of Change

5. Gaining a Tradition     109
6. Transforming the Tradition     130

## Section III. John Frederick Wolle: Bach for Americans

7. Mastering the "Divine Art"     167
8. Creating The Bach Choir     192
9. Creating a Bach Festival     237
10. J. Fred. Wolle: Academic and Organ Virtuoso     285

11. Church Composer ... 324
12. Permanently in Bethlehem ... 341

## Appendices

A. Compositions by Peter Wolle ... 377
B. Compositions by Theodore Wolle ... 392
C. Compositions by J. Fred. Wolle ... 395
D. Glossary ... 407
E. Chronological Listing of Positions Held by Peter,
    Theodore, and J. Fred. Wolle ... 409
F. Genealogical Table of the Musical Wolles ... 411

Bibliography ... 412

Index ... 421

# Illustrations

| | |
|---|---|
| 1. Peter Wolle, 1792–1871 | 20 |
| 2. View of Nazareth, Pa., 1795 | 24 |
| 3. Nazareth Hall Square after 1841 | 35 |
| 4. Page from *Hymn Tunes*, Peter Wolle | 82 |
| 5. Central Moravian Church, Bethlehem, after 1867 | 88 |
| 6. Theodore Francis Wolle, 1832-1885 | 108 |
| 7. Chapel of the Bethlehem Women's Seminary, Late 19th c. | 126 |
| 8. Program from Philharmonic Society | 137 |
| 9. Choir Loft and Original Organ, Christmas 1861, Central Moravian Church, Bethlehem | 149 |
| 10. "Asleep in Jesus," Theodore Wolle | 154 |
| 11. J. Fred. Wolle, 1863-1933 | 166 |
| 12. Jedediah Weiss, 1878; J. Fred Wolle's Grandfather | 169 |
| 13. Francis Wolle, J. Fred. Wolle's Father | 172 |
| 14. J. Fred. Wolle with His Mother, Sisters and Brothers | 174 |
| 15. Cover from the Mass in B Minor Premiere Program | 228 |
| 16. The Bach Choir on the Steps of Central Moravian Church, 1803 | 264 |
| 17. Central Moravian Church Trombone Choir on the Steps of the Central Moravian Church | 268 |
| 18. J. Fred. Wolle's Birthplace and Meeting Place for the Bach Choir Board, Church Street Bethlehem | 273 |
| 19. J. Fred. Wolle at the Organ Console, St. Louis World's Fair | 300 |
| 20. Charles Schwab, President of Bethlehem Steel Corp. | 318 |

21. Henry Drinker, President of Lehigh University                348
22. Packer Memorial Church, Lehigh University, Bethlehem         351
23. J. Fred. Wolle Conducting the Bach Choir, Packer
    Memorial Church, 1917                                        354
24. Central Moravian Trombone Choir in the Belfry of
    Central Moravian Church, Bethlehem                           359

## Acknowledgments

FOR EXPERT ASSISTANCE and advice whenever I needed it, I wish to thank those in charge of the Moravian institutions that hold documents related to the Wolles: Rev. Vernon H. Nelson, archivist, and Rev. Albert H. Frank, assistant archivist, The Moravian Archives in Bethlehem, Pennsylvania; Rev. Thomas Minor, head of Reeves Library, Moravian College, Bethlehem, Pennsylvania; Susan Dreydoppel, director, Moravian Historical Society, Nazareth, Pennsylvania; Jan Ballard, curator, Moravian Museum in Bethlehem; Jean Doherty of the Lititz Moravian Archives, Lititz, Pennsylvania; Dr. Nola Reed Knouse, director, Moravian Music Foundation, Winston-Salem, North Carolina. Marie Boltz, Special Collections, Lehigh University, Bethlehem, Pennsylvania, was eager to supply me with anything I needed regarding Lehigh University – including parking permits. Without the help of people at all levels of administration in the North Carolina State Archives, I would not have been able to flesh out the years Theodore Wolle taught in the South. The research librarians at the Chicago Public Library were most helpful with material related to the World's Columbian Exposition, Chicago, 1891–1893. My thanks also to Moravian College for a sabbatical leave to work on writing this book.

I am deeply indebted to a number of individuals who contributed in various ways to the completion of this book. My good friends Dr. Herbert Rubenstein and Dr. Barbara Wright read the manuscript in its early stages. Herbert gave me valuable and thoughtful advice of all sorts, and Barbara searched for ways I could make the players in this story vital people. Both became nearly as interested in the lives of these

Wolles as I was. An author cannot ask for more. Three members of the Wolle family were particularly generous. Mrs. Robert Taylor gave me a number of her husband's books on Bethlehem history. As a result, most information I needed was constantly at my fingertips. Mrs. Jane Hammond was always delightful and supplied family photographs. Her sister, Mrs. Mary Baker, shared her devoted genealogical work with me. Mrs. John Ferguson, a relative of Dorothy Doster, was most helpful in talking with me about the crucial role Mrs. Doster played in founding The Bach Choir and instigating and preparing the American premiere of Bach's Mass in B Minor. That Mrs. Doster was *the* true founder of the choir is now perfectly clear. Finally, Robert Steelman, Moravian College Music Department, always made himself available when I needed help in translating from German script.

    I was truly fortunate that members of my immediate family gladly accepted Peter, Theodore, and J. Fred. Wolle into our inner circle. Jan, my wife, was particularly welcoming, and my nieces, Nora and Laura Bellows, wept with me as I read to them about the wonderful communities the Moravians had created so that these men could flourish.

    That my idea became a manuscript, which then became a book, is largely due to Dr. Philip Metzger, Lehigh University Press, my editor, and to Mrs. Judith Mayer, his assistant. Both of them beautifully maintained that delicate balance between encouragement and exactness. They were always patient, polite, gracious, and believed in the importance of my subject.

    Finally, I must express my admiration for the Moravian legacy that has surrounded me daily for over twenty years. I have derived constant pleasure and inspiration from the community these Wolles helped make into such a beautiful place. It has been a privilege to have worked and lived where they worked and lived. I am confident that Bethlehem will continue to nourish me, as it did them, for the rest of my life.

Paul S. Larson<br>Bethlehem, Pa.

## *Introduction*

THE WOLLE FAMILY of Bethlehem formed a multigenerational musical dynasty rare in the history of Western music. From 1800 to 1933 they produced three outstanding musicians, beginning with Peter Wolle, a notable composer and performer whose lifelong musical contributions continued beyond his call as a Moravian pastor and bishop. Theodore, his son, also became a prominent and versatile musician and teacher; the most lasting musical achievement of the family, however, was made by John Frederick Wolle, nephew of Theodore, who became the first conductor of the Bach Choir in Bethlehem, Pa., and the founder of the first Bach Festival in America, which the Bach Choir of Bethlehem still presents each spring.

For their entire lives, Peter, Theodore, and J. Frederick served the Moravian Church as organists, choirmasters, composers of sacred music, music teachers, and instrumentalists. Through their impact on the Moravian music tradition, the founding and continuation of the first Bach Choir and the first Bach Festival in America, the family has exercised significant influence on the history of music in America.

The activities of the Wolle dynasty mirrored a profound change in Moravian culture, as the Moravians adapted to ever-encroaching democratization, commercialization, and secularization. They ceased to be explicit cultural leaders in their communities, which were being overtaken by extremely wealthy, capitalistic newcomers.

Moravians had founded their communities in the 1730s and 1740s as Christocratic communes with Christ as the Chief Elder. Usually, the towns were closed to non-Moravians. The residents, all members of the worldwide mission of the Moravian Church, were missionaries themselves, or provided basic needs for those in the mission fields, furnished shelter for church visitors, and instructed the children. They worshiped God together until each member of the community "fell asleep in Christ."

Peter Wolle was raised in the closed community of Nazareth, Pennsylvania; his wife grew up in a similar community: Salem, North Carolina. They married and ministered to Moravian congregations in North Carolina and in Pennsylvania. As the nineteenth century unfolded, however, Salem and Bethlehem became the two administrative centers of the Moravian Church in America and experienced similar, profound transformations. From tightly controlled religious communities, each became a city of power and wealth based on industrial capitalism. Salem grew into a center of the American tobacco industry, and Bethlehem became the site of The Bethlehem Steel Corporation, the nation's second largest steel producer.

Peter was excited by the changes he witnessed. To him they meant progress. During the Civil War, Theodore, employed in the South, worked within these changes to become the family's first independent musician. By the time J. Frederick became an adult, these economic and social forces had reached fruition. He understood the changes well and, skillfully shaping them to his advantage, he brilliantly capitalized on both the growing industrial wealth and the secular musical need they produced. Still remaining a devout Moravian, he promoted, performed, and conducted the music of Johann Sebastian Bach throughout America.

While Peter, Theodore, and J. Frederick shone as musical leaders, other Wolles established, managed, and contributed to industries that developed in Bethlehem. Augustus Wolle bought an iron deposit near Bethlehem. Rather than erect blast furnaces at the mine, he built them along the Lehigh River across from the center of Bethlehem, making the area the site for future steel making. In 1860, he became the president of the board of The Bethlehem Rolling Mills and Iron Company.

Then, Asa Packer, founder of the Lehigh Valley Rail Road, which transported hard coal to Philadelphia and New York City, joined the board. Packer lacked high-grade durable rails and wanted Wolle's company to manufacture them for his railroad. Soon the majority of the board represented Packer's interest, and The Bethlehem Rolling Mills began producing rails. Wolle's company produced much more than steel rails and soon became The Bethlehem Steel Corporation with worldwide sales of iron and steel. Packer also selected Bethlehem as the administrative center of his railroad empire. Almost overnight, Bethlehem became a place of wealth and political influence.

Asa Packer next founded a university on the hill above his rail center and Wolle's iron company. While one purpose of the university was to train men to run this rapidly expanding complex, Packer made it clear he had established a university and not a school of engineering. Religion and the humanities, including music, held important places in the education of the young men who attended there.

While Peter and Theodore watched the growth of this industrial/university enterprise, Lehigh University and The Bethlehem Steel Corporation figured most prominently in the musical career of J. Frederick. He was Lehigh University's first professor of music, organist, and choir director, and Lehigh became the permanent home of The Bach Choir and the site of the annual Bach Festival. Henry Drinker, Lehigh's president from 1905 to 1920, promoted the choir on his campus, and Charles Schwab, President of Bethlehem Steel at the same time, both eagerly supported the choir's performances and generously contributed money and influence to its activities.

The Bethlehem Steel Corporation became one of the nation's leading steel producers, and the Bach Festivals became one of the nation's leading musical events. Thus, Bethlehem came to occupy a significant position in American industrial and artistic life through most of the twentieth century.

Prominence in music and industry was not new to Bethlehem. Neither was a close relationship between the two. Industry and musical culture were interrelated from the beginning, because for nearly a century after its founding, everything in Bethlehem had been owned and sponsored by the Moravian Church. Colonial leaders who visited Bethlehem to witness its progressive industries praised the music they heard throughout the town. The Wolle family reflected this interdependence of music and industry. Correctly summarizing the play of these forces, a Wolle wrote

> So it goes. In the last half of the nineteenth century the old culture of Bethlehem [the culture of the Moravian Church] and the new one of business and industry became represented within the Wolle family. Francis [father of J. Frederick] and J. Fred. identified with the old; Augustus and Clarence A. [one of the first graduates of Lehigh University] with the new. One group made money; the other spent it. One made "culture"; both enjoyed it. Both were creative...each needed the other, not as audience and client, but as source[s] of inspiration.[1]

While the musical culture so essential to Moravian communities was unique in America, those communities were not isolated. Thus, the careers of these Wolle musicians came to mirror the fundamental shift in the patronage of sacred music that occurred in America during the nineteenth century, as performance and its support moved from church to academe and concert hall. Major factors in that transformation were the growing secularization of Western society and the great wealth that industrial capitalism generated. While Peter remained a Moravian cleric, Theodore, his son, was a music professor and a concert pianist and violinist. Though a devoted Moravian, he served other Protestant denominations as an organist and choirmaster. J. Frederick, also a lifelong Moravian, was a music professor, an organist, and choirmaster serving Episcopal, Lutheran, and Methodist churches, and was one of America's great virtuoso organists. Mainly, he conducted The Bach Choir, a choir with no religious affiliation but with vital connections to The Bethlehem Steel Corporation and Lehigh University.

In this biography I have tried to present persuasive evidence for the view that the Wolle family was an important agent in the development of American musical culture. At the same time, I want to describe ways in which Western musical practice and American social currents played out in the lives of members of the Wolle family. Finally, it was my intention to focus the lens of a historical revisionist on their musical lives. That nineteenth-century Idealism was foolish is not supported by the activities and creations of the Wolles. These musical Idealists composed works and led performances of high quality throughout the nineteenth and well into the twentieth century. In addition, the view that the American Moravian music tradition was not limited to the eighteenth century should become evident as the Wolles's story is told.

## NOTE

1. "The Wolle Genealogy," "Concluding Remarks." Unpublished typescript in the author's possession.

*Part One*

Peter Wolle: Founder of a Dynasty

Peter Wolle, 1792–1871
(Jane Hammond)

Chapter One

## *A Moravian Novice*

"We can give nothing before we have something."
—From a talk given by Nikolaus Ludwig von Zinzendorf.[1]

DURING THE SUMMER of the year 1795, Brother and Sister Wolle traveled from their mission station in the Virgin Islands to Nazareth, Pennsylvania, with their three-year-old son, Peter. His parents brought him to Nazareth, a Moravian community, to enroll him in the Nazareth Day School, where he would begin his Moravian education. Peter's parents were insuring he would be correctly and fully inducted into the *Unitas Fratrum*, the Church of the United Brethren. Also, Christian Jacob, Peter's older brother, was to be admitted to Nazareth Hall as a boarding student. He had resided with Brother and Sister Moehring, managers of the general store in Nazareth, while he attended the day school. Christian was old enough to begin the second level of Moravian education. His time with the Moehrings had worked out well. Br. and Sr. Wolle were pleased, so they arranged for Peter to take his brother's place. As Christian left the Moehrings for Nazareth Hall, Peter moved in with them as his new parents.[2]

The Protestant sect the Wolles were members of had originated in Moravia and experienced a renewal in Saxony on the estate of Count Ludwig von Zinzendorf. Almost immediately these Moravians established missions throughout the world, including colonial America and islands in the Caribbean. In the year 1740, Moravians went to the northeastern frontier of Pennsylvania to build a school for Negro children on a "barony" owned by James Whitefield, the famous minister. Later they purchased the barony called Nazareth and promptly built Bethlehem in 1741 on its southern border. For many years, the two communities were one; however, when Peter arrived in Nazareth, they were nominally separate. Both communities were closed to outsiders. All property belonged to the Moravian Church, and businesses and trades were community-owned. Each town was organized into groups of single women, single men, married men, married women, boys and girls, and children. These groups were called choirs. By Peter's arrival, families lived together. Children were educated in Moravian beliefs and practices in special schools. While each community had a day school for children, a boarding school for girls was in Bethlehem, and one for boys was in Nazareth.

Peter did not see his parents again for seventeen years. This early separation from them affected him profoundly. Later, when he was a teacher, one of his pupils was separated from his parents. Peter was so moved that he wrote in his diary, "The boy is destined for Nazareth Hall. Poor boy, he is to be pitied, as there is very little hope to be entertained that he will again see his parents, his father intends to send him to Germany, that he may there continue his studies."[3] Near the end of his life, Peter again recalled his early separation and confided, "To have been separated at so early an age, and for so long a time . . . from my parents, was an experience which I often lamented as interfering with the development of the finer feelings of filial love."[4]

Peter's Moravian education began in earnest as he learned six lessons that were required for membership in the Moravian *Bruedergemeine*. The first came soon after Peter began to feel at home with Br. and Sr. Moehring. It was one of the most painful lessons he would face.

### The First Lesson: The Meaning of Life and Death

Socialization is a "process in which a novice transitions toward becoming a member of a social group." This process is one in which cultural bases of social life as well as what constitutes competency in membership in a social group are consistently communicated to the novice.[5]

Four members of the trombone choir climbed the spacious stairs of the Nazareth *Gemeinhaus*. Carrying a trombone the size of a trumpet, the first trombonist took a card marked *Sopran* from a wooden rack on the wall beside the stairs. The musical notes on the card were beautifully drawn. The player attached the card to his instrument, opened the door, and stepped onto the balcony. A broad river valley appeared. Forested mountains far to the south outlined the end of the valley against the sky.

The next Brother carried a slightly larger trombone. He took the card marked *Alt* from the rack, attached it to his instrument, and followed onto the balcony. The Brother with the tenor trombone took his card, and the man with the largest trombone, the bass, did the same. The door closed as each took his place.

The four trombonists looked at the beautiful town below them. The square in front of the *Gemeinhaus* was bordered on one side by the Single Sisters' *Chorhaus*, on the other by God's Acre, the cemetery. To the left, the houses of the Nazareth families surrounded a second square. Gardens, pastures, and trees arranged in patterns surrounded the community. Visitors to Nazareth often commented on its beauty.

Silently the trombone choir prepared to transmit a message from God. Each inhaled deeply. As they began to play, the *Passion Chorale* sounded. Christ's announcement spread over the valley. One of the Moravian brothers had "fallen asleep in Christ," it said.

*From our band a Pilgrim's gone*
*Before us to his rest:*
*We all are nearing to that home,*
*His lot is with the blest.*

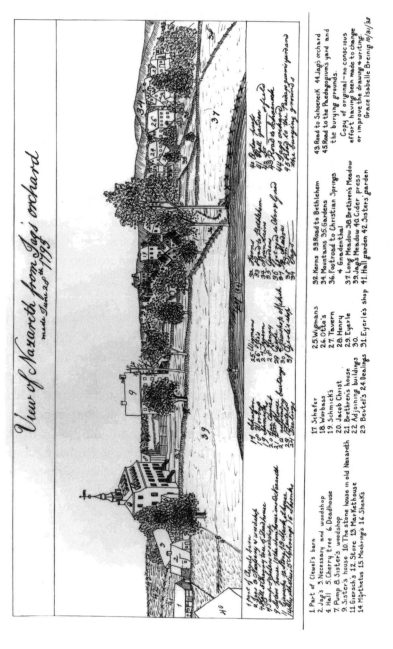

View of Nazareth, Pa., 1795. Note Moehring's House, no. 15
(Moravian Historical Society)

Everyone stopped immediately, gripped by the message the trombones were delivering. Their message forced each person to think about the meaning of life and death. Little Peter Wolle watched those around him and knew that he must also listen to the trombones and understand what they were saying. They taught him his first Moravian lesson: "Death was the most desired state. Live your life preparing for it."

The second chorale sounded, and everyone recognized its message immediately. A married brother had passed on.

*Jesus ne'er my soul can leave,*
*This is my consolation,*
*And my body in the grave,*
*Rest in hope and expectation,*
*That this mortal flesh shall see*
*Incorruptibility.*
*The first chorale repeated, and it touched every heart.*
*When I shall gain permission*
*To leave this mortal tent,*
*And gain from pain dismission,*
*And let me when expiring*
*Recline upon Thy breast*
*Eternal life and rest.*

The first chorus was repeated, and when the trombones ceased, everyone listened as the valley grew still and peaceful.

Each player watched spring spread again over the valley as if from another world. Without a word the brothers turned, passed through the door, returned their music to the rack, and replaced their trombones in the storage cabinet. The announcement of the passing of Peter's surrogate father was complete. Brother Moehring was "asleep in Jesus."

Br. John's body was moved from his home into the corpse house. Peter went there with Sr. Moehring "to gaze upon the face before its final disappearance in the earth."[6] Br. Moehring's body was attired in white, "the garb of death expressive of peace and joy to the soul departed."⁷ During the night a light burned "for the lifeless body, still within the precincts of the living."⁸

As Sr. Moehring and Peter sat in the *Saal* with the rest of the community, everyone singing dirges and hymns, Peter heard the important events in Br. Moehring's spiritual journey on earth as his memoir was read. The *Gemeine* left the *Saal* and stood before the corpse house singing hymns accompanied by the trombones. The body was taken up, and the musicians led the procession to God's Acre. Standing at the grave site, everyone sang with the trombones, as the body was lowered into the ground beside the graves of the other married men who had "passed on." Flat stones marked their graves "while the bodies of the departed sleep beneath the turf, adorned with smiling flowers, expressive of heaven and typical of its realized joys, the living footsteps are seen to pace the walks above, with thoughts chastened by the sacred spot."⁹

The living returned to the *Saal* for a love feast, a sacred song service without a sermon when bread and a beverage were served. When Peter went to live with the Moehrings in the fall of 1795, they were strangers, but they soon became his new parents. Now, Peter had lost two fathers within a year; his real father to the temporary earthly mission, and Brother Moehring to the lasting Heavenly Kingdom.

Sixty years later, Peter, then a Bishop, attended a reunion at Nazareth Hall and heard a fellow alumnus describe the meaning of life and death the trombones had taught him when he was four years old. The speaker said

> I cannot refrain from turning to all to remind them that there is another and an eternal [reunion] . . . at hand; and that it is infinitely better, infinitely greater and more glorious. Oh that all of us, from the youngest former scholar even to the eldest, could but have a share therein, and meet again before the "throne of God and of the Lamb!"¹⁰

Peter Wolle echoed these beliefs himself when he lay dying. His family gathered around him heard him say he was going to his Saviour. To one of them, who said that he might not yet be received, he remarked, with great assurance: "No!—that will not be the case." He had the desire to depart and to be with Christ, which is far better. In the morning he said to one of his sons: "Today I will take flight."[11]

Moravian beliefs had shaped his whole life.

On 14 November 1871, the Bethlehem Trombone Choir played the same chorales announcing Br. Wolle's passing to the Bethlehem Congregation that were played when the Nazareth Trombone Choir announced the death of Br. John Moehring.

## The Second Lesson: Memory, Music, Worship, and Sacred Texts

> The main purpose of our little ones' work and leisure, in their daily services in the chapel, in their classrooms, is to proclaim their Saviour's life and to extol their beloved Martyr's death, which themes they never tire to hear and to sing.[12]

Peter, the little novice, walked down the street, rounded the corner, and entered the Nazareth Day School. Though he had no knowledge of what awaited him, the Moravian community had determined that he was the right age to learn the second Moravian lesson, one he would be taught in school. His teachers were among the finest in America, for they had been educated in European Moravian schools. The curriculum they followed for the children focused on the Bible with Jesus as the central figure. Students learned their lessons by memorizing, singing, reading, and writing sacred texts and hymns. "A Bible verse which the children commit to memory can be a highly effective instructional medium to bring them [the children] to a saving knowledge of the Lord Jesus Christ."[13]

Peter's school day began with the "Quarter Hour," a devotional service in which his teachers read and recited Bible stories and verses, delivered inspirational messages, and everyone sang hymns. A Nazareth diarist described how the children "learned a great number of verses and sang them with feeling and blessing, making the Lord's presence seem very close."[14] Student *Singstunden,* little singing hours "in which the children sang with their hearts overflowing with love for their dear Saviour's suffering," were held regularly.[15] It was reported that when some children from the countryside sang "worldly" songs "one of the youngest children told them that their songs were nasty. . . . 'Be quiet and I'll sing nice ones for you.' Then our children sang some of their hymns, and the occasion became a charming *Singstundenchen*."[16] Singing hymns from memory was as important as learning to read the Bible. Peter's second Moravian lesson, the intersection of memory, music, worship, and sacred texts, was soon as much a part of him as breathing.

Music filled the school day, for the Brethren believed that music directly influenced character. Words were the language of the mind, but music was the language of the soul. God spoke to humans through sacred texts, but He communicated with the soul through music. Count von Zinzendorf added to the belief by stating that God spoke through Holy Scriptures, but He was praised through music. Moravians also held that music was a powerful way to embed religious beliefs in people's minds, because verses were easily memorized when they were sung. As a result, music was particularly important in teaching young children how to read. After they learned the alphabet, they spelled words from the Scriptures, from hymns, and from the Daily Text for children.

> Copies of the hymn collection were distributed to all pupils in town and country schools and it [sic] was so joyfully received by all the boys and girls that "they could find time neither to eat nor drink; they spent the whole day reading familiar verses and discovering new ones. That was the first book that the children were ever given to read outside of the regular school hours."[17]

A teacher in Nazareth told of the students' desire for the Daily Text, a selection of Bible verses and inspirational thoughts defining each day of the year, and described how it was used to teach children of different levels to spell, write, and read:

> because there was no school [the next day] . . . many children came and begged me for the Text of that day and of the next. The little children were so loveable! Since they could not yet read handwritten materials, I made a copy of the Texts . . . . The older children copied the Texts for themselves.[18]

In the afternoons, Peter and his classmates produced goods for the community. A visitor described this time when the pupils learned to live quiet, productive lives. "Upstairs are the school-rooms. One room contained children between 3 and 4 years old picking cotton, so orderly and still. For any noise they made you might have been in an empty room."[19]

While the orderly, pleasurable learning that permeated the Nazareth Day School was expressed in many diaries by Moravian teachers, their accounts were corroborated by outsiders. For example, a workman who was repairing a Moravian school building told one of the teachers how

> He never failed to marvel at the quiet and order of the school. . . . He had once been in another school and asked the teacher how he could stand the talking and terrible noise in the classes. The latter replied that the problem had no solution . . . children in this country were an entirely different breed from those in Europe. . . . The workman said that he had never seen such a difference anywhere.[20]

In addition to the hymns Peter sang in school, he was surrounded constantly by the newest and best music available in America. Several times a week he heard this music in the church services he attended. Frequently, he listened to two or three anthems accompanied by instruments in a single service. Some of the newest and best European orchestral instruments available anywhere were owned by members of the Nazareth *Gemeine* and were played in the *collegium musicum*, the instrumental group that provided sacred instrumental music along with the trombone choir. While Peter was in Nazareth, there was a concert in Nazareth Hall nearly every week through the winter. The concerts consisted of symphonies, concertos, extended choral works, and pieces played as solos and by chamber groups. In the chapel, hymns were accompanied by one of the finest organs in America, built by David Tannenberg, the greatest American eighteenth-century organ builder.

The first phase of Peter's instruction was comprehensive, orderly, pleasurable, highly moral, consistently supervised, and richly musical. At the Nazareth Day School, he learned the second lesson: the interrelationship of memory, music, worship, and the sacred texts.

### The Third Lesson: Order and Discipline within a Christian Community

> . . . a school in which the moral and religious training of youth is shaped after the teachings of Christ, and by no means subordinated to the acquisition of mere human knowledge. . . . The best lesson the youth of the republic could learn, would be that which might be drawn from the training of the steed, which, let him be the most perfect form, agile limbs, and purest blood, would be entirely valueless unless his noble instincts were curbed, molded, and directed to some practical turn by his master man.[21]

In the year 1800 after four years in the Nazareth Day School, Peter left Sister Moehring's care and moved into Nazareth Hall to begin the classical component of his Moravian Christian education. "The Hall" became his new home. Peter was assigned to a "room company" with fifteen boys. The company studied, ate, played, and worshiped together. According to the school's regulations, and every parent received a copy, "A particular attention will be paid that the scholars are constantly under inspection, not only in school hours, but also at all other times."[22] The teachers accompanied the boys on walks, to the playground, to the chapel, and to the dormitory. "The system of constant supervision enables the preceptors to guard them [the students] from hurtful influence, which, might not as readily be done otherwise."[23] The teachers were well qualified for this intense supervision, for they had experienced it themselves in the Moravian schools they attended in Europe. Because each teacher was either a candidate for the ministry or already a clergyman, everyone modeled the behavior expected of the boys.

Academically, the students were divided into three departments: primary, intermediate, and senior. Each boy was assigned to specific subjects "according to grade of merit and proficiency," rather than according to his age or to his room company.[24]

Classes began at 7:30 A.M., with an hour of German or English. The languages were spoken on alternate days, with all other lessons and all conversations in the language of the day. As a result, the students became bilingual. A half-hour devotion followed, then there were classes in Latin, geography, or natural history. Instruction in arithmetic, geometry, bookkeeping, and mathematical geography was spread throughout the week. At noon the boys rejoined their room companies and ate in their apartments. The boys' diet was "plain and wholesome. For breakfast, bread and butter and milk, now and then tea or coffee; at dinner, boiled or roasted meat, with suitable vegetables; for supper, bread and butter, milk, salad, etc."[25] These meals were prepared by the Single Sisters living next to the school. Everyone ate in silence. Classes resumed at 2 P.M. with writing and drawing lessons followed by French. Organ, piano, flute, and violin instruction was given to those who wanted it and to those who showed particular musical talent. The pastor taught religion two afternoons a week.

Twice a year public examinations were held. In the morning of the examination day, the boys read from the Bible in German and English, translated and conversed in French and German, read essays on topics in history, mathematics, geography, and recited speeches, poems, and classical prose in English, Latin, and German. In the afternoon, the students played instrumental music, sang, and exhibited their work in geometry, drawing, and writing.

During the school year, contact with families was discouraged. According to a school regulation, "It is earnestly wished that the visits of the scholars to their parents, relations and friends . . . may occur as seldom as possible, because they frequently dissipated the mind of youth and cause more damage than pleasure."[26]

Describing the students, a visitor to Nazareth Hall wrote, "It is a truth that there is not undue confinement nor restraint. There is in their manners an elegant ease and simplicity that is charmingly prepossessing."[27]

Peter learned the value of order and discipline well. This lesson was grafted onto his religious education, and he became a refined, disciplined, engaging Christian gentleman.

### The Fourth Lesson: The Daily Reality of Christ

> He testified . . . Christ was so near to him, that he seemed to behold Him with this bodily eyes.[28]

Peter's schooling was only one component of his induction into Moravian society. Simultaneously, he moved through the community "choir system." Because they believed that different ages and different genders required different spiritual instruction, support, and guidance, Moravians organized their members into choirs by age, gender, and marital status. A choir was usually maintained as a household with its own code of behavior, leaders, and residence. A *Chorhaus* was "a school for piety, virtue and industry."[29] The adult choirs were independent economic units in which young people served as apprentices.

Peter joined the Little Boys' Choir when he was five years old. He attended lessons and meetings especially for his choir. While singing was an important part of the meetings, other activities were included.

> When the children have had some practice in singing they shall have a short song service once a week of a Liturgy that is partly sung. Occasionally the memoir of a child shall be read, which will have more affect on their hearers than a sermon.[30]

Each choir had a spiritual leader and a warden. The spiritual leader conducted the choir's daily devotional exercises and planned and led the frequent love feasts and choir celebrations. He/she constantly reminded the choir members of their responsibilities, assisted individuals in times of spiritual struggle and doubt, disciplined disorderly members, and met monthly with each person to discuss the state of his soul. The *Pfleger* (spiritual leader) of the Single Brothers' Choir was also a member of the Overseers' Committee, a type of town council. The warden was responsible for the practical and external concerns of the choir. She/he kept the financial records, integrated the community activities for the choir, and coordinated the many trades and apprenticeships.

Though the choirs came together for regular sacred services, each choir had its own festival day. The festival day for the Little Boys' Choir was June 24. The Nazareth Diary contains an account of an evening celebration of such a festival in which Peter probably participated. "The little boys celebrated today their choir-festival. In the evening after the festival, the boys sang on the balcony of the Gemeinhaus their songs of praise to the Lord."[31]

At the age of twelve, Peter joined the Boys' Choir. The intensity of Peter's spiritual devotion at that time was recounted in his obituary.

> ... there [in Nazareth Hall] he not only studied with diligence and great pleasure, but also received so deep an impression of the Saviour's love that he lived with Him, in a daily fellowship and was often accustomed to retire to the dormitory, where he would cast himself between the beds, on the floor, and pray earnestly to the Lord.[32]

Also, Peter would leave the playground, find a solitary place in the woods, "and kneel down behind a tree to ask God to bless him."[33]

At this age, the gender separation in Moravian communities became a reality for Peter. Not only was he enrolled in an all-male school, he was a youth in a community in which all contact between males and females was strictly controlled. When Peter entered puberty, he experienced his first serious spiritual crisis. The exact nature of the crisis was not revealed, but he "yielded to the sinful prompting of his heart."[34] His teacher, David Moritz Michael, helped Peter resolve his struggle, and the reality of Christ was affirmed for him during the communion that followed his confirmation.

> . . . he received, while partaking of the Lord's supper . . . a full measure of pardoning and sanctifying grace. He testifies, that, in that hour, Christ was so near to him, that he seemed to behold Him with his bodily eyes.[35]

Peter's spiritual life was now fundamentally set. The lessons were learned. He never again doubted the living reality of Christ.

At the age of seventeen, he became aware of how the will of Christ, expressed through the Lots, governed the life of each Moravian. Christ's will decided community membership, and those who did not follow His decisions were dismissed from the church and required to leave the community. A month after Peter joined the Single Brothers' Choir his oldest Brother, John Frederick, a member of the same choir, requested permission to marry. However, the Lot did not sanction his choice. When John married anyway, he and his wife were "excommunicated for refusing to marry by lot."[36] The rapidity and decisiveness of the dismissal sent a clear message to Brother Peter. The reality of the power of Christ to shape earthly events was decisive and the decisions were executed fully.

### The Fifth Lesson: Christian Service and Music

A month after Peter came to Nazareth from St. Thomas, David Moritz Michael arrived from Neisky, Germany to teach in Nazareth Hall. Peter could not have known, but that coincidence profoundly affected his life, for Michael was a fine educator and administrator, an outstanding violinist, and one of the great Moravian composers. In Germany he had been among the first rank of musicians.

Also, he was the head of a Moravian boarding school for boys that was renowned for its high academic standards. Assigned to Nazareth Hall as a music teacher and to the Nazareth *Gemeine* as the music director, Michael's first mission was to raise the standard of music in Mora-

Nazareth Hall after 1841
(The Moravian Archives, Bethlehem)

vian communities in America. Because all future Moravian male leaders attended Nazareth Hall and participated in the musical activities Michael directed, his instruction insured that they were well educated in music. His second duty was to make the *collegium musicum* in Nazareth an outstanding musical group. Michael, 44 years of age, had had years of experience as an excellent teacher, was familiar with the latest developments in German music, and was a gifted composer. He was at the height of his powers when he arrived in Nazareth. In addition to all of these attributes, Michael was a perfect model of how a Moravian musician should conduct his life. He exemplified Christian musical service.

Michael's arrival in Nazareth was also important for the history of American music, for under his leadership, Nazareth became a musical center. He brought the best European music with him and insisted on a standard of performance and instruction typical of Moravian schools in Europe but rarely found in America. He took over the *collegium musicum* immediately. It was modeled after German court orchestras, featuring violins, divided into firsts and seconds, violas, violoncellos, flutes, oboes, horns, and trumpets.[37] Though the *collegium* was centered in the Choir of the Single Brothers, students attending The Hall, whether Moravian or not, played and sang in the group. In the year 1798, Nazareth census included the statement that "music in the meetings of the Congregation and the choirs [included] 30 brethren and boys. . . ."[38]

When he entered The Hall, Peter surely joined the *collegium musicum*. As a member of a group devoted to performing sacred music, Peter was involved daily in worship through music.

Michael initiated a greatly expanded concert series in the year 1796, and by 1799–1800, the group played twenty-one public concerts during the winter season. These concerts were in addition to the weekly church services that included as many as four anthems with instrumental accompaniment. This schedule was all the more remarkable since Nazareth was a community of just over 300 residents including students. It is doubtful if so much concert and sacred music could be found anywhere else in America.

Peter would have performed in these concerts, which consisted of major orchestral, chamber, and vocal works. For example, on 4 January 1799, the *collegium* performed the Symphony No. 2 by Eichner, a piece for two choruses by Reichart, a symphony by Pleyel, and compositions for two clarinets and two horns. The next week, the concert contained a symphony by Gyronwetz, a sonata for the piano by Hoffmeister, Psalm 143 by Doles, and pieces for winds from Mozart's *The Magic Flute*.

Michael was also a composer. In an analysis of a psalm set to music by Michael, which was performed in Nazareth, a historian of Moravian music wrote, "Even Michael himself was probably unaware that his setting for soloists, and chorus of Psalm 102 was the first extended cantata-like work written by an American Moravian composer, and quite possibly the earliest work for these performing forces written in America."[39] This account is only one example of the energy, capability, and creativity Michael brought to Nazareth.

In the year 1804, Michael left his position at Nazareth Hall and became the *Vorseher* of the Nazareth Single Brothers, a path Peter would follow later in Salem. Michael continued to serve on the Nazareth town board.

Four years later, Michael asked permission to leave Nazareth, and the diarest recorded that on 6 February 1805, to the choir of the single brethren and boys, it had been announced, that Brother D. Moritz Michael, who had asked for some time to be relieved from the office of an attendant and warden in the single brethren's choir, had his request granted.[40]

The Nazareth diarist summarized Michael's contribution to that community.

> April 19th, 1808. . . . Br. D. M. Michael moved from here to Bethlehem to stay. He served faithfully in the Institute [Nazareth Hall] for 9 years, and in the single brethren's choir he had served faithfully 3 years. During the whole time he had been director of the music for the congregation to the pleasure of the congregation.[41]

In Bethlehem, Michael became the *Vorseher* of the Single Brothers. With his presence in Bethlehem, musical prominence shifted from Nazareth. The notable performance of Joseph Haydn's *Creation*, possibly the American premiere, took place soon after Michael arrived in Bethlehem. Peter's oldest brother, Jacob, played the double bass in that performance. Peter may have heard that premiere or sung in the choir. Peter, now one of the finest musicians in the area, surely participated in the Bethlehem performances under Michael, for Nazareth and Bethlehem were within walking distance.

In 1816, Peter's brother Jacob informed him that Michael was leaving for Germany. In his diary, Peter responded to his brother's news, "I learned the old Michael, that dear man who taught me so much music, was about to go to Germany. I wish him a good journey and much pleasure once he gets there."[42] Peter had been fortunate enough to receive instruction in violin and composition from one of the finest musicians in America, and he had been in daily contact with a Moravian musician who was first a spiritual servant to the community.

John Bechler was Peter's second great spiritual music teacher. He replaced David Moritz Michael when he went to Bethlehem. Bechler had received his education in the Moravian Seminary at Barby, Germany. Describing his intense interest in music, he wrote, "Among the various branches of learning in which I was instructed, I felt a particular love for music; where upon I devoted every moment of time left by other duties to the various branches of this charming art with the greatest delight."[43] He learned to sing, "to play various stringed instruments, and more particularly the piano and organ."[44] Upon his graduation from Barby, Bechler became a teacher, a path identical to the one Peter was to follow. Bechler recorded that "the Elder's Conference gave me to understand that I would endeavor to train a considerable number of efficient organists for the service of the Church [in America]."[45]

Bechler was twenty-two years old and was assigned to teach in the newly founded Moravian Theological Seminary housed in The Hall. In a description of his time at Nazareth, Bechler spoke of the importance music occupied in his life there.

I entered upon the duties assigned to me with great diligence, However, I soon found, after faithfully attending to them, that I had plenty of leisure left to follow private pursuits of my own choosing; consisting, principally in efforts to improve my knowledge of the English language and in taking up the classics again; while I instructed others in the art and began to compose pieces.[46]

Along with being responsible for teaching other subjects to the three seminary students, Bechler pursued his charge to create "efficient organists" for America and selected Peter to be one of his organ students. Peter was fourteen years of age. With a Tannenberg organ in the *Saal,* Bechler and his students had one of the best organs in America at their disposal. The Moravians placed more importance upon the organ than any other Christian denomination in eighteenth-century America. Therefore, an organ was found in every important building in their communities.

• • •

Though there were many Moravian composers who played the organ, they created no distinctive body of literature for the instrument, for the Moravian use of the organ was unique. Christian Ignatius Latrobe, the most influential eighteenth-century Moravian musical spokesman, described the uniqueness in the preface to his chorale book. "To be able to play a voluntary [a solo organ piece] is by no means an essential part of the qualifications of an organist among the Brethren. The congregation will often prefer hearing Hymn-tunes in its stead."[47] Rather than playing extended preludes, offertories, and postludes, Moravian organists led congregational singing, kept the pitch of the hymns, and were part of the *collegium musicum.* An organist must be modest and not call attention to his finger dexterity.[48] While the Moravian organists did not indulge in display, great demands were placed upon their memories and upon their improvisational skills. For example, one of the most frequent Moravian services was the *Singstunde,* the singing hour. In that service, the pastor selected hymns with verses that expressed a central idea for the service. The hymns were unannounced and usually only a few verses from any place in the hymn were sung. The pastor began singing, and the organist, recognizing the tune immediately, began to accompany the congregational singing. At one time more than four hundred melodies were in use; each with many verses. Not only did the organist recall a melody instantly from hearing only the beginning of the verse, he played in the key the pastor was singing. Thus, either perfect or excellent relative pitch was required to accomplish an instantly correct match. Latrobe described each of these skills.

> The organist should be able to play the Hymn-tunes in most, if not all, of the different keys extempore; because, upon many occasions, the verses sung by the minister, according to his own choice, are taken from a variety of hymns, and it would be next to impossible to turn continually to the Tune-book, without detriment to the singing; especially as such single verses are often given out. He should be acquainted upon their being given out, or sung, without previous notice, he may assist the weak singer, . . . if left to his choice, or in the key the singer himself pitches upon.[49]

Knowing the hymn melodies and the verses associated with each of them was only the beginning. The correct bass for each hymn had to be remembered, and the alto and tenor parts improvised. Using a system called "figured bass," numbers signifying the pitches appropriate for the alto and tenor harmonies were written above or below the bass. When the hymn tune was added, four-part harmony was the result. Mastering this system and memorizing the many bass lines required talent and many, many hours of practice. All of this knowledge had to be automatic, for the speed of the hymn left no time to think about the harmony before it was played.

Moravian organists also improvised interludes between the phrases of a hymn. Again, Latrobe, in his description of this practice, urged moderation.

> In adopting the German practice, the Brethren have however endeavored to simplify it. The interlude of a skillful Lutheran organist, however, fine as a composition, is too apt to perplex the hearer by its length and the richness of its combinations.[50]

John Bechler wrote a set of "Rules for Interludes," consisting of numerous examples explained in the language of music theory.[51] As well as learning to realize a figured bass and to improvise interludes, a knowl-edge of music theory was part of the instruction Peter received from Bechler. "Rules for Interludes," for example, was unintelligible without a mastery of music theory.

While hymns were accompanied by the organ and occasionally by the trombone choir, anthems were accompanied by the *collegium musicum,* which included the organ. The organ parts in the *collegium* fall into two categories: those with a bass that was figured, and those in which the harmony and some of the other instrumental parts were notated. When there was only the figured bass, the organist improvised the harmony and filled in for instruments that might be missing. Occasionally, there were short solos for the organ in an anthem, but the organ remained an accompanying instrument rather than a solo one.

From the above, it is clear Moravian organists possessed prodigious musical memories. They improvised relatively simple choral harmonizations and fully independent orchestral parts often at sight. Frequently, they directed the choir and the instrumental ensemble and had a fluent, accurate, practical knowledge of Western music theory. No other denominations held a higher standard of performance in concerts, sacred services, and practical playing than the Moravians.

• • •

Nowhere in America could Peter have received such a fine, thorough musical training; first as a singer in school, then as a string player with David Michael, and then as an organist with Bechler. Though the lasting significance of the organ instruction could not have been known to Bechler, organ playing became one of the strongest branches of the

Wolle musical dynasty. Peter passed the skills he learned in Nazareth on to his son, Theodore, and Theodore passed them on to his cousin John Frederick, who became one of the great organists of his time.

Not only did Peter emerge from Nazareth Hall a highly proficient organist, he also learned to compose. Michael and Bechler were both notable composers and taught Peter this art – one that also passed through three generations of Wolles. Again, Nazareth was an ideal place for anyone with a talent for composition. Michael left a large body of sacred and instrumental music, and John Christian Bechler was the most prolific Moravian composer of his generation in America. For years, Peter, the novice, was in daily contact with such men. Already as a child, Peter heard their music frequently in church and at school. As a young man, he played and sang their compositions with the composers conducting.

Learning the violin taught Peter how to write for orchestra. Playing the organ taught him how to shape musical lines that moved correctly, efficiently, and expressively. He learned to ornament melodies, and many hours of religious instruction through singing hymns filled his mind with passages from the Bible and with verses he could use in his anthems. A study of music theory taught him how to construct appropriate and effective musical details. Like many composers before him, Peter also learned by copying music. He began this practice early, for at least two Bechler anthems have parts copied by Peter.[52] Finally, he had many opportunities to compose and to hear his works performed. A young composer could not ask for more. Peter's compositions are such an important, though still largely unrecognized, part of the Moravian music tradition that a later chapter is devoted entirely to his music.

To Peter, it was of the utmost importance that his teachers were models of how Moravian musicians and composers led lives as Christ's servants. Michael, in addition to being a musician and composer, was the administrator of the Single Brothers' Choir, a complex organization. He was secretary of the town council. Bechler, also a notable musician and composer, taught classical and Biblical languages, history, and sacred texts in the first Moravian Theological Seminary in America. Both men always provided spiritual support and counsel. Michael and Bechler composed and performed when they had the time or when the occasion required music. Expert and talented as they were in music, they were clerics first and musicians second. Peter followed their paths exactly.

### The Sixth Lesson: Serving the Community

> ... in the afternoon the visitors talked with William Henry van Vleck and Peter Wolle ... regarding the continuation of their studies here, in order to be prepared for service in the boarding-school and for other service of the Lord.[53]

When Peter was fourteen years old, he had to become either an apprentice and learn a craft or a trade, or study to be a teacher. The Director of Nazareth Hall selected the second route for Peter, and so he joined two of his friends in the first class of the Nazareth Theological Seminary. The plan was for them to attend the seminary for three years, become teachers, and possibly be ordained as pastors.

The seminary was founded "with a view to educated classical teachers, as the procurement of such from Europe was attended with heavy expenses."[54] Therefore, new subjects were added to those the boys had previously studied: Greek, Hebrew, ecclesiastical history, and Biblical exegesis. Classes met every day from 9:00 to 11:00 in the morning and from 2:00 to 4:00 in the afternoon. On Saturday mornings there were two one-hour classes from eight to ten o'clock.

The supervision, care, and guidance already surrounding Peter intensified. The three students moved into the apartment of one of the professors who was charged to care for them "in every respect" and to "win their confidence, and in the building up of their character accustom them to habits of industry and have regard for their conduct."[55] Peter's professor, fortunately, was John Bechler. Thus, Peter lived with one of the best musicians in American, who cared for him in "every respect."

After three years, his lessons learned, he was ready to serve God and the *Bruedergemeine* in what ever way Christ chose. He was prepared to follow, and in 1810, Peter, age eighteen, joined the faculty of Nazareth Hall.

## NOTES

1. Arthur J. Freeman, *An Ecumenical Theology of the Heart* (Bethlehem, Pa.: The Moravian Church in America, 1998), 208.
2. "Nazareth Diary," 22 August 1792. (Manuscript, Nazareth, Pa.: Moravian Historical Society, n.d.).
3. Peter S. Seadle et al., trans., *The Diaries of Peter Wolle*, vol. 10 of *The Three Forks of Muddy Creek* (Winston-Salem, N. C.: Old Salem, Inc., 1984), 83.
4. "The Late Bishop Wolle," *The Moravian*, 23 August 1871.
5. Linda S. Gibson, "Toward a Description of Teacher-Child Dispute Process in a Mainstream Nursery-Age Classroom: Negotiating Rules and Relationships" (Paper presented at the 15th Annual Ethnography in Education Research Forum, The University of Pennsylvania, February, 1994).
6. Henry James, *Sketches of Moravian Life and Character* (Philadelphia: J. B. Lippincott & Co., 1859), 147–48.
7. Ibid., 148.
8. Ibid.
9. Ibid.
10. William C. Reichel, *Historical Sketch of Nazareth Hall from 1755 to 1869* (Philadelphia, Pa.: J. B. Lippincott & Co., 1899), 36.
11. *The Moravian*, 23 August 1871.
12. Mabel Haller, *Early Moravian Education in Pennsylvania* (Nazareth, Pa.: Moravian Historical Society, 1963), 236.
13. Ibid., 219.
14. Ibid., 226.
15. Ibid., 225.
16. Ibid.
17. Ibid., 227.
18. Ibid., 217–18.
19. Ibid., 63.

20. Ibid., 24.
21. James, *Sketches,* 173.
22. William C. Reichel, "Nazareth Hall: A Moravian Boarding School for Boys," *Transactions of the Moravian Historical Society*, 1875–76, 1. Also, Appendix in the same journal, 9.
23. Ibid., 26.
24. James, *Sketches,* 175.
25. Reichel, *Historical Sketch,* 9–10.
26. Haller, *Early Moravian Education*, 27.
27. Ibid., 9.
28. *The Moravian*, (November 1871), 186.
29. Haller, *Early Moravian Education*, 277.
30. Rosamond C. Smith, *The Choir System in Salem* (Winston-Salem, N.C.: Old Salem, Inc., 1980) Vol. 5 of *Three Forks of Muddy Creek*.
31. "Nazareth Diary," 22 August 1792, 180.
32. *The Moravian*, (November 1871), 186.
33. Ibid.
34. Ibid.
35. Ibid.
36. "The Wolle Genealogy, Concluding Remarks." (Typescript, Nazareth, PA: Moravian Historical Society, n.d.).
37. "Nazareth Diary," 686.
38. Ibid.
39. Karl Kroeger, "A David Moritz Michael Psalm 103," *Moravian Music Foundation Bulletin* (1976), XXI, 2:10.
40. "Nazareth Diary," 870.
41. Ibid.
42. Seadle, *Diaries*, 39
43. *The Moravian,* 26 June 1857.
44. Ibid.
45. Ibid.
46. Ibid.
47. Donald M. McCorkle, "Prelude to a History of American Moravian Organs," *American Guild of Organists*, reprint October, 1958.
48. Ibid.
49. Ibid.
50. Ibid.

51. Kroeger, "Psalm 103," 5–6.
52. Those anthems are "Die Gnade Des Herrn Jesus Christ," and "Kommt Ach Kommt, Ihr Gnaden Kinder."
53. "Nazareth Diary," 861.
54. Ibid., 873.
55. Haller, *Early Moravian Education,* 78.

Chapter Two

*Serving as a Teacher*

The question was prepared [for the Lot] DOES THE SAVIOUR APPROVE THAT AN ATTEMPT BE MADE TO ESTABLISH A BOARDING SCHOOL FOR BOYS IN SALEM? Answer YES. Steiner will try to procure an outline of the plan followed at Nazareth.[1]

WHEN PETER HAD BEEN CHOSEN to join the first class of the Moravian Theological Seminary, the church leaders and his parents had in mind that he would ultimately become a pastor. Because Moravian pastors were spiritual teachers rather than preachers who made Christian converts, a prospective pastor had first to be a successful teacher. Wolle had taught two years at Nazareth Hall under the supervision, guidance, and the eyes of his superiors. They watched him develop and saw that he was outstanding. Therefore, they chose him to lead the new school and sent him to Salem with their approval.

Not only had Peter been an outstanding teacher during his apprenticeship at Nazareth Hall, his membership in the Single Brothers' Choir had been exemplary. He could receive counsel from his superiors and in turn counsel others wisely, and he had held his sexual feelings in check. That was important, for there was proof he could withstand the temptations that might arise from a close contact with the political and personal events in school, in the Moravian community, and in the outside world.

Wolle's musical drives could also be controlled. He would bring the "Divine Art" to the Salem *Gemeine,* playing and singing to further the spirituality of his students and the congregation. However, playing and composing music for pleasure would remain a pastime and not the dominant focus in his life.

Each of Peter's achievements had been carefully prepared and provided for by the *Bruedergemeine*. Things were going as they should; one step at a time, with each step carefully and fully mastered before the next one was taken. Now a new school for boys had been founded in Salem, and a teacher was needed. Br. Wolle was selected for the position. He reported his response in his diary.

> On the 21st of June I received a call as First Teacher to the Institute for Boys and School for Local Boys in Salem. . . . Since I must believe that the Saviour has meant for me to be a servant in His house, I regard this as a step which will bring me closer to this goal. . . . That of all the learned Brothers here [in Nazareth] I was chosen for this office was indeed most humbling. In it I recognize the wondrous guidance of the Saviour.[2]

The year was 1814. Br. Wolle was twenty-two years old.

Br. Wolle packed his possessions, bid farewell to his students and friends in Nazareth, and left for Bethlehem on the first stage of his journey to Salem, North Carolina. He stayed for a week in Bethlehem, "the beloved place," with his widowed mother and his brother, Jacob.[3] He spent time with friends and with his teacher David Mortiz Michael. Departure from Bethlehem was painful, and when he left on Thursday, 3 October 1814 he wrote, "in spirit, torn from the embraces of what was most dear to me."[4]

The journey to Salem took three weeks. Not that Peter lingered along the way, but his geniality and curiosity, the political events he encountered, and an accident turned the trip into an interesting tour.

Wolle traveled west to Lancaster, Pennsylvania, where he was the guest of a Moravian family and visited a cotton factory that impressed him. He played the fortepiano for acquaintances of a fellow traveler. After crossing the Susquehanna River, he traveled south to Baltimore, Maryland, where he watched fortifications being constructed in the event that the British would attack again, for war (the War of 1812) was in progress.

Wolle's affability and curiosity emerge from his diary accounts. With dinner guests in Baltimore, he played duets and string quartets, and then, "I retired to rest in the most elegant inn in the U.S."[5] He visited the battlefield at Bladensburg and viewed the Capitol and other public buildings in Washington, D.C., in ruins from British attacks. Passing through Alexandria, Virginia, Peter proceeded to Richmond. From there he went to Raleigh, North Carolina, where he was delayed a few days because the stagecoach was damaged in an accident. While it was being repaired, he occupied his time shopping for books. The wife of the owner of the bookshop in Raleigh had been a student at the Girls' Boarding School in Salem, and she offered him "any book for my leisure during my stay. I borrowed Willimans travels, which I found very entertaining. I felt myself quite at home, and spent time quite agreeably."[6]

When the coach was ready, Peter traveled west and passed through Chapel Hill. Two days from Salem, he watched a military muster in Hillsborough and viewed some waxworks. "These were tolerable but the music accompanying was most wretched and enough to scare abody [sic]."[7] The last evening of the trip was spent in an inn only a few miles from Salem. On 25 October, Wolle arrived in Salem to take up his position as a servant in the "house of the Saviour." Salem greeted Brother Wolle with a love feast. Then, he was introduced to the young boys as the head teacher of the new school.

Salem was built on a tract of land called Wachovia in the mountains of North Carolina. The land purchase was finalized in 1751, and in 1753 a group from Bethlehem arrived to settle the wilderness. They divided Wachovia into three communities. Bethabara was settled first and was a closed church community. Bethania was founded next. There, Moravians and non-Moravians lived together on property owned by the Moravian Church. Salem was the final settlement, founded in 1756.

The community was perfect for Wolle. Everyone wanted the newly formed boys' school to succeed. There, he could grow as a teacher. Although Salem's musical life had been vibrant before Peter arrived, it was modest then compared to Nazareth and Bethlehem. Every improvement that furthered Salem's music was welcomed by the community.

Wolle was also perfect for Salem, having emerged from Nazareth a congenial gentleman, polite, refined and cultivated, well-mannered, moral, spiritual, and always intellectually curious. He was an aristocratic Christian who enjoyed to the fullest the fruits of a community life that valued education, refinement, sociability, and prosperity. Moravian pietism was never rooted in self-denial. On the contrary, community service was shaped by aristocratic-like ideals without the political, social, and physical excesses that characterized European aristocrats. The Salem *Gemeine* could not have received a better teacher for their boys' school. People who sent their sons to be educated in Salem wanted a person like Br. Wolle to be their teacher.

The educational plan the Salem Elders had received from the Nazareth *Gemeine* for their new school articulated three principles. First, the curriculum was defined by the European tradition of a classical education constrained by Moravian pietism. Second, the teachers were fully committed to the curriculum and were specially trained to teach it. Finally, the students were publicly examined at the end of each term by community members. The basic goal for the school was expressed in the Salem town diary.

> It is the intention that the older boys and the larger among the little boys shall have more opportunity to progress in useful knowledge, in the hope that some of them can be trained for service in the Unity [the Moravian Church].[8]

The breadth of knowledge and intellectual rigor required to teach effectively in such a school was daunting, but Wolle was ready to undertake it. When the first day of school arrived, Monday, 31 October 1814, Br. Wolle wrote in his diary, "And so I began today with my service for the school."[9]

The school day was divided into two parts. Academic work occupied the boys in the morning. Astronomy, geography, arithmetic, history, English and English orthography, and German were studied. Geography covered the United States, Europe, Asia and the Pacific Islands, maps, and the globe. Natural history included lessons about electricity, magnetism, light, hydraulics, and many species of animals. Human his-tory was devoted to a detailed study of the Peloponnesian War, Roman civilization, and the American Revolution.[10] Wolle instructed the older boys in Latin, natural history, geometry, singing, and violin.[11]

The afternoon was for recreation. Wolle alternated responsibility for the students' afternoon recreation with the other instructor. When the weather was warm, students and the teacher on duty went bathing, boating, and gathered berries, nuts, and other fruits. There were other activities that Peter reported in his diary.

> In the afternoon I went for a walk with the children in the [Single] Brothers' Meadow, where we extracted the juice from the maple trees. Some of them went fishing for the first time this year but were not very successful.[12]

One afternoon, the group watched a house raising.

Wolle always played energetically with the children. He particularly liked winter sports and described them in his diary.

> The ice on the street continues; I made use of it to provide some fun for the children who had asked me for it. We went to the congregational tree orchard behind the church and slid down the hill on sleds and on boards.[13]

He expressed his disappointment when winter conditions were not agreeable, and "Because of the bitter cold I did not go for a walk with the children although the ice on the mill dam exerted a strong attraction."[14] Whenever possible the boys and their teacher played ball.[15]

In the late afternoon, Wolle taught the violin, piano, and organ to boys who were talented and interested. He also conducted sacred song services.

Because the school was a boarding school, the boys were supervised each evening. While evening supervision was seldom mentioned in his diary, the entry for 10 February 1816 gives the idea that it was probably usually moral in tone. "Read to the children this evening a play for children called 'He who digs a trap for others, will fall into it himself'."[16] When it was evident that the boys were not kept busy enough in the evenings, more education was demanded by the parents. In 1815, the town's diarist recorded an anti-idleness policy enacted by the town council.

> The room hitherto reserved for them [the older boys] in the [Single] Brothers house shall still be held for them, but shall stay locked so they do not loiter there just when they wish, without supervision. Evening classes shall be held there Monday and Friday, from seven to half past eight o'clock, with instruction given in reading, writing and reckoning. All the boys shall attend religious instruction on Tuesday evening, every fourteen days. On alternate Tuesday evenings instruction will be given in history and geography.[17]

The pastor led the religious services.

By closely following every facet of the school's curriculum, Wolle upheld the Moravian tradition of a classical Christian education. However, his approach to instruction was consistently innovative, for he employed teaching methods that were rare in early nineteenth century schooling.[18] While lecturing remained the norm for most subjects, to enliven the study of language, Wolle's students kept diaries.[19] In all subjects, he moved at the speed of the students without blaming them for their errors or their ignorance. "I examined my scholars in the first rudiments of arithmetic, in which some were very deficient, so that I could proceed but slowly."[20] The students were reminded of the relevance of diligent study by appealing to their personal relationships with the Brothers and their responsibility to their Savior.

> 2 January 1815. School started again today. . . . I admonished the children that they should now try and please us with their most intense attention in their studies and diligence in their work and a generally peaceful behavior; but that they could not do this without asking the Saviour daily for strength to their [lives]. I presented to them the advantages of diligence for all that remained of their life.[21]

Wolle wrote how he employed peer teaching. "Carried out a plan I had made some days ago, namely to have some of the older boys instruct the younger ones."[22]

In the natural science lessons, things were not just talked about, principles were demonstrated rather than given as facts to be memorized. For example, "carried out all sorts of experiments today . . . strewed sand on a piece of glass. I also drew a violin bow across it – did the same with water in a glass."[23] Sometimes food was used as an extrinsic reward. "In my arithmetic class I gave away the peaches. . . . I gave them to the best students in order to increase their zeal."[24]

Wolle made the recreational walks in the afternoons instructional as well. He used the time for nature study, and as a time when he could insist on correct language usage. In his diary, he described the way he accomplished that.

> They played quoits. This word had been introduced to them as more proper than quote in the German orthography lesson when they wrote their diaries, and consequently an edict was announced to which they were prohibited from every using the latter again under pain of death.[25]

Br. Wolle also took the boys on an all-day outing for the first time. He enjoyed preparing for it, and the boys were very excited. From his description of the day, it is clear that the congenial atmosphere that characterized the recreational time pervaded all Wolle's teaching.

> This was finally the day when we could go on a trip in the stage with the children, which they had anticipated for such a long time. It had never been done before. . . . We left at 1/2 to 8 and at 10 o'clock we arrived . . . in Bethania [a neighboring Moravian village] . . . as can be expected, the children were very cheerful and happy during the whole journey. . . . First we went to [Dr.] Schuman's, where they were smoking meat. Also, the organ with the four registers . . . made a short while ago, was played by me and by most of the children. After a good dinner, we all went to church where the organ was played, and then we climbed onto the steeple from where one has quite a panoramic view. – Then afternoon coffee at Bro. and Sr. Pfohl's . . . we gave permission to leave by 3 o'clock. We stopped for a few moments in Bethabara [another Moravian village] in order to drink some of Bro. Kummer's good cider. At a quarter to six, we then happily arrived back in Salem.[26]

It is clear from Wolle's diary that the students did not always behave perfectly. A number of entries described disruptions and his response. "In Latin class I put on my suite of armor . . . and expressed my indignation about the laziness of several of my pupils quite clearly."[27] Never one to hold a grudge however, in another place he wrote how

> This morning I flew into an immoderate rage at my boys, on account of their continual talking and chattering and other things, at a time when their action should be directed to their school tasks. My anger continued the whole morning and only the ridiculous stories in their daybooks could again make me assume a more friendly look.[28]

Sometimes unruly children came into the school. "Joshua Boner, who must be brought to school by force, there was a little fray at noon."[29] "Little Charles Eberhard was today enrolled in school. He has been very badly brought up. . . . He promised to do all sorts of good things."[30]

Unfortunately, Wolle did not see eye to eye with his teaching colleague, who was entirely traditional in his teaching. "I believed he knew no other way to keep order in school than with a ruler."[31] His class of young boys was often totally out of control. "There was constant noise and confusion so that in the end I was forced to close the door between the two rooms."[32] When the other teacher was sick, and he was frequently indisposed for long periods of time, Wolle gladly taught both classes.

A little over a year after Wolle became a teacher at the boys' school, the first public examination took place. This examination was always an important community event, and a full account of the activities was recorded in the Salem Diary.

> The EXAMINATION was continued in the *Saal* of the Gemein Haus. The parents of the children attended and other invited guests. The children spelled and read in German and in English. Questions were asked in natural history; and they repeated a memorized dialogue of civil history, which gave a brief review of the Roman Empire. The first class [Wolle's] distinguished itself in these, and in the geography of the United States; and gave pleasure by the recitations of poetry. Several played on the FORTE PIANO and showed specimens of their writing. Especially did we enjoy the singing. In general it was noted with pleasure that they took part freely and gladly, which was hardly to be expected as none of them had participated in such an Examination before. At the close there was a pleasant lovefeast.[33]

By contrast, Wolle's account of the examination was modest, for it was appropriate for Moravians to understate their achievements.

> The weather was very inclement, so that only a few could appear for the affairs of this interesting day. At 1/2 to 10 we started with the singing of some verses, as one can see on the special bulletin about the program of this day. Those present were the parents of the children, the members of the Conference of Elders, several Sisters from the

Institute [the boarding school for girls], and a few friends. Everything proceeded to general satisfaction, and the children were not at all shy or bashful as one might have expected.[34]

Always the faithful Moravian servant of Christ, Brother Wolle wrote, "I renewed my resolve this morning to attend to all of my obligations faithfully before the eyes of the Lord."[35]

The positive attitudes of the students' parents towards him reflected his success in teaching their sons. He learned what they thought the first time he collected the tuition from them. Again he modestly recorded their responses in the diary couched in terms of devoted Christian service. "The satisfaction which parents manifest with the discharge of my present duties makes me blush – all praise be given to Him, who has given me the power of acting in a satisfactory manner."[36]

At the start of the year 1816, six years after he began teaching in Salem, Wolle looked back and wrote, "Most of the time with JOY AND PLEASURE . . . I find myself in the happiest of situations."[37]

In May, Wolle's status changed dramatically. During his monthly spiritual talk with the pastor, he was asked if he would lead the Salem Single Brothers' Choir. Wolle had proven he was a successful teacher and spiritual leader of youth within schools; he was now being asked to lead older boys and adult males. If he proved to be a good leader then, he would probably be called to be a pastor. He accepted and a search for his successor in the school began.

Johann Gottlieb Herman, a teacher in a Moravian school in England, took Wolle's place. When he received the news that Herman was on his way to Salem from England, Wolle wrote, "I felt a very lively pleasure in receiving that intelligence, my boys on the contrary were not delighted."[38]

When they learned they were losing their great teacher, it was understandable that Peter's students were not pleased. The group had been privileged to have a teacher who carried out daily the educational ideals of the two great Moravian education theorists, John Amos Comenius and Nicholas von Zinzendorf.[39]

Herman was introduced to the school children on 30 January 1817. They were "admonished to further industry and obedience by Brother Van Vleck, the Pastor."[40] Before Wolle left the school, he, the boys, and the new teacher "held a very agreeable lovefeast together."[41]

Three days later *Pfleger* Brother Wolle was presented to the members of the Single Brothers' Choir. "After a fervent prayer by Br. Van Vleck he was blessed for this office."[42] Soon after Wolle assumed his new position, he gave his first sermon in Salem "speaking in German."[43] Those who supervised the community were pleased that Br. Wolle's path was working out so well.

## NOTES

1. Adelaide L. Freise, ed. *Records of the Moravians in North Carolina*, vol. 7, 1809–1822, (Raleigh: State Department of Archives and History, 1974), 3123.

2. Peter Seadle, et al., trans., *The Diaries of Peter Wolle* (Winston-Salem, N.C.: Old Salem, Inc., 1984), 1, Vol. 10 of *The Three Forks of Muddy Creek*.

3. Ibid., 1.
4. Ibid.
5. Ibid., 2.
6. Ibid., 3.
7. Ibid., 4–5.
8. Friese, *Records*, 3221.
9. Seadle, *Diaries*, 6.
10. Ibid., each of these subjects is mentioned throughout Seadle in various places.
11. Friese, *Records,* 3241.
12. Seadle, *Diaries*, 24.
13. Ibid., 51.
14. Ibid., 49.
15. Ibid., 58.
16. Ibid., 58.
17. Friese, *Records,* 3274.
18. Seadle, *Diaries*, 99.

19. Ibid., "We had much pleasure with the children's diaries this morning because of droll remarks and of faulty spelling," 96.
20. Ibid., 93.
21. Ibid., 18.
22. Ibid., 30.
23. Ibid., 18.
24. Ibid., 36.
25. Ibid., 30.
26. Ibid., 45.
27. Ibid., 52.
28. Ibid., 68.
29. Ibid., 86.
30. Ibid., 96.
31. Ibid., 34.
32. Ibid., 99.
34. Ibid., 44.
35. Ibid., 32.
36. Ibid., 88.
37. Ibid., 47.
38. Ibid., 91.
39. Ibid., 91.
40. Friese, *Records*, 3326.
41. Seadle, *Diaries*, 100.
42. Friese, *Records*, 3326.
43. Ibid., 3327.

Chapter Three

## *Serving as a Musician and a Composer*

> He devoted himself to the composition of that excellent hymn book . . . has remained a standard in our church.[1]

NO SOONER had Br. Wolle arrived in Salem than he began playing music in the church. Describing his second day in Salem, he wrote, "I have already served here twice as organist."[2] A few days later, he was playing chamber music in the afternoon.

> After the mid-day meal, we played some music. P.W. [Peter Wolle] played the first clarinette, Bro. Meinung the second, Bro. Matth. Reis [also Reuz] first horn, Bro. Biehahn [Byhan] second horn.[3]

The music he played with his friends was wide-ranging. "Coffee I drank with them [the Reichels], and yet there was so much time remaining that Sr. Frederica sang an aria by Mozart, and Gotthold [Reichel] and myself played a Sonata for 4 hands by Kotzeluch."[4] Because Wolle alternated evenings supervising the students, there was time for chamber music. "Gotthold [and] I visited at Schweiniz's. Played a double-sonata [sonata for four hands] in addition to variations by Beethoven and Genlinek."[5] Wolle also played for his own pleasure when he was alone. He described how "a vehement desire for exercising my fingers on the Piano forte seized upon me and till the time of walking, I played 122 pages of Variations by Mozart."[6]

Within the first month, Wolle performed symphonies with the Salem *collegium musicum* in which he played the violin, and he wrote that, "Afterwards we played our trombones in the Brothers' House."[7]

Because people had many duties, musical ensembles did not always have the required instrumentalists. If a person was missing, the group simply played without the part. When Wolle "Played Quadros [quartets] in the evening," he wrote in his diary, "because Br. Wierling was called away, we had to play in three parts."[8]

Neither were the performances always as perfect as Wolle would have liked.

> Because it was impossible to go outside, we made music in the Church in the afternoon ... played two symphonies by Haydn which, however, were not well received, but mainly because the bass-player did not play his part very well.[9]

Commenting on the music for a love feast, Wolle wrote, "The music was not well chosed [sic] and was performed very poorly."[10] While the quality of musical performances was often irregular, when everything worked out, Wolle took great pleasure in the result. One evening service received very high praise from him, a person who had heard the best music expertly performed in Nazareth and Bethlehem.

> What distinguished this day ... from others is the Liturgy which was sung in the evening meeting, the finest that I ever heard sung. Not only the completeness of the Choir, consisting of 6 Sisters and 3 Brethren, but also the great number of people assembled.[11]

The arrival of a bassoon brought Wolle particular joy. When it was added to the *collegium,* he wrote, "we played a considerable time, till the lips refused obedience."[12]

A year later the music director for the community resigned, and Brother Wolle was offered the post. "Today I was assigned the position of Musical Director."[13] As Salem's musical director, Wolle selected and prepared the music for the church services as well as performed it. He

## SERVING AS A MUSICIAN AND A COMPOSER

filled his diary with musical information about each type of service. At the same time the Salem town diary contained many detailed accounts of Salem's musical life.

There were numerous congregational services throughout the week, and music was an essential part of each one. The "preaching service" was similar to what is now a Sunday service. Many hymns with organ accompaniment were sung by the congregation, liturgies were included, and one or two concerted anthems, i.e., choral music accompanied by an orchestra, were performed.

The *Singstunde* was to celebrate special occasions of every sort. Usually, the *Gemeine* attended at least one a week. In that service the pastor extemporaneously chose hymn stanzas to form a unified message; however, that practice appeared to be disappearing in nineteenth-century America, for Wolle was disturbed when he was not told what hymns would be sung and expressed his displeasure in his diary.

> In this matter I must object to the fact that he does not announce the numbers of the verses that he is going to sing ahead of time. This causes a paging around in the books until already half the verse is sung.[14]

• • •

By Wolle's time, it was apparently acceptable for the organist to play directly from a chorale book, rather than from memory. Therefore, the organist needed to know the number of the hymn tune, so it could be located in the chorale book. One or two concerted anthems or solos might be sung at this service, also. Wolle described a *Singstunde* that was the culmination of a particularly moving day.

> In the evening solemn *Singstunde*, during which the following pieces were sung: *"Frohlocket und jauchzet"* ["rejoice and be exultant"] *"Gott stehet in der Germein Gottes"* ["May the Lord stand with his congregation"], and *"Seelige Gemeine, Jesu segne dich"* ["May Jesus bless the congregation of those who have gone Home"]. The entire day was

truly festive and I must say that the peace from above and the closeness of the Saviour could be felt strongly.[15]

Love feasts were held when the need arose and were not necessarily musically demanding. Wolle described one, "During a happy lovefeast there was a short address, and a hymn was sung that had been composed for the occasion."[16] However, festival love feasts included an "Ode," the most elaborately planned musical form in the Moravian Church. Also called a psalm, the ode was comprised of hymn texts and scriptural excerpts that were chanted or sung as anthems.

> At the lovefeast an ode was sung by the choir and the congregation alternately; the ode had been prepared in advance and printed, and dealt with the joy of the Lord.[17]

Musically, the ode resembled the Lutheran cantata though it was less formal, and there was a greater opportunity for congregational singing. Odes were not as centered on the choir and usually involved a litany that was sung and spoken.

> Various other types of music might mingle with these: antiphonal chants for combinations of choir, congregation, of liturgies; solos and duets; chants or recitatives sung by the liturgist or a soloist in the choir.[18]

Because of the number and variety of services, six or seven concerted anthems might be performed during a week. A single Sabbath might have included three or four such anthems. A festival love feast had two as did a *Gemeinstunde*. A *Singstunde* in midweek might add one or two more anthems. In his diary, Wolle complained about rehearsing the amount of music that was needed to celebrate Easter, "At 3 o'clock there was a rehearsal for the 18 musical pieces that were to be used during these days. Almost too much at once."[19]

When the entire church year was considered, the need for music in a small Moravian community such as Salem was startling. In addition

## SERVING AS A MUSICIAN AND A COMPOSER

to weekly services, three Christian festivals were observed with very special services. They were Great Sabbath (the Saturday before Easter), Easter, and Christmas Eve. The following account is of a Christmas Eve service.

> The children had a lovefeast at five o'clock in the afternoon. . . . Br. Van Vleck moved his forte-piano into the church, placing it near the minister's table, so that he could play the accompaniment for the choir anthems "Glory to God in the highest," and "Beautiful Child."[20]

In addition, there were church festivals celebrating important events in the history of the Moravian Church. New Year's Eve and July 4th were also sacred services. Independence Day always included a variety of music. The following is Wolle's account of 4 July 1816.

> At 1/2 past 6 the musical band assembled and performed very elegantly some marches and hymn tunes. – At 10 o'clock was english Preaching. Bro. Schweintiz delivered an excellent discourse. We sang from the choir: "Come joyful . . ." and "Praise Jerusalem. . . ." The horns accompanied by the Posauns [trombones] and Clarinets! – At 8 o'clock Bro. von V. kept the morning prayer. I played. At 2 o'clock a private party had a refreshment of wine sangrie and sugarcake. . . . At 1/2 past 4 we again made some music in the square but soon quitted [sic] because Meinung's clarinet would not come to order, [work correctly] and people did not seem to mind us! – In singing meeting [*Singstunde*] a few pieces were sung. . . . The day was most elegant.[21]

Each of the choirs celebrated its own festival day. Even ceremonies with children included concerted hymns and anthems.

> At ten o'clock there was a sermon for children, and during the service the little boys sang verses of blessing for the little girls. . . . In early evening, in the Boarding school, they sang their praises, accompanied by several wind instruments.[22]

Days celebrating very special events required elaborate music. Salem remembered its Fiftieth Jubilee during Brother Wolle's second year as music director. The account of that celebration offers a comprehensive picture of the musical service required of him.

> Scarcely had the sun risen in its glory – for the day was unexpectedly pleasant . . . when the trombonists announced the festal day. . . . At nine o'clock the congregation assembled for the early service. After a hymn with instrumental accompaniment Br. Van Vleck explained the reason and the occasion for the observation of this festal day . . . petitions were offered that He would continue to reign over this town and its inhabitants, and would work out ever more fully His thoughts and peace therein, and especially that on this day of blessing He would permit His presence to be felt in our midst. At two o'clock was the festal lovefeast, during which a printed ode was sung with full instrumental accompaniment, the musicians from Bethabara assisting.
>
> Following this service large and smaller groups took pleasant walks to various points near Salem, while wind instruments were played from the balcony of the church.
>
> In the evening at seven o'clock there was a happy singstunde, with hymns sung by the congregation and by the choir. The church was beautifully illuminated, with a pyramid of fifty candles in front of the minister's table, and twenty-five candles burning on each choir gallery, in addition to the usual five chandeliers.[23]

An even more elaborate service was held for the centenary of the Salem *Gemeine*. The musical activities that took place during that single day are listed:

> Chorales by the trombones at four o'clock [a.m.]
> The choir opened by singing the invitation. [by Buckler]
> At half past ten . . . the choir sang. [by Nemine]
> At two o'clock . . . a new ode was used.
> At half past seven . . . the choir sang [by Ghastlier]
> In closing the choir sang the Old Testament Benediction.

Pupils marched around the square singing hymns accompanied with wind instruments. The musicians continued to play chorales in front of the Brothers' House.[24]

In addition, services were held throughout the year within each choir. Thus, every *Chorhaus* had an independent musical group. People in each choir were awakened by singing with instrumental accompaniment. Birthdays were celebrated with musical announcements and love feasts.

Visits and departures of residents or guests often included sacred concerts of instrumental music and concerted anthems. President George Washington's visit to Salem was announced by brass. "The intelligence being received here on the 31st May . . . at his approach the sound of trombones, trumpets and french horns was alternately heard."[25]

In contrast to music played for the enjoyment of the musicians, church music required rehearsals. Yet, there is no record in the diaries that the *collegium musicum* practiced regularly. Wolle does write about rehearsals for special occasions.

At 3 o'clock was the rehearsal of the music for the holidays. The sisters choir consisted of 6 persons; they seem to have been excited to new endeavors, to fill up vacancies that have been occasioned of late.[26]

• • •

One of the great legacies of the Moravian Church to American music is the immense collection of manuscripts that grew from the constant need for large amounts of sacred music. The published music catalogue of the Salem Congregation includes approximately one thousand compositions. The catalogue covers about one hundred years of musical activity in Salem and is restricted to anthems and liturgies that survived. How much music was discarded, destroyed, removed from the collection, or taken elsewhere is not known. It is clear, however, that the collection was larger than it presently is. The collection adds a thousand more items associated in some way with Salem.[27]

Keeping the music filed, catalogued, and stored was one of Wolle's primary responsibilities as music director. "Spent the morning putting the musical materials that Bro. Reuz had passed on to me in order," Wolle wrote in his dairy.[28] The music required constant attention, updating, and revision due to the large number of services. The catalogue and the filing system existed before Wolle arrived in Salem.

As music director, Wolle followed in the footsteps of the most famous Moravian American composer of the eighteenth century, Johann Friedrich Peter, who served as Salem's music director from 1780 to 1790 and was followed by other prominent Moravian musicians. Wolle now had the opportunity to complete his personal musical education by becoming intimately familiar with the music holdings of the congregation and by selecting music that fit the capabilities of the Salem *collegium musicum*. As always, Wolle did his job well, and his contribution to the management of Salem's music was notable enough for the editor of the Salem music catalogue to write in 1980:

> His [Wolle's] volumes of *Musikalische Texte,* written in a hand that rivals Johannes Reuz's for neatness and legibility, contains the most complete record of texts performed in Salem. Entries sometimes even indicate the composer or call number for a given anthem. He also kept the bound catalogues current.[29]

Because printed anthems were generally unavailable to Moravian congregations, sacred music was copied by hand. Making these copies was one of the duties of the music manager. Wolle wrote of his preparation of manuscripts, "Copied music all afternoon, most for 'The Song of the Bell'," and, "This morning I was principally employed in copying some notes."[30] By identifying Wolle's handwriting, scholars established that he added many manuscripts to the Salem collection while he was the music director. "He seems to have played a leading role in the music program in many ways from 1814–1819 . . . and copied a great deal of music."[31]

In addition to his responsibility for the notated music, Wolle supervised Salem's musical instrument collection. Concerted anthems regularly required an orchestra including an organ, a number of violins, violas, violoncellos, and basses; often two horns, two flutes, two trumpets, and clarinets were added. In addition, there was the trombone choir of at least four players. The school and the choir houses contained fortepianos. Most, if not all, of these instruments belonged to the community. Wolle recorded numerous times when he tuned or repaired them. In one case, he did both on successive days. "[Wednesday] asked me to tune the piano in the Saal in the Sisters' House," and, "[Thursday] This afternoon I fixed the piano in the Sisters' House."[32] He also repaired harps, clavichords, organs, polished the bassoon, and made clarinet reeds.

After being music director in Salem and the leader of the Single Brothers' Choir for four years, Wolle moved to the next level of sacred service in Moravian communities: he became associate pastor in Bethania, Salem's sister settlement in Wachovia. The Salem diarist recorded Br. Wolle's decision and the events that followed.

> Br. Peter Wolle has accepted the post as associate pastor of Bethania, trusting in the help of the Lord. He proposed marriage with the single Sr. Maria Theresa Schober, and as the Conference has no objection the LOT was tried and the affirmative drawn.[33]

• • •

Marriage was a requirement for anyone entering the Moravian ministry, and Peter's marriage to Maria Schober was a fortunate one. She was an excellent companion, a loving mother, a sensitive leader of the women in the community, and a fine musician. Br. Wolle outlived Maria and never ceased to mourn her loss. Maria's importance in this biography looms large in the next section, for she was primarily responsible for her son Theodore's musical education.

Wolle's transfer to Bethania meant that he left his musical duties at Salem. Never again did he have full responsibility for the music in a

Moravian community. At that moment, the balance between musical service to the church and pastoral duties shifted. From then on, Br. Wolle's duties as a cleric would far exceed his activity as a musician and as a composer.

Like other aspects of his musical talent, composition came naturally to Peter. Whether he was a teacher, a pastor, or a bishop, when he wanted to compose, he sat down and did so. Soon after he arrived in Salem, for example, he wrote in his diary, "Wrote a letter to my mother this morning. In the afternoon composed a minuet and trio for two clarinets and horns."[34] Another day he wrote, "for the last hour, I let my class occupy itself, and composed a bit."[35] When recuperation from an illness gave him leisure from teaching, he composed for the group he played with in the evening. "I felt tolerably well today, nothing of fever and the heart in good order. I composed a march for clar., horn and bassoon."[36] In another diary entry, Peter described how his natural gift and the ease with which he composed fit into his gracious lifestyle at Salem. "After I had finished straightening up, I got to work copying my piece and finished just in time for coffee."[37] Many years later, when he was retired in Bethlehem, he recorded the events during a very pleasant musical evening. "We had some music at our home, – father Weiss, James & myself tried for the first time my new composition, recently ushered into the world, it was approved of. We also sang a number of our choral hymns."[38]

The ease with which he composed did not mean that Peter composed without thought. On the contrary, he considered every aspect of the composition. He recorded part of that process when describing an anthem he wrote in the year 1816.

> Yesterday evening I again had the urge to do some composing and searched through the entire hymnal and the supplement and then finally found something in the latter that I liked, namely, "Schmueke und erfahre, Gnadenwahl neu." Now I had to think for a long time which key and which measure [meter] I should choose for this piece. After much thought I selected "A" as the key and 3/4 time as the measure. I seemed to make quite a good beginning, and by this

evening managed, in a little time left to me after taking care of my classes, to write 38 measures that I like quite well.³⁹

The completed anthem, more than ninety measures, is scored for four voices, two violins, viola, violoncello, bass, and organ.

Unlike the previous generation of Moravian composers, Wolle even considered profiting from his compositions. He confided to his dairy, "Composed a few little songs the morning. Was encouraged by the favorable general acceptance of Buckler's songs to make a similar collection in the hope of being able to profit from it."⁴⁰ He continued to work on this "Anthology," and wrote, "Yesterday and the day before yesterday, I carried the Musical Anthology I was preparing around with me, but I am still not finished."⁴¹ Nine days later it was complete, and the following week he played selections for the Single Sisters. Unfortunately, there is no record of this anthology, though later in his life, Wolle did publish a number of songs for profit.

• • •

Like every aspect of Moravian life, the musical style acceptable to the community was already in place when Wolle began composing. He carried on a European tradition transplanted in America by his composer/teachers who had been trained in Europe. They also composed in the manner they had inherited, and conveyed it to Wolle and to his generation.

The Moravian composer Christian Gregor (1732–1801) codified the style. His compositions were models of the way to do things. He was very prolific, composing over five hundred and sixty anthems, many arias and duets, and a book of chorale tunes that became the standard chorale book for Moravians until well into the nineteenth century.

It was a later Moravian composer, Christian Latrobe, who described this musical canon. "Correctness and Simplicity, the two grand sources of beauty in the performance of Music . . . ought chiefly to be attended to."[42] He added "elegance" to the list when he described the sacred compositions of one Moravian minister.[43] Reminding the reader that musical instruments played an important part in the worship of the Moravian Church, Latrobe stated that "moderation, but sufficient skill" was required to perform Moravian music. Thus, musical accomplishments were never to display virtuosity. Writing specifically of anthems, Latrobe summarized the Moravian aesthetic for both voice and instruments.

> . . . that neither in the vocal, nor instrumental parts, any attempt is made to exhibit the skill of the performers by a display of extraordinary powers of execution, which might lead the attention of the congregation into an improper channel.[44]

Writing in a treatise on church music, a relative of Christian Latrobe explained what the "improper channel[s]" might be.

> In this light may no gift be said to be a great gift . . . but he who possesses none, may be comforted in his poverty by the consideration, that he presents none for the assaults of Satan. The very knowledge and love of the [musical] science, enticing musical men from their attention of spiritual enjoyment to fix or mingle the dross of human gratification with the pure gold of devotional feeling, becomes a snare: while the want of it preserves the uninitiated from any dread of the temptation.[45]

Simplicity and elegance became the compositional practice for Moravian sacred music. Such music did not detract the listener from the devotional mood, and the singers and instrumentalists were not required to practice long hours, keeping them from their primary spiritual work. There is another reason for the musical simplicity that pervaded the style. Christian Latrobe discussed it. "Vocal fugues also, are not used in the Church, as being unintelligible to the congregation, who wish to understand the words of the Anthem."[46]

On first hearing, Moravian sacred music may sound like simplified Haydn, Mozart, or Schubert. But the differences between the music of Moravian composers and those of the Viennese classical school were intentional; they were not simplifications or made out of lack of understanding. For Haydn and Mozart, and other composers of their generation, set musical forms that regulated the musical design of a composition. Sonata form was the dominant one. In a sonata movement, classical symmetry prescribed that specific key and thematic relationships were observed. For example, a major practice was to have the opening key and musical material, i.e., the exposition, return before the piece ended, i.e., recapitulation. Between the exposition and the recapitulation, both the themes and the keys underwent transformations that were often very elaborate, i.e., the development. But the key and the themes must be recapitulated for formal reasons. That was the practice in vocal compositions even when there was a text with no repetition.

In their sacred music, Moravian composers consciously ignored the formal aspects of musical classicism that inevitably obscured the text. For them, the text determined the form of an anthem or an aria. Different words required new music. There were no elaborate or even simple thematic developments. Musical repetition confused the meaning of a text, and frequent changes of key captivated the musical mind, diverting attention from the soul. Thus, Moravians created a unique musical practice to express Zinzendorf's Christian theology rooted in Protestant pietism. A twentieth-century scholar summarized this aesthetic when she wrote, "textual content must not be overshadowed by musical complexity."[47]

Three musical analyses follow, revealing how skillfully Wolle applied the Moravian compositional style to a variety of compositions, how knowledgeable he was of the general canons of Western musical composition, and how precisely he applied those canons.

Wolle's earliest extant compositions were composed when he taught in Nazareth Hall. Two pieces were signed by him and dated [see Appendix A, #3 and #22]. The earliest composition [#22] was composed on 24 June 1812. It is an *arietta*, a favorite vocal form for Moravian composers. These sacred "airs" were "more complicated than a chorale and less elaborate than an anthem. Gregor's *ariettas* were simple enough for congregational singing, yet appropriate for choral use. *Ariettas* are not lengthy compositions."[48]

Wolle's *arietta* was only twelve measures long with the first two measures repeated. He scored the song for two violins, viola, cello, and organ. The text was in both English, "Jesus makes our heart rejoice," and in German, "Jesus unser Hort ist treu." The graceful, innocent melody is in the key of G Major. The melody was shaped with just enough subtle rhythm and pitch variety that it sounded innocent but was not repetitious. The vocal range of an octave was traditional for simple songs. Even the most untrained singer could sing an octave. Wolle placed a small climax, appropriate for such a short piece, in the eleventh measure where the melody reached its highest point on the pitch G above the treble staff. The melody had been moving to the high G from the fourth measure. Wolle also prepared for the climax by modulating to the key of D Major at that point. The other harmonies are conventional and unadorned.

Consistent with the Moravian need to express the text, Wolle not only composed a direct, uncomplicated melody, harmonized with simple chords, he skillfully placed an evocative yet delicate instance of word-painting early in the song. This word-painting can be understood only within the context of the full English text.

> *Jesus makes our heart rejoice;*
> *We're his sheep & know his voice.*
> *He's a shepherd kind & gracious*
> *& his pastures are delicious.*
> *Constant love to us he shows,*
> *yet our worthless names he knows.*[49]

The sentiment of the poem was of joy and assurance in the fact that Jesus, as a shepherd, knows and loves all his sheep. This was a typical expression of Christian pietism. The message was direct, uncomplicated, with heartfelt rather than rational appeal. Wolle had captured all the elements of belief in his melody and in his harmony. However, he went musically much beyond simply composing a literal setting of this text. He harmonized the words "our heart rejoice" and "know his voice" with a musical formula called "horn fifths," a distinct progression of pitches created in which horns played in harmony. Horns symbolized pastoral scenes because of their association with hunting. They were also a symbol of royalty. By incorporating these musical references within the texture of his *arietta*, Wolle expressed musically the belief that Jesus the King was at the same time Jesus the gentle, all-knowing shepherd. Wolle's use of the device was even more subtle, for he not only set the words "and know his voice" to the horn motive – that in a sense would be expected – but he placed the horn fifths with the phrase "our hearts rejoice" earlier in the poem. Thus, the "heart" already felt Jesus, the shepherd, and rejoiced in that feeling before the shepherd Jesus was known to the mind. Peter's musical insight at that place was truly admirable and completely Moravian with the pietistic dictum "heart before mind."

In order to assure that the musical reference to Jesus the shepherd was completely audible, and thus openly expressive of the text, Wolle placed the horn fifths in all four voices. Because horn fifths are only two-voiced, the result was that the soprano and the tenor sang the same part while the other part was sung by the alto and bass. By placing the horn fifths in all the voices, Peter abandoned the rules of harmonizing a melody in four parts. Such a departure from traditional part-writing was acceptable only because of the unusual pastoral reference associated with horns. Already in this "simple" air, Wolle, still a young man, showed he had attained the theological and musical education required to compose a perfect Moravian setting of a text. The effect of natural innocence conveyed through the horn call must be heard to be fully appreciated.

A further example of his skill as a composer was the occurrence in the eighth measure of four descending eighth notes. He used that musical gesture to express the words "how delicious." Consistent with Western musical practice that every musical element plays a part in every musical event, Wolle also employed the subdominant chord to harmonize these words. Normally, composers used the subdominant chord earlier in such a composition. However, Wolle withheld it until the text demanded special attention. To refresh the harmony at that place by using a new chord emphasized the "delicious" nature of the pastures attended by Jesus, the shepherd. At the same moment Wolle also changed the accompaniment from a figure of moving eighth notes called an Alberti bass to a slow harmonic bass of single quarter notes. This change intensifies the sentiment "how delicious" by slowing down the musical motion. Finally, the climax of the melody mentioned above occurred on the word "Yea," exactly where the climax should be, just before the conclusion of this charming, very skillfully designed, pietistic sacred song.[50]

Bro. Wolle was most prolific as a composer while he served as a teacher, as the *Pfleger* of the Single Brothers' Choir, and was responsible for the musical activities of the Salem community. Two anthems composed in the year 1815 show his ability to create both a purely traditional Moravian choral piece and an anthem with an expanded harmonic palette that still remained within the Moravian canon.

The traditional anthem "Come, Joyful Hallelujahs Raise" was composed for Salem's 4th of July service, 1815.[51] The Salem Diary contained an account of activities that characterized the sacred nature of the celebration.

> July 4. The anniversary of the declaration of independence by the United States was observed in solemn manner. In the morning at ten o'clock there was English preaching, which opened with an anthem, with musical accompaniments, which had been written for the occasion. After a prayer for our dear fatherland and its welfare Br. Reichel spoke to the large congregation on Ps.[alm] CVII drawing attention to the great mercies and blessings by the Almighty which had been poured upon us and our fellow citizens. In the evening there was a sacred singstunde.[52]

Wolle's anthem was composed for the typical Moravian choir with parts for two sopranos, alto, and bass. The importance of the occasion called for an impressive sound, so Wolle added two flutes, two clarinets, and two horns to the usual instrumental ensemble. The key of the anthem, E flat Major, expressed the patriotic solemnity appropriate for the event. Wolle composed only simple voice lines and harmonies, avoiding extended sections of counterpoint so that the words were always clear. The music was easy enough for amateur singers and instrumentalists to learn with little rehearsal. The anthem was through composed, i.e., with new music for new words so that the text remained prominent. Yet, the musical invention must not intrude in any way, or call attention to the composer's craft. Self-expression by the composer was not the issue. The Moravian remained at the service of the community in his musical composition, as he did in every other facet of his life.[53]

Though "Come, Joyful Hallelujahs Raise" was nearly devoid of word painting, Wolle did compose a word picture at the climax of the anthem. The final verse told the singers

*O tune thy harp, and strike thy lay,*
*America, Columbia, America, Columbia,*
*America, Columbia, America, Columbia!*

Wolle harmonized the first, third, and final "America, Columbia" with tonic and dominant chords. However, the second "America, Columbia" Wolle set apart by having the words in unison. Thus, every harp was tuned to strike "thy lay," and that "lay" was "America, Columbia." Wolle extended the meaning further when he used the same pitches for "America" and "Columbia." Two different words had the same meaning.

This anthem is exactly as Latrobe had described when he wrote

May the proper character of the anthem be ascertained. It should be simple, spirited, in good taste, marked with devotional feelings, rich in melody to attract, and solemnizing that attention abound in ecclesiastical harmonies, its performance should be modest and yet animated, free from affected ornaments and characterized by . . . truth of expression.[54]

This anthem was sung often in Moravian communities throughout Wolle's life.

"Fuer Mich, O Herr" was composed in 1815 for the Lenten season, the most important time in the Moravian Church year. The Moravian meaning of Christ's sacrifice shaped Br. Wolle's composition in every sense. A detailed analysis of the piece is beyond the scope of this biography; however, some of the most expressive moments show Wolle's complete command of the musical resources available to composers in the early nineteenth century.[55]

This text expressed the wonder Moravians felt when contemplating that their personal salvation came from Christ's suffering and death. The transformation of suffering into the wonder of salvation was captured by the poet in the construction of the verses beginning with "For me," and moving to "What a wonder," and concluding with "For my sake, for my salvation." This progression is clear in the full text of the anthem:

*For me, For me,*
*O Lord, O Lord, my God and Saviour,*
*Didst Thou suffer alone,*
*Forsaken, sadly struggling,*
*In bitter anguish with grim death.*
*What a wonder, a wonder!*
*What a wonder, does my spirit,*
*Uplifted behold!*
*Life, life itself,*
*Life itself bows low in the dust of death,*
*For my guilt, for my guilt,*
*For my sake, for my salvation.*

Wolle set the mood at the beginning of the anthem as *Grave,* indicating the composition was slow and profoundly serious. He selected the key of E flat Major, a key chosen to express heroic, solemn events. In the Western harmonic system, the key of E flat Major is directly related to, and interchangeable with, the key of C minor, which is associated with noble suffering and mourning.[56] Throughout the anthem, Wolle moved from one of these keys to the other, at times harmonizing the word "death" in E flat Major, and then using the key of C minor. In this way he expressed the belief that Christ's death was a happy event for Moravians, and the happiness came from suffering. In his choice of keys, Br. Wolle embedded the interdependence of death, suffering, and the triumph of salvation.

The interconnection between the sacrifice and the wonder expressed in the text was also part of the anthem's formal structure. "For me, For me," opens the anthem. After a rather extended musical development when the phrase "What a wonder, a wonder!" appeared in the middle of the composition; Wolle set the new words to the same pitches and in the same key he used at the beginning of the anthem. In this way, he made clear that the "wonder" was "For me." The harmonic and melodic repetition resembled sonata form with its statement, development, and return. While formal melodic repetition normally was avoided in Moravian anthems because of the canon "new word, new music," Wolle selected the sonata form for this piece because that form best expressed the theological meaning "a wonder for me."

To express the belief that Christ's salvation was for everyone, Wolle used another musical device. He composed the anthem for two choruses. The two groups of singers began by conversing; chorus II singing "For me," softly and in a very declarative rhythm. Chorus I responded "For me," softly, very lyrically, an octave lower.[57] The two choruses remained separate as long as Wolle expressed the suffering of Jesus. However, after the two groups echoed "What a wonder!" the choruses merge. The "wonder" has taken place. The sacrifice was for everyone. The result was a moment of insightful expression. The antiphonal drama in the first part of the anthem reached a full resolution in the joining of the choruses. Wolle created a totally satisfying merger of form and poetic expression to serve the sacred meaning of the text.

Still, the most distinctive aspect of this anthem was its harmonic richness. In order to intensify the expressiveness of the music, Br. Wolle employed excursions into distant keys and unusual dissonances used by pre-Romantic composers: a sudden shift into the key above and a family of chords called augmented sixths. The sudden shift into the key above the tonic was called a Neapolitan. An example of a Neapolitan would be a D flat chord in the key of C Major or of C minor.

Yet, Wolle used a Neapolitan a number of times in an anthem only seventy-three measures long. He placed the first Neapolitan chord on the word "suffer" in the line "didst Thou suffer alone, forsaken." The second use was even more dramatic. A highly theatrical pause followed the phrase, "for my sake," just before the conclusion "for my salvation." This moment summed up the meaning of the anthem. Bro. Wolle harmonized the word "for" in "for my sake" with a Neapolitan. It is a stunning touch emphasizing the reason Christ's suffering occurred. Again, the effect must be heard to be appreciated.

Chords that increased dissonance were the augmented sixths. There were three types: Italian, French, and German. The German sixth was the most dissonant and for that reason was rarely used in the late eighteenth and early nineteenth centuries. These chords were not used by Wolle's teachers at all. Wolle used the German Augmented Sixth chord as skillfully and effectively as he used the Neapolitan. He repeated the line "Life bows low in the dust of death" three times. At this place, the voice underlay of the translation differs from the German. The English translation reads "the dust of death." However, the original German is *zum Todes Staube,* literally, "to death's dust." Wolle wanted the emphasis on the word "dust," rather than on "death." He placed the augmented German sixth on the second syllable of *"Todes,"* "death," stressing that it was from earth's dust that salvation was generated. This salvation was reconstructed from dust – from nothing. In many ways this is the most telling moment in the anthem, for Br. Wolle coupled it with an instance of fine tone painting. "Life itself bows low in death" began on a high pitch and descended to a low one for the word "death." Then, unexpectedly, the melody ascended the D Major scale on the word "dust." We hear the generation of salvation from death's dust in the music. It was moments of compositional control such as these that placed Peter Wolle on an equal footing with other composers in the Moravian tradition.

However, "Fuer Mich, O Herr" remained unique. While Wolle did compose other anthems throughout his life, they are all conservative. Wolle may not have exceeded the border of "ecclesiastical harmonies" advocated by Latrobe; he reached the limit for himself. Wolle never again composed an anthem using these chords. It remained for his son, Theodore, to perform and compose truly Romantic music.

Even though he composed a considerable amount of sacred vocal music, Wolle was remembered by Moravians chiefly for his contribution to Moravian hymnody. Referring to Wolle, the editor of *The Moravian* wrote, "He devoted himself to the compilation of that excellent hymn book, which was subsequently published and has remained a standard in our church to the present day."[58] Wolle also compiled a booklet containing the melodies of favorite Moravian hymns. Both of these collections were completed during the time he was a pastor in Philadelphia and in Lititz. The book of chorales was of greater importance than the tune book, but both works address a change that was taking place in American Christian churches: the loss of an aural hymn-singing tradition. Learning hymn tunes by ear was replaced by learning hymns from printed music. Also, harmony was no longer improvised as it had been in the past. In the "Preface" to the *Choral-Buch* in 1784, Christian Gregor described the practice of improvised harmony. "The basses [bass lines] have been for the most part set to harmonize best with the long-standing custom in the singing of the Brethren, where many sing a special kind of middle part, or seconding."[59] Congregations needed notation that followed the canon of correct ecclesiastical part writing to guide them when they sang harmony.

Two other changes came about. Many more people were playing the piano and the harmonium, and accompanying hymn singing in the parlor. These amateurs were not trained to realize harmony from a figured bass. For them, harmony had to be fully written out. Also, non-Moravians were interested in using Moravian tunes to sing texts from their denomination, but they had no way of coordinating the two.

Each of these changes was clearly delineated in the "Preface" of Wolle's *Hymn Tunes, Used in the Church of the United Brethren, arranged for Four Voices and the Organ or Piano-forte; to which are added Chants for the Litany of that Church, and a Number of Approved Anthems for Various Occasions*. Wolle also introduced changes in the traditional notation and articulated the religious pietism that undergirded the whole enterprise. Because of its importance the complete "Preface" is given.

> The collection of Church Tunes contained in this book is presented to the public by the publisher at the earnest solicitation of many of his friends. He has had respect more immediately to the congregations and members of his own denominations, desirous that through his humble instrumentality their psalmody in the house of God might become improved, and divine worship thereby be rendered more engaging. Yet would he flatter himself, that among Christians of other persuasions many will be found who approve of our church music, the slow and solemn movement observed throughout being in their estimation best suited for the holy worship of the Lord. And the tunes being adapted to the hymns of the United Brethren's Hymn-book, which is known to possess a very rich variety of meter, this very circumstance will render it the more easy to find tunes corresponding with most of the meters used in the collections of other churches. The tunes are all carefully arranged for four voices, and the accompaniment of the Organ or Piano Forte is brought down to the capacity of a moderately skilled performer, whereby a facility is offered for executing them, both in the house of God, and in the domestic circle, with that correct harmony which constitutes the superior beauty of that species of music, and which is in a special manner adapted to religious purposes. With little difficulty, it is presumed a choir of singers might be trained in every place, to lead the congregation in singing

the songs of Zion: and not infrequently might a few persons unite in the habitations of the righteous, with the aid of this book, to raise harmonious anthems to the Most High.

It has been deemed expedient, with a view to the better appearance of the work, to substitute quarter notes (crotchets) in place of half notes (minims) as has been the general custom: it may therefore be proper to remark, that this change is not designed in the least to accelerate the tempo to be observed in singing the tunes, which on the contrary require throughout a slow movement.

To facilitate the adaptation of these tunes to hymns contained in the collections used by other Christian denominations, it may be observed that C. C. corresponds with our tunes 14, 590, 593; L. M. with 22, 166; S. M. with 582, 595; for the particular meters, a comparison of any given hymn with the verses in this collection would in most cases lead to the discovery of such tunes as would fully answer the purpose.

That this publication may, under the divine blessing, become an aid to devotion, and a means of advancing God's glory in promoting the cause of truth and piety, by tending to impress the sentiments to which the voice gives utterance upon the heart, and thus preparing the pilgrim here below, for uniting, when once arrived at his blissful and eternal home, with the saints above in the song of Moses and the Lamb, is the sincere wish and prayer of the publisher,
Rev. Peter Wolle[60]

The hymn book contained one hundred twenty-one tunes printed in four parts. Wolle notated the voice parts in score, i.e., each voice with its own staff. The top staff was the tenor and the "second treble" staff was the alto part. The third staff, the "first treble," was the hymn tune with the text of the first verse of the hymn above it and the appropriate harmony below in small print. The "base" line completed the vocal four-part score. That part also included the figures indicating possible chord tones for the harmony. Using Wolle's score, a choir, members of a congregation, or a family group could sing their written voice parts and produce "that correct harmony which constitutes the

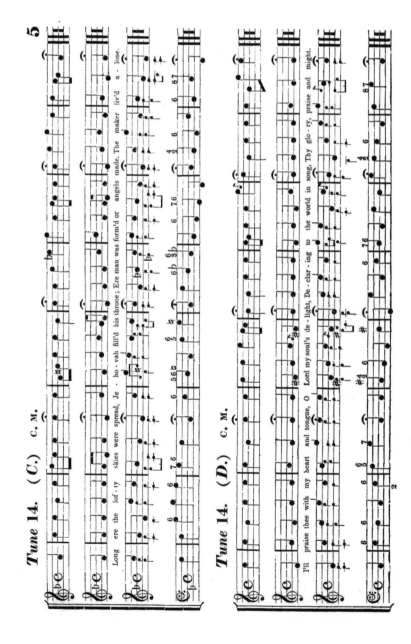

Page from Peter Wolle's *Hymn Tunes*, showing layout of voice parts

superior beauty of that species of music" Wolle spoke of in his "Preface."[61] In addition, there was a self-standing keyboard part on two staves for the two additional sections;"Chants of the Church Liturgy" and "Anthems," completed the volume. These anthems were divided into "Anthems I. For Passion Week., II. For Easter., III. For Christmas., and IV. For other Festivals of the Church." Seven anthems, mostly by Moravian composers, were included along with one composed by Wolle specifically for this collection, "Sing Hallelujah, Christ doth live."[62] With the addition of chants and particularly anthems, Wolle greatly expanded the usefulness of a tune book and supplied a basic source of vocal music for the entire church year.

By the beginning of the year 1835, Wolle had conceived of his book of hymn tunes. This book came to be his most significant and most original work. Stressing that it would contain only tunes in "current use" in America, Wolle described his plan in a letter written 23 January 1835 to Theodore Schulz, a Salem friend. The "Melodies will appear in 4 voice settings, for soprano, alto, tenor, and bass, each voice part with its own staff. The setting will be correct and beautiful." Wolle explains that while every congregation would desire chorales that are correctly sung in four parts, for Moravians, "No such book exists." He wished to place a book in every hand that could be used to train everyone to sing to the Lord "correctly and beautifully." Such a book, costing no more than a dollar, could also be used in Moravian boarding schools. Before he began the book, however, he was interested to know if his colleagues found the idea a good one. Would Schulz support this project and would he kindly find out what others thought?[63]

A few days later, Wolle wrote about his plan in a letter to John D. Anders, president of the Provincial Elders Conference, at that time the governing body of the Moravian Church in America. Wolle reported that he already had a draft of ninety-three chorales, which he listed by number, and had informed members of every Moravian congregation regarding his project which was intended "to improve the singing in our churches."[64] In addition, Wolle informed Anders that arias and other pieces would be added that would be a departure from previous books of hymn tunes. In a long postscript, Wolle mentioned that it had been suggested that he examine a tune book by a European Moravian, Bishop L. Hueffel. It was similar to the one Wolle was planning; Wolle was not aware of that tune book and could Anders please send him a copy?

Wolle received a copy and wrote to Anders. Wolle had examined Hueffel's book with a very critical eye and found it wanting. "I would rather be a student learning from my good elders . . . and the melodies will be set in the way I learned them in my youth [from Michael and Bechler, who were following Gregor]."[65] Hueffel departed from the traditional figured bass, there were many printing errors, the tenor part was too high, and the ranges were too difficult for ordinary singers. In conclusion, Wolle would submit his book to Homman and Hupfelt, famous Philadelphia musicians, for their endorsement.

Understanding what Hueffel did that aggravated Wolle provides a key to appreciating what Wolle achieved in his tune book, and why it was so important to his contemporaries.

Both Wolle and Hueffel faced the same problem: how could congregations add correct harmony when singing hymns in church and at home? As was discussed above, "figured bass" or "thorough bass" was a system devised for keyboard players so that harmony could be added by improvising inner parts using numbers as cues. This was called "realizing" the figured bass. The bass part was written in the bass clef and played with the left hand – only one pitch at a time. The right hand played everything else in the treble clef; usually three pitches at one time. Figured bass was never sung. On occasion the bass was too low, and tenors and altos found the treble too high.

Hueffel retained the two-hand division of the figured bass, but he eliminated the improvised realization. In its place, he composed a realization that he expected the singers to sing. Thus, what the keyboard players played and what the singers sang was the same.[66] Wolle was correct when he stated that the result was not for "ordinary" voices. Hueffel had compromised the integrity of both the singers and the keyboard player.

Wolle, however, retained the integrity of both. He kept the traditional figured bass created by "his elders," suggesting a possible realization with the addition of small notes – keyboard players trained to improvise could do so, while those who were not able had a harmony part to play. To insure that the sung harmony would be "correct," Wolle created a harmonic setting for voices that simultaneously meshed with the figured bass. In addition, Wolle added a full text so that it did not have to be memorized. As a result, Wolle's book of hymn tunes was useable by the trained church organist, the parlor pianist, the singer in the church choir, the congregation, and a group singing hymns at home. Finally, the book was inexpensive, and for many years, Wolle's *Hymn Tunes* was advertised in *The Moravian* for seventy-five cents at the Moravian Book Store in Bethlehem.

The first edition contained a number of "Recommendations" written by others attesting to the worth of Wolle's work. Writing in Bethlehem, 17 March 1836, seven of the most important Moravian clerics in America wrote

> We, the Subscribers, having examined this improved edition of the United Brethren's Tune Book, take great pleasure in recommending it as a work of much merit, for its unexceptional-harmony according to correct principles of Thorough Bass, and as a useful, practical guide for the student of the fundamental principles of music, as well as the more advanced Organist; and being, moreover, persuaded that this work fully answers one of its principal objects, which is, to afford facilities to choirs for executing our church tunes in four parts correctly, as also to promote harmony in singing, at family devotions and in private circles, we confidently recommend it, in both these respects, to all our congregations in this country, and to persons generally who take pleasure in religious psalmody.[67]

Two non-Moravian musicians from Philadelphia verified the correctness of the harmony and the high quality of the book.

> . . . having been requested by the Rev. Mr. Wolle to examine a few pages in manuscript of the work on Psalmody which he is about publishing, take pleasure in stating, that, as far as their examination extended, the arrangement and harmony appeared unexceptional [i.e., not in the romantic style], and the music generally better adapted to the service of the church than is to be found in most publications of a similar character.[68]

The organist in the Moravian Church in Philadelphia, where Wolle was the pastor, concluded his recommendation by stating "the theoretical as well as practical knowledge of the present author will need no further recommendation than an examination of his labor will spontaneously beget for him."[69]

*Hymn Tunes* was reprinted in the years 1857, 1872, 1883, and 1889 by the Moravian Publication Office.

A touching reference to the importance the hymnal held for Peter and his family was found in private Wolle family papers. Agnes Wolle, the daughter of Theodore, Peter's son, gave a copy of the *Hymn Tunes* to a family relative. On the cover Peter had written, "This book was presented to Theodore F. Wolle on entering School at Nazareth, it being at that time quite familiar to him, – by his father P. Wolle. June 23, 1842."[70]

Even though both Hueffel and Wolle were revered by their contemporaries for creating "enduring monuments," by the end of the nineteenth century both of their hymn books were obsolete.[71] The figured bass gave way to four-voice settings on two staves. The lower staff with the bass clef was for the bass and tenor voices. The upper staff with the treble clef was for the soprano and alto.

• • •

Wolle completed his *Hymn Tunes* while he was the pastor of the Moravian Church in Philadelphia. His next position was in Lititz, another Moravian community situated in Central Pennsylvania. If his hymnal proved to be his most important musical service to the Moravian Church, it was in Lititz where Wolle was elevated to the highest level of clerical service. There he was consecrated the first Moravian bishop in America. The report of the ceremony in the church diary, written by Wolle because he was the pastor, is appropriately modest and to the point. It simply states that the service was held 28 September 1845 in the evening officiated by Bishop Benade. No reasons for his election were recorded. That was not unusual at the time. Even now the reason a bishop is elected is not recorded. Only the results of the election appear. As a result of his office, Bishop Wolle made a number of trips to Germany, served on various church committees, officiated at high-level meetings, ceremonial occasions involving the Moravian Church, as well as interactions with other denominations. Thus, Wolle gained the distinction of being one of the rare clerics in the history of the Christian church who was both a bishop and a composer.

Twenty years after Wolle published this collection of hymn tunes, his second contribution to Moravian hymnody appeared in print. The title was in German and in English: *Sammlung der gebraeuchlichen Choral-Melodien der evangelischen Brueder-Gemeine* and *A Collection of Customary Moravian Hymn-Tunes*. It was much more limited in its purpose. Wolle stated the need for the booklet in a short preface.

> This collection of Hymn-Tunes, used in our Moravian Church, is published for the purpose of making our members and friends more familiar with them, and with a view of rendering the congregational singing, in the service of the Sanctuary, more full, harmonious and elevating.[72]

The collection was comprised of one hundred twenty-one melodies. Texts were not included, and each melody was identified only by its traditional Moravian tune number. The booklet "was prepared . . . in 1856 to assist choir members at funerals and on other occasions where an instrument was not available, and when everyone sang in unison."[73] However, the "Notice of New Books" in *The Moravian* indicated that this little volume had other uses.

Central Moravian Church, Bethlehem, after 1867
(The Moravian Archives, Bethlehem)

It is admitted by those who are competent to judge, that our Moravian Collection of Choral-Tunes contains some of the finest specimens of devotional music that can be found any where. The above little volume, offered for sale, at the low price of 15 cents, will be found of great service to those who desire to acquaint themselves with Moravian singing, especially our children and youth.[74]

These pages could be used to learn the hymn tunes by following them during the service or practicing them at home using a piano, or a melody instrument such as the flute. Hymnals with texts, tunes, and harmony are so familiar to present-day churchgoers, this little manual is a curiosity to us. However, it provided Moravian hymn tunes very cheaply to anyone who was interested in them. With these two volumes, Wolle had addressed the needs of the market for nearly a century.

In addition to the hymn collections, Wolle published two semi-sacred duets for the secular music market. They were printed in Philadelphia but were undated. Both songs had simple but well-crafted melodies with very easy piano accompaniments. Though one was based on a text by Byron, there was no touch of Romanticism in the music. The songs were simple and unadorned. They possessed nothing to distinguish them from hundreds of other songs composed for the developing market of the middle class, which wanted music with elevating texts for wives and daughters to sing in parlors and at school. However, the songs were valued by the Wolle family as they valued the *Hymn Book*. The printed copies of the songs in the collection of the Moravian Music Foundation are both signed, "Henrietta Regina Shober a present from her Grand Father Rev. G. Shober." Rev. Shober was Peter's father-in-law and a fine musician himself. He thought enough of the songs to give copies to his daughter; in turn, she thought they were important enough to be passed down in the family for three generations.

In the tradition of his forebearers, Brother Wolle became a cleric who was a musician, not a musician who was a cleric. The next generation would change that tradition and greatly expand the musical influence of the family.

## NOTES

1. *The Moravian*, 23 November 1871.
2. Peter Seadle and Irene P. Seadle, trans., *The Diaries of Peter Wolle*, vol. 10 of *The Three Forks of Muddy Creek* (Winston-Salem, N.C.: Old Salem, Inc., 1984), 4.
3. Ibid., 5.
4. Ibid., 74. Gotthold Reichel was the *Pfleger* of the Salem Single Brothers.
5. Ibid., 7. Lewis David von Schweinitz was the administrator of the Moravian lands in North Carolina. He was a renowned botanist who was known as the father of modern mycology.
6. Ibid., 62.
7. Ibid., 11.
8. Ibid., 18.
9. Ibid., 22.
10. Ibid., 67. Much of the diary Br. Wolle wrote in Salem was written in English, and there are occasional errors. It is to be remembered that Br. Wolle's first language was German, which at that time was the first language of Moravian communities in America.
11. Ibid., 69.
12. Ibid., 86.
13. Ibid., 21.
14. Adelaide L. Friese, ed., *Records of the Moravians in North Carolina*, vol. 7, 1809–1822 (Raleigh: State Department of Archives and History, 1974), 3240.
15. Seadle, *Diaries*, 35.
16. Ibid., 65.
17. Friese, *Record*, 3139.
18. Ibid., 3240.
19. Francis Cumnock, *Catalogue of the Salem Congregation Music*. (Chapel Hill: The University of North Carolina Press, 1980), 9.
20. Seadle, *Diaries*, 25.
21. Friese, *Records*, 3665.
22. Ibid., 77–78.
23. Friese, *Records*, 3084.
24. Ibid., 3290–91.
25. Ibid., 3502–503.
26. Ibid., 3051.

27. Seadle, *Diaries*, 93.
28. Ibid., 7.
29. Ibid., 26.
30. Cumnock, *Catalogue*, 43.
31. Seadle, *Diaries*, 28.
32. Cumnock, *Catalogue*, 43.
33. Seadle, *Diaries*, 12.
34. Ibid., 18.
35. Ibid., 81.
36. Ibid., 54.
37. Peter Wolle, "Diary," 5 October 1862.
38. Ibid., 52.
39. Seadle, *Diaries*, 13.
40. Ibid., 13.
41. Christian Ignats Latrobe, *Anthems for One, Two or More Voices Performed in the Church of the United Brethren*. (London: 1811), 2-3.
42. Ibid., 2.
43. Ibid., 3.
44. John Antes La Trobe [sic], *The Music of the Church* (London: R. B. Seeley and W. Burnside, 1831), 311.
45. Christian Ignats Latrobe, *Anthems*, 3.
46. Martha Secrest Asti, "The Moravian Music of Christian Gregor (1723–1801): His Anthems, Aria and Chorales." (Ph.D. dissertation, University of Miami, 1983), 168.
47. Ibid., 171.
48. Another translation from the German made by Bishop F. W. Foster in 1789 is the one in the Moravian hymnal: "He's a shepherd kind and gracious." The final line is "Yea, my very heart He knows." See *Hymnal and Liturgies of the Moravian Church*, 1923, hymn #486, 330.
49. It should be noted that the repetition of the first two measures of Peter Wolle's arietta melody resembles the form of the German hymn tune, which repeats the first two measures. However, measures 5–6 were also repeated as well as 7–8. Peter Wolle was naturally aware of the hymn, which dates from a *Herrnhut Choral Buch*, 1735.
50. Barbara Jo Strauss, "A Register of Music Performed in Concert, Nazareth, Pennsylvania from 1796–1845: an Annotated Edition of an American Moravian Document." (Masters thesis: University of Arizona, 1976), 229.
51. Friese, *Records*, 3259.

52. There are no known examples of musical compositions by Moravian women during the eighteenth and early nineteenth centuries.

53. Latrobe, *Anthems*, 51.

54. *"Fuer mich, O Herr"* was the only anthem composed by Wolle that has been published (H. W. Gray Co.), and is accessible to interested readers. Because the translation by Helen Dickenson follows the original German text very closely, the English edition was used in this analysis. When the English text under lay differs from the original German, those differences are indicated.

55. Wolle's arietta *"Mein Tod"* described the suffering at Golgotha. The key was C minor.

56. The expressive directions, "With astonishment" and "Incredulously" in the published edition are not in the original manuscript though they are not out of place in the mind of the author.

57. *The Moravian*, 23 November 1871.

58. Translation by Karl Kroeger from Christian Gregor's *Choral-Buch,* 47.

59. Peter Wolle, Preface to *Hymn Tunes Used in the Church of the United Brethren; Arranged for Four Voices and the Organ or Piano-Forte* . . . Bethlehem, Pa.: Moravian Publication Office, 1872).

60. Ibid.

61. Unpublished letter "Peter Wolle, Philadelphia 13 February 1836 to Rev. John. D. Anders, Bethlehem," box "P.U.C. 1827–1840 Letters from Philadelphia," Moravian Archives, Bethlehem. Translation from the German by the author.

62. All references in the paragraph from an unpublished letter "Peter Wolle, Philadelphia 23 January 1835 to Theodore Schulz, Salem." For source see note #61. Translation from the German by the author.

63. All references in the paragraph from an unpublished letter "Peter Wolle Philadelphia 27 January 1835 to Rev. John. D. Anders, Bethlehem." For source see Note #61. Translation from the German by the author.

64. Unpublished letter "Peter Wolle, Philadelphia 17 February 1836 to Rev. John. D. Anders, Bethlehem." For source see Note #61. Translation from the German by the author.

65. *Auszug aus den bisher in der evangelisher Brueder-Gemeinen gegraechlichen Choral-Buche mit angeschreiben Stimme der Choral-Melodien*, [ed.] C[hristian] G[ottlieb] H[ueffel] (Gnadau, 1831).

66. Peter Wolle, Preface to *Hymn Tunes*.

67. Ibid., Charles Hommann (1803–1872) was a prominent composer, violinist, and teacher in Philadelphia and elsewhere. Charles E. Hupfeld (1788–

1864) was Hommann's brother-in-law. He was also a violinist and teacher in Philadelphia. While not a Moravian, Hupfeld was "a frequent summer visitor to Bethlehem." See *Charles Hommann Chamber Music for Strings*, eds. John Graziano and Joanne Swenson-Eldridge, (Madison, Wisc.: A-R Editions, Inc., 1998), Introductions, vii–xx.

68. Peter Wolle, Preface to *Hymn Tunes*.

69. Private genealogy papers of Robert S. Taylor, Peter Wolle: 8. In the possession of the author.

70. *Nachrichten aus der Brueder-Gemeine* 1842 (Gnadau, n.d.), 904.

71. Peter Wolle, *A Collection of Moravian Hymn Tunes,* (New York: 1856), 2.

72. Ibid.

73. Ibid.

74. *The Moravian*, 7 March 1856.

Chapter Four

*Service Completed*

> I am released from much official burden, & thus I shall be permitted to spend the remnants of my days in comfort.[1]

WHEN HE WAS SEVENTY YEARS OLD, Bishop Wolle retired and settled in Bethlehem where a number of his sons and relatives lived. Always energetic and mentally alert, he soon assumed an unofficial duty as the proofreader of the church's publications. The printing office was in Bethlehem, and the Moravian Church was an active publisher. The Bishop proofread books for daily spiritual guidance, textbooks for the Moravian schools, histories of the Church of the United Brethren, printed music, and the weekly newspaper, *The Moravian*. Calling upon his many years of experience as a pastor and as a musician, he frequently assembled printed liturgies for special services held in Bethlehem's Moravian Church, and one of his first proofreading duties involved supervising the edition of a new hymnal. In successive diary entries, the Bishop indicated that he spent a great deal of time proofing. "Read proof." And then written a few days later, "Afternoon spent in reading the book proof from NY."[2] *The Moravian* required the most attention, and when someone substituted for him, the Bishop wrote curtly in his diary, "Read the Moravian of the week, which has passed through N. Happen's hands as proofreading, I found no less than 70 typographical errors!"[3] The editor of *The Moravian* pointed out the debt the staff of the paper owed to the Bishop's continuous vigilance and dedication when he wrote of the Bishop's death.

> In this office we shall miss our departed brother greatly. When failing strength precluded other more active mental labors, he volunteered to undertake proofreading and such other tasks as were in accordance with his tastes and strength, and which younger men would have found irksome, and performed them with a regularity and correctness which rendered them doubly valuable. He was faithful both in that which was much and in that which was least.[4]

The Bishop's direct association with *The Moravian* kept him abreast of what was happening in the Moravian Church, in Bethlehem, and in the wider world.

As a part of his leisure, the Bishop took afternoon walks – weather permitting – to socialize and to keep himself informed about what was happening in town. Always a curious man, he watched with great interest as Bethlehem became an industrial city, noting every alteration and construction in his diary. What he saw impressed and pleased him. During his first year in Bethlehem he witnessed the construction of the iron works on the site that would soon become a center of iron manufacturing. Following an afternoon walk along the Lehigh River, he wrote, "then I pursued my way across the bridge & walked the R.R. tracks past the Zinc Works, down to the commencement of the Rolling Mill & Foundry building of A[ugustus] Wolle & Co. There is nothing there now. They expect to get the Furnace ready by May 1."[5] A month later a relative, Jedidiah Weiss, ceremoniously ignited the plant's first "Bethlehem furnace."

Of course, the Bishop knew that the most dramatic developments in Bethlehem involved members of the Wolle family in some way. From his perspective the Bethlehem that was expanding throughout the area was still under Moravian control. It was not some new entity, and the town was clearly developing with the supervision of the Wolle family. Two of his sons, James and Comenius, were employed by Augustus Wolle, the Bishop's nephew. The Bishop was a stockholder in Augustus' company and went regularly to the factory office to collect his dividends.[6] The influence of the family extended far beyond the building of the iron industry. Other Wolles were on the boards that oversaw the installation of the new utilities providing the town with water and gas. Family members were stockholders in the companies that built the bridges that spanned the Lehigh River and were members of the board of the new "public" school.

There are only a few references in the Bishop's diary that suggest he felt that the "others" moving to town would reshape the community in ways that might threaten the hegemony of the Moravians, and that the changes that were taking place might not ultimately be to his liking. The Bishop's reaction to the founding of Lehigh University across the river near the iron works does seem somewhat ambivalent. He chose not to attend the opening ceremonies, but wrote in his diary, "The Packer [Lehigh] University was opened; I did not feel disposed to accept the invitation to be present, nor had I time. I am told there were many there. No doubt a full account will be published."[7]

The University, the iron works, and the railroad reflected an expanding wealthy enclave building mansions on the south side of the river. The Bishop's account of the effect of the hailstorm on these properties hardly disguised some disapproval. "The hot houses of the *rich folk* [author's italics] of the other side of the river, had some 4 or 6 thousand panes of glass broken by the hail stones."[8] On the other hand, a month before his death, the Bishop experienced the opulence that coal transport and steel production brought to Bethlehem and, with his taste for refinement and comfort, he approved.

> I had just put my foot on the step [of the passenger car] when it moved off. On entering I was struck by the elegance and grandeur of the new style R. R. equipment; cushioned seats for single persons, & turning on pivots, – costly curtains to the windows, – elegant lamps suspended & everything magnificent.[9]

The expansion of Bethlehem also meant new churches built for new denominations. Though he retreated more and more from the ceremonial duties expected of a Moravian Bishop by refusing invitations to be present at groundbreakings, it is interesting to note that he remained on excellent terms with the clergy of other denominations. However, he did comment on the lack of musical resources existing in South Bethlehem, "the Roman Catholic Church in Bethlehem South was consecrated today. It is said that for the performance of a mass of Mozart, they had engaged a choir from Philadelphia."[10] Nearly every Sunday the choir of the Moravian Church sang music as elaborate as a Mass by Mozart with instrumental accompaniment. Also, when a Moravian organist bowed to a non-Moravian musical practice and played a long organ voluntary during the consecration ceremony of the new Episcopal Church in "Bethlehem South," the Bishop expressed his disdain. "The organ is of considerable capacity. Our Br. Bleck at the opening played a voluntary of such length that I grew tired of it."[11] Such an emphasis on the performer was still out of place in the Moravian Church; it bored the Bishop and would not have pleased Latrobe, either.

The Civil War fueled the prosperity the Bishop watched. While the Wolle family profited financially, the war affected the Bishop himself very deeply. Two of his sons were directly involved. Comenius joined the Pennsylvania regiment when the Confederate Army moved into Pennsylvania, and the Bishop was grief-stricken. In one of the most moving entries in his diary, the Bishop expressed how he felt when Comenius departed.

> It was quite heart rending for me to bid him farewell! No one can tell what trials & dangers await these our men. Possibly I may never again see my son; or perhaps see him mutilated. I could speak but a few words of admonition to him on giving him a parting kiss. I wept bitterly. Since my dear wife's departure nothing has so deeply . . . affected me. May my dear Lord & Saviour take my son into his kind protecting care.[12]

Comenius never saw active duty and returned safely to Bethlehem, taking up a high administrative position in iron mining and production.

Theodore was the other son directly involved in the war. He was living in the South when the war began and served briefly in the Confederate Army. For most of the war, he taught in North Carolina. His decision to remain in the South troubled the family greatly. Not only was communication with Theodore difficult because of his enemy status, his father and brothers could not understand or easily accept that Theodore was supporting the Southern cause. When the Bishop heard that Theodore had enlisted in the Southern Army, he wrote in his diary, "Alas! that my son should be found in the ranks of the nation against their country. How awfully misinformed & deluded the people in the South are!"[13] Two days later he continued to record the consternation of the family.

"Henry [Theodore's brother] is quite violent in his condemnation of Theo's course, & surely we have cause to be disappointed, or rather pity for him for being so awfully blind as they are in the South."[14]

The Bishop was kept informed as to the progress of the war by reading daily newspapers and through correspondence and visits with Moravians living in Salem and Bethania, his first stations. He witnessed volunteers mustering in front of the Moravian Church, troops being transported to and from the South, saw railroad cars of wounded men, and attended the funerals of local soldiers. When Bethlehem mourned the death of President Lincoln, Bishop Wolle, the oldest surviving Bishop in the American Moravian Church, occupied a prominent place in Bethlehem's funeral service held in the Moravian Church. He reported every detail of this public event in his diary.

> At 1/2 p. 10 A.M. the multitude was gathered . . . the band first played a funeral dirge. . . . Then the procession was formed. It was headed by the band, who repeatedly made their mournful notes be heard. After the band came the clergy, the Town Council, & then the citizens, females & males, – always 6 abreast. The first set of clergymen consisted of the 4 bishops . . . then the other clergy of the place . . . . It took considerable time till the multitude had entered the church [Moravian Church], & it was just about 12, when the services were opened. . . . The Choir opened with our *"Herr, Herr Gott &c."*

& later sang another piece. [A description of each address follows with the Bishop adding his critical comments.] The service lasted till nearly 1/2 p. 1 P.M.[15]

Bishop Wolle survived the Civil War without personal loss. In fact, the prosperity that war brought to Bethlehem directly benefitted him. His son James was able to build a new house with profits from the iron company, and included a spacious apartment for his father, and the Bishop was delighted to live with his son's family. By the end of the war, three sons had settled permanently in or near Bethlehem, and the Bishop was surrounded by congenial, caring families in his final days.

Wolle had expressed the concern that his early separation from his parents might have prohibited his ability to be a good father. Yet, his diaries show the family was consistently a concerned and loving one. Family members visited one another almost daily, they ate together frequently, and spent evenings pleasantly in conversation, playing music and singing hymns. There was frequent physical illness within the family, and the Bishop expressed concern about the stress his sons experienced from working long hours. They occupied important positions in the area's rapidly growing industrial enterprises. The Bishop's diaries written in Bethlehem reveal a happy man who was an important part of a prosperous family and community.

Throughout most of his life, Wolle's musical activity was in response to religious needs. That did not change during his retirement. When an organist was needed in church or at conferences, he responded, "I was obliged once again to take his place; I made one mis-take!"[16] James bought a new piano and the Bishop reported his polite submission to requests to be the first to play it. "I was made to give it the first touches when it stood in its destined place."[17] Unexpectedly, a violinist was needed in the church orchestra, and the Bishop responded dutifully. "I was called from my seat below to play violin, in the absence of the proper performers; I managed to get through."[18]

He did purchase a melodeon, a small reed organ, because he still needed to play music for his own satisfaction. "It will prove a means of pleasure to me in the remnant of my days."[19] Soon after the instrument arrived, the Rev. Potter, an Episcopal Bishop living in Bethlehem, called on Bishop Wolle and asked him to speak at the groundbreaking for a new church building. Wolle declined the invitation, but Rev. Potter saw the new melodeon and invited his fellow cleric to his apartment to play the melodeon he had recently purchased. Bishop Wolle was a bit chagrined when

> I played a little, but felt quite ashamed of my performance when I heard him play in quite a superior manner. I never knew how the pedal can be used as a swell, – having had no acquaintance with such instruments before.[20]

The next day, Wolle returned for an informal lesson on Potter's "Harmonium." The Bishop described how he listened to Potter demonstrate and then he imitated him. Wolle became satisfied with his melodeon and said he played it often, surely with more expression now that Rev. Potter had taught him how to make the harmonies loud and soft by using the pedal as a swell.

Bishop Wolle often attended concerts and musical "Entertainments." He had a very discriminating ear that had been trained by his excellent teachers and by his long experience playing and singing. Nearly every diary entry about music included some critical judgement as to the quality of the performance.

In Bethlehem in the 1860s there was a great deal of music to catch the Bishop's ear. The Bethlehem *collegium musicum* had become the Philharmonic Society. The group still included a chorus with an orchestra, which, in addition to performing regularly in the Moravian Church, gave an annual series of public concerts. Shortly before his death, the Bishop wrote about such a concert, "I was glad to be able to attend the Concert given by the Phil. Soc. to a perfectly crowded house. I never heard better music."[21] In the tradition of the *collegium musicum*, the Philharmonic Society concerts included extended choral works such as "The Creation" by Haydn and music by contemporary composers: Beethoven, Mendelssohn, Spohr, and Rossini. Wisely, the Society repeated its concerts when the works were unfamiliar. There were times when even the Bishop's refined ear found the music too new, and he took advantage of the repeated concerts for a second hearing. For example, after listening to a new work by Robert Schumann a second time, the Bishop wrote

> I went to the Concert to hear the "Paradise & Peri" performed. I cannot say that I was much pleased. The music is too artistic for me and abstruse. . . . In the evening the oratorio of "Paradise & Peri" was performed for the third time. It was the second time that I heard it, & now I enjoyed the music very much, – some parts are exquisitely beautiful.[22]

The Moravian schoolgirls had a first-class music faculty, and the students presented musical "Entertainments" frequently. The Bishop was as willing to mention a lack of quality in a performance at the seminary as he was to comment on excellent playing and singing.

> Great entertainment given by the pupils of our Boarding school . . . the chorus was good, the teacher Agathe deserves much credit, – some duets, & trios sung by the girls also very good. . . . But some of the performances on the piano were too long and tedious.[23]

Other musical performances the Bishop felt were truly memorable! In the following diary entry, he expressed his love for musical criticism using his fine writing:

> . . . each played in the most wonderful manner on their instruments; most difficult passages, with the greatest perfection; when all together engaged the forte and piano most striking by contrast; the piano so soft that you could scare hear it close to them. The whole was superb! I don't know that I can hear better music.[24]

Bethlehem clearly continued to be a center of fine musical performances. Bishop Wolle's diary contained ample evidence that Bethlehem residents neither lost their capability to perform excellent music nor their desire to listen to and support it.

In addition to formal concerts and services in the church, there was always the pleasure of house music – particularly when the household was a family of musicians. When Augustus Wolle invited Peter's family to supper, and the party finished eating, the men

> repaired to the office, to smoke their cigars, [and] having returned, the rest of the evening was devoted to musical performances at the piano by Theo, the Van Vlecks, & they all played well, & it was quite a treat to me. The company broke up near 10 o'clock.[25]

Unexpectedly, an old ailment required medical attention. A rupture "had grown to such size, that when I showed it to James . . . he was astonished and alarmed."[26] A suitable truss was not available and ten days later, the Bishop completed his diary, writing "nothing particular – very feeble" and "I'm too sick all day to read or to write."[27] The editor of *The Moravian* wrote, "In the morning he said to one of his sons: 'Today, I will take flight.'"[28]

The final sentence in Bishop Wolle's diary, one he had kept for over forty years, was written by another hand. "Died on 14th 1 1/2 A.M. [1871]."[29] Bishop Peter Wolle was 80 years old.

The Bethlehem Trombone Choir assembled and blew from the steeple of the Moravian Church announcing the passing of the Right Rev. Bishop Peter Wolle. The Moravian congregation listened to the chorales that reported everyone's "passing," heard that the deceased was a married man, and finally, the faithful were advised "remember your own mortality is the purpose of your life." The chorales were the same that Peter Wolle, as a novice, had heard over seventy years before, when the Nazareth Trombone Choir announced the death of John Moehring. Their message had not changed.[30] It was the same as the one he had learned when he was very young: a servant of God was called to a higher realm. The trombones now sounded for him. The purpose of Bishop Wolle's life, a "time for which we are held responsible," was achieved. He was "asleep in Jesus."

The Bishop's funeral was significantly different from John Moehring's. Moravians were no longer the only residents of Bethlehem, as when Peter and his parents had stopped there in the eighteenth century on their way to Nazareth. Non-Moravians were not foreigners as they had been when Peter, the novice, watched his parents leave for the West Indies. Ministers, representing denominations and churches that were unknown to Moehring, "were seated in front of the pulpit."[31] The Moravian Church was now one among many.

The music sung at Bishop Wolle's funeral was also very different. In Moehring's time, the music had been composed by Moravians. Peter had become one of those Moravian composers. The music for his funeral was not only music of a different style, more importantly, the intent of the music had changed. What it expressed was different. *The Moravian* reported that at Bishop Wolle's funeral the choir "sang with great power and pathos the beautiful, 'Blessed are the dead,' from [Ludwig] Spohr's 'Last Judgement'."[32] Spohr was not only not a Moravian composer, the "Last Judgement" was not composed for a church service. A profound change in the purpose of sacred music had occurred. Previously, sacred music was for worship in Christian churches. "Sacred music" could now be removed from the church and become "religious music" that could be performed anywhere. This change made it possible later for Bethlehem to be called the "American Bayreuth," when performances of the Bach Choir gained an international reputation.[33] Bayreuth was the place Richard Wagner's sacred music drama *Parsifal* could be experienced.[34] Bethlehem was the place in America where Bach's church music could be heard in the equivalent of a sacred opera house – Packer Memorial Church at Lehigh University.

It was music for the concert hall, not for church worship. Spohr's complete work would have lasted far too long, so only one section of "The Last Judgement," "Blessed are the dead," was sung.

Nineteenth-century composers like Spohr responded to the secularization of Western society as sacred music was moved from churches into concert halls and opera houses. Even in Bethlehem, Spohr's complete "Last Judgement" had been performed by the Philharmonic Society a number of times in public concerts. Yet, the music was still "sacred" so that a section could also be sung during a church service. The funeral of Bishop Wolle was an indication that the musical mobility of religious music was no longer questioned by Christians.

The music had also become very rich harmonically. The resulting complexity was now desired by the Moravians. It was no longer an appropriate musical gesture for the choir to sing one of the Bishop's own anthems at his funeral. That music would have sounded too simple and have been too unexpressive. The Bishop's music lacked drama. It was not grand enough to carry the occasion.

• • •

The early nineteenth-century social contract that had defined Moravian communities and that had been so ideal for Peter Wolle's spiritual growth and musical education had changed in many ways. That social contract, however, had worked well throughout his life. It nurtured a man who was able to pass an extraordinary musical culture onto his son, who then settled in Bethlehem and instructed John Frederick. Other Wolles, led by Augustus, founded the industries that drew wealth and prominence, and cultural aspiration, to Bethlehem.

Making religious music dramatic, a sense of handing down a unique musical tradition, and new wealth combined with cultural aspirations in Bethlehem, were the new social contracts needed to transform Moravian Bethlehem into America's Bayreuth. Everything was in place for that transformation to come about, and Bishop Peter Wolle had built a firm foundation on which the changes would take place. Theodore, the second powerful member of the Wolle musical dynasty, had already taken the Bishop's place.

## NOTES

1. Peter Wolle, "Diary," 29 May 1861.
2. Ibid., 12 February 1861, 16 February 1861, and 20 February 1861.
3. Ibid., 11 July 1861.
4. *The Moravian*, 23 November 1871.
5. Peter Wolle, "Diary," 27 February 1861.
6. Ibid., 8 September 1864. "I walked to the Rolling Mill to draw my dividend of stock."
7. Ibid., 1 September 1866.
8. Ibid., 11 April 1871.
9. Ibid., 10 October 1871.
10. Ibid., 30 October 1864.
11. Ibid., 19 April 1865.
12. Ibid., 29 June 1863.
13. Ibid., 11 May 1861.
14. Ibid., 13 May 1861.
15. Ibid., 19 April 1865.
16. Ibid., 25 February 1863.
17. Ibid., 29 September 1866.
18. Ibid., 13 April 1865.
19. Ibid., 22 July 1864.
20. Ibid., 22 November 1864.
21. Ibid., 2 March 1871.
22. Ibid., 7 and 28 February 1867.
23. Ibid., 14 June 1861.
24. Ibid., 16 January 1863.
25. Ibid., 28 September 1865.
26. Ibid., 29 October 1871.
27. Ibid., 9 and 10 November 1871.
28. *The Moravian*, 16 November 1871.
29. Ibid.
30. Ibid., 16 August 1866.
31. Peter Wolle, "Diary," 16 August 1866.
32. *The Moravian*, 23 November 1871.
33. *Public Ledger* (Philadelphia), n.d. "Music lovers from all parts of the world have gone to the Bach Festivals each year, until now Bethlehem appears

to the musical world in the light of an American Bayreuth." Clipping in the Archive of the Bach Choir of Bethlehem.

34. There were few performances outside Bayreuth until 1914 when Wagner's copyright expired. The performances in the U.S. before 1914 were "illegal," for Wagner had stated *Parsifal* could only be played in Bayreuth.

*Part Two*

Theodore Wolle: Continuing the Legacy
in the Midst of Change

Theodore Francis Wolle, 1832–1885
(Jane Hammond)

Chapter Five

*Gaining a Tradition*

At his majority, he came South. . . . There we first met him, and learned to love him.[1]

THEODORE'S CAREER as a musician began with the celebration of his mother's birthday on 19 January 1842. At that time the Wolle musical dynasty entered the second generation, for Theodore's birthday gift was a musical one: his organ debut. He performed that evening for the first time in public during "the English service." Theodore was ten years old, and of all the gifts Maria Wolle received that day, his touched her the most. The debut was such a success it prompted his father to write, "Mother's Birthday, distinguished with us by the circumstance that *our Theodore played the organ in Church* for the first time, in the English meeting in the evening: he performed *very well*, and astonished all who heard him."[2]

Two weeks after his mother's birthday, Theodore played for "the German service." Everyone in Lititz, the Moravian community where Peter was the pastor, knew that Theodore was gifted; a gift both parents saw in him when he was very young. His mother, herself a fine pianist, taught him piano, organ, and the church repertoire. His father was a model of a Moravian Church musician; skilled and creative in music but always serving the greater good of the religious community.

Every day Theodore practiced hymns from his father's *Hymn Tunes*, and in a year he had memorized most of them. Playing the piano was easily transferred to the organ, and by the time he made his church debut, he was able to play all 136 chorales from memory.

Not only was Theodore talented; he had the total musical support of his family; he was living in Lititz, a Moravian community that provided him with the high level of musical culture he required to develop fully. There was music constantly in church services throughout the week and during religious holidays when the Lititz *collegium musicum* performed anthems composed by Theodore's father and other Moravian composers. Reverend Wolle recorded such an occasion in his diary. "In the evening was music singstunde, among the pieces performed was my own: Come joyful, Hallelujah Raise."[3] Also, the Lititz *collegium musicum* gave concerts frequently. "Our Musicum," wrote Reverend Wolle, "gave a Concert. The pieces performed were 1. Symphony of Haydn all but the Finale . . . 8. Finale of the Symphony."[4]

In addition, there were many recitals played by the students and the faculty of Linden Hall, the highly esteemed Moravian boarding school for girls in Lititz. Theodore's parents took him to these musical events. His father wrote, "An evening Entertainment in the Boarding School; Mother & Theodore present, head-ache prevented me."[5] Also, guest artists who visited Lititz gave concerts that Theodore heard. Reverend Wolle mentioned many of the concerts in his diary, for example, "The Shaws gave a concert in the evening: Mr. Gregor & Theodore went."[6]

Theodore's early academic education was in the Lititz parochial school and mirrored the one his father had received. Soon after his organ debut, when he was ten years old, his parents enrolled him in Nazareth Academy. On the 7th of July 1842, Father Wolle dropped Theodore off at Nazareth Hall. Emma, his sister, attended the Moravian Seminary for Girls in Bethlehem. Theodore's older brothers, Nathaniel, class of 1831, and James, class of 1838, had graduated from The Hall.

The plan of Br. and Sr. Wolle was for Theodore to become a teacher in a Moravian school and then a pastor. Like the rest of the family, Theodore, i.e., beloved of God, would be inducted into the

*Unitas Fratrum*. Theodore became a member of the Children's Choir in Lititz, and then he joined the Young Boys' Choir when he went to Nazareth. When he was thirteen years of age, in the year 1849, both his spiritual initiation and his religious education continued when he was chosen to enter the Moravian Theological Seminary in Nazareth. Four years later, in 1849 during his apprenticeship in Bethlehem, Theodore was accepted into full church membership following his confirmation and his first communion.

His general education was the same his father had received. However, unlike his father and older brothers, Theodore's opportunities to play in the Nazareth *collegium musicum* were limited by the fact that concerts had ceased in 1841 and did not begin again until 1845. However, Theodore's piano and organ instruction continued, and the violin was added.[7] Since he learned instruments easily, he soon played the violin as proficiently as he played keyboard instruments. He joined the *collegium* as soon as he was able. At the same time, he studied the clarinet.

While he was at The Hall, he received a number of letters from his brother James. They were filled with bits of advice offered with goodwill. For example, in one letter James reported, "Mother says she hopes you will have your hair cut before you appear in public at the examinations or else they will think they are going to have a bear dance, when you appear on the stage."[8] Naturally, the family expressed interest in Theodore's musical training, and James added, "She [Theodore's mother] also says, you must by all means bring those pieces of music along that you play for the examination if you possibly can, & also all other music."[9] Theodore's father added a note to another letter written by James. After granting Theodore permission to come home for the Christmas holiday, his father wrote, "Bring your Clarinet with you that we may see how you have improved."[10] James wrote extended descriptions of the routines the family followed in Lititz. "Mother does nothing that I know of, but scold me for having dirty hands. . . . Father does everything as usual, eats his meals at regular times, goes to bed at 10 & then rises at 6, preaches on Sunday, & in short there is nothing out of the way in any of his motions."[11] The letters also contained many instances of romping affection. "More affectionate most affectionate, Brother Jim, more Jimmy mostly James."[12] Playful flights of fancy are also present, as when James describes a cart he would build to pick Theodore up when he came home for Christmas. The two family cats, Billy and Bawby, would pull it. Father Wolle joined in the fun in a postscript.

> You will leave Naz[areth] on Monday the 22nd for Bethlehem, where I trust some of your relatives will give you a bed to sleep on, & some food to keep you alive, till Tuesday morning, when you proceed to Reading where Jim's new contrivance will meet you!... Much love from all. . . . Your affectionate Father, Peter Wolle.[13]

• • •

When he was twelve years old, Theodore changed the direction of his studies, chose not to follow in his father's footsteps, and instead decided to work as a Moravian tradesman and to serve the community as a musician. He left the seminary in Nazareth in 1847 without completing the theology curriculum and was apprenticed to William Luckenbach, a cabinetmaker in Bethlehem. Although it is not known why Theodore chose a path different from the one his parents had laid out for him, he was following the pattern of many of the Single Brethren who were both craftsmen and musicians. Theodore fulfilled the full term of his apprenticeship and left the workshop when he was twenty years old.

As with everything he did, Theodore excelled in cabinetmaking. (Two pieces of fine furniture survive in the possession of a Bethlehem member of the Wolle family.) Much later he used these skills when he designed a new organ for Central Moravian Church.

Following the model of a craftsman/musician, Theodore was musically active during his Bethlehem apprenticeship. He played second violin in the Philharmonic Society, tuba in the town band, and was an organ substitute in the Moravian Chapel. However, his participation in

Bethlehem's musical life was his real apprenticeship. It prepared him to become a performer and music teacher.

After a year in Bethlehem, Theodore again took an unexpected step. He accepted a position teaching music in a female seminary in North Carolina. He gave up his woodworking trade and never returned to it for a livelihood. By moving to a town with no Moravian Church, he also left the confines of the Moravian community, though he never ceased being a Moravian. Theodore wrote to his father about his new position, and Peter noted in his diary, "A letter from Theodore informed of his engagement with the Principal of Green[s]borough Female Seminary as music teacher for $50 per month."[14] Peter recorded his pleasure at Theodore's prospects in the South. "Theodore has a bright prospect opening to him as music teacher in Greensborough N.C."[15] The next week, 15 July 1853, Theodore left Lititz for Greensborough "for his new & untried field of labour." The following month Theodore wrote his father an eleven-page letter, "the first from Greensboro, his new situation." Peter commented in his diary, "The letter was written well & contained very welcome information. Theodore was well, had commenced his operations as Professor of Music, & was happy."[16] Peter was pleased with his son's success. At the same time, Peter the proofreader always remained aware of the correct language usage. Eventually, this high standard of language usage proved profitable for Theodore, for when his father died, Theodore replaced him as proofreader on the staff of *The Moravian*.

• • •

Greensborough, with a population of over one thousand inhabitants, was the county seat of Guilford County in rural North Carolina.[17] The town was laid out in a grid; four streets intersected to form a square where the courthouse was located. Because it was the county seat, Greensborough had a number of lawyers' officers and in addition "five hostelries, several dry-goods stores and a number of apothecary shops."[18] A contemporary visitor noted, "It had two banks [along with] some very handsome private residences and quite a number of excellent institutions of learning."[19] There were two churches in the town: Methodist and Presbyterian. Major industries were established during the 1830s and 1840s, producing cotton cloth and tobacco products from raw materials grown in the surrounding area. Similar to Moravian communities, Greensborough "afforded abundant facilities for the acquirement of a complete education."[20] There were three schools in the town: Greensborough Female College, Greensborough Male High School, and Edgeworth Female Seminary. The two women's colleges were on adjacent sites with "large and commodious buildings, beautifully situated, and in a highly prosperous condition."[21] A Friends' co-educational boarding school was outside the town.

A prior governor of the state, John Motley Morehead, and his family lived in "Blandwood," a Tuscan mansion, which was the social center of the area. Morehead had been instrumental in establishing both women's seminaries. The Methodist Episcopal Church founded the Greensborough Female College in 1846 to train female teachers and provide young women with a refined education. The refinement of the college was exemplified by Rev. Mr. Turner M. Jones, president of the college, "a gentleman of great suavity of manners, agreeable and pleasant in the social circle."[22] He taught mathematics and ancient languages. While the "Ornaments" were important, a newspaper reporter stressed "a highly intellectual training – a thorough discipline of the mind is sought to be attained as of the first importance after the cultivation of moral and religious feelings."[23] The second year Theodore was on the faculty of the college, there were over one hundred pupils studying the natural sciences, *belles lettres*, French language and literature, drawing & painting, and music. Students paid $22.50 a term for piano lessons, and guitar lessons cost $21.00. The college was furnished with nine pianos. Commenting on the enlightened Christian discipline at the college, a reporter wrote, "The student is induced to act from principles instead of fear of punishment." In a telling sentence, he wrote, "jewelry is not allowed to be worn by students."[24]

In addition to the principal, there were eight other faculty members – four professors, an art instructor, and three assistants in music. The prosperity of the school was attributed to the high quality of the faculty. "The promise of increased prosperity is evidence of a well merited confidence in the ability and fidelity of those who are engaged in the arduous and responsible duty of instructing the young ladies."[25] In a newspaper article describing the college, a report extolled the faculty, mentioning Theodore specifically. "The corps of teachers had never been stronger – [made] by such men as Professor . . . Wolle."[26] Music was the only full-fledged department in the college, and Theodore was the head. "The Professor of Music, Mr. Wolle, is well known as Composer of Music and thoroughly educated in the department over which he presides."[27]

In addition to their studies, the young ladies attended Sunday services in the Methodist Church, "when the weather is suitable," and "when the weather is inclement, there are religious services held in the College Chapel."[28] Theodore played the music for the chapel services on the "new and superior melodeon."

Each spring there was a graduation preceded by a public examination and a concert in which the students performed vocal and instrumental music and presented recitations. A concert program led by Theodore and his assistants appeared in a local newspaper as a part of an account of the graduation events at the college. There were piano solos and duets, accompanied vocal solos, and the chorus sang with men from the church choir. The selections were: "Gondolalied," "Come to the Forest," Forest Glade Polka," "Les Adieus," "Then You'll Remember Me," duet; "Morning Star Waltz," song; "The World as It is," "Snow Flake Waltz," chorus; "Now Vanish before the Holy Beams," from *Creation* by Joseph Haydn, and "The Lord's Prayer."[29] The following spring the program did not appear in the paper, but there was a glowing account of the concert with compliments to Theodore.

> It was certainly the most interesting concert ever given at the institution. Those who have charge of the music department in the

College have given indubitable evidence that they well understand the art of getting up a rich treat for public entertainment.[30]

The next year, 1858, with 157 students enrolled in the college, the graduation concert impressed those who attended it even more "and did credit to the skill and taste of the several instructors."[31] The audience was large, "There were estimated to be at least a thousand persons present. . . . The commodious chapel was densely crowded; and all appeared to be pleased."[32]

The high value placed on music in the education of the young ladies at Greensborough College was not unique in the southern states. Many schools provided similar instruction in music. This instruction was rooted in the belief, held widely throughout the nineteenth century, that music refined the character of the listener by educating the soul. This philosophy was expressed in an article, "Music," printed in 1858 in *The Patriot*. After a number of references to the joys of music, the writer concluded

> Music refines the taste, enobles [sic] the mind, comforts the mourner, calms the troubled spirit, makes man more content with his lot and more lenient towards his fellow man. If it was more generally cultivated, there would be more contentment and happiness and less enmity, selfishness and sin. Those best love music who have great souls.[33]

Theodore felt at home with this belief. He had been raised with it.

In the spring of 1860, Theodore resigned his position at the Female College and became a music professor at Edgeworth Female Seminary. A newspaper report of the concert in the spring of 1869 made clear that Theodore had been largely responsible for increasing the quality of the musical performances during the six years he was at Greensborough College. "The concert came off at night. It was a pretty general remark that it was the most interesting one given in the institution and reflected great credit on Prof. Wolle and his accomplished teachers in the Music Department." [34]

Edgeworth was very familiar to Theodore, for only a brook separated it from Greensborough College. John Morehead had established Edgeworth a year before he became governor of the state. He not only paid for the school; he had it constructed on his estate across the street from "Blandwood." He wanted to provide a refined education for his daughters while he kept them close to home. Morehead was a Presbyterian, but the seminary was nondenominational. "We do not consider Edgeworth a sectarian Institution, though it is under Presbyterian influences – never the less it has received the patronage of the various Christian denominations," wrote a reporter in a detailed newspaper description of the school.[35]

Edgeworth was a four-year school with the academic year divided into two sessions of five months each. By the 1850s many schools, similar to those established in Bethlehem and Nazareth a century earlier, were founded to educate females in the South.

Edgeworth promoted a rigorous curriculum that included spelling, reading, writing, grammar, rhetoric, composition, *belle lettres*, arithmetic, algebra, geometry, astronomy, natural philosophy, intellectual philosophy, mineralogy, botany, and chemistry. As in Moravian schools, Edgeworth was well-established and with a particularly fine reputation in music and art. "Ornamental" courses were: piano, guitar, harp, painting with oil or watercolors, crayon drawing, and modern and ancient languages for which there was an extra charge. "The young ladies of Edgeworth have always heretofore been noted for their superior musical performances."[36] In addition to instruction in singing, private voice lessons were available. As the Professor of Music, Theodore conducted the school chorus. If he needed male voices, men from the local church choirs joined the young ladies. When Theodore arrived at Edgeworth, the original single building had been expanded to accommodate an increase in students. A new, large addition included a sizeable chapel and special rooms for musical instruction. Nine fine pianos were placed throughout the building. The faculty resided in a smaller building connected to the school.

Each morning there was a chapel service with a scripture reading, prayer, and hymn singing. Theodore accompanied the hymns on a melodeon.

Theodore taught young ladies to play the piano and the violin. He prepared them for parlor music, a skill refined young ladies were expected to possess. Parlor music consisted of piano solos and duets, performances by instrumentalists and singers accompanied by the piano, and singing the popular songs of the day. A reporter shed light on the reason seminary concerts were such an important part in training young ladies to play parlor music. "Permit us here to say (without any reflection on that prince – or princess – of the parlor instruments, the piano,) . . . that women's living voice, skillfully attuned in that control of sweet sounds, excels all the music of the world."[37] The faculty also performed, and many evenings Theodore entertained the young ladies and their guests in the "concert hall" with his own brilliant piano playing.

At graduation, there was a student concert at Edgeworth. The program of a similar concert a few years before Theodore joined the faculty appeared in print: "The Lord's Prayer," composed by Glover; song, "The Sunny World;" "Variations on an Air from La Norma," by Hunder; duet, "Tyrolieune" from "Guillame Tell," by Vollweiler; song, "Forget Not the Loved Ones at Home:" duet, "The Fairy Sisters," by Coppola; duet, "Variations on a Theme Allemand," by Herz.[38]

A fictional account of life at Edgeworth contains a description of a musicale which makes clear they were cultural events with opportunities for young people to meet.

> Friday night we had a Musicale at Edgeworth. Mrs. Morgan [the Principal's wife] says that they usually have two or three a year. Certainly I found this first one to be delightful. Everyone in the Morehead household is always invited to our entertainments as well as many townspeople. A delegation of young men from the Greens-

borough Male Academy attended. And this certainly put the Edgeworth girls in a twitter.

All our music students performed, and we asked several members from the Methodist and Presbyterian church choirs to join with the Edgeworth faculty and students in chorale singing, Professor Schneider directed.

I had been asked to sing a solo and was very happy to do so. As you know singing is my panacea for all the ills in the universe. Also several of the Edgeworth students performed on the piano and did it most creditably.[39]

There were occasional concerts in which the music faculties from both women's seminaries participated. Naturally, Theodore was active in those programs, which provided an opportunity for him to play chamber music on the violin as well as on the piano. In addition to events at the seminary, there were social occasions at "Blandwood," at other residences in the town, and at plantations in the area. Theodore's abilities as a pianist of the first rank and an expert accompanist must have put him in constant demand for recitals, parlor music in the evenings, and other social events. He probably played violin for dances as well.

Theodore was also the organist and choir director for the Presbyterian Church, a position automatically assumed by Edgeworth's Professor of Music. The church had an excellent organ, and Theodore expanded his liturgical knowledge to include Presbyterian hymnody. The church had a fine choir, but there was no tradition of concerted music so Theodore accompanied the anthems on the organ. The teacher in *Letters from Edgeworth* was a member of the Presbyterian Church Choir, and she described her experience as a choir member in her fictional correspondence. "The church has newly installed a pipe organ, the only one for miles around, and it thrilled me to join in singing to its glorious tones."[40] When services were held in the chapel of Edgeworth, Theodore played the melodeon.

A statement in *The Moravian* summarized Theodore's musical activity and his importance during the time he lived in Greensborough. "The eleven years spent in Greensboro' were devoted with unflagging energy to the study of music, and he attained an enviable reputation as a player. As a teacher he was conscientious and thorough."[41]

Theodore had become the first Professor of Music in the Wolle family, making him the first Wolle to make his living as a musician and a teacher. Being a music professor was now a family option, and J. Fred. Wolle, Theodore's cousin, a member of the next generation, would take that option. Such positions for musicians were increasing in America, and there were many by J. Fred's time.

Theodore's professorship in Greensborough College was a departure in another way. He was the first member of the family to be employed outside the Moravian community. The Female College was a Methodist college. That his son was not serving the Moravian Church with his music was of no concern to his father. His reaction to his son's non-Moravian employment was deeply rooted in Moravian theology, which was ecumenical in its relationship with other churches.

Though Theodore had not followed his father's plan to serve the Moravian Church as a cleric, composing or performing when required, he had taught very successfully for seven years in Greensborough. He had adapted to a new world for musicians in America.

• • •

When Theodore took his first music professorship in Greensborough, the American Civil War was eight years in the future. No one could have foreseen how greatly his decision to teach in North Carolina was to strain the Wolle family. Moravians were constantly traveling between their communities in the South and in the North, sometimes living for extended lengths of time in one area and then in the other. Even worldwide, they were a large extended family. That individuals, a Moravian family, or a Moravian congregation, were suddenly divided between North and South seemed unthinkable, but as the war began in

April 1861 the Wolle family took positions that divided them clearly into Union and Confederate. Theodore adopted the Southern cause. His father and brothers were ardent Northerners.[42]

Theodore was twenty-nine years old when the Civil War began. He had taught at Edgeworth nearly a year. Yet, within a month it appeared as if he had enlisted in a band led by a relative, Charles Schober. Theodore had played tuba in the Bethlehem Band, so he could have been a bandsman. The news of Theodore's enlistment reached his family through Nathaniel, the oldest son. Peter's first reaction was strictly political. He wrote in his diary

> information had been received that Theodore had enlisted as a member of a band, under the command of Chas. Schober and was to go to Richmond! Alas! that my son should be found in the ranks of the nation against their country. How awfully misinformed & deluded the people in the South are.[43]

A few days later Peter heard the same news from a relative, along with the reaction of one of Theodore's brothers, to Theodore's decision. While their politics were similar, this time Peter took a more forgiving tone with his son.

> Theodore had joined the Salisbury Band, & would go to Richmond! Henry is quite violent in his condemnation of Theo's course, & surely we have cause to be disappointed, or rather pity him for being so awfully blind as they are in the South.[44]

A week later the picture had changed dramatically, for "accounts were received that Theodore is not in the war but is engaged in teaching music as heretofore in Greenborough [sic]."[45] That was May 1861. When the conflict began, Governor Morehead was reported to have said, "If the boys must fight, we must see that the girls get an education."[46] The Governor vowed that he would keep Edgeworth, his own school, open in spite of the war, and Theodore was one of his most important faculty members. Morehead may have intervened to keep Theodore from conscription, thus keeping his Edgeworth faculty intact.

By September Peter had a clearer picture. The whole family was relieved to hear that Theodore was not a Confederate soldier.

> . . . warmer intelligence has been received concerning Theodore, that he had been to Richmond with a band, but that now he was teaching music in the Presbyterian Institute at Greensboro [Edgeworth] – to that we can think easier on his account.[47]

That information was fully confirmed in December, 1861, and the next year a conscription law was enacted in the South that granted exemptions from military service for all teachers and professors. Thus, Theodore was safe at Edgeworth.

Like all Moravians, Peter revered the birthdays of all family members. He wrote his sentiments regarding Theodore at this time of conflict in his diary and also reported the first of many doubts and frustrations that arose between Theodore in the South and the rest of the family in the North.

> Theodore 30 yr old today! We all remembered him, & wished him well, & I particularly commended him to the care, guidance & benediction of our good Lord. Almost a year has passed by since I received the last letter from him! Whether the blame rests alone upon him, or is in part attributable to the war of N. S. I cannot say.[48]

Early in 1863, the family received indirect information regarding what had happened to Theodore during that year.

> Theodore had spent Christmas at Salem; further, that he was at his regular business at Greensborough, I presume as Prof. of Music in the Edgeworth Seminary, – & that he was exempt from military duty. All this is gratifying indeed; but that he never writes, – while Salemites know how to send letters to Northern friends, I cannot understand or approve.[49]

Theodore had in fact written a long letter to his father, but it was delayed since it went by way of the Bahamas. "We were happy to read this morning a long letter which had arrived last evening from Theodore."[50] Peter responded to Theodore's letter almost immediately, but the letter was received back from the dead-letter office at Washington, confounding matters.[51] However, a family friend from Salem had spoken to Theodore in Greensboro and reported he was out of danger.

Six months passed before the family heard more news. It came as a package of letters delivered by people who lived in the same house with Theodore for two years. Peter wrote, "Theodore has been kept in health and constant activity. The Lord be praised for all this goodness towards him!"[52]

Apparently, at the end of the term, classes were suspended with the intention of reopening the seminary in the fall of 1863. That did not happen, and the sale of the furniture at Edgeworth, along with the nine fine pianos, was announced in *The Greensborough Patriot* in 9 June 1864. When the faculty of Edgeworth was disbanded, Theodore was offered a position teaching music at a female seminary in Lincolntown, N.C. An advertisement for Lincolntown Female Seminary, "this excellent school," appeared in *The Greensborough Patriot* in the summer of 1863 lauding its academic quality and safety because it was situated in the mountains of North Carolina. "Lincolnton [sic] possesses many advantages as a pleasant place to live and Prof. Landen [the principal] is an able and competent instructor."[53] Landen and Theodore were apparently close friends.[54] Piano lessons are mentioned in the advertisement as one of the musical offerings at the school. They were taught by Theodore. His duties were basically what they had been at Edgeworth.

When the exemptions for professors were cancelled in 1864, Theodore was apparently conscripted a second time, and he again joined a military band. Years later, Theodore's daughter, Agnes, remembered being told by her father that he was on a train to the front when he was taken off to be Professor of Music at the "Institute for the Deaf & Dumb, and Blind" in Raleigh, North Carolina. Theodore's obituary stated "a safer position, in the military sense, was opened to him in the State Institute for the Deaf and Dumb and Blind, at Raleigh."[55] Peter recorded in his diary that "influential men" had intervened.

> . . . brought information concerning Theodore that he had been conscripted, – but through the interposition of influential men, his friends, he had another appointment under the Southern government given him in some public institution at Raleigh.[56]

There is no doubt that Theodore had influential friends, beginning with ex-governor Morehead. Everyone known to Morehead was known to Theodore at least indirectly. In addition there were all the people in the Greensboro area whom Theodore had befriended, as well as students who could speak on his behalf. However, the action was not outside the law, for the exemption of teachers for the blind and deaf continued, and when Theodore moved to his new position in Raleigh in the fall of 1864, Peter recorded the event in his diary.

Theodore also experienced a change of situation, a result of the war,

> – narrowly escaping military service in the Confederacy, & obtained a situation in Raleigh in the Deaf and Dumb Asylum, with which the Institute of the blind is connected.[57]

A month before the end of the war Peter received a letter from Theodore. "He was in good health & comfortable in his position at the Deaf and Dumb & Blind Asylum at Raleigh."[58] Suddenly there were doubts. On 19 April 1865 Peter read in the newspaper that Raleigh had capitulated. Not knowing that the war was nearly at an end, he asked, "How does Theodore fare now?" A few days after the war Peter wrote in his diary, "In the morning I was pleased to receive a letter from Theodore written on Maundy Thursday; in it he speaks of coming north; having borrowed $200 from Col. Selfridge."[59]

The war was over, but the school did not permit Theodore to visit his family in Bethlehem until the school term was ended. "We were glad to be delivered from our uncertainty as to his movements," responded Peter.[60] Theodore arrived in Bethlehem on 30 June 1865. This is the complete diary account of that joyous meeting.

> Fair day till toward evening heavy rain set in. On the evening the greatest satisfaction to welcome to my embrace after a separation of 5 years & six months my son Theodore, whose later years were spent in N. Carolina, in the last place at Raleigh. On his arrival at the Depot, it rained hard; there being no room in the omnibuses, which were surrendered to the ladies, James was obliged to accompany his brother on foot. Comenius had come down to greet his brother, & had arrived at our house a good while before then. It got late till we could take our supper. Then the evening was spent in happy conversation.[61]

Theodore had not only survived the Civil War in the South, he had survived because he was a Professor of Music.

It was decided that Theodore would reside in Bethlehem. There was an opening in the Moravian Seminary for Girls, where Theodore's uncle, Francis Wolle, was the principal. Theodore returned to Raleigh to resign his position. He then traveled to Salem where he and Adelide Francesca Susedorff, a member of the Salem Moravian community and a teacher at the Salem Girls' Academy, were married within a few days. They set out for Bethlehem and arrived there 16 August 1865, a week after their marriage.

Theodore and his new bride were in Bethlehem with the Wolle family. Summarizing the year 1865, Bishop Wolle wrote in his diary, "My son Theodore left the South, & with a dear wife Aggie has settled here as Professor of Music in the Boarding School, & organist in the Chapel."[62]

Thus, the Wolle family continues as a dynasty; numbers of successive generations of the same family who shape events in their own

Chapel of the Women's Seminary where Theodore Wolle often played. Late 19th century. (The Moravian Archives, Bethlehem)

times so strongly they alter the time in which they live, assume places in history, and shape the future.

## NOTES

1. "Obituary. Prof. The. F. Wolle." Unidentified newspaper clipping in the possession of the author.
2. Peter Wolle, "Diary," 19 January 1842.
3. Ibid., 4 July 1841.
4. Ibid., 31 March 1840.
5. Ibid., 3 February 1842.
6. Ibid., 19 May 1840
7. There was a violin school in Lititz and possibly Theodore began his study there. Peter noted in his diary, "Violin School commenced with And.[rew] Raus & Levin Clewell in connection with Br. Fetter." 28 January 1842.
8. James Wolle, letter to Theodore, 2 June 1845. Archives of the Moravian Church in Bethlehem, Pennsylvania.
9. Ibid.
10. Ibid., 3 December 1845.
11. Ibid.
12. Ibid., 9 February 1847.
13. Ibid.
14. Peter Wolle, "Diary," 28 June 1853. The Greensborough Female College was also known as the Methodist Female College. The school is now Greensboro College.
15. Ibid. The varied spellings of Greensborough, N.C. are the result of spellings that Peter Wolle used in his diary. I chose not to use today's spelling when writing about the nineteenth century.
16. Ibid., 20 August 1853.
17. This spelling of the community was the one current when Theodore was a resident there. It may differ from the one Peter Wolle used. The accepted spelling now is Greensboro.
18. Mary Lewis Rucker Edmunds, *Letters from Edgeworth*, (Greensboro, N.C.: The Greensboro Preservation Society, 1988), 27.
19. *The Greensborough Patriot*, (Greensboro, N.C.), 25 August 1855.

20. Ibid., 31 March 1855.
21. Ibid.
22. Ibid.
23. Ibid., 6 June 1851.
24. Ibid., 13 March 1855.
25. Ibid., 29 July 1854.
26. Ibid., 31 March 1855.
27. Ibid.
28. Ibid.
29. Ibid., 19 May 1855.
30. *Patriot and Flag,* (Greensborough, N.C.), 29 May 1857.
31. Ibid., 28 May 1858.
32. Ibid.
33. Ibid., 17 July 1857.
34. *The Greensborough Patriot,* (Greensborough, N.C.), 22 June 1860.
35. *The Patriot,* (Greensborough, N.C.), 24 March 1855. The Greensborough newspaper was known as *The Patriot and Flag, The Patriot, The Greensborough Patriot* at different times. However, it was the same paper.
36. *The Greensborough Patriot,* 22 June 1860.
37. Ibid.
38. Ibid., 7 June 1851.
39. Mary Lewis Rucker Edmunds, *Letters,* page 34. This is a fictional account of life at the seminary just prior to Theodore's arrival there. It is, however, contemporary with his teaching position in the community. The story is in the form of letters written by various individuals who would have attended the school or worked there.
40. Ibid., 38.
41. *The Moravian,* (Bethlehem, Pa.), "Wolle," 1 April 1885.
42. Though there are Wolle family anecdotes, and some official records, the primary firsthand accounts of the family during this time survived in Peter Wolle's diary. However, he remained deeply concerned about Theodore throughout the war. That concern makes it possible to use his diary as a major source for many of Theodore's actions during the war, if not his reasons for the actions.
43. Peter Wolle, "Diary," 11 May 1861.
44. Ibid., 13 May 1861.
45. Ibid., 24 May 1861.
46. Mary Lewis Rucker Edmunds, *Letters,* page 124.

47. Peter Wolle, "Diary," 14 September 1861.
48. Ibid., 12 February 1862.
49. Ibid., 2 March 1863.
50. Ibid., 19 May 1863.
51. Ibid., 22 July 1863.
52. Ibid., 4 January 1864.
53. *The Greensborough Patriot*, 11 June 1863.
54. *The Moravian*, 1 April 1885.
55. Ibid.
56. Peter Wolle, "Diary," 25 December 1864.
57. Ibid., 31 December 1864.
58. Ibid., 29 March 1865.
59. Ibid., 30 April 1865.
60. Ibid., 18 May 1865.
61. Ibid., 30 June 1865.
62. Ibid., 31 December 1865.

Chapter Six

*Transforming the Tradition*

Prof. Theodore F. Wolle, who . . . held a front place in music. . . . There are many of his remaining musical associates and people of Bethlehem generally, who will concur in the tribute due him in these pages.[1]

[A] brilliant pianist, and ingenious mechanic, a fine business man, an almost perfect proofreader, a faithful teacher, and a master of epistolary English.[2]

BISHOP WOLLE MET HIS SON with his bride at the railway station 16 August 1865. The person who stepped off the train in Bethlehem with his new wife was not only a secure and skilled musician, he had a broad experience in leading and teaching others. "At about 1/4 p. 11 Theodore & his Aggie . . . made their appearance. We bade Aggie most heartily welcome to the circle of new relations," wrote the Bishop.[3]

After living through the Civil War in Greensborough, Raleigh, and Salem, Bethlehem seemed idyllic to Theodore and Aggie. There was no devastation or hunger. On the contrary, prosperity and growth were everywhere. The Civil War, new industrialization, and the secularization of the community – for the Moravian Church no longer owned and controlled the community – had created a building boom; a real estate agency was opened to meet the demand for buying, selling, and renting property. *The Moravian* reported that "Building of all sorts is being briskly carried on in all [parts] of the town. In Market street some very fine houses are going up."[4] New civic services were becoming available: bridges, gas and gas lighting, and water. Commerce was active. Anthracite coal was profitably transported to New York and Philadelphia from mines in the mountains north of Bethlehem by the Lehigh Canal. The canal flowed through Bethlehem parallel to the Lehigh River. Eighty-one canal boats passed through Bethlehem in one day in October 1866.[5] When the canal was surpassed by the Lehigh Valley Rail Road, South Bethlehem became a major rail center.

Industrial expansion was in full swing, and a resident in Moravian Bethlehem wrote proudly, "A walk to the 'other side' [South Bethlehem] always reveals some new improvements in the busy, pushing town."[6] The expansion was driven by the manufacture of zinc and iron, and by the railroad. The Pennsylvania and Lehigh Zinc Works had been operating in South Bethlehem since 1853, producing the first sheet zinc in America. Then iron production was introduced. Local writers saw beauty in the "great prosperity" of the Bethlehem Iron Company. "This splendid works went into operation in South Bethlehem in the year 1866."[7] The Lehigh Valley Rail Road daily transformed South Bethlehem into a complex network of iron rails flowing in every direction. To the north a cement industry flourished, and in the mountains there were slate quarries. A contemporary financial report stated that the "demand for slate continues and the speculative excitement is without abatement."[8] The residents of Bethlehem were surrounded by growth and change.

Other qualities of Bethlehem, moral atmosphere and age, were explicit as the trustees promoted their Lehigh University to parents and to students. An announcement soliciting students for the opening class read, "It is also most important to state that perhaps no town in the country has purer and healthier moral atmosphere, in which to train young men, than this old Moravian settlement."[9] The University opened its doors in the fall of 1866 after purchasing Christmas Hall, the South Bethlehem Moravian Church, for classrooms and to house its first students, in another move that exemplified shrinking Moravian influence. At the same time a very large stone building in the German Medieval style was constructed to house science laboratories. Though the University might appear to be a German technical school, the resemblance was only visual. This was a University, with a curriculum tied to Bethlehem with its tradition of a Christian liberal arts education.

Across the river from the University and the industrial complex, many of the Moravian buildings from the eighteenth century were in use. To Bethlehem visitors the town remained a "quiet Moravian town" in spite of the postwar development taking place along the river. Using a surprising metaphor, one railroad passenger described a romantic impression of Bethlehem after the two-and-one-half hour train ride from Philadelphia.

> We saw the town of the Moravians, at the mountains' feet, like a nun kneeling before the altar, with flashing spires and slate-roofed dwellings, affording a finer view of neat and quiet towns . . . we passed on through its clean well-kept streets, looking upon its numerous and substantial churches, and wandering far out of Bethlehem.[10]

To this day Bethlehem retains this combination of prosperity, growth, historical interest, and serenity.

Other "old" buildings had greatly changed their appearance. The expansion of the Moravian Seminary for Young Ladies engulfed the House of the Single Brethren so completely that the colonial building was no longer recognizable except for its "ancient" Mansard roof.

Like the rest of Bethlehem, the Seminary prospered during the Civil War, "money being abundant," and the number of pupils "slowly but steadily increased."[11] By 1865 there were 318 students in attendance there. Many more applied, but the school had become selective and prestigious. Only half were accepted.

While he was principal of the Bethlehem Young Ladies' Seminary, Theodore's uncle, Reverend Sylvester Wolle, another musical member of the family, enhanced the music faculty by hiring musicians from Europe. One of the historians of the Moravian Seminary wrote, "the increasing demand for superior instruction in music had dictated the wisdom of seeking abroad the requisite talent for teaching."[12] Rev. Wolle hired not only instrumentalists, but "the call for higher culture in vocal music induced the appointment of several exceedingly able European singers."[13] In 1860 Madam C. Dressler joined the music faculty. She was "a highly accomplished singer, who in earlier years had attained no inconsiderable renown at various courts of Europe, and still excelled in her favorite art."[14] Theodore accompanied her on the piano until her death in 1869.

Bethlehem's musical life had not suffered during the war. Its high musical culture continued at a level equal to performances in major cities in America, and Central Moravian Church provided some of the best sacred music outside of Philadelphia, Boston, and New York City. The Moravian Trombone Choir continued to play important announcements from the church belfry. In addition to the music during the Moravian services, everyone could hear excellent concerts of "the world's finest music" performed by professors in the Seminary and prominent musical guests from out of town. The Philharmonic Society continued its public concert series, though some felt the group was not as good as it had been earlier in the century.[15] Other local civic groups sponsored concerts by outside artists.

For Theodore there were unlimited musical opportunities for which he was ideally suited. His talents were the most comprehensive in the family: he mastered the piano and the violin, conducted, understood the organ both as a musician and as an engineer, and was devoted to teaching. Like his father, Theodore was an expert in English-language usage. Soon after he arrived in Bethlehem, he began work as a proofreader with his father. Many Moravians admired him as much for his "almost perfect proofreading," as they did for his "brilliant" playing.

During their first few days in Bethlehem, the couple stayed with Theodore's brother James until a house was vacated for them. The evening after they arrived, "Francis & wife came to salute Theodore & wife."[16] Rev. Francis Wolle was principal of the Women's Seminary, having taken Sylvester's place at the beginning of the Civil War.

Within a short time, Theodore began to influence every facet of musical life in Bethlehem, assuming positions he would occupy for the rest of his life.

When the Seminary opened in September, Theodore began his musical leadership as Professor of Music. He joined at least nine other music faculty members who were teaching vocal and instrumental music. Theodore instructed students in piano, violin, and organ, accompanied other faculty members, and played both the piano and the violin in concerts. In addition to his daily teaching, coaching students, and rehearsing with other faculty, the professors prepared the students for the "Musical Entertainments." As at Edgeworth, they consisted of a variety of solo and ensemble vocal and instrumental pieces interspersed with recitations. The "Entertainment" that concluded the first year of Theodore's teaching at the Seminary was typical. The women's chorus sang a piece by Mercadante, and, with male voices added, an oratorio chorus by Mendelssohn. Pianists played a "Polonaise" by Chopin, a "Romanze" by Mozart, and "Andante with Variations" by Schumann, among other piano pieces. There were four vocal soloists. Miss Selfridge impressed people the most. Not only did she sing a difficult aria by Bellini, "she executed one of the piano parts in Gloria's bravoura [sic] arrangement of Belisario."[17]

• • •

A number of times during the school year the Seminary faculty gave "Grand Musical Soirees." These evening concerts included chamber music, instrumental solos, and songs. Theodore played both the piano and the violin in a "Soiree" soon after he joined the Seminary in a program consisting of "Quintette in C Major," by Beethoven; "Trio for Piano, Violin and Claironet [sic]," by Mozart; violoncello solo "Souvenir de Suisse;" piano solo "Faust Waltz," by Liszt; violin solo "Concerto No. 3," by De Deriot; "Andante and Variations," by Schubert; "Quintette in A, Op. 18," by Mendelssohn, the "Allegro."[18] In addition to his teaching and performing at the Seminary, Theodore was soon teaching privately in a nearby community. His wife often went with him to these lessons.

Early in the first fall, Theodore became organist at the Moravian Chapel and joined the church orchestra as a violinist. Though the chapel, built in 1751, was much smaller than the Moravian Church, the position of organist was a demanding one. There were two German-language services every Sunday in the chapel with a choir. Bishop Wolle described a busy musical Sunday for Theodore and other family members.

> Theodore played the organ there [in the Old Chapel] very acceptably. At the lovefeast at 2 P.M. he accompanied Br. Bechel [the chief organist] at the first violin; Br. Silvester [sic] was in the choir.[19]

Weekday services normally took place in the chapel as well, and there could be as many as two per week. Theodore joined the other master musician and composer living in Bethlehem, Francis Hagen, and the Bishop was particularly pleased with his son's perfection when he wrote, "In the evening we had a delightful and blessed meeting in the Chapel. . . . Mr. Hagen, liturgist, an efficient choir & large congregation present, – led by Theodore on the organ, without a mistake!"[20] In the yearly statistical account of the Moravian Congregation in Bethlehem, *The Moravian* stated "the whole number of public services in the year was four hundred and sixty-one."[21] There were 899 communicants residing in Bethlehem at the time.

Theodore also played second violin in the Philharmonic Society, which presented a number of concerts each year. The society, with its roots in the *collegium musicum,* continued as an extension of the Moravian Church; however, members were no longer only Moravians. The Philharmonic Society, like the *collegium musicum,* performed a major sacred vocal composition in each concert. An 1869 program was typical. The first part consisted of ensemble pieces and chamber works:

Overture-La Concertola. Orchestra.
Fantasia-Piano-Chopin. Prof. Warner.
Trio-Piano, violin and violincello [sic]. Mendelssohn

(By Messrs. Wolle, Graber, and Bleck.)
Marchia-Piano-Raff. Prof. Warner.
Quintette-Larghetto & Ronda [sic]. Beethoven.

(Wolle, Graber, Bleck, Chas. Roeper, and
B.E. Lechman [Lehman]).[22]

Since secular music was also played, the society did not perform in the sanctuary. The second half of the concert was a "Stabat Mater," by an unidentified composer. The Philharmonic Society played two other concerts for the benefit of the Young Men's Christian Association. The next year, 1870, Theodore was elected a member of the board and became concertmaster. James Wolle continued as the secretary/treasurer, a position he held for many years. In 1870 the orchestra numbered twenty-six players, and the singers consisted of twenty-nine females and thirty-three males. The society also arranged concerts by prominent outside performers. The "Mendelssohn Quintet" from Boston was frequently engaged.

In addition to public music, there was always music in Moravian homes. Families sang hymns accompanied on the harmonium or melodeon, and there was "elevating" vocal and instrumental music involving the piano. The Theodore Wolles were not long in Bethlehem before Theodore was playing for musical evenings. One evening the couple was invited to dine with Bishop Wolle and others at the home of their relative, Augustus Wolle. He was the family industrial entrepreneur who founded the iron industry in Bethlehem and developed slate quarries. The evening must have been typical of many that occurred in an era when all music was live, usually performed by amateurs, and often centered around the parlor piano. "Supper over, the men repaired to the office, to smoke their cigar[s;] having returned, the rest of the

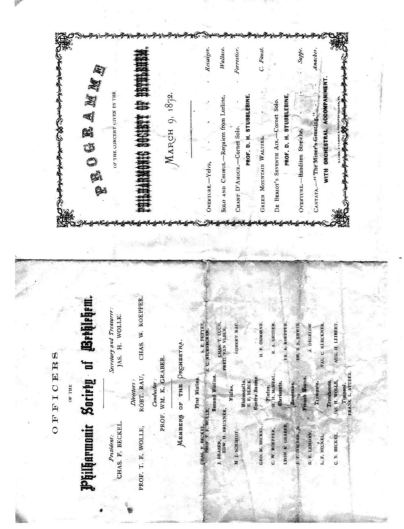

Front and back of a Philharmonic Society program showing positions of two Wolles
(Archives of The Bach Choir of Bethlehem)

evening was devoted to musical performances at the piano by Theo, the Van Vlecks, & they all played well," wrote the Bishop with his usual judgement of the quality of the music he heard. "The company broke up near 10 o'clock."[23]

At a more moving event in the life of the family, Theodore played a part in a birthday celebration for his Uncle Frederick. The Bishop recorded the occasion in his diary. "Remembered my father's dying days, 53 years ago, on his son Frederick's birthday. . . .The family of Theodore spent the evening with us; he gratified us by his performance on the Piano."[24]

• • •

As Theodore and his wife were settling in Bethlehem, the idea of progress was taking hold in American society. An era was dawning across America, which Theodore's contemporaries called "the ceaseless materialistic striving of a young nation."[25] Evidence of American material progress was everywhere for Theodore to see, and in the area of Bethlehem, much of it involved his relatives. But the idea of progress was not limited to the materialism of industry and science. Many believed that America was progressing just as rapidly in the arts. "Let no man complain of stagnation in the progress of art in this country!" wrote the editor of *The Moravian*. Everything was being reshaped and redefined in "this eventful epoch of the world's history."

Within a year of Theodore's arrival, his influence in Bethlehem's musical progress was recognized in an unusually long review of an entertainment at the Ladies' Seminary. The "thanks of the community are due to Professors Wolle and Graber, and to Madame Dressler, whose excellent musical judgement and faithful labors combined to make it a great success."

That event was a microcosm of musical growth in America. "In order to measure the progress of art in our own country with some degree of accuracy, let those interested note the performances of amateurs within the social circles nearest them." While some have expressed "that the 'divine art' can never become a national characteristic in restless America," a quick review of music "in our nation" revealed each step in musical progress.

> Little by little, youthful amateurs, now imbued with a growing love of the art, dropped the drumming quickstep for Huenten's pretty variations, then those of Herz's more difficult technicalities, until passing through Stakosch and Thalberg, they reached Chopin and Beethoven; or, they vocalized the *Zauberfloete* in lieu of Sir Henry Bishop's ballads. Where in those days of musical unripeness, one young miss astounded her circle with the brilliancy of Herz, there are now hundreds who faithfully study Mendelssohn, Beethoven, Schumann, or Mozart.

In Bethlehem the issue was not a matter of increased musical skill or more refined musical taste, those were already in place, it was "how much more comprehensive have become the ideas of the teachers – how much more elevated the standard for the pupil." One hundred years before, Bethlehem had been nearly unique in musical America. After the Civil War, with burgeoning musical performances everywhere, Bethlehem had become more comprehensive, and that progress was led by the faculty of the Seminary.

At the conclusion of the evening when Principal Francis Wolle spoke, he tied the musical progress to another Moravian tradition, the importance of women in music.

> Some words were bestowed upon the noble mission of women, especially at this eventful epoch of the world's history, and, in conclusion, he eloquently alluded to the principles of Christianity and virtue, which had ever been the foundations of the administration of the school and of the instruction there imparted. Seldom have we seen so rapt an attention as we saw elicited by these remarks.

Though the idea of continuous progress in the arts began to be questioned near the end of the century, in 1883 a writer in *Scribners*

*Monthly-Century Illustrated Monthly Magazine* felt comfortable presenting a balanced view affirming progress in music.

> This our nineteenth century is commonly esteemed a prosaic, a material, an unimaginative age. Compared with the foregoing period, its amusements are frivolous or sordid, and what mental activity it spares from making of money it devotes to science and not to art. These strictures . . . have certainly much truth to back them. But leaving out of sight many minor facts which tell in the contrary direction, there is one great opposing fact of such importance that by itself alone it calls for at least a partial reversal of the verdict we pass upon ourselves as children of a nonartistic time. This fact is the place that music – most unpractical, most unprosaic, most ideal of the arts – has held in nineteenth-century life.[26]

The reviewer in *The Moravian* wrote not only of musical progress, he raised the fundamental aesthetic question facing those concerned with culture in America following the Civil War, namely, whether it was possible to reconcile a "vital idealism within an absorbing utilitarianism."[27]

• • •

Idealism, and its tenet that the purpose of music was to ennoble the listener and the performer, was not yet under direct attack at the Moravian Seminary. The issue was only raised. Later, direct attacks would come, and a defense would become necessary. But in the year 1866 even a student's performance of an operatic selection had to submit to the sacred surroundings of the Moravian Seminary Chapel, where it "would doubtless have been greeted with the outburst it invariably elicits in the Opera houses, but for the sacred locality of its performance. A previous attempt at demonstrative approbation had been promptly checked by the Principal."[28]

In his "Historical Notes on Music in Bethlehem," Rufus Grider, flautist, librarian of the Philharmonic Society, and Theodore's contemporary, clearly stated what the purpose of music had been to the founders of Bethlehem.

> Music was an institution of the church . . . especially fostered as affording intellectual enjoyment, perfectly innocent, exerting a refining influence upon the human heart and delighting the senses. All who could learn were expected to engage therein. It was believed that whoever was able to calculate could be taught music.[29]

The connection between music and mathematics referred to by Grider was rooted in the belief that music was "sounding number," a long-standing Christian absorption of Greek Platonism. That belief elevated music to the position of the "divine art." Another member of Grider's generation viewed the purpose of music in early Bethlehem in terms of the philosophy of Idealism. "Thus, they contrived to form a frame of the Beautiful around their toil and labor; an idea which does not suggest itself to this age of progress."[30]

For Theodore and other Moravians, "the beautiful" was still "of God." Though "subordinate to the spiritual. . .'What God hath joined together let no man put asunder' – the beautiful and the goodly, aesthetic and religion," wrote the editor of *The Moravian* in the year 1873.[31] An earlier injunction to the leaders of the Philharmonic Society, again in *The Moravian*, that the purpose of the Society was "to cultivate a taste for really good music" and to offer "a series of concerts in which equally the beautiful and classical music shall form the programme" met with agreement within the Wolle family. The reason for their acceptance was that for them the beautiful and classical music reflected one another. Both described "good" music. And "good music" was "Godly" music. For Theodore and his circle, cultivating a taste for good music in the public was a spiritual service to the community. Therefore, while the program of a concert included what were termed "miscellaneous" compositions, the core of the concert was always a sacred work in German.

While the Seminary chapel was clearly a sacred place, the applicability of aesthetic idealism in Bethlehem's music life came under open attack regarding the concerts of the Philharmonic Society held in the auditorium of the Moravian Parochial School. Defending the position of the Society, and at the same time adapting it to new realities, became the responsibility of Theodore, a director and concert master, James, secretary/treasurer, and trombonist, along with others, as they transformed the Philharmonic Society to serve musical needs of the "new" Bethlehem, of the "Bethlehems" as they began to be called. Interest in the concerts of the Society lagged, and a meeting to reorganize the group was held on 8 October 1870 in which the Wolles assumed a major role for shaping the future of the group. James was elected secretary/treasurer, and Theodore became the concert master as well as a board member. The Society's historian wrote, "The Society seems to have taken a new lease on life. Efforts are now made, not only to improve the rendering, but also to bring in new material."[32]

That there was no longer agreement regarding the purpose of music began to be voiced in the community. While the members of the Philharmonic Society held that beauty and goodness were the same, and that they created their programs to express that belief, individuals from the Bethlehems questioned that belief and the music the Society programmed. "*The Times* is of the opinion that the public would prefer less German and not quite so much scientific music," was reported in *The Moravian*. The readers of *The Times* understood "scientific music" meant music with complicated harmonies and no clear melody with a light accompaniment, in short, Romantic music. The complaint that the texts were in German would have surprised musicians like Theodore who were bilingual. However, they defended the use of German texts on practical and aesthetic grounds, for "there is very little really good music in English suitable for the Philharmonic."

The issue of "scientific" was defended on two fronts: from the point of view of the audience and of the performers. Occasionally, listening to a waltz or a ballad is "pleasant," but listening to nothing else "would be tiresome to an audience."[33] Also, the editor of *The Moravian* questioned that "a Society of amateurs, who meet for their own improvement, could be kept together at all, for waltzes were simply not worth playing week after week. This view harks back to the purpose of music for Moravians, as stated by Grider. Amateur musicians were to have the opportunity to perform music for their own spiritual improvement. Thus, the Philharmonic Society existed first for its members. They were to be uplifted by the music they played. The players were not professional musicians with a "job" to entertain an audience. Their concerts were spiritual offerings to the community, which in turn would be uplifting through the musicians' performances of great music.

While reasserting the basic purpose of the Society, "the Society should, and we have no doubt it does, regard itself as an educator of the music taste." The Society must bring "the taste of the public up, rather than let its own standard down for the sake of gratifying a desire for 'popular' music."

The purpose of the group was changing from edification to education. Theodore and other members of the board were faced with the most profound musical problem of the era: how to refine the taste of the public when the only educational agent was the concert itself. Perhaps more information about the music and the composer offered a solution for the "uninitiated public." The editor suggested that short notes "containing an analysis of the music, the composer, etc." be added to the program. However, since every part of the Moravian church year was articulated by special music, the Philharmonic Society "should constitute itself the guardian" of yearly concerts on Whit-Monday, "an old Moravian institution." Yet, the Whit-Monday concert was not well attended. Promotion for the final concert of the season made clear that both "classical and popular selections" of a "miscellaneous character" would be played, and for the first time the term "music-loving public" was used.[34]

What Moravians had taken for granted, i.e., a shared ability to understand "good" music, was no longer the case. Every Moravian spent years in school, and Sunday after Sunday being educated musically. Now people with little or no experience in listening to "good" music were buying tickets, attending the concerts, and were unable to understand either the texts or the music, let alone be uplifted and refined by the experience.

Theodore and the Philharmonic board had heard the message, and they performed a completely "miscellaneous" concert at the end of the winter season in the year 1871. Other concerts retained the emphasis on "good" instrumental works and vocal music with sacred texts. The arrangement worked, and *The Moravian* reported at the conclusion of the 1872 season that the series was successful, and

> It is a pleasing thing that in musical matters *at least* [author's italics] the old traditions of Bethlehem are so well preserved, and the old life perpetuated, and we imagine there are few if any communities of its size where so large and well trained an orchestra, and chorus of amateurs can be gathered together, and that from every station in society and of every age.[35]

The issue remained unresolved, and in the season of 1873 the continuation of the "old tradition of Bethlehem" required a more intensive defense with the admission, now in the concert program itself and not just in *The Moravian*, that "certain classes of music it [the Society] cannot touch." Those who did not understand the Society's music should listen to "traveling minstrels and such like."[36] Not withstanding, the cantata that spring was "The May Queen," a piece that was both secular and in English. A new thought was introduced in the report of the concert. This was the idea of civic pride, an expression that would become commonplace in the following years. "Bethlehem may indeed feel proud that it can gather together so large a number of skillful and intelligent amateur musicians."[37]

Not only presenting good music to an informed audience, but the musical education of a relatively uninformed but interested public became a new responsibility of the Philharmonic Society. Their concert series was a culture course offered by the newly established Young Men's Christian Association. Yet another deep-seated problem emerged: the lack of young trained instrumentalists. The Philharmonic Society for the first time required a formal feeder group if it was to survive. To meet this need, in 1877 E. C. Ricksecker, a music professor at the Seminary, organized the Amateur Philharmonic Society. It was made up of local young men. *The Moravian* made clear, however, that the justification for such a group was still the ennobling power of music.

> How much better it is to spend the evening [rather than] frequent those places, at which unfortunately so many young people congregate exposing themselves to dangers which threaten both soul and body. . . . The best coffee, sandwiches and very superior Moravian Sugar Cake were served.[38]

Doubt that the Philharmonic Society would survive was mentioned for the first time in the press in the year 1879. "They have made wonderful advances in proficiency, and have done a good work in cultivating a taste for really good music – and it were a great pity if their labors and mission were to stop here."[39] That fall, the society discontinued rehearsals, because there were not enough people attending the practices regularly. The fault was due to another broad social problem. "Too many irons in the fire, is the burden and excuse of the average American citizen of this day, and the pleasant recreation of an hour or two of practice . . . is unfortunately the first duty to be sacrificed."[40]

For four years there was no Philharmonic Society. Then in 1883 the group was reorganized. Professor Theodore F. Wolle was elected the president. The orchestra had twenty-five members and rehearsed each Monday evening. The first concert was recorded in the church diary, "A concert given by the Philharmonic Society, for the first time in several years."[41] When Theodore died the following year, the Society ceased, until J. Fred. returned from Germany to replace Theodore as organist and choirmaster of the Moravian Church.

The transformation of the Philharmonic Society into the Choral Union, which the new group was called, was due mainly to the charismatic leadership of J. Fred. Wolle. The story of that transformation is told in the next section of this family biography. However, Theodore and his circle had made the Philharmonic Society a group ready to serve the needs of a wealthy capitalistic community where they remained true to many Moravian musical beliefs. As he had done by providing his cousin, J. Fred., with the possibility of serving as a professor of music, Theodore now offered him a further option: becoming a conductor for the whole community.

• • •

After a number of years as chapel organist, in 1871 Theodore became the organist and choirmaster of Central Moravian Church. It was in this position that he made significant transformations in the Moravian organ tradition and in the role of a Moravian organist. These changes were embodied in replacing the Central Church organ, and its presentation to the public in the year 1874.

The original organ was installed in 1806, when the church was built. Off and on, there had been talk of replacing the organ, but nothing was done until Theodore became the organist. The next year the trustees formed a committee with "Theo. F. Wolle" as an advisory member.

Theodore and his contemporaries proposed two reasons for the replacement of the original organ. First, they argued the tone of the organ was no longer what it had been; and second, the original instrument was mechanically out of date. They presented a petition to the trustees containing a "large number of signatures from among the clergy and the laity of the congregation."[42] The trustees were "instructed to take immediate steps for the procuring of a new organ adequate and proportionate in power and quality to the size and requirements of our church." Their arguments were compelling enough to convince the trustees that a new organ was necessary, and they set aside a budget not to exceed $10,000.

It is doubtful that the tone of the organ had decayed. What had taken place was a change in musical taste. The organ sound the congregation and the organist desired was different from what their ancestors had preferred. Moravian organs were designed to lead congregational singing and to accompany instrumental ensembles. The ranks of pipes were selected for those two purposes. Moravian organs were not solo instruments; therefore, they did not contain ranks of pipes with dominant individual tone colors. Their tone was unassuming.

By 1870 organ preludes were desired that were longer, more expressive, with greater virtuosity than the brief, simple improvised voluntaries advocated by Gregor. The new preludes were often transcriptions of orchestral works, or they were compositions for organ that made the instrument sound like an orchestra. In addition, to accompany expressively the anthems that Romantic composers were writing, an organ had to increase and to decrease the volume of tone, i.e., crescendo and diminuendo, either slowly or rapidly. The organist must dramatically vary the timbre of the organ. The original Central Moravian Church organ was not capable of "nuanced" performances because it had been built to create a sound world that was quite different.

The explosion of technology that occurred in the nineteenth century not only opened new possibilities that were evident in Bethlehem's industries, organs were affected as well. Thus, a reporter wrote that the old Moravian organ was "sadly out of date as regards the many improvements which have been perfected in the organs as well as nearly all the other musical instruments during the past 67 years."

The new organ was entirely Theodore's design. The editor of *The Moravian* informed its readers that Theodore was the mind behind the new organ, and that mind was so well-informed in the area of organ building that everyone who saw the plan, including one of the best organ building firms in America, could only praise Theodore's design, adding nothing to it.

> It is proper to state that the entire specifications of the organ, so far as relates to the disposition of the manuals, the number, character and combinations of the stops in each manual, the arrangement of the combination pedals, the introduction of the "tell tale" into the organ desk, and other minute details is the production of the present organist, Theo. F. Wolle. This specification was first laid before the organ committee and they approved it without alteration or amend-

ment. It also received the unqualified approbation of the various organ builders to whose examination it was submitted.

A New York organ builder, Jardine & Sons, was given the contract to build the organ.

Theodore was not only an exceptional organist, he was conversant with the organ as a machine. It was one thing for the organist to make his musical desires known to an organ builder; to design all the specifications was highly unusual. He was following in the footsteps of the great eighteenth-century Moravian organ builder, David Tannenberg. Theodore was indeed an "ingenious mechanic." In fact he was the last Moravian organ engineer in the line of Klemm and Tannenberg.

Every part of the organ was listed in a description of the instrument in *The Moravian*. The organ contained 2,161 pipes, none silent. The organist, facing the pulpit, set at a desk with three manuals with fifty-eight keys, twenty-seven pedals, and forty stops. "The stop heads are of the oblique patterns with ivory faces, the name and the number of feet being neatly engraved on each face." The exposed pipes were painted "a beautiful shade of lilac, with neat and chaste ornamentation in gilt." The final cost of the instrument was $8,000, under budget by $2,000.

The organ was dedicated on Christmas Eve, 1873. Theodore began the service with a voluntary "in which he brought out the various stops and the general power of the instrument . . . and then passed over into the beautiful strains of a Christmas Eve anthem, sung by the choir ["Stille Nacht"]."[43] The pastor wrote that Theodore gradually changed the voluntary into the accompaniment of the anthem that was "sung with great effect."[44]

Now that there was a Moravian orchestral organ capable of being a solo concert instrument, Theodore set in motion the second profound change he made in the Moravian organ tradition. He organized a public concert to introduce the organ to the "citizens of the town" for the benefit of the "good causes of the Congregation."[45] Thus, he became an organ recitalist.

Choir loft and original organ, Christmas, 1861
Central Moravian Church, Bethlehem
(The Moravian Archives, Bethlehem)

Expecting a sold-out house, the tickets were color-coded according to the seating location in the sanctuary "to keep order in the large crowd."[46] The ticket sales were very rapid; by the date of the recital the newly decorated and expanded sanctuary, seating over one thousand people, was in fact sold out. The clergy and their wives were seated in the pulpit area.

The "Grand Organ Concert" was held the evening of 15 January 1874. It was "grand" in every way. Two of the finest organists in the United States were featured performers: David Wood, the blind Philadelphia organist who was later J. Fred. Wolle's organ teacher, and G. W. Morgan, organist at two of the most prominent Episcopal Churches in New York City. Theodore deferred to the esteemed guests and played only one piece. Singers from the Philharmonic Society joined the Moravian Church Choir.

Each piece demonstrated the orchestral, recital qualities of Theodore's instrument. The selections also showed the variety of the organ literature played in the 1870s. Dr. David Wood, one of the early exponents of Bach's music, began with Passacaglia in C Minor. This colossal composition introduced the audience to the magnificent new organ in their community and to Bach at a time when he was still a "new" composer. The audience also heard a virtuoso player without peer in his day in a church where virtuosity was not cultivated. To demonstrate that the organ could sound like an orchestra accompanying a choir, Wood and the large chorus performed "The Heavens are Telling" from Joseph Haydn's *Creation*. Wood played the orchestral parts on the organ. That chorus also was selected because of its special association with Bethlehem. At the time it was believed that the American premiere of Haydn's *Creation* had occurred in Bethlehem. The Haydn chorus tied the organ concert to a long tradition of musical innovation and lent the program a sacred character. The concert broadened the Moravian tradition; it did not replace it. Therefore, it could still rightfully take place in the church. The concert was not just a secular recital to showcase the new organ.

Wood continued in the grand manner: an organ sonata by Mendelssohn, pieces by Schumann, and a *tour-de-force* by Meyerbeer, "Fackeltanz," exploiting the varied capabilities of timbre and dynamic range of this new orchestral instrument. There was absolutely no connection between what the audience heard that evening and what they would have heard ten years before in the same sanctuary. Moravian services would continue with a more modest use of the organ, but Theodore had crossed the bridge into the modern outside world with its Romantic taste for musical richness and nuances, and the music of Bach. Central Moravian Church had not only entered the world of Romantic music, the Moravians were again in the forefront, for they had the most modern organ in the area.

Theodore played an offertory by a Romantic composer, and the second "star" took his place on the organ bench. Prof. G. W. Morgan began with the Toccata and Fugue in D Minor by Bach, a composition equal in scale to the Passacaglia in C Minor. Morgan played two original compositions, "Handel's Lesson" and a piece that surely demonstrated the orchestral capabilities of Theodore's organ, "Sad Sea Waves." The pièce de résistance, however, was Rossini's overture to *William Tell*. Each section of this overture evoked a grand passion: dawn, pastoral scene in the Alps, storm, and the famous musical depiction of the battle for Swiss independence. This transcription of an orchestral piece for the organ exploited all the possibilities of the new instrument.

This concert was significant not only because it signaled a new view of the organ's function in Moravian services, but because it moved the Moravian Church and its musicians again on to center stage culturally in the Bethlehems. In addition, it was the first step leading to the problems with the Bach Festivals held two decades later in the same church. Tickets had been sold to a church event, only slightly sacred, held in a Moravian sanctuary. Reserved sections were created in a congregation where any sign of rank was avoided. The pulpit area was used for concert seating, albeit for the pastors and their wives. Professional soloists who were not local performed for a congregation that had built and sustained a high musical tradition rooted in amateur musical participation by its own members. Every one of these innovations later became major issues, until the Moravian Church no longer hosted the Bach Festivals early in the 1910s.

While no documentation confirms J. Fred. Wolle's attendance at the concert, it seems difficult to imagine he was not at such an important musical event. He was twelve years old at the time; old enough to appreciate the importance of the occasion and the power of the music played that evening. If he were present, it may have been the first time he heard Bach's organ music, and the importance of the evening for his whole musical career cannot then be underestimated. In addition this concert may have been the occasion when J. Fred. met Dr. Wood, his future organ teacher and the man who trained J. Fred. to play Bach's music. At least, the concert established that Wood was known to Theodore, and that Wood was well aware of music in Bethlehem. Later, when J. Fred. Wolle was proficient enough to benefit from Wood's instruction, Theodore may have been the contact for the lessons.

In the years following the first public recital on the new Moravian organ, there was an increasing number of organ concerts held in various area churches. Organ recitals became popular musical events as the organ took on an orchestral character. Theodore played these recitals usually with other organists. He was involved with a number of organ dedications, for there were many new churches being built in the Bethlehems. In this way Theodore was the first Moravian who played recitals and not just sacred services. For Theodore the number of recitals remained modest, and they focused primarily on inaugurating new instruments. However, again, Theodore paved the way for organists in the future. It was possible for a Moravian to think of giving recitals on the organ.

It was probably because of Theodore's expert knowledge of organ technology that the story was told that J. Fred., as a youth, approached his cousin to learn about organ construction rather than for organ instruction. Theodore refused to instruct J. Fred. about the mechanics of the organ unless he submitted to a rigorous, disciplined, and systematic musical study of the instrument. J. Fred. agreed. In addition to learning how the organ functioned, he mastered harmony, improvisation, the sacred liturgies of the Moravian Church, and began to practice part of the immense volume of organ literature being written by Romantic composers. The time for self-instruction was over, and the link between the generations was forged. The match between J. Fred's talent and Theodore's teaching was so fine that, when Theodore began to show signs of illness, he transferred J. Fred. to David Wood. It was a tribute both to Theodore and to J. Fred. that Wood accepted him immediately as a student.

## TRANSFORMING THE TRADITION 153

• • •

The Moravian tradition of composition had not ceased with Bishop Wolle. Fine Moravian composers were not found only in the eighteenth century as later critics contended when the Romantic style fell out of favor. Theodore among others carried that tradition into the new Romantic era.

In Greensborough Theodore was already a recognized composer, and records exist of other compositions. In 1867 his father wrote, "Theo's choir piece, 'Blessed are the dead &c.' was beautiful – I had my seat in the organ gallery."[47] A number of years later a piece by Theodore was mentioned in a concert in the Women's Seminary, " an English farewell song composed by one of the graduates, and set to music by Prof. Theo. Wolle."[48] In a description of the memorial service for President Garfield "Asleep in Jesus," Theodore's only surviving composition, was mentioned by the pastor. "The choir sang "Asleep in Jesus," to music composed by the organist, Prof. T. F. Wolle, and Spohr's 'Selig sind die Todten'."[49] What was musically significant about this service was that Theodore's composition was paired with a piece by Spohr, one of the great European composers of the era. Theodore's work was considered fine enough to be included in an important, impressive community event when only the finest music was required. In the eyes of his contemporaries, Theodore was a composer of importance. He composed pieces that were on a par with those by the foremost European composers.

"Asleep in Jesus" was sung at another important event: a community memorial for the death of President Grant held in the Moravian Church.

> On Saturday afternoon, August 8 [1885], a 2:30 service in memory of General Grant was held in the Moravian Church. . . . After a chorale had been played by the Trombonists [sic] followed by an organ voluntary and a double quartet of male voices (Flemming's "Integer Vitae"). . . . The choir sang the anthem "Asleep in Jesus" composed by the late Prof. Theo. F. Wolle.[50]

## 154 THEODORE WOLLE

"Asleep in Jesus," by Theodore Wolle, as printed in *Hymnal and Liturgies of the Moravian Church*, 1923.

# TRANSFORMING THE TRADITION

Theodore's anthem was programmed again at a solemn occasion and paired with the finest recognized contemporary sacred music. The pastor's description of this memorial service was also informative. "The choir sang the beautiful anthem "Asleep in Jesus," composed by the late Prof. Theodore F. Wolle, and on this occasion for the first time since his funeral."[51] "Asleep in Jesus" continued to express the feelings of the community. "Asleep in Jesus" remained a favorite of the Moravians for many years. It was only recently deleted from their hymnal.

The anthem was composed in the year 1877. Theodore dedicated it "respectfully inscribed to my esteemed friend, Robert Rau."[52] Rau was the first tenor in the Moravian Church Choir who also played with Theodore in the trombone choir. The anthem was copyrighted by Theodore's widow in 1897.[53]

The poem, a popular hymn throughout the second part of the nineteenth century, was by a Scottish writer, Margaret Mackay. Mackay visited the burying ground in Pennycross Chapel, Devonshire, England where "the quiet aspect of Pennycross comes soothingly over the mind."[54] She was inspired by a tombstone inscription she saw there "Sleep in Jesus."

The poem is in three verses. Theodore set it unaltered.

*Asleep in Jesus! blessed sleep,*
*From which none ever waked to weep;*
*A calm and undisturb'd repose,*
*Unbroken by the last of foes.*

*Asleep in Jesus! Oh! how sweet,*
*To be for such a slumber meet;*
*With holy confidence to sing,*
*That death hath lost his venom'd sting!*

*Asleep in Jesus! peaceful rest,*
*Whose waking is supremely blest;*

*No fear, no woe, shall dim that hour
That manifests the Saviour's pow'r.*[55]

"Asleep in Jesus" is a 58-measure motet.[56] It is a gem composed by a musician who possessed extensive musical knowledge, and who brought a deeply inspired Moravian understanding to the Scottish text.

Theodore begins his piece, marked "Calmly," with a quiet, four-measure organ introduction. From an octave emerges two pitches, then a second rest and two more pitches. These pitches are like soft footsteps which come from a perfect world; symbolized musically with the octave at the beginning. Later in the song this pattern is set to the words "No fear, no woe" (measures 48–50). The soul steps without fear or woe from earth into heaven.

The key of the anthem is G flat Major, a key very rare in Western music. Theodore is expressing the transporting of the soul from earth into heaven by musical means. G flat Major has six flats and is very distant from C Major, with no flats, that is associated with earthly enterprise. Theodore skillfully and knowingly selected a key that in his time was as far away from earthly activity as possible.

Four voices enter singing "Asleep in Jesus!" in harmony (measures 4–7) like a lullaby. The soul is welcomed home. A traditional musical gesture for sighing expresses the word "weep" (measure 12) at the end of the poetic line followed by a very calm section of "undisturbed repose" (measures 15–17). Yet, at this point Theodore greatly extends the ranges of each voice signifying the expansiveness of the heavenly peace. A brief, quiet, organ response completes the first verse of poetry (measures 21–23). This phrase is similar to one Theodore uses later for "Oh! how sweet." He harmonizes this organ phrase with a very "sweet" chord progression; one that came to be associated with the close harmony of barbershop quartet singing.

The second verse begins with a trio of female voices singing *a cappella*. *A cappella* means "as in the chapel." It refers to unaccompanied choir singing in the Vatican. Instruments were not used there because they were considered inferior to voices. By setting the beginning of the second verse *a cappella*, Theodore used this ancient musical device to signify we are hearing the voices of angels. The women sing the lullaby "Asleep in Jesus!" like angels (measures 22–24). They rock the soul like mothers as they transport it further into the heavenly kingdom symbolized by the new key, D flat, the key associated with sublime darkness.[57] The soul is accepted into heaven and has begun its transformation. The key of D flat reenforces that transformation.

The setting for the line, "To be for such a slumber meet" (measures 26–29), contributes toward making this anthem a gem. The poetic line begins in the same key but the organ enters with an independent bass line to signal a new event. Theodore accents "such" and emphasizes it by using a chord that is totally foreign to the key of D flat (measure 28).

Theodore thrusts us with no warning into the key of A Major, a great distance from five and six flats and quite distant from C Major. There are relationships however, for A Major is one half-step above G flat. The effect of moving up a half-step is to elevate the listener, as the soul is carried near the center of heaven. The key of A Major is traditionally a bright key, "golden, warm, sunny," and Theodore has its light intensely suffuse the heavenly landscape.[58] The soul is on a higher spiritual plane. Theodore harmonizes "Ayslum" (measures 29 and 30) with the A Major chord. He then uses one of the richest chords in the Romantic palette to complete the word "slumber." This chord, an augmented sixth chord, leads to "meet," which Theodore harmonizes with a G sharp Major chord. With these chords using six sharps, he places us as distant from C Major on the sharp side as we were at the beginning of the anthem when we were in G flat with six flats. This atmosphere is flooded with heavenly light.

The next two lines are "With holy confidence to sing, That death hath lost his venom'd sting!" The soul has entered eternal life, where there is no longer death. Theodore connects the line ending with the word "meet" with the line "With holy confidence" with deep expressiveness. Again, he does this with great skill. "Meet" is sung on the pitch G sharp. "With holy confidence to sing" is sung on the pitch A flat. G sharp and A flat are the same. Further, the new words are harmonized in the key of D flat. The world of heavenly light and the world in which the soul is free from death are the same world and have nothing to do with the world of the living, C Major. Only an inspired composer with great musical skill, knowledge of music history and theory, and with a profound understanding of Moravian theology creates such moments. The addition of men's voices and a deep organ pedal part strengthens the growth of confidence expressed in the poem.

Theodore then adds greater depth to the words "With holy confidence to sing" by another musical device. In music more than one meaning can be expressed simultaneously by means of polyphony, i.e., different voices singing different melodies at the same time. In this section the soprano holds the same pitches, while the other voices sing the text to the music used for "Oh! how sweet" (measures 25 and 26). By repeating this musical phrase, Theodore expresses how sweet it is to sing with holy confidence. He not only achieves something the poet was unable to do, express two ideas at the same time, he enriches the poet's meaning. Theodore creates a phrase of heightened expression without calling attention to his musical methods. Thus, he synthesizes the Moravian aesthetic established by Gregor and the Romantic style.

The second verse ends with the word "death" on the highest pitch in the whole composition and the greatest concentration of Romantic harmony expressing the words "hath lost his venom'd sting!" as the melody descends to a D flat chord.

In setting the third verse, Theodore varies the music he composed for the first verse in subtle, lovely ways. The verse is introduced by the organ with music similar to the opening of the anthem, but Theodore shortens it and places the step figure in the forefront (measures 39–41). The phrase "blessed sleep" (measures 7 and 8) becomes "peaceful rest" (measures 43 and 44). Theodore harmonizes both verses basically the same way, but he uses a richer Romantic chord to highlight the word "peace." The passage in the first verse, "A calm and undisturbed," (measure 13–15) is very smooth, expressing calmness. In the third verse, the comparable place in "No fear, no woe, shall dim" (measures

48–51), Theodore sets off this idea by separating the words with rests. He uses musical silence effectively to confirm the meaning of the text. After the voices cease, the organ echoes the rhythm of "the Saviour's pow'r" for that power is what for a Moravian makes all the beliefs expressed in the anthem possible. The pitch G flat is sounded four times, while the altos enrich the calm with a final altered Romantic chord.

Unfortunately, "Asleep in Jesus" is the only proof that Theodore was a fine American composer of sacred music in the Romantic style. Because the piece is currently out of fashion, the tradition of Moravian composers appears to be broken. However, that tradition was not broken, it was only silenced. And Theodore Wolle's importance as a first-rank composer was silenced as well.

· · ·

Theodore's musical presence had been felt everywhere in Bethlehem including in the Moravian Trombone Choir. During the last years of his life, he was a faithful member who, like his father, frequently ascended the stairs to the church belfry with his brothers. Theodore played the bass trombone using an instrument that had belonged to his uncle, Jedidiah Weiss. Later, in the year 1881, Bethlehem received a set of trombones built especially for the Moravians, and Theodore was the first to play the new bass instrument. In the pastor's report of the arrival of the trombones, the name of each player is mentioned.

> During this week our set of trombones especially made for the Congregation in Boston, arrived. They are beautiful instruments. The present faithful trombone choir consists of the following brothers: Ambr. H. Rauch, Robert Rau, Aug. H. Siebert, Edward Hunt, & Theo. F. Wolle.[59]

Two years later Theodore could no longer ascend to the church tower easily. He began to be short of breath and became too weak to join his brothers when they played. His disease was diagnosed as consumption. He was 49 years old. The trombone brothers now played the announcements without him, even though "after his jubilee birthday, on February 12, 1882, he rallied somewhat, and appeared to regain that cheerful and joyous habit of mind which was so characteristic of his whole life."[60] His strength returned only for a short time; in the fall of 1884, Theodore weakened again. He played the Christmas service but was unable to begin the New Year at the organ bench. The 11th of January Theodore played "this afternoon for the first time since Dec. 26, he having been confined 'to the house,' then 'to his room,' and then 'to his bed'."[61]

During the evening of March 30, 1885, the trombone choir announced Theodore's departure. "The Master's call came on Monday afternoon, March 30, at 3 o'clock."[62] The pastor recorded Theodore's passing, "Bro. Theodore F. Wolle, for many years the faithful and efficient organist of the congregation, departed this life at 3 o'clock this afternoon after a lingering illness of consumption."[63] Three days later it was recorded, "On Maundy Thursday 10:30 A.M. the funeral of Bro. Theodore F. Wolle was held in the church."[64] The choir sang "his beautiful anthem, 'Asleep in Jesus'." He was buried in God's Acre. His widow had Psalm Thirty-seven, line thirty-seven, carved in his flat gravestone, "The end of the upright man is peace."

Almost immediately the Elders of the Moravian Church in Bethlehem sent a letter to J. Fred. Wolle in Munich requesting that he return to fill Theodore's position as organist. That summer J. Fred. was in Bethlehem, and in the fall he was seated on the organ bench about to take the Wolle dynasty toward its musical high point.

• • •

The ease with which J. Fred. moved into the position vacated by Theodore's death was not only due to J. Fred's extraordinary musical talent. Theodore's deep involvement in every major music issue of his time helped J. Fred. to assume positions of leadership in Bethlehem's musical institutions. Theodore had paved the way in every instance. He spent his adult life participating in the shift from church to college and university patronage. His teaching involved him in the growth of private musical instruction, i.e., private music student and the inception of the teaching studio. New trends in musical performance occupied him as well: the mechanical development of the organ into a solo "orchestra" far from Moravian roots, and the expansion of choral music sung by amateurs. The deep philosophical and aesthetic issues of the time were part of his thinking: the idea of musical progress, the promotion of "good music" and the cultivation of musical taste in audiences, and the question of what type of music constituted a concert. Finally, there was the compositional achievement of creating Moravian music in the Romantic style, a style based on the expression of personal emotion and mood through harmony rather than through melody. In "Asleep in Jesus" Theodore left the mark of his time on Moravian music, a time much different from his father's. Romantic ideas had introduced profound changes in the way all musical elements were used and heard, but particularly how listeners heard the interrelationships between melody and harmony. In Romantic music, harmony drove the meaning of the music rather than melody. "Asleep in Jesus" clearly exemplified these changes.

Theodore continued the creativity, vitality, and importance of Moravian music in American culture, added to it, and passed on the Wolle heritage of musician, organizer, engineer, and scientist to the next generation. These are reasons why J. Fred., in one of his rare public statements, told a reporter "that he is largely indebted to his cousin, the late Theodore F. Wolle, who was his predecessor as organist of the Moravian Church."[65]

## NOTES

1. Joseph Levering, *A History of Bethlehem, Pennsylvania 1741–1892*, (Bethlehem, Pa.: Times Publishing Company, 1903), pages 708–9.

2. "Obituary." Unidentified newspaper clipping in the possession of the author, given to him by a member of the Wolle family.

3. Peter Wolle, "Diary," 16 August 1865.
4. *The Moravian*, 3 May 1866.
5. Ibid., 4 October 1866.
6. Ibid., 18 October 1866.
7. Ibid., 9 August 1866.
8. Ibid., 17 January 1876.
9. Ibid., 14 June 1866.
10. Ibid., 23 August 1866.
11. William C. Reichel and Wm. H. Bigler, *A History of the Moravian Seminary for Young Ladies at Bethlehem, Pa.* (Lancaster, Pa.: The New Era Printing Company, 1901), 265.
12. Ibid., 261.
13. Ibid., 261–62.
14. Ibid., 262.
15. See Rufus Grider, *Historical Notes on Music in Bethlehem, Pennsylvania from 1741 to 1871* (Philadelphia, Pa.: John L. Pile, 1873).
16. Peter Wolle, "Diary," 17 August 1865.
17. *The Moravian*, 29 April 1866.
18. Ibid., 4 January 1866.
19. Ibid., 10 September 1865.
20. Ibid., 1 November 1865.
21. Ibid., 17 January 1867.
22. Grider, *Historical Notes*, 31.
23. Peter Wolle, "Diary," 28 September 1865.
24. Ibid., 20 November 1866.
25. All quotations in this section are from "The Progress of Music in our Country-Entertainment Given by the Young Ladies of the Seminary," *The Moravian*, 19 July 1866, except when noted otherwise.
26. Joseph A. Mussulman, *Music in the Cultured Generation,* (Evanston, Ill.: Northwestern University Press, 1971), 195.
27. *The Moravian*, 19 July 1866.
28. Ibid.
29. Grider, *Historical Notes*, 3.
30. Ibid., 4.
31. *The Moravian*, 15 May 1873.
32. Ibid.

33. Ibid., 23 March 1871. All other quotations in the paragraph are from this source.
34. Ibid., 1 June 1871.
35. Ibid., 22 May 1872.
36. Program "The Winter Evening Entertainment," Thursday, February 13 1873. Archives of The Bach Choir.
37. *The Moravian,* 29 May 1873.
38. Ibid., 13 November 1877.
39. Ibid., 23 June 1879.
40. Ibid., 27 November 1879.
41. "Diary of the Bethlehem Congregation," unpublished manuscript in the Moravian Archives, Bethlehem, 9 February 1884.
42. *Daily Times*, (Bethlehem, Pa.), 24 December 1873. The article "New Organ in the Moravian Church" is the source of all quotations regarding the planning and the structure of the organ.
43. *The Moravian*, 8 January 1874.
44. "Diary of the Bethlehem Congregation," 24 December 1873.
45. Ibid., 15 January 1874.
46. From a program of the recital reprinted in *The Moravian Music Foundation Bulletin* 26, no. 3 (1981): 70.
47. Peter Wolle, "Diary," 14 January 1867.
48. *The Moravian*, 11 July 1872.
49. Ibid., 29 September 1872.
50. Ibid., 12 August 1885.
51. "Diary of the Bethlehem Congregation," 5 August 1885.
52. Theodore F. Wolle, *Asleep in Jesus* (Bethlehem, Pa.: Comenius Press, 1897).
53. Ibid.
54. Samuel W. Duffield, *English Hymns: Their Authors and History,* (New York: Funk & Wagnalls Company, 1886), 47.
55. This is the text of the hymn as it appears in the published edition of Theodore Wolle's *Asleep in Jesus.*
56. A motet is a polyphonic sacred vocal composition.
57. John R. Parker, *A Musician's Biography: Or Sketches of the Lives and Writing of Eminent Musical Characters* (Boston: Stone and Fovel, 1824), 42–44.
58. Ibid., 42–44.

59. "Diary of the Bethlehem Congregation," July 1881.
60. *The Moravian*, 1 April 1885.
61. "Dairy of the Bethlehem Congregation," 11 January 1885.
62. Ibid., 30 March 1885.
63. Ibid.
64. Ibid.
65. *Bethlehem Globe,* 18 May 1901.

*Part Three*

John Frederick Wolle: Bach for Americans

J. Fred. Wolle, 1863-1933
(Special Collections, Lehigh University)

Chapter Seven

## *Mastering the "Divine Art"*

Dr. Wolle is the full accomplishment of a century or more of materials and people who went before him.¹

There seems to be nothing too stupendous for our neighbor Bethlehem to undertake and that entertainments of this kind are so well attended may be attached to the fact that the "Divine Art" has always been held in such high esteem in Bethlehem from the earliest times.²

FRED STOOD STIFFLY near the window staring at the belfry of the Moravian Church waiting for the trombone choir to appear. He went to the window to watch for the trombones after his mother had called the family together and told them, "Your Grandfather Weiss has gone to Jesus." Fred knew the trombones had to play the announcement to the town, and he wanted them to tell him of his grandfather's death, not his mother. His grandfather had often told him, "The trombones announce to everybody that the soul has left the body."³

Fred followed every movement of the Brothers in his mind as he stared at the belfry door and waited for them to appear.⁴ First they unpacked their trombones stored under the benches in the organ gallery. Then, they climbed the stairs to the church attic and walking under the huge old beams that supported the church roof, they ascended the stairs to the belfry door. Fred knew the path so well because he had helped his Grandfather Weiss unpack his bass trombone many times, had climbed to the attic with him, and had walked with all the Brothers to the belfry stairs. Freddy was not allowed in the tower, so he waited at the foot of the stairs and watched his grandfather take the varnished card of beautifully written notes from the storage rack and fix it to his trombone. Grandfather Weiss then climbed the stairs and disappeared through the door. The beautiful chorales flooded Freddy's special place below the belfry stairs, and he was engulfed by the music.

Fred tried to remember when he first met his grandparents, but he couldn't. But Bishop Peter Wolle noted Freddy's introduction to the family in his diary, "to vesper we had father and mother Weiss & Francis [Fred's father] & wife (with the little fat John Frederick.)"[5] The trombones intertwined Fred and his Grandfather. Then in school Grandfather Weiss taught Fred to sing along with the other children.

The door opened. The first Brother stepped out. His trombone was covered with a black mourning cloth. Seven other Brothers followed. Their trombones were draped in the same way. The players stood in a circle. Each one with his trombone raised and pointing outward.

When he saw the Brothers take their first breath, Fred's heart was gripped. The music now proved that his grandfather had "gone home." By the end of the first chorale, Fred was sobbing. He loved his Grandfather Weiss. *Princeps* [sic] *facile* of musician, everybody had called him.[6]

The second chorale began, and all knew the deceased was a Widowed Brother. Brother Weiss' death had come as a surprise to the community, for he had not been ill. Yet, Fred had heard people say to his parents, "Brother Weiss never recovered from when Christ took Sister Mary last year." Only a month ago, Fred listened to his Grandfather sing in the church choir during a Children's Festival celebrating Fred and the other children. At home after the service, his father told the family, "It was remarked and conceded that Jedidiah Weiss was still the most effective basso belonging to the choir."

The trombones repeated the first chorale "to remind us all we will die." Grandfather Weiss had told Fred, "Think about your own death as you listen to us play." Fred, ten years old, thought about dying. His heart relaxed, for like everyone else in Bethlehem, he knew that his grandfather and grandmother were happy in Jesus. He left the window as the last Brother left the belfry. As he moved across the room, he stopped crying.

Jedediah Weiss, J. Fred. Wolle's grandfather, 1878
(The Moravian Archives, Bethlehem)

The Service for the Dead was held in the Moravian Church on Friday, the 5th of September, 1873. Fred sat with his brothers and sisters, father and mother, and his other relatives. The funeral began with the choir singing *a cappella*; just pure angel-like voices floating above the congregation from the organ gallery at the back of the church. Fred listened. After a long silence, his cousin Theodore accompanied the first hymn, and the large congregation sang their parts perfectly. Bishop de Schweinitz, the father of Fred's closest friend, Paul, read "a brief memoir."

Never before had Fred heard all of the reasons his grandfather was called *Princeps facile* of musicians, or how great the Weiss family had been from the beginning of Bethlehem.

All the Weisses were musical, and Jedidiah's father had been one of the first organists in the Bethlehem chapel. "All the sons inherited the divine gift," said the Bishop, but Fred's grandfather was the most gifted. When Brother Jedidiah Weiss came to Bethlehem, he was indentured to the local clock maker and silversmith, a man who was also very musical. Jedidiah excelled and was soon building clocks, making silver pieces, and finally running the business. With the help of the master craftsman, he had helped to place the clock in the church belfry, where it tells time to this day.

But, it was not as a clock maker or silversmith that Brother Weiss was revered. He played a number of wind instruments, including the trombone, "for upwards of fifty years."[7] When Haydn's oratorio *Creation* was performed for the first time in Philadelphia – the same work had been sung many times in Bethlehem – everyone said Jedidiah was the only person who could play the bass trombone required for the orchestra. So, he traveled to Philadelphia to play the part, and the performance became a legend in Bethlehem. He was even more famous as a singer. His vocal range was unusually large, and he was considered the greatest singer in a community where everyone learned to sing. Fred had heard him singing solos many times in church and at the concerts of the Philharmonic Society. His grandfather's reputation went beyond Bethlehem into the "towns and rural districts of the neighborhood – in a number of which his services were repeatedly engaged to educate vocalists for the sanctuary."[8] Fred heard the Bishop add, "as the clock on the cupola, significantly, we thought, struck Two in the still hours of the early morning of the 3rd of September, the spirit of the good old man, without a struggle left its tenement of clay and went to God who gave it."[9]

Now the orchestra in the gallery joined the chorus. Fred thought of what a great musician his Grandfather had been and wondered, did he also have the "divine gift"?

After the ceremony, Fred took his place with the family in the funeral cortege. The double trombone choir with instruments still draped in mourning was first. The Philharmonic Society was followed by the *Liederkranz* and the clergy. The "remains of the deceased in the rosewood casket – surrounded by a cross of white gladioli" were next. The relatives and friends followed the casket, leading some two hundred "young ladies of the Moravian Seminary, and a large concourse of residents of the Bethlehems, and the towns of the valley."[10]

The trombones led the cortege, playing chorales so familiar to those present they could not help singing them. They did not turn into "God's Acre," the old Moravian cemetery, but moved on to Nisky Hill, the "new" cemetery, for Bethlehem was no longer a closed Moravian community.

At the graveside, the shrouded trombones played the final chorales; members of the Philharmonic Society and the *Liederkranz* sang a requiem. The editor of *The Moravian* reported, "Thus on a lovely autumn day, amid the perfect glories of the earth, of air and sky – with Choral harmony . . . the old musician was gathered to his fathers."[11]

After his grandfather's funeral, Fred was improvising again on the melodeon in the cellar of the seminary, practicing the piano, singing at school and church, and listening attentively to the concert and sacred vocal and instrumental music he heard all around him.[12] Like his musical relatives, Fred lived in a community where he could be rapidly and thoroughly inducted into the Western musical tradition. Fred always remembered that the town and the church were his first music teachers. When he was much older, a reporter asked J. Fred what inspired him to devote his efforts to the works of Bach, he answered as if the combination were inevitable, "I was born and raised in Bethlehem and brought up as a member of the Moravian Church."[13]

• • •

John Frederick Wolle was born in one of the musical centers of Bethlehem, the Seminary for Young Ladies. His, father, the Rev. Francis Wolle, was the principal of the Seminary, and Fred was born in one of the Seminary buildings. Approximately two hundred and thirty girls and young women attended the school, and Fred heard them practice their music lessons and listened to them rehearse for concerts. He went to those concerts and heard the young ladies sing solos and choral music, play instruments, and recite poetry. In reality, Fred lived in a music school.

Fred's sister, Helen, was mentioned in a review of a faculty concert that appeared in *The Moravian*. "A quartette at the beginning and another at the close the latter being piano, Miss H. Wolle, Bethlehem, organ, Miss Jordan, Philadelphia, violin, Prof. Graber, violoncello, Mr. E. F. Bleck) were brilliantly performed."[14]

When Fred's father had an organ installed in the Chapel of the Seminary, Fred taught himself to play it by figuring out what his fingers and feet needed to do to make the hymn tunes he had memorized sound right. Soon, he was substituting for Helen at the chapel services. Later, he took over Helen's position. He played the morning chapel service before he rushed off to classes at the Moravian Parochial School nearby.

Central Moravian Church, directly across the street from Fred's home, was still the center for sacred music in the community. Fred became a part of a large congregation singing chorales, some of which he would later recognize in the works of J. S. Bach. Fred heard anthems nearly every Sunday performed by a choir with orchestra in which his relatives sang and played instruments.[15] They regularly performed sacred music by Haydn, Mozart, Beethoven, Mendelssohn, and Spohr. In addition, Theodore, his cousin, was the organist and choirmaster who played the recently installed organ he had designed. When Fred played church with his friend Paul, the Bishop's son, Fred

Francis Wolle, J. Fred.'s father
(The Moravian Archives, Bethlehem)

improvised on the melodeon or the organ and imagined he was his Cousin Theodore playing hymns and voluntaries in the large church.

Fine singing was stressed in the Moravian Sunday School and a singing master was specially appointed for the various age groups. The children, including Fred, sang at Sunday service in the large church on special occasions, or gave public concerts. A newspaper reporter described such an event and mentioned Fred's sister, who was the organist for the Sunday School.

> The Sunday-school of the Congregation of Bethlehem invited the parents and friends of the children to a very pleasing "Concert Entertainment," on Easter Sunday afternoon . . . the singing by the classes . . . was very spirited and correct. . . . To Bro Jos. Rice, the chorister of the School, and Miss Ellen [Helen] Wolle, the organist, the success is mainly due.[16]

These events were the first concerts Fred participated in.

Vocal instruction was also taken seriously at the newly formed Moravian Parochial School which Fred attended. Grandfather Weiss had been the singing teacher there. Fred made his first public appearance in the school as a singer when he was thirteen. "Freddie Wolle Sings a Solo in an Olde Folkes concert," read the report in the local newspaper. "Freddie sang the solo in an arrangement of "Massa Is In the Cold, Cold Ground," and joined in a "singing" dialogue with Fannie Eggert. Their performance "brought the house down," and they received an encore. In a music sketch "Waste not, want not," Freddie sang the solos.[17] When he graduated from the school at the age of sixteen, he sang well, played the organ, read music, played the trombone in the Moravian Trombone Choir and the viola in the Central Church orchestra.

Fred's musical education outside the church and the church school was also rich. He attended concerts of the Philharmonic Society and became acquainted with much of the finest sacred and symphonic music of the nineteenth century. Again, Fred saw his relatives involved in

J. Fred. Wolle (2nd from right) with his mother, sisters, and brother
(The Moravian Archives, Bethlehem)

ambitious and excellent musical performances. Many were members of the Philharmonic Society. Theodore was the first violinist, Timothy and Jedidiah Weiss sang arias in performances of oratorios and Masses, and Jedidiah played the bassoon and trombone.

Touring artists and chamber ensembles frequently gave recitals and concerts in Bethlehem, and young Fred attended the programs with his family. A typical program performed by the Mendelssohn Quintette Club from Boston included compositions by Thomas, Schubert, Ole

Bull, Mendelssohn, Paganini, Arthur Sullivan, Adam, and other nineteenth-century musicians. Groups came from New York and Philadelphia as well, playing concerts that were taken very seriously by Bethlehem music lovers.

Bethlehem not only enveloped Fred with quality performances, the town provided him with excellent formal instruction. Though Fred began teaching himself at an early age, his improvisations were buttressed by lessons with local teachers from the Seminary. His first three teachers were Helen, his sister, Caroline Brown, head music teacher at the Seminary, and Theodore Wolle.

Fred was seven years old when he began studying piano with Helen. She was ten years older than her brother and had just joined the Seminary faculty as a teacher of painting and music. Hilda Doolittle, H. D., the famous American author and imagist poet, wrote of Fred's lessons with Helen, her mother. She "gave all her music to Uncle Fred., that is what she did. . . . It was Mama who started being the musician, and then she said she taught Uncle Fred."[18] Helen told people she had given Fred "the gift," and when Hilda was older, the problem of the "gift" loomed large.

> But where did he get the gift, just like that? Why didn't Mama wait and teach us music like she did Uncle Fred when he was a little boy? Mama gave all her music to Uncle Fred. . . . That is why we hadn't the gift, because she taught Uncle Fred; she gave it way, she gave the gift to Uncle Fred, she should have waited and given the gift to us.[19]

While Helen told everyone she gave her brother the gift, J. Fred. spoke of Sister Caroline Brown as "his music teacher."[20] Sister Brown taught singing, the piano, and conducted choirs at the Seminary for more than fifty years. Lessons with her began in 1873, when she was sixty-eight years old. She was one of the many gifted Moravian women who remained single; living as a member of the Choir of the Single Sisters in a stone building on Church Street near the Seminary.

In addition to lessons on the piano, Sister Brown provided Fred with the image around which his "gift" began to take shape – the life of the composer, organist, and choir director, Johann Sebastian Bach. Fred never forgot his discovery of Bach, and many years later described the moment precisely.

> One day . . . my music teacher . . . loaned me the parts of Grove's Musical Dictionary . . . I began to read through the A's and then the B's and then the name of Bach held my attention. I read that Bach had composed the Passion music. Not only were the Biblical stories the same as I had heard in my own church every Holy Week, but chorales, I found, were introduced throughout the Passion music which were the same I had been hearing in the Moravian Church.[21]

Yet, Bach's music was missing from Fred's life. As he sorted through the many manuscripts stored in the church attic, Fred found no compositions by Bach. Much later he told a reporter, "Strange to say, I have not been able to find that the organists and orchestras of my early days here played Bach's music. I found only lots of music of Mozart, Haydn, and others, but not Bach."[22]

Moravians were not familiar with Bach for the same reason that he was largely unknown to most Americans. His music was rarely heard in America. Fred had to wait until he was twenty years old before he had the opportunity to study Bach's music from an organist who was one of the first to play it in the United States.

Not only was J. Fred. born and raised in a community where his musical talent could flourish and be cultivated, his parents were highly gifted people, even though they were not musical.

Fred's father, Francis Wolle, was born in 1817 into what the Wolle's still call the "business side of the family." His interest in science surfaced very early in his education. "Francis was educated at Nazareth Hall, where he completed his first scientific study. He kept a notebook containing information about butterflies and spiders with many illustrations."[23] Not surprisingly J. Fred. also was fascinated by spiders, and they remained one of his lifelong interests. Upon graduation Francis was apprenticed to his father who managed the Moravian general store in Bethlehem. However, Francis became a teacher instead of a store manager, first in Nazareth Hall and next at the Moravian Parochial School in Bethlehem. There he married a young widow, Elizabeth Seidel, who was teaching at the Women's Seminary. Elizabeth was the daughter of Jedidiah Weiss.

It seemed that Francis would continue to be a teacher, but in the year 1851 he had a stroke of genius rooted in his memory of his apprenticeship and the drudgery of cutting and pasting paper bags every evening. He made a model of a machine that would make paper bags which he patented in 1852.[24] He resigned his teaching position and formed the Union Paper Bag Machine Company with four of his relatives. Other patents followed in 1855, 1856, and 1857. The machines were licensed, and by 1860 they were producing "nearly all of the country's paper bags."[25] Basking in his prosperity, Francis took a six-month tour of Europe, unfortunately leaving the business in the hands of his family associates. When he returned, he had been squeezed out of the business. Years of litigation followed, but Francis never profited from his invention which "revolutionized retailing and merchandising methods. Eventually, it changed the shopping habits of a nation."[26] At his death *The Moravian* called Francis "an inventive genius."[27]

Francis was without a fixed income, and his older brother, the Rev. Sylvester Wolle, Principal of the Young Ladies' Seminary, arranged for Francis to be his assistant. He found himself again in education but as an administrator. When Sylvester retired, Francis became the principal. "He carried the school through the trying years of the war, the unsettled period of inflation and the dark days of the panic and financial depression in the seventies."[28]

It was during this time that Reverend Francis – he had been ordained by his uncle, Bishop Peter Wolle – published a series of articles and books based on his observations of algae. The series of articles was important enough to make national news in *Harper's Weekly*. *The Moravian* quoted from that influential magazine.

> We clip the following item of interest from Harper's Weekly of June 16th [1877]. "Rev. Francis Wolle, of Bethlehem, Pa., has published in the Bulletin of the Torry Botanical Club, the description of one hundred species of fresh water algae found in the United States, additional to those given by Dr. H. C. Wook, Jr. of Phil., in a memoir published some years ago by the Smithsonian Institution, a few of them are new, but for the most part they have been previously described by European authors, a number of them, By Dr. Alexander Braun, whose death was recently noticed.[29]

When Francis published this study, J. Fred. was ten years old. As he approached the age of twenty-one, his father published his first book *Desmoids of the United States*. Another soon followed. Francis's grandson summarized the importance of his grandfather's achievement.

> Wolle became such an important pioneer in the field of microscopic botany that for fifty to seventy-five years after his death the most important infusorial scientists of the United States came to visit his grandson, Philip, at his farm in Maryland, in order that they might consult his grandfather's library, the notebooks in which he recorded his original observations, and his correspondence with scientists of similar interest in all parts of the United States and Europe.[30]

In spite of the difficulties he encountered in his innovative research, Francis conveyed his sense of scientific wonder to his family. Hilda Doolittle, his niece, described how he lovingly introduced her to this world in a way that was nearly mystical.

> When Papalie [Francis] lifted us, one in turn, to kneel on the chair by his worktable, we saw that it was true what he said, we saw that where there is nothing, there is something. We saw that an empty drop of water spread out branches, bright green or vermillion, in shapes like a branch of a Christmas tree or in shapes like a squashed

peony or in the shape like a lot of little green-glass beads, strung on a thick stem.[31]

In praising his father, J. Fred. related similar experiences: "We, his children, gathered about the table while he conjured up, as with a magic wand, exquisite forms from the medium most unpromising, can but thank heaven again and again for the influence of such a father."[32] "Leaving a very rich legacy and having changed all of our lives, Francis Wolle died 10 February 1893 after many months of failing health."[33]

Elizabeth, J. Fred.'s mother, was also unique and impressive. In addition to being a woman of "graceful Christian culture," Elizabeth Wolle incorporated a strong musical spirituality into her Moravian pietism.[34] She was born in Bethlehem 27 May 1824 and graduated from the Ladies' Seminary with the desire to join the Single Sisters' Choir. Hen-ry Seidel dissuaded her, and she married him in 1842 when she was eighteen years old. Seidel was the pastor in a small Moravian community in New Jersey, Hopedale. It was during her marriage to Christian, as Elizabeth called him, that she had a religious mystical experience that was so profound she never forgot it. When she was elderly, a small woman who still wore the same cap as the founders of Bethlehem, Elizabeth told the story to the child Hilda Doolittle.

Christian and Elizabeth had found a manuscript recording a meeting that took place soon after the founding of Bethlehem. Henry Seidel translated the text that was written in Hebrew and Greek, and Elizabeth "just picked out notes (that she carefully looked up in the old folios) that John Christopher Pyrlaeus had indicated to her, down the side of the page."[35] As she and her husband pieced the details together, they discovered that the purpose of the meeting was to unite the Christian "Holy Spirit" and the Indian "Great Spirit." Elizabeth then described the experience she had as she studied the manuscript.

> She herself became one with the . . . initiates and herself spoke the tongue – hymns of the spirits in the air – of the spirit of sunrise and

sun setting, of the deer and the wild squirrel, beaver, the otter, the kingfisher, and the hawk and eagle.[36]

Siedel died suddenly and Elizabeth returned to Bethlehem with her daughter Agnes and began teaching at the Ladies' Seminary. Grandmother Wolle told Hilda the secret that Christian left with her: a secret Elizabeth feared would be lost. "Mamalies said, 'Christian explained the secret to me. . . . It was simply a belief in what was said – and, lo I am with you always, even unto the end of the world.'"[37]

In Bethlehem Elizabeth met Francis, who apparently proposed to her almost immediately, but she refused him. ". . . he did not want to offend dear Sister Elizabeth Caroline, who had so recently lost her husband. He would wait. But he feared that she had been carried away by some feverish phantasy."[38] When Elizabeth spoke of her experience with Christian, Francis told her, "he could not doubt her word nor question the reality of the experience [but] there had been strange forces at work, in this great land from the beginning, and the Indian ritual in the early days was not understood."[39] However, he took her by the hand "and said that he will not speak again of these things that have troubled her unless she herself particularly wants it, and that he will tell no one of it."[40]

When she was twenty-four years old Elizabeth married Francis and stopped teaching. She became a mother and housewife while Francis embarked on his paper bag factory and the business that he shared with his relatives. After the failure of his part of the business deal, Elizabeth became a perpetual hostess and manager of the staff and kitchen of the Seminary. People found her gracious. Charlotte Beck, a teacher at the Seminary when Elizabeth was the hostess of the school, wrote in her diary, "I encountered Mrs. Wolle, who I lighted into the kitchen, for which service she rewarded me with some cake. Mrs. W. is really kind to us, I wish I had more time to visit her."[41] Charlotte attended a tea with other teachers given by Mrs. Wolle when, "I think we all enjoyed ourselves very much, I know I did. It was not stiff at all."[42] Much of J. Fred.'s later success was due to his ability to mingle graciously with people of wealth and power. He probably learned that from his mother, for he had been raised in a home where Victorian social skills were practiced daily with a gracious informality.

While Francis witnessed only the beginning of his son's rise to fame, his mother lived during the time of the great organ recitals in Chicago and St. Louis, the early performances of the Bach Choir, and her son's appointment as professor at Berkeley. She not only watched the music tradition of her family and her husband's family being carried on, she saw it surpassed by the activity of her youngest son.

J. Fred.'s nephew, Francis, in his autobiography described the closeness J. Fred. felt for his mother:

> Fred. the other son who stayed in Bethlehem, lived only five houses away from his mother and was always solicitous of her, dropping in to see her for a few minutes every day on his way to or from organ practice. His wife Jennie and daughter Gretchen when they had errands to do, also stopped by and offered to shop for her, and at least once a week they had her with them for dinner.[43]

In her "Obituary," the editor of *The Moravian* wrote "she became very widely known and endeared to the hearts of many hundreds of pupils from all parts of the United States and foreign countries."[44]

From his father J. Fred. experienced greatness based on the persistence and exactness of science. In his mother, J. Fred. saw a well-educated, charming, very devoted spiritual person with Moravian mystical beliefs. He was well prepared for the world he was about to enter: the world of eminent musicians, conductors, teachers, industrialists, and wealthy patrons.

Like other Moravian boys, J. Fred. had either to continue his schooling or become an apprentice. There must have been discussions about becoming a musician, but Fred was not given that choice. His father said that Fred could enter Lehigh University or be an apprentice in the local pharmacy. Fred chose the pharmacy to work with Mr. Rau, also one of Bethlehem's best singers. Rau agreed to take Fred as an apprentice. A news reporter sedately wrote much later about J. Fred.'s apprenticeship, emphasizing Fred's early single-minded and intense concentration on musical things.

> When Fred had the choice of college or apprenticeship . . . he chose the latter because it would give him more time to devote to music. In fact, he became so absorbed in transcribing manuscripts that customers came and went, without disturbing his oblivion.[45]

Following his failed apprenticeship, J. Fred. joined the faculty of the Moravian Parochial School, teaching mathematics and geometry. But, very soon he was provided with two musical opportunities. The first was a full-fledged musical theater production, and the second was an organ position in a newly built Episcopal Church. Both opportunities articulated lifelong positions for Fred., and they led to his becoming a self-supporting musician, which he was determined to be.

In the year 1882 when he was twenty years old, J. Fred. directed and conducted *The Flower Queen*, a cantata by George F. Root. It was not a simple literal performance of the cantata, however, for J. Fred. shaped every element of the production. He provided "alterations, additions and improvements . . . [and] of course there will be full orchestral accompaniment composed and arranged by Prof. J. Fred. Wolle [the title because of his position at the parochial school] leader and director of the whole affair."[46] The production was the first exercise of his organizational ability, which was extraordinary throughout his life. He had not only created a chorus of "a large number of Bethlehem's fair young ladies," but brought together some of the best voices in town to be soloists. One was the principal singer in the Moravian Church Choir. Another, "whose voice had never been heard in public without winning hearty applause," was Miss Flora Richsecker, who often sang with the Bethlehem Philharmonic Society. The newspaper report continued, "And these are by no means the only soloists, but the principal ones." A long review of the performance closed with a request.

On the whole the cantata was a grand success, and the performance of the girls reflected great credit on themselves and on their instructors. Bethlehem has always had the name of being a musical town, but lately it had depended upon a reputation won long ago. The event of Saturday night had made a break, now let the ball be kept rolling. Let the next thing be the production of some grand chorus from the masters.[47]

Buoyed by the success of "The Fairy Queen," J. Fred. organized a new chorus for the performance of major choral works. *The Moravian* found the organization news worthy, and reported

Friends of music will be glad to hear of the organization of the Choral Union, which will be conducted by Prof. Fred. Wolle, the rehearsal to be held in the Hall of the Parochial School. Considerable enthusiasm was manifest at the first meeting. . . . We hope the new Society will be a worthy successor of the old Philharmonic.[48]

Within a few months The Choral Union performed sections from Haydn's "Creation." Performances followed one another rapidly, and the editor of *The Moravian* expressed his pleasure. "Under the efficient management the Union had made rapid progress, and its concerts are highly appreciated by the lovers of music in Bethlehem."[49]

J. Fred.'s reputation spread beyond Bethlehem, and he assumed the leadership of the choral society of nearby Easton. Again, *The Moravian* reported "under the efficient leadership of J. Fred. Wolle. . . . This society has made rapid progress, one of the choruses will be sung by 150 voices."[50]

At twenty-one, J. Fred. was the conductor of two choral societies. He was given a desk and Bach's complete organ works in the "Peters Edition" as a token of esteem by the Bethlehem singers. The Bach gift must have pleased him very much. That gift also indicated that his interest in Bach was common knowledge. The singers in Easton responded with another gift, and

> During a recent meeting of the Choral Society in Easton, its Director J. Fred. Wolle, was presented with a handsome baton, made of ebony, heavily tipped with gold, ivory handle and an inscription place. Evidently Mr. Wolle's services are as highly appreciated in Easton as in Bethlehem.[51]

Within two years J. Fred. had become a notable musician in the area, and *The Moravian* summarized his achievements. "Mr. Wolle has done much to develop and regulate the musical taste and ability of Bethlehem. His greatest success so far has been the development and training of the Choral Society of Bethlehem and Easton."[52]

At the same time as J. Fred. was becoming established locally as a choral conductor, the other facet of his career began. When he was nineteen years old, J. Fred. took a position as organist at the newly built Episcopal Church. Not only was he independent, he was introduced to another musical tradition. In addition he came in contact with many individuals who would support the activities of the Bethlehem Bach Choir when it was organized in a number of years. The Episcopal position in Bethlehem may also have led to his next teacher, Dr. David Wood, who was the organist of St. Stephen's Episcopal Church in Philadelphia.

Wood was "Philadelphia's greatest organist in the mid-nineteenth century, excelling in the interpretation of the works of Bach, many of which he played for the first time in Philadelphia."[53] Wood owned the first complete set of Bach's organ works brought to Philadelphia.[54] On May 8, 1894, Wood gave the first all-Bach organ program in Philadelphia. During the thirty years he taught organ at the Philadelphia Musical Academy, he introduced a number of generations of fine organists to Bach's music.

Dr. Wood was asked to instruct J. Fred. and he agreed. J. Fred. could not have been more fortunate as Wood could teach him exactly what he most wanted to learn. He later described that experience with Wood to a reporter.

I began to study organ. My first lesson was on a little fugue of Bach's. For some reason or other this piece took hold of me, and I asked my teacher to give me Bach compositions entirely. . . . I seemed to feel that I was coming back to something that I had known or heard before.[55]

J. Fred. informed his students by engraved note that he would begin studying in Philadelphia.[56]

J. Fred. studied with Wood for only a short time, but the lessons had a profound effect on him. He never forgot the debt he owed Wood. Wood attended the premiere of Bach's B Minor Mass, in Bethlehem, conducted by J. Fred., who responded to a note from Wood about the performance,

> Your kind note touches me too deeply for expression. Coming from you who embody Bach's spirit, and have Beethoven's head, the letter is the greatest treasure I possess. . . . It was your masterful inspiration which led me to the study of Bach.[57]

Nearly thirty years after J. Fred. had taken his first organ lesson, he was moved to write to Wood's widow, "If I have accomplished anything, or if I ever do anything worth while, may it reflect all the glory back to my dear old friend and teacher."[58]

• • •

Hartley Wolle, J. Fred.'s oldest brother and an administrator in the newly formed Bethlehem Iron Works, offered to pay for a year's study abroad, and J. Fred. left for Munich in July 1884. He went, possibly at Wood's suggestion, to study organ and composition with Joseph Rheinberger. According to the renowned conductor Hans von Buelow, Rheinberger was "unrivalled in the whole of Germany and beyond. . . one of the worthiest musicians and human beings in the world."[59]

What attracted J. Fred. was the fact that Rheinberger was one of the greatest European organists and Bach interpreters of the nineteenth century. In addition he was a very successful and prolific composer. At the height of his career, Rheinberger was one of the most highly sought-after teachers. As a composer he shared the pinnacle of nineteenth-century music with Wagner, Liszt, Brahms, and von Buelow. He occupied one of the highest musical positions in the German-speaking nations as the director of the conservatory in Munich. He was also in charge of music in the royal chapel, which meant he had direct contact with the Bavarian and other European nobility. In addition Rheinberger's wife was an aristocrat who was also a poet of note.

Rheinberger accepted only four organ students each year. After a rigorous examination he selected J. Fred. to be one of them. Moving from Bethlehem to Munich and being accepted immediately by one of the foremost German musicians attests not only to J. Fred.'s musical superiority, even genius, but also the superiority of the Moravian organ tradition still vital enough in the late nineteenth century to provide the background J. Fred. needed to move immediately into the highest circles of musical excellence. The lessons with Wood had expanded J. Fred.'s organ technique and clearly solidified his devotion to Bach, making him ready for success in Munich.

When asked to summarize his organ lessons with Rheinberger for the press, Wolle said only, "I asked him . . . to give me only Bach compositions."[60] However, a friend of Wolle related, "there was a fundamental difference in temperament and viewpoint between a teacher who regarded the organ as strictly an ecclesiastical instrument to be played without emotion and a pupil whose whole thought was, and is, that the organ – and all music – would express human feeling."[61] In addition to the organ technique he learned from Rheinberger, which must had been immense, Wolle learned he did not want to play Bach the way Rheinberger did. Thus, he solidified his philosophy, one from which he never deviated. When he left Rheinberger, Wolle was no longer an organ student. He was an organ scholar capable of working independently to perfect his artistry. His rapid rise to fame as an

American virtuoso was the result of Wolle's successful synthesis of talent, excellent training, and a rare but convincing view of the organ as an instrument for the expression of human feelings.

At the time J. Fred. was in Munich two schools of taste and composition contended for supremacy in German music. One school was conservative: rooted in the works of Bach, Mozart, Beethoven, and Mendelssohn. The "New German School" was embodied in the works of Wagner, and Liszt, and others. The music of the New German School was unfamiliar to J. Fred. for, like the music of Bach, it was seldom performed in Bethlehem. The Philharmonic Society program contained no music by Liszt or Wagner.

Rheinberger belonged to the conservative school of German music and composition. However, 'It was typical of his generous nature that, although he himself disliked the work of Wagner and Liszt and was no partisan of the New German School, he never tried to influence the young artists in his care through his personal views."[62] J. Fred. benefitted greatly from his teacher's tolerance. He not only studied music by Bach and Rheinberger, he came to know the music of Wagner. How this happened is unknown. That it happened is obvious from the fact that he left Bethlehem not knowing Wagner's music and on his return began playing Wagner's works, transcribing them for organ, lecturing on them in Bethlehem, and eventually conducting them and using the vocal scores he owned frequently enough to nearly wear the bindings out.

To us, J. Fred. is associated only with the music of Bach; however his contemporaries had quite a different view. To them J. Fred. was also an interpreter of Wagner's music. When J. Fred. returned to Bethlehem he transcribed sections of Wagner's *Ring* cycle for the organ, played the transcriptions in his organ recitals, and was part of a series of lectures designed to introduce *The Ring* to Bethlehem. Later, when he lived in California, J. Fred. conducted symphony concerts devoted entirely to the music of Wagner. The memorial service for J. Fred. held in Central Moravian Church began with the organist playing J. Fred.'s arrangement of "Siegfried's Funeral March" from Wagner's *Ring* cycle.⁶³ To J. Fred.'s friends, music Wagner composed for the death of Siegfried, the Germanic hero, was considered the most fitting memorial for J. Fred. Music by J. S. Bach was not performed in the memorial service.

On June 5, 1885, as he was about to leave Munich, J. Fred. heard a performance of Bach's *The Passion According to St. John*. Though he did not care for the performance, he was stunned by the music. "The Bach music impressed me far more than the actual performance of it by the chorus. . . . It was given by opera performers in that city [Munich]," J. Fred. recounted.⁶⁴ Years after his description of this event, he quoted Keats as the best expression of the effect the passion music had on him.

*Then felt I like some watcher of the skies,*
*When a new planet swims into his ken.*⁶⁵

When he returned to Bethlehem, J. Fred. conducted the American premiere of Bach's *Passion According to St. John* in Bethlehem.

Though J. Fred. was Rheinberger's student for only a year, he remained in the memory of his renowned teacher. A Bethlehem choral conductor told the following anecdote. An American musician went to Munich to study the works of Bach with Rheinberger. "You could have saved yourself the trip. The person who knows the most about Bach lives in Bethlehem, Pennsylvania. His name is J. Fred. Wolle!"⁶⁶ Rheinberger told him.

Early that spring J. Fred. was notified that his cousin Theodore was dead. The position of organist and choirmaster in Central Moravian Church was vacant, and the elders offered it to J. Fred. if he would return. The pastor recorded, "He was written to & his services engaged immediately after the death of our latter organist. Prof. Theodore F. Wolle."⁶⁷ He accepted, though he fortunately remained in Munich until his year of study was up. Otherwise, he would not have heard the Bach performance, and everything would have been very different. J. Fred. left Bavaria knowing he had a secure position as a musician for which he was now eminently prepared. The church diarist recorded the event,

"Our new organist, Br. J. Fred. Wolle, today entered upon his duties. . . . He recently returned from Europe where he was under the instruction of the celebrated organ master Joseph Rheinberger."[68] He was the second member of the Wolle family to occupy that position. J. Fred. had gained a vision in Munich of what he wanted to do for the rest of his life – conduct Bach's music for Americans as well as play it. His formal education was completed. Now he would become the fullest musical flowering of the Wolle family.

## NOTES

1. Elmer L. Mack, *Why a Bach Choir in Bethlehem* (Bethlehem, Pennsylvania: printed privately, 1973), 5.
2. *The Bethlehem Times*, 13 January 1874.
3. John Frederick was known as Freddy when he was a baby, as Fred when he was a child, and, for the rest of his life as J. Fred. However, his name appears in various ways: J. Fred., J. Fred, and J Fred. He seemed to prefer J. Fred. That is how his name appears in the programs of the Bethlehem Bach Choir, as well as on his personal scores. For this reason this author uses J. Fred., although other versions of the name may appear in the various quotations throughout the text. I have also used "Freddy," "Fred," "J. Fred.", "Professor Wolle," and "Dr. Wolle" to indicate his approximate age in the narrative.
4. The opening section of this chapter is based on the actual arrangement of Central Moravian Church in Bethlehem, Pennsylvania. The area of the church described is still the same, and today's trombone choir follows the same route as in the nineteenth century.
5. Peter Wolle, "Diary," 4 November 1863.
6. See "Jedidiah Weiss and His Musical Family," *Moravian Music Journal* 28, no. 1 (Spring 1983): 8–12, for an extended article on the Weiss family.
7. *The Moravian*, 11 September 1873.
8. Ibid.
9. Ibid.
10. Ibid.
11. Ibid.

12. Francis Wolle, *A Moravian Heritage* (Boulder, Colorado: Empire Reproduction & Printing Company, 1972), 40. "J. Fred. found an old melodeon in the Seminary basement on which he played hymns and made improvisations as preludes to them."

13. "How Wolle Came To Take Up Bach," unidentified newspaper clipping in The Archives of The Bach Choir of Bethlehem.

14. *The Moravian*, 6 July 1871.

15. Rufus Grider, *Historical Notes on Music in Bethlehem, Pa.* (Winston-Salem: The Moravian Music Foundation, Inc., 1957) lists the Wolle musicians: August Wolle, Silvester Wolle, Julius H. Weiss, Frank L. Wolle, Edward Wolle, Augusta E. Wolle, Elizabeth Wolle, Amelica N. Weiss, Ellen Wolle, Emily Wolle, and Mary Wolle.

16. *The Moravian*, 21 April 1870.

17. Elizabeth Myers, news clipping n. d. and no source in a file "J. Fred" in the Archives of The Bach Choir of Bethlehem.

18. H. D., *The Gift* (New York, N.Y.: A New Direction Book, 1982), 12.

19. Ibid., 11–12.

20. "How Wolle Came To Take Up Bach," n.d.

21. Ibid.

22. Ibid.

23. Francis Wolle, *Moravian Heritage*, 21.

24. Ibid.

25. Ibid.

26. Ibid.

27. *The Moravian*, 15 February 1893.

28. Ibid.

29. Ibid., 28 June 1877.

30. Frances Wolle, op. cit., 26.

31. H. D., op. cit., 11.

32. Francis Wolle, op. cit., 27.

33. "Dairy of the Bethlehem Congregation," 10 February 1893.

34. *The Moravian*, 4 April 1906.

35. H. D., *The Gift*, 87.

36. Ibid., 87.

37. Ibid., 85.

38. Ibid., 97.

39. Ibid.

40. Ibid., 59–97.

41. "Diary of Charlotte Beck, 1861–1886," 3. A copy in possession of the author.
42. Ibid., 17.
43. Francis Wolle, op. cit., 39.
44. *The Moravian*, 4 April 1906.
45. *The Allentown Morning Call*, 29 May 1937.
46. *The Bethlehem Globe-Times*, 28 August 1882 and 31 August 1882 are the sources for these accounts.
47. *The Daily Bethlehem Times,* 4 September 1882.
48. *The Moravian*, 4 October 1882.
49. Ibid., 12 December 1882.
50. Ibid., 28 November 1883.
51. Ibid., 2 January 1884.
52. Ibid., 25 June 1884.
53. Robert Cerson, *Music In Philadelphia* (Westport, Conn.: Greenwood Press, 1970), 106.
54. *Dictionary of American Biography*, vol. 4 (New York: C. Scribner's Sons, 1928–58): 455.
55. "How Wolle Came to Take Up Bach," unidentified.
56. Program Book no. 6: 107, the Archives of The Bach Choir of Bethlehem.
57. Ibid.
58. Ibid.
59. Stanley Saide, ed., *The New Grove's Dictionary of Music and Musicians,* Vol. 15 (London: Macmillian Publishers Limited, 1980): 791–92.
60. "How Wolle Came to Take Up Bach," unidentified.
61. Ibid.
62. Stanley Saide, ed. *The New Grove's Dictionary of Music and Musicians,* Vol. 8, ( London: Macmillian Publishers Limited, 1980), 791.
63. *The Moravian,* 18 January 1933.
64. "How Wolle Came to Take Up Bach," unidentified.
65. Raymond Walters, "Bach at Bethlehem, Pennsylvania," *The Musical Quarterly* 21, no. 2 (April 1934): 184.
66. Related to the author by Professor Richard Schantz, Bethlehem, Pa.
67. "Diary of the Bethlehem Congregation," 2 October 1885.
68. Ibid.

Chapter Eight

## *Creating The Bach Choir*

... it will be remembered to the honor of Bethlehem that Bach's Mass in B Minor here received its first complete and successful American production.[1]

J. FRED. SAT ON THE ORGAN BENCH in the choir gallery overlooking the people assembled in Central Moravian Church. He caught the eyes of singers seated on both sides of him, the women in white and the men in black. The singers were mostly young people. Two of them, Agnes and J. Samuel, were his relatives. Everyone knew each other well, for Bethlehem was still a small town, and together they had rehearsed Johann Sebastian Bach's Mass in B Minor with J. Fred. for more than a year. This group had become "The Bach Choir."[2] It was about to give its first public performance.

An orchestra of area instrumentalists spread out from the organ console down to the rail of the choir gallery. Like the singers, the players were all acquainted and knew J. Fred. well, for he had conducted most of them already either in the church orchestra or in the Bethlehem Choral Union.

The Trombone Choir waited in the church belfry for the tower clock to strike the hour of four. In the sanctuary "every available seat was occupied," the pastor reported in the church diary.[3] The silence was charged with reverence and excitement. The clock chimed. After the fourth tone, the Trombone Choir played the first chorale. The sacred service had begun.

Everyone in Bethlehem heard the chorale, sounding from high in the belfry, announce this important community event. Those inside the church were uplifted as J. Fred. had been when he was a young boy standing below the belfry listening to his Grandfather Weiss play with his other Brothers. Then there were four trombonists, now eleven Brothers played. Their sound was even more stirring and, for many Moravians, it was still the voice of God.

The first chorale, "Our Father in His Heavenly Kingdom," ended. After a pause the congregation heard the second chorale floating into the sanctuary through the large medallion in the center of the ceiling. No one stirred. When the second chorale ceased, there was a very long silence as the Trombone Choir descended from the belfry and reassembled behind the choir. The eleven Brothers in place, J. Fred. and every other musician breathed deeply preparing to respond to the final sacred announcement played by the trombones. The third chorale, Martin Luther's "A Mighty Fortress is Our God," sounded.

As the trombones reached the final chord, the chorus and the orchestra burst forth with the opening chord of Bach's Mass. The trombones had proclaimed God as a mighty fortress, and the singers cried out "Kyrie eleison!," "God have mercy on us!"[4] The Mass had begun. "The effect was grand," the pastor recorded.[5] For many, God, through the trombones, had spoken the Mass into being. For others, the joining of the Moravian Church and the music of Bach and the Bach Choir had been seamless. "It was brilliantly done," wrote a music critic in attendance.

The date was 27 March 1900. The American premiere of Bach's masterpiece was taking place.

During the performance of the Mass, J. Fred. was totally involved in conducting and playing the organ. However, earlier he must have thought about the events that preceded the premiere. The route had not been easy. The territory was uncharted, and J. Fred. lost his way a number of times. Retracing the journey, there is no striking sense of inevitability to it; no sense that The Bach Choir had to come into being. In fact, at first, J. Fred. did not even take credit for founding the choir, though he accepted that attribution later.

If J. Fred. returned from Munich with a vision to develop a choir to sing Bach, no record remains. However, there are many accounts that finding ways to rehearse and to conduct the B Minor Mass occupied J. Fred.'s thoughts for a long time, and without him the American premiere would not have been in Bethlehem. Much had to take place before performing the Mass could have even occurred to J. Fred.; he found the Bethlehem Choral Union in disarray. Though Theodore had taken over the group, he became ill soon after J. Fred.'s departure. When Theodore resigned, Professor Graber, the conductor of the Philharmonic Society, took his place and the concerts reverted to the programming that had existed before the Bethlehem Choral Union. They began with a section of light music followed by an extended sacred choral work. The concerts were both entertaining and edifying. Under J. Fred. the Bethlehem Choral Union sang a single work such as Haydn's *Creation* and Spohr's *The Last Judgement*. A concert was a unified musical event designed to uplift and cultivate those who attended. That was the view of the Moravians and the view of the Romantics. Both shared the belief that beauty edified the performers and the audience. Rapt attention was expected from everyone. The reward was a spiritual experience.

In September the Bethlehem Choral Union was formally reorganized. Its purpose was "the promotion of musical culture, and the social enjoyment of its members."[6] That the "promotion of musical culture" addressed a community need was echoed in a newspaper article describing the Choral Union's first concert. "That this society exerts a beneficial influence upon the music of the community, generally, but upon the music of the churches specifically cannot be questioned."[7]

J. Fred. launched into evening rehearsals that required discipline, hard work, and commitment from the members. He made clear that rehearsing and performing music was not mere entertainment. The rewards of art were not gained easily or casually. Like manufacturing, artistic activity required energy that was highly focused, controlled, and carefully sequenced. Special groups of devoted people were required for the constant attention music needed. Throughout the nineteenth century, new institutions such as the Bethlehem Choral Union were founded to "produce" concerts, as, similarly, new industries were built to produce and transport products. As the giant mills that dominated Bethlehem forged works of iron, the Bethlehem Choral Union forged works of art. These musical forces were set in motion by a conductor who constantly controlled and supervised them. J. Fred. was a musical foreman like his brothers were foremen in the iron works.

Performing music had become serious work. Edification was not free of effort. Unlike the eighteenth century when music was for pleasure and amusement, in the nineteenth century "devotees," ordinary citizens with devotion beyond the ordinary, joined together to produce music. This view was clearly expressed when *The Daily Bethlehem Times* reported, "The Choral Union has been rehearsing regularly since last September, and fruitful and hard work has been accomplished by the devotees of the art."[8] Membership in the Bethlehem Choral Union demanded not only intense work but required a high level of commitment to the group. The Union's "Constitution and Bylaws" spelled out clearly that the Union must come before every other social obligation.

> Active members shall hold the stated meetings and rehearsals of this Society of paramount obligation to all other social engagements, and shall be in their places promptly at 7:30 on evenings to practice.[9]

Everyone responded enthusiastically to J. Fred.'s leadership and management of the Choral Union. "Never has the attendance at rehearsals been more regular or more punctual; never has the Day School Hall resounded with such spirited singing as at present," *The Daily Bethlehem Times* reported to its readers.[10]

The first concert was on 9 February 1886, five months after J. Fred. became the new conductor. It was not a complete departure from previous programs, yet there was the seed of the new programming. The Choral Union sang a sacred piece by Mendelssohn and the secular cantata, *The Rose Maiden*. There were no entertaining pieces. Though the concert included a local violin soloist who "won the admiration of the audience," her solos were in the intermissions. The two serious works focused the audience on the chorus and on its conductor.[11] J. Fred.'s name began to pervade the newspaper accounts of the Union's concerts. The group "reflected the music aptitude of J. Fred. Wolle, the accomplished and talented director. . . . Before leaving the halls, Mr. Wolle received the hearty congratulations of his friends and the patrons of music on the excellent performance."[12] The success of the concert was due to the conductor. J. Fred. had a following, and an audience existed beyond the Moravian Church. The Bethlehem Choral Union and J. Fred. were serving the whole area.

Because the next concerts and the rehearsals were in the hall of the Moravian Parochial School, the question whether the concerts were sacred or secular was not asked. In the flush of excitement caused by J. Fred.'s return, no one could have foreseen that the answer to that question when it was asked would destroy the Bethlehem Choral Union and even put the founding of The Bach Choir in doubt.

For the second concert the Choral Union performed a new major sacred oratorio, *Christophorus*, by Rheinberger, J. Fred.'s Munich teacher. The newspaper reporter had already asked, "Shall it [the Choral Union] be encouraged to attack the more modern 'Christophorus'? It remains for the public to decide."[13]

J. Fred.'s second concert exemplified the edifying concert style with only one sacred choral work. The audience was expected to work to enjoy it, for *Christophorus* was "of the difficulty, for the conservation of the well-trained musical mind to grasp."[14]

As J. Fred. rehearsed the chorus, the press prepared the public for the concert. This promotion was another sign of changed times. Previously, a discrete announcement had appeared on the front page of the

Bethlehem newspaper a day or two before the performance, a paid advertisement was on one of the inside pages, and, after the concert there was a favorable account on the front page. Concerts were announced, not promoted. Before the performance of Rheinberger's *Christophorous*, a number of front-page articles appeared in *The Daily Bethlehem Times*. Readers were introduced to the soloists through short press releases; the story of St. Christopher was told, and there was a review of the public dress rehearsal as a preview of the concert. Interested listeners could become familiar with the music before the concert, by attending the dress rehearsal. The reporter gave a musical tour of the work. He told his readers that "the orchestra can be heard at its very best in the overture, when they commanded the whole attention of the audience."[15] In addition, the audience now took an active part in the concert. They served the performers, for they "encourage those who participate," and those who attended were assured that they "would in turn be amply repaid for this attendance."[16] The final promotional article appeared the day before the concert. Entitled "The Devil's chorus," it concluded with enticing details about the upcoming performance.

> Great preparations are being made for the concert. The stage will be decorated with choice flowering plants loaned to the Choral Union for the occasion. The reserved seat tickets are very nearly all taken . . . . There will evidently be one of the largest audiences present at this concert that has ever before attended any of the concerts of the Choral Union. The orchestra and the Choral Union had a very successful joint rehearsal on Saturday evening in the presence of a large number of their friends. It is urged upon all that in order to fully understand parts of "Christophorus" that they get librettos, which cost five cents each.[17]

The new promotional spirit was obvious in the difference between the way the concerts were reported in the two local newspapers. *The Moravian* continued to report the concerts as events, giving less and less information over the years. There was no preparation of its readers.

While Moravians did not require descriptions of the music, the general public did need information and interpretations: what was being played, by whom, where, and when, and how the listeners should feel about the music. *The Daily Bethlehem Times* not only reported and promoted the concerts, it provided the broad reading public with even more information about the music. As the performance became largely a community, rather than church, event, the secular newspaper became a promoter of culture, a product for a special cultivated group of "music lovers" to support and to consume. These concerts were attracting an audience that was not necessarily prepared at home or at school to appreciate and to understand the music they would hear as the Moravians were.

The performance of Rheinberger's *Christophorus* took place on 18 May 1886. This was probably the American premiere of a work J. Fred. would conduct frequently during his life. Typically, *The Daily Bethlehem Times* devoted nearly a column of front-page space to a report of the concert, taking "much pride and pleasure in chronicling the event as a perfect success." The singers were discussed, and a "debt of thanks" was paid to J. Fred. Wolle, "the efficient and enthusiastic leader," who "by his intelligent interpretation, has shown himself to be master of the situation." The orchestra was praised, as well; the new music of the "Wagnerian school" was described as "so startling in its modulations and constant surprises interspersed with the thrilling bursts of joy and gladness." (Rheinberger would had been shocked and dismayed to be called a member of the "Wagnerian school.") The reporter expressed his pleasure with the audience's concert manners: there was no applause between pieces and no calls for encores.[18]

When to applaud and when not to applaud was often discussed in subsequent performances of the Choral Union. In addition, the practice of encoring a movement passed out of fashion. The composer's creation became an object that was not to be interrupted. This idea was expressed by a reviewer who made clear that calls for encores through applause were now inappropriate. Although encores could be politely granted by the artists, "rapt attention" now pervaded a concert.

A most pleasing feature of the concert was the rapt attention of the audience. A number of parts were encored and kindly repeated, but the general feeling was that any applause would be disturbing to the effect, or that not a note should be lost.[19]

The Bethlehem audience had begun to revere the music and behave quietly during public concerts, as they had previously done in church. Characteristically, *The Moravian* report was modest, for "Our space prevents anything like a detailed description or criticism."[20]

At the general meeting of the Choral Union in June 1886, J. Fred. was reelected the conductor. The Union "is in a very prosperous condition."[21] In the fall J. Fred. began rehearsals for a Christmas concert. *The Moravian* reported it was "pleasant to chronicle the fact that the Choral Union, with recruited members, will undertake the study of Handel's Messiah."[22] By performance time, however, many problems arose. The first came about when the Choral Union applied to the Moravian Board of Elders for permission to perform *Messiah* during the Advent season in the church rather than in the parochial school. "After some hesitation it was decided to grant the request inasmuch as such concerts have been held in the Church before and no general rule has been adopted by the Board forbidding such things."[23] No tickets were to be sold at the door, however, and any profit was "devoted to church causes." General admission was 75 cents, reserved seats were $1.00, with seats in the gallery $1.25. A large platform was erected in the front of the church "tastefully decorated with beautiful flowering plants and bunting."[24] This platform, however, was a major reconfiguring of the church with the result that the performers became the focus rather than the music. Central Moravian Church was designed with a choir loft in the rear of the church with the choir out of sight so that the music floated down from a height as from heaven. The basic issue was articulated by the pastor. Was this a concert or was it a religious service? His position was clear.

> Though the character of the composition is irreproachable and the order was very good, yet it is regretted that the Board of Elders must

feel constrained to grant the use of the Church for concerts, & it is to be hoped that it may not occur often.[25]

While the "concert" took place in the church, the issue surrounding such events was not finally resolved until the church board refused to host the Bach Festival in 1913, because it was not a sacred service.

The report of the concert in *The Daily Bethlehem Times* was dramatic. It was clear how far from a sacred service the performance was. There were ninety singers and thirty instrumentalists. J. Fred. had involved more musicians than he had done previously, and he became a center of attention.

> Prof. J. Fred. Wolle . . . mounted the stand, his baton poised for a few moments in the air, and the magnificent orchestra struck the overture . . . indeed it was hard to feel one was live in the flesh, so glorious and heavenly was the music. . . . That he trained and drilled the performers and conducted the entire rendition of the great masterpiece of Handel is the greatest praise we can express.[26]

Readers of *The Moravian*, however, were presented with a mixed "review." Issues that were disturbing the Moravian congregation were compounding and were brought into the open. That the issues were important was clear from the fact that one-and-a-half columns were given to the review. Normally a report of a concert was about one-half a column, and the previous concert had not been reviewed at all due to "lack of space."

What was the allegiance of the Union to the Moravian Church when they were singing music that was traditionally sung by the Moravian Church choir? Should concerts be permitted in the church at all? Why were instrumentalists and vocal soloists from elsewhere rather than from the community? There were no reserved seats for a church service, yet reserved seating had been sold for the concert. Was it right to use profits from a concert for charitable causes? *The Moravian* continued we suggest that the wisest course for the future will be to rely absolutely on home talent for orchestra and soprano and contralto soloists. There must be some reason why a musical community which was able to get one together for "the Messiah"; for those musicians are still with us. Let the reason be found and removed. . . . There are at least three sopranos in our community who are fully competent to render the solos of "the Messiah" in a satisfactory manner. If special practice is needed, it would be only just to make a financial remuneration in these cases, as had been customary since 1867.[27]

The review concluded with a number of suggestions that would make future performances of the Choral Union more acceptable to the Moravian congregation. The paper concluded

Our proposition, therefore, is that the Oratorio be sung annually at Christmas-tide, in the Hall of the Parochial School until some other easily accessible place is available; that local talent be relied upon to furnish both orchestral and soloists, omitting some of the solos for bass and tenor, if need be; that the tickets to all seats be reserved at a nominal price, so that no one may have a financial excuse for absence; and that the net proceeds be devoted to St. Luke's Hospital. That would bring about an even more notable concert.[28]

Through his skill as a manager, J. Fred. made sure that such concerns did not impede the development of the Choral Union and its concerts. He had resumed his position as conductor of the Easton Choral Union when he returned, which made it possible for them to perform together a number of times. J. Fred. combined them to repeat Rheinberger's *Christoforus* in the hall of the Moravian school. All of the issues that were sensitive to the congregation were avoided. Whether or not a performance was a concert or a sacred service was sidestepped by not holding the performance at the school. The concert was given primarily by local talent. The problem of "correct" concert decorum did not arise, because the previous audience had already agreed the "applause would be a disturbing effect." The large numbers involved assured that it was impressive. Prior to the concert there was an enthusiastic news release emphasizing the grandeur of the event. "This will be the largest chorus that will ever have sung, not only in the Day School Hall, but the largest ever heard in Bethlehem."[29]

This concert showed that J. Fred. was firmly rooted in the Romantic aesthetic of grandeur and the awesome. The platform was extended to accommodate the double chorus. In the school such a change posed no religious problem. There was a public rehearsal to help the audience become more familiar with the work, but only for those with prepaid admission. The dress rehearsal was not a substitute for attending the performance.

With characteristic excitement, the reporter from *The Daily Bethlehem Times* wrote

> From the moment Mr. J. Fred. Wolle raised his baton in the opening overture to the close of the last chorus, the hearers were held by the charm which only the most delightful music can lay upon an audience.[30]

*The Moravian* contained a brief, cool notice within which J. Fred. was not even mentioned. In a later edition, the readers were informed that in rehearsing their next piece, Mendelssohn's *Elijah*, the Choral Union was not undertaking much more than what the Moravian Church choir sang routinely. "It would be the first rendition of the entire oratorio in our town, though many of the choruses are familiar to attendants at the services in the Moravian Church."[31] The concert took place in the Moravian Church and was treated as a sacred service. No tickets were sold at the door, though there were reserved seats and the audience was "respectfully requested to abstain from applause."[32] The church was filled. *The Moravian* was pleased, and devoted considerable space to a report that focused on the soloists and the music with little mention of J. Fred. Leaders in the Moravian Church like J. Fred. were traditionally granted only modest recognition for their service, as no Moravian should stand out.

> For the first time there is a glimpse of J. Fred's conducting style in *The Daily Bethlehem Times*. His style of directing is forcible, yet graceful; his management personality enables him to at all times have his forces in hand, while his musicianly interpretation commands the admiration of all.[33]

The reviewer pointed out another quality many people commented on during J. Fred.'s career: his persistent determination to go beyond what he had previously achieved. "Prof. Wolle's leadership . . . had showed careful and intelligent drilling and determination to excel all previous work before the public."[34] Another significant fact, civic pride, was reported in the review. J. Fred. "deserves the sincerest thanks of all good Bethlehemites for affording us the opportunity of hearing *Elijah*."[35] Armed with his successes, J. Fred. was prepared to attempt more difficult works – the monumental, unknown "Passions" composed by J. S. Bach.

Four years had passed since J. Fred. had heard Bach's *St. John Passion* in Munich. After his experiences with the concerts of the Choral Unions in Bethlehem and Easton, J. Fred. felt he was ready to conduct the work that had moved him so deeply. He was one of very few conductors in America who even dreamed of undertaking such a task.

The moment was right. There was a well-trained chorus under his baton. His superiority as a conductor was unquestioned. Money could be raised to cover the performance, as long as the sale of the tickets did not take place in the Moravian Church. This made it possible for J. Fred. to hire professional soloists and to supplement the Bethlehem orchestra with additional players. Finally, the large secular audience of "music-lovers" had been cultivated to respond to concerts of sacred music in a reverent manner. He began preparing the Bethlehem Choral Union for J. S. Bach's *Passion According to St. John*, for what would be an American premiere of that work.[36]

Exactly when J. Fred. began to rehearse this "Passion" is unknown, but by May 1888 the date was set for a performance in early June. It was called a concert, not a sacred service, and was held in the Moravian

Parochial School, not in the church. Thus, once again, earlier problems were avoided. Further distance from the Moravian Church was evident in *The Moravian*'s announcement of the concert. It was to be a community event rather than one involving the church. A number of areas around Bethlehem that included various European ethnic groups and diverse church congregations had come together because of the growth of the population. Earlier concerts had proven that "music-lovers" lived throughout the area, not only in the Moravian section. Thus, this concert was for the "the music-loving people of the Bethlehems."[37]

The editor of *The Moravian* did not mention the importance of the performance. The announcement neither mentioned the quality of the work, the musical difficulties involved in rehearsing and performing it, nor that this performance was an American premiere. The editor only noted, the "efforts of the Choral Union [ensure] a most enjoyable treat."[38]

On the other hand, reporters for *The Daily Bethlehem Times* were eager to determine if the Choral Union concert was in fact going to premiere the "St. John Passion." Critics in New York City were asked and the staff of the paper "awaited [their responses] with interest."[39] One critic referred the reporters to the conductor of Boston's Handel and Haydn Society. That conductor said that he had performed only sections of this "masterpiece" in concert. As far as he was aware, the Bethlehem performance would be the American premiere. The announcement "brought forth much applause."[40]

With feelings of civic pride aroused, a reporter attended "A Successful Rehearsal" a week before the concert. The music excited him, and he wrote not only of the high quality of the composition but of the importance of Bach's music in general. "We feel no hesitation in assuring the public that they will be fully repaid for this attendance . . . with the breadth and dignity of style possible only with music of so elevated and a sacred character."[41] The reporter pointed out the difficulty of learning the work, for it was "one of the severest tests of the capabilities of the chorus, whose powers of execution it tasks to the utmost . . . prepared, not without strenuous effort by our ambitious and painstaking singers."[42]

He was correct. The Bethlehem Choral Union possessed no experienced singers of Bach. Everyone was moving in unchartered waters under J. Fred.'s youthful direction. The independence of the voices, the density and complexity of the sound, the often tortured quality of the harmony and dissonance, the emotionally charged asymmetrical melodies with unusual accompaniments, the difficult rhythms and entrances made the undertaking an awesome one. Even today this *Passion* is not undertaken lightly.

In addition to teaching the choir their parts, other musical difficulties arose that required J. Fred. to adjust this premiere to American circumstances in the 1880s. *The Daily Bethlehem Times* reported that no wind and brass parts were available in America.

> So rare is the St. John "Passion" performed in this country that after several unsuccessful attempts to procure the orchestral parts the directors [the officers] of the Choral Union were obliged to send to England for them, and could even then procure only the stringed quartette, the other parts existing only in manuscript.[43]

J. Fred. apparently had assumed he would have no difficulty locating the parts. Finding them unavailable must have come as a shock. J. Fred. was forced to play the missing parts on the organ and the piano from the score. The lack of parts was further evidence of how *avant-garde* this enterprise was.

For J. Fred., playing the missing parts greatly complicated the performance. Bach's organ part was notated in figured bass, so J. Fred. had to improvise the harmonies using the pedal and the keyboard and at the same time integrate the other parts into his playing. One hand was only occasionally free to conduct. All of his excellent musical education was put to the test.

As it was, J. Fred. lacked enough string players to balance the size of the chorus. The paper reported, "the orchestra did its duty quite satisfactorily, even though weak in numbers . . . the gentlemen soloists had not before undertaken such ambitious works."[44] Singing Bach recitatives is an art in itself. Because there had been so few performances of Bach's choral music, there was no tradition in America for this style of singing. As a result, the soloists were unable to sing all of the recitatives. Events of the *Passion* recounted in the recitatives were mostly narrated and only occasionally sung by a male soloist who recited the text chant-like over very sparse chords played by J. Fred. on the piano. As a substitute for the singing, "Rev. Edwin G. Klose read the connecting parts of the Scripture narrative very expressively."[45] The many chorales in the work were sung without accompaniment, even though Bach had clearly notated parts for orchestra. While J. Fred.'s adjustments would be unacceptable now, they did not disturb the listeners at the time for they had no prior experience with the work. A reporter wrote of this premiere

> From the sweet strains of the orchestral prelude to the majestic chorus which marked the end of the work the audience was rapt in wonder at the exquisite beauty of the composition and the skill with which the large body of singers and players rendered the work under the magic influence of Prof. Wolle's baton.[46]

The reviewer concluded by expressing a feeling of pride in the fact that this premiere had taken place in Bethlehem.

> In short, Bach's "Passion," as rendered by the Bethlehem Choral Union, was a thorough success and Prof. Wolle and his faithful assistants can feel very proud of the first rendition on this continent of this magnificently set story of the "Passion" of our Lord Jesus Christ.[47]

What had J. Fred. achieved? He had proven that Bach could be sung in Bethlehem. His monumental choral works could be performed in a small American community without the musical resources and experienced musicians that were available in a European city like Munich and without the financial backing of a system of aristocratic and church patronage. The music-loving citizens of the Bethlehems sang, played, bought tickets, and listened to one of Bach's most complex and expressive choral works. Also, J. Fred. learned he had the musical understanding and the managerial skills demanded for such a complex artistic undertaking. With this performance J. Fred., then only twenty-five years old, made his first significant contribution to music in America.

The Moravian Church diarist, however, noted a fact not mentioned in the newspaper that must have given J. Fred. and the officers of the Choral Union pause. "The audience was not large."[48] The concerts for the rest of the season and the next year were designed for audience-building to secure funds. The music was decidedly more popular. Handel's *Messiah* was presented during the Christmas season as *The Moravian* had requested when the Choral Union previously sang this oratorio.

This Christmas concert was significant for a number of reasons. The orchestra was dramatically smaller. Also, the soloists and instrumentalists were probably all local volunteers. The result was a concert that cost far less and included more neighbors and friends, which ensured a larger audience. Of greater importance is the fact that the concert was held in the Fountain Hill Opera House rather than in the Moravian Parochial School. Fountain Hill was an adjoining town where most of the newly wealthy industrialists, engineers, and managers had built their mansions. It was the social center of the Bethlehems and was controlled by a group of people who had no direct roots in Moravian culture. The Choral Union was no longer an extension of the Moravian Church Choir. It was growing more independent and drawing its support from music lovers among the industrialists who were not Moravians. This group offered greater financial support and was not restrained by decisions of the Moravian Church Elders. At the same time, J. Fred. was making connections that proved essential to him in the future. A number of years later these music lovers of the Bethlehems ensured both the founding and the survival of The Bach Choir.

Financial support by the Fountain Hill group for the *Messiah* was raised by selling memberships in the Choral Union. Each associate member received two reserved seats for the *Messiah* and for two succeeding concerts. The list of members was printed in the program. J. Fred.'s father was an associate member as were other Moravians; however, the steel industrialists and railroad owners were most prominent. The printed program also contained an announcement of the next concert. It was Max Bruch's "popular, secular" dramatic oratorio, *Arminius*. The associated members would "materially aid the Society in producing *Arminius* in a style commensurate with [its] merits."[49] The precision J. Fred. demanded of the singers for the *Messiah* was such that "they can sing their parts by heart."[50] This is the first time this hallmark of the performances was mentioned by the press.

The review of the concert in *The Moravian* was brief. Recognizing that the concert-going public now included "the Bethlehems," "the members of the Choral Union deserve great encouragement from the music loving people of the Bethlehems."[51] Even though *The Daily Bethlehem Times* printed a number of promotional articles, they did not review it. There is no record as to the success of the *Messiah* concert.

Six months later, the Choral Union sang *Arminius*. J. Fred. correctly judged the public's desire for concerts of grand secular choral compositions. The reporter of *The Daily Bethlehem Times* picked up the point and wrote in his promotional article, "The bright brilliant music of the secular oratorio stands out in full relief to the more somber music of the religious oratorios."[52] The concert exemplified the new philosophy of programming adapted to secular ends. *Arminius* occupied the whole evening, but the audience was permitted to respond with applause between numbers. The secular subject did not require listeners to sit reverently for the entire evening. As a result, "The audience received the solo parts and chorus with rapturous applause and one encore after another followed."[53] While reviews do not mention the orchestral groups, a "renowned" bass from New York City was a vocal soloist. In spite of the "rapturous response of the audience," *The Daily*

*Bethlehem Times* concluded "that it wasn't the financial success it should have been is regretted."[54]

J. Fred. reacted immediately to the financial problems. He presented a concert that included choruses from previous oratorios, instrumental performances by students that were "encored several times," and a guest violinist "received with meritorious applause."[55] While the concert was one in the old entertainment style, and must have been difficult for J. Fred., it worked. A month later "fully 500 people, among whom were a great many of our musical critics, enjoyed the excellent miscellaneous concert." The reviewer from *The Daily Bethlehem Times* concluded his review with welcome news. "From all appearances it was also a financial success."[56]

Financial success had become an issue now that the concerts were no longer under church patronage. As capitalistic interests became patrons, financial success or failure became a factor in judging artistic success or failure. The news media was making this clear to its readers by including statements about the box offices as news items.

The December concert in 1889 was even more miscellaneous. Performing with the Bethlehem Choral Union was a glee club from nearby Easton, a cellist from New York City, a string quartet of Bethlehem players, and a vocal soloist, Miss Agnes Wolle, one of J. Fred.'s aunts. A sacred piece, *Christus*, by Mendelssohn, concluded the concert.

While this concert was in most ways entirely traditional, one aspect of the event was unique. The audience was polled to determine the pieces that might be performed in the future. *The Daily Bethlehem Times* described the procedure. "Blank slips will be distributed with the librettos, upon which the voter may write one name selected from the list in [the] program, the result to be announced at the close of the concert."[57] This was the final nod to public taste.

Mendelssohn's *Elijah* was chosen for a concert given the following February. However, J. Fred. wanted to ensure that his group did not need to perform if there were not enough voices, so a statement was included, "under the proviso that 100 voices can be obtained for the chorus."[58] The reporter noted in his review, "It was the prevailing opinion last night that the chorus should be much stronger in its tenors and basses."⁵⁹

True to its promise "the Bethlehem Choral Union is rehearsing 'Elijah' and will shortly give another of its grand musical treats to the lovers of good music," reported *The Moravian* some months later.⁶⁰ The performance never took place. Instead, a program designed purely for fund-raising was offered "under the auspices" of the Bethlehem Choral Union. Various selections were played for the audience on a phonograph with a "funnel eleven feet long, and a diameter at the mouth of four feet."⁶¹ About six hundred people attended, and the applause for a recording of Europe's most celebrated banjoist was "so vociferous that Prof. Ivans was compelled to repeat it."⁶² The Choral Union sang two selections. The program was not mentioned at all in *The Moravian*. But the church diarist expressed disapproval. The Easter season was the most sacred time of year for Moravians, and a phonograph concert was not an appropriate substitute for a performance of *Elijah*.

> On the evening of Easter Monday the Bethlehem Choral Union gave a mixed concert in the hall of the Parochial School House gotten cheaply for the purpose of replenishing the depleted treasury of the Society. A sensation was added in the shape of phonography renditions given by a person who is traveling about with an instrument and gathering dimes. Financially the effort was a success.⁶³

Moving in the contrary direction, J. Fred. began his next Bach project – a performance of the *Passion According to St. Matthew*. When he requested permission for the performance in the church, the old problems arose, but this time with greater urgency. The diarist wrote that the Board of Elders, after some discussion of the case, "concluded to grant the petition of our organist."⁶⁴

There were two new conditions. The first was "if they succeed in the effort to master it."⁶⁵ Such a condition was surprising, for it might imply that the previous Bach performance had been considered so poor with its compromises that the capability of the Choral Union and J. Fred. were being called into question. If they could not sing *Elijah*, how could they sing Bach? Were the elders really prepared to withhold their permission if the work was not mastered? An awkward situation was developing. A second condition was even more limiting. The elders had greatly tightened their restrictions involving financing sacred concerts they were associated with. " No selling of tickets or taking money at the doors will be permitted. The money will be raised by special subscription and tickets will be issued to subscribers only."[66] Tickets were not sold at all but were given to subscribers. A later editorial in *The Daily Bethlehem Times* made clear that there could not even be a "special subscription" as stated by the pastor. The money had to come from season subscriptions. The Moravian Elders had eliminated every possible connection between money and a Bach performance in the church.

As the performance neared, there was not enough money to sign contracts. *The Moravian* was silent as a number of appeals for subscribers appeared in *The Daily Bethlehem Times*. In an interview with J. Fred. the question was raised, was there an audience to support Bach performances? In response J. Fred. contradicted public perceptions of Bach's music he must have heard after the "St. John Passion." Bach's music was not "dry and abstruse," he insisted. Instead, it was lucid and simple. He continued

> While, undoubtedly to many minds the name of Bach carries with it the idea of dryness and abstruseness, Bach's biographer, Spitta, says in a few words enough to dispel such an impression. Here it is: "St. Matthew Passion," as a whole, is . . . a popular work.[67]

The interviewer added, "The present status of the Choral Union and the "Passion" music is rather precarious. I believe Professor Wolle's enthusiasm, if nothing else, will carry both of them through."[68] More appeals for subscribers appeared. The subscription prices had been raised, and a concerned reader wrote to the editor, "Does this subscription price of five dollars for the series seem too high? We have heard the idea expressed."[69]

Suddenly, the Choral Union's complete season was in danger. First the initial concert was postponed, then, it was canceled entirely. Finally, the Bach performance was abandoned. The year was 1890.

The Bethlehem Choral Union was nearly ruined. When the chorus did appear a year later, the reviewer expressed surprise.

> It was an agreeable surprise to find that our excellent Choral Union, which only a few weeks ago seemed in such danger of closing its useful career, had started out once more on the high road to success.[70]

There was no mention of the split within the Choral Union: half the group was rehearsing in North Bethlehem and another section met in South Bethlehem. That split grew wider. A few days after the December concert, the South Bethlehem section appeared alone to sing in the Fountain Hill Opera House. The wealthy part of town seemed able to support its own chorus.

The year 1894 was the 150th anniversary of the founding of Bethlehem. With characteristic ingenuity, J. Fred. used the occasion to revitalize his plans to perform the *St. Matthew Passion*. What better way for the Moravian congregation to celebrate its musical heritage than by sponsoring a community performance of Bach? All parties readily agreed that the anniversary was the appropriate time for such a grand undertaking, and J. Fred. began preparing for a performance during the Easter season. It would be a service in the sanctuary with no applause.

The Moravian elders modified their previous position regarding ticket sales to cover the performance, which the pastor noted "were heavy." While the elders insisted on the sale of advanced subscriptions, these were for the "Passion" performance alone, not for the Choral Union's complete season. Each subscriber "invited" a certain number of "friends." Tickets were not mentioned. The elders must have remembered that their decision for a season subscription ticket had destroyed the "Passion" performance two years before and had caused the Choral Union's season to collapse.

Since the 150th anniversary was a community celebration, J. Fred. selected instrumentalists only from Bethlehem and neighboring Allentown, and two of the vocal soloists were popular area singers. J. Fred. rehearsed the two Choral Unions separately, one in the North and one in South Bethlehem, combining the groups for the performances. In that way, singers from each of the Bethlehems participated. In addition, J. Fred. added one hundred children, selecting them from both the Lehigh University Chapel Choir and the Moravian Parochial School.

Adding children was a particularly clever gesture. Here was concrete proof that his idea of Bach's music was correct. It was not "dry and abstruse" as people thought. Children could sing it. The *St. Matthew Passion* was "lucid and simple," as J. Fred. had told the newspaper reporter. This music was for everybody. Like the two Choral Unions, the two children's choruses could be rehearsed separately and combined just before the performance. The addition of the children greatly increased the monumentality of the production at no additional cost. Also, the size of the audience was immediately increased with the addition of parents, families, and relatives who would not otherwise attend a performance of Bach.

After the first full rehearsal, the church diarist expressed a feeling of pride as the preparations were taking place "in our church" led by "our organist." Though it was an important community musical event, it was a Moravian one, and there was no question that Bach's music was a "masterpiece." They were performing the very best.

> Monday evening the two large choruses of the augmented Choral Union, one of Bethlehem and one of South Beth. which have been practicing the the great masterpiece of sacred music, the Passion According to St. Matthew, by John [sic] Sebastian Bach, under the leadership of our organist, Br. J. Fred. Wolle, with a view to its rendition in our church, had their first rehearsal in the Church.[71]

The diarist's usual reserve disappeared when he described the performance. He was overwhelmed by J. Fred.'s "achievement" and the "devout spirit" of the listeners.

> It was a magnificent success and a fitting introduction to the Holy Passion Week. This 150th Anniversary year of Bethlehem, crowning a century and a half of music fame with the greatest achievement yet reached. The church was entirely filled . . . and the devout spirit in which the noble composition was listened to was like that which pervades the congregation during the solemn liturgy of Good Friday. It was felt that such a thing as applause would be profanation. It was a privilege to be present.[72]

J. Fred. had made this performance of the *Passion* work in every way.

*The Daily Bethlehem Times* agreed with the pastor. This was the "most impressive Lenten service ever held in Bethlehem . . . a triumph thoroughly worthy of the glory of the sesqui-centennial years."[73] Though there had been doubts, J. Fred. dispelled them all. He also solved the multiple problems involved in realizing a service on such a large scale involving children and community singers accompanied by a local orchestra. The newspaper reporter described the ideas held by the public prior to the service and the significance of the performance.

Many of the listeners had gone to the service with misgivings. They thought

> the effort too great, the undertaking too ambitious. The identical "Passion Music" had been rendered but twice or thrice before in America, and then only by large thoroughly drilled, semi-professional city choruses. For a place of Bethlehem's size to undertake it they deemed altogether too audacious. They dreaded the possible result. And with their acute critical faculties sharpened to the excitement they awaited the denouement with fear and trembling. . . . But they need not have quaked.[74]

This report made clear there had been intense reservations about the performance. People wished for *Elijah* or *Messiah*, pieces they knew. The name Bach "scared them." They were "repelled" by the fugues, and the story would be "dreary." The *St. Matthew* service changed all of that. Now "novices could enter into its rendition with keen delight," and the only regret was that it was "too brief. It lasted exactly two hours."[75]

J. Fred. received surprisingly little credit for the performance, though he had trained the choirs "excellently," and they sang with "marked evenness, symmetry [balance?] and expression." A number of chorales were "most inspiring," and the final chorus was "soul stirring." The reporter felt the male voices were "overshadowed" in sections, but J. Fred. was not blamed. "This was probably unavoidable by reason of the conductor's material."[76]

In addition to the "Passion," Bach composed three other monumental choral works: The *Christmas Oratorio*, Magnificat, and the Mass in B Minor. Probably confident in his own musical and managerial powers following the great success of the *St. Matthew Passion*, sure of the skills of his singers, and certain of the support of the "music-lovers of the Bethlehems," J. Fred. began to rehearse the Mass in B Minor, a work that had never been sung in its entirety in America.[77] An unexpected reaction awaited him. One account is that J. Fred.

> wanted the Choral Union to undertake Bach's greatest work, the MASS IN B MINOR; but, considering it too difficult, the singers balked. Dr. Wolle was relentless, and refusing to lead in the singing of any other music compositions, the Choral Union was disbanded.[78]

Writing while J. Fred. was still alive, the official historian of the Bach Choir recounted how

> after the singers of the Choral Union gave the *St. John Passion* in 1888, it was four years before Wolle could get them to sing the *St. Matthew Passion*. When he proposed the B Minor Mass, they utterly balked. They wanted to sing easier things. Their conductor was adamant; it was to be B Minor Mass or nothing. It was nothing, so far as the Choral Union was concerned.[79]

J. Fred.'s nephew provided a more intimate description of the reaction of the members of the Choral Union. When the singers were asked why they were losing interest and why others were no longer coming to rehearsal, they said they "got stuck in so many places and the music sounded so awful . . . they would not take his reproving, nagging sessions any longer."[80] The secretary of the Choral Union, Mrs. Ruth Doster, approached J. Fred. with their complaints. She pleaded with him, "Please, please do give in, Fred, for this season at least do something just a little less difficult."[81] J. Fred., in a rare public show of stubbornness, replied, "The Mass or nothing" and continued the rehearsals. Soon no singers appeared. "The director in grief and disappointment broke his baton – and never thereafter did he use one in directing."[82]

Six months after the successful performances of the *St. Matthew Passion*, the Bethlehem Choral Union ceased to exist. J. Fred. had moved too far, too fast, and in youthful passion, too stubbornly. More than ten years later, J. Fred. gave his side of the story in a newspaper interview. He simply wanted nothing to do with music as entertainment.

> . . . several times rehearsals were taken up, but for one reason or another had to be dropped. At last I washed my hands of the whole movement, declined to have any part of any musical entertainment until the mass [sic] should be produced.[83]

Bethlehem Moravians made no move to save the Choral Union. However, "the general opinion of the Fountain Hill people was that the entire abandonment of a musical organization would be a kind of stigma on Bethlehem."[84] Those who were recent citizens of Bethlehem were feeling a greater sense of cultural pride than those whose families had founded the community. J. Fred. worked with a number of the most influential new industrialists on a plan to organize another chorus. The group presented the idea to William Sayre, an owner of the Lehigh Valley Rail Road and one of South Bethlehem's philanthropists. Mr. Sayre not only supported the idea, he agreed to chair the organizational meeting. During that meeting, J. Fred. "gave a short account of the rise and fall of the Choral Union" and "deplored the lack of interest that caused its downfall and rejoiced that the entire extinction of musical enthusiasm would not be permitted."[85] Sayre was elected president of the new chorus, and J. Fred. was appointed the music director. The concerts "will probably take place in the Fountain Hill Opera House, which the majority seem to regard as the most convenient auditorium"[86] J. Fred. held the first rehearsal the same evening in a room in the administrative building of the Lehigh Valley Rail Road.

The musical separation from the Moravians appeared to be complete. While "it is the desire that all those who have musical talent shall become members," the new group was organized and sponsored by non-Moravians. It was not a union of church choirs as the Choral Union had been. It was a secular group. Therefore, the problem of concert vs. sacred service could not arise. The newly formed Bethlehem Oratorio Society rehearsed and performed where the industrialists lived and worked, the area, naturally, "most convenient" for them. But the office building and the Fountain Hill Opera House were not only convenient to the homes of the members – both buildings housed institutions generated by the industrial growth of Bethlehem. These buildings were symbols of Bethlehem's new wealth, power, and now cultural influence. Members of the Choral Union had rehearsed and performed in the Moravian Parochial School and the Moravian Church. But the center of musical patronage had shifted, and a concert became a social event for the Bethlehems.

That fact was not lost on the newspaper. The headline of the review of the first concert read, "The Wealth, Beauty and Fashion of the Bethlehems Grace the Fountain Hill Opera House."[87] The social attributes of the audience were expanded into a full paragraph. People were there to support their own kind and to be seen doing so as well as to be among the critical-music-lovers social set.

> The audience was one of the most select, cultured, and critical that the opera house has ever contained. All of the Fountain Hill and Bethlehem society was there. Nearly everyone in town who understands and appreciated music of a high character was there and many out of

town people attended. The auditorium was completely filled and there was a generous sprinkling in the balcony.[88]

All of the performers were local. The concert consisted of ensemble numbers except for one solo, arranged by J. Fred., "which fairly took the house by storm. The applause for several minutes was thundering. She [the soloist] bowed, but this was not enough, and she repeated the German part of the song to appease her admirers" for encores were allowed.[89] The performers were enthusiastically supported in every way. The eighty-voice Bethlehem Oratorio Society sang "The Patriotic Hymn" by Dvořák. Even J. Fred. was caught up in the importance of the event, and he responded with uncharacteristic, uncritical abandon to the newspaper stating, "This chorus is the best music ever undertaken by any society in Bethlehem and the splendid manner in which each individual helped to carry out all the parts won for every member of the society new and fresh laurels."[90] One of those singers was Mrs. Ruth Doster who supported J. Fred. in the Choral Union and emerged later as the organizer of The Bach Choir. For the next concert, this "most select, cultured, and critical audience" was promised a performance of *Faust*, "which has hitherto been heard but once in this country."[91] The work referred to was probably the oratorio by Robert Schumann.

Documents from the time reveal that the Choral Union did not "quietly pass out of existence" as one of the historians of the Bethlehem Bach Choir wrote.[92] Rather, it was replaced by the Bethlehem Oratorical Society, a new choral group that represented a genuine shift in the cultural hegemony of the area. The sense of violation the new choral group created in the Moravian community was not apparent until the expansion of the Lehigh Valley Rail Road made it necessary for the Oratorical Society to move rehearsal out of the railroad's administration building. A new building was under construction in the center of Bethlehem where the Oratorical Society was going to rehearse. Because the structure was not ready when the chorus was to move, the group approached the Board of the Moravian Parochial

# CREATING THE BACH CHOIR

School, composed entirely of members of the Moravian Church, with a request to use the school hall until the new building was finished. The Board granted permission, but the report in the church diary concluded with a statement that expressed what the church had felt when the society had been founded. "Like some other organizations in this town it finds it of advantage or even necessary, after experiments in other quarters, to come back to the Moravian Church for aid and comfort."[93]

The Moravian community had the last word it seemed. The choral group was back in the fold after "experiments in other quarters," and Brother J. Fred. had returned as well. The diarist stressed that the Oratorical Society "is under the directorship of Br. J. Fred. Wolle, our organist."[94] Br. Wolle had maneuvered a difficult political situation with his usual skill.

The *Faust* performance never took place. The Bethlehem Oratorical Society, which had been organized with the support of many of the most prominent people in Bethlehem and had caused such excitement with its first concert, did not perform again. Apparently, the chorus had never been more than a scaled down Choral Union and, like that group, it was now "defunct." It appeared that J. Fred.'s association with community groups had ceased again.

J. Fred. now concentrated his performance of Bach within the Moravian Church where his remaining group, the church choir and orchestra, "assisted by a few friends," was willing to rehearse sections of Bach's *Christmas Oratorio*.[95] This next major Bach performance took place in the Central Moravian Church in 1894. From the point of view of the choir, J. Fred.'s idea was a fine one. The work was easier to sing than the Mass, there was a story, and it contained many familiar chorales that appealed to everyone. It was also significant that it would be sung in English. On the other hand, the Mass in B Minor was in Latin, told no story, and contained no familiar chorales. Also, J. Fred. was certain that the Moravian Church would patronize a performance of the *Christmas Oratorio*. It was appropriate sacred music because it "suitably introduced the Christmas season," and the elders were willing to meet expenses by "a collection, entirely voluntary and without appeal" during the intermission.[96] No tickets or public subscriptions were considered. This performance was a church service open to the general public. The problems that had plagued J. Fred. were solved again. The church diarist reported that

> The Board of Elders met this evening. The increase of the force of the church choir was discussed and a plan, to render Bach's Christmas Oratorio, by the choir on some evening shortly before Christmas was approved.[97]

The church was filled for the service. There were representatives from all the churches in town and the important music lovers were there. It was a Christmas event that drew everyone of importance into the church. After the performance, the pastor wrote

> A programme containing the words of the oratorio was in the hands of the audience. The body of the church was densely filled; and the galleries were crowded. . . . The people who had gathered for the occasion represented all the churches of the towns, and all those who make any pretence of musical attainment, or love of music. . . . As no admission had been charged, and yet expenses were connected with the rendition of the production, a collection, entirely voluntary and without appeal was taken during the intermission, which amounted to $194.50. The oratorio suitably introduced [the] Christmas season.[98]

*The Daily Bethlehem Times* briefly announced that the performance would take place. Their readers were informed "A collection for defraying the expenses of the performance (there is no charge for admission) will be taken during the intermission."[99]

Though only "Parts I and II" of the oratorio had been sung, J. Fred. had organized and conducted another major performance of a Bach work in Bethlehem. The fact that this had not been a performance of the complete oratorio did not minimize the undertaking. With one exception all previous performances in America were only of the first two parts. The American premiere of the complete work had to wait until 1903, when J. Fred. conducted it in Bethlehem.

It is curious that J. Fred. stressed mainly the big works by Bach. He did not have his singers perform Bach's cantatas, of which there are over two hundred. The scores and parts were available for many of them. The cantatas' musical demands on the chorus are not always great, and Bach wrote cantatas for the entire church year so there was always music that was appropriate for any church service. Also, the music was Protestant. J. Fred. did have the choir sing a few sections of them. They sang two choruses from cantatas in 1893, 1894, and 1896. The "Crucifixus" from the Mass was sung in 1894 for the first time. After the *St. Matthew Passion* was performed in 1894, various choruses were used throughout the church year. However, it does not seem that J. Fred. had developed a plan to systematically build a Bach repertoire. A willingness to conduct cantatas could have furthered his vision to ultimately conduct the Mass, because his singers would not have been overwhelmed by unfamiliar music and the performances would not have incurred expense that the church was unwilling to pay. For six years, Bach performances in Bethlehem nearly ceased. J. Fred.'s insistence on performing only Bach's expansive works jeopardized Bach performances in Bethlehem and, thus, in America.

Though the struggles over musical patronage described above were centered in Bethlehem, during the nineteenth century religious works took on such a scale that it was beyond the financial capacity of individual churches to perform them. Concerts halls and universities became the patrons of these sacred choral compositions. Moravian communities still continued to give extensive church patronage to music. That was the reason that the struggle in Bethlehem between the church and the wealthy industrialists lasted so long. Ultimately, even in Bethlehem, the wealthy won. However, unlike other communities in Bethlehem, the battle was not only financial. The Moravians would simply not allow their church to be used as a concert hall.

• • •

J. Fred. had to wait eight years from the performance of the *Christmas Oratorio* before he realized his desire to premiere the Mass in B Minor. Whether J. Fred. returned to Bethlehem from Munich with a "vision" to perform the major choral works of Bach in America is not known. However, by 1894 a pattern had emerged that the pastor noted in his diary. "The Passion Music according to St. John by Bach, had been rendered in Bethlehem April 8, 1868; and the Passion according to St. Matthew, by Bach, had been given in Bethlehem, April 8, 1892; and then came this evening worthily followed by the Christmas Oratorio."[100]

The next monumental Bach choral composition performed in Bethlehem was the Mass in B Minor. It was the result of a collaborative effort of the non-Moravian industrial group and the Moravian Church. The movement to form a group willing to learn the work was spearheaded by Mrs. Ruth Doster, the secretary of the defunct Choral Union. She had pleaded with J. Fred. to hold off on the rehearsal of the Mass, but he had refused. Now she came to him with a plan.

Her mansion was a center of musical activity in Bethlehem, where friends gathered to sing and to study music. Mrs. Doster asked J. Fred. to work with them, and he replied that he would only conduct a group willing to sing Bach's Mass. If anyone could have succeeded in reviving Bach in Bethlehem, it was Ruth Doster. She was a Moravian, a leader of Bethlehem's cultured social set, and one of J. Fred.'s neighbors. Moreover, "she was a diligent . . . student of Bach's music."[101] She formed a group of approximately thirty singers who wanted to study the Mass by singing it. This group joined with the Moravian choir, and this combined chorus rehearsed following the weekly practice of the church choir. There was also a plan to commemorate the 150th anniversary of Bach's death by a public performance of the Mass in the year 1900.

When Mrs. Doster was interviewed by a critic attending the Third Bach Festival, he reported

> now she talks of the work of that winter, but ever and again her lips tighten in a line that tells why, when she had finished "writing saucy

postals," and talking to her friends "until they ran away from me," the Bach Choir – the real Bach Choir – had become an organization.[102]

Years later, J. Fred. gave Ruth Doster a photograph on which he wrote, "To the organizer of the Bach choir Mrs. W. C. Doster from its leader, J. Fred. Wolle."[103]

The organizational meeting of the "Bach Choir" took place on the evening of 5 December 1898. A month later, the first rehearsal was an event important enough to be recorded in the church diary.

> Monday evening the augmented choir organized Dec. 5, 1898 under the direction of Br. J. F. Wolle, as the "Bach Choir," to learn the Mass in B Minor by John Sebastian Bach, had the first rehearsal of the new year in the church.[104]

J. Fred. had asked himself again and again why his attempt to teach the Mass to the Choral Union had failed. He realized he must devise a way to relieve the drudgery of learning this music with "its well nigh insuperable difficulties, and almost inaccessible height of artistic plan," just as his father had invented a way to relieve the drudgery of individually gluing paper bags. J. Fred. must teach the singers this new music in a new way. He was convinced the community singers were capable of singing the music, even though few had worked on such a demanding score before in America.

J. Fred. did devise a new, unique, and effective teaching method. He reasoned that the tedium the members of the Choral Union had experienced was because so much complex and unfamiliar music had to be learned before the group experienced the exciting climax of a movement. The climax was the moment when the music made the most sense, was the most impressive, and the most beautiful. J. Fred.'s nephew wrote that his uncle Fred "frequently told me with glee, 'I taught them the Mass backwards.'"[105] The group first learned the last four measures of a chorus. When they had mastered the ending, they sang the section with confidence and experienced a sense of fulfillment. J. Fred. then moved the singers a few measures back into related but unfamiliar territory. They worked on the new section but sang through to the end, always ending with music they already knew. Thus, J. Fred. conducted the rehearsals by adding new measures to the conclusion. Led this way even the first rehearsal filled the singers with a feeling of success and excitement. Within a short time large sections of music, with "well nigh insuperable difficulties," were mastered. In addition, the singers soon had the music memorized. The repetitions were never boring, because they contained familiar music.

J. Fred. had changed in another very basic way since he had conducted the Bethlehem Choral Union. After he broke his baton at the last rehearsal of that group, he used only his hands. His gestures became so subtle and refined everyone had to concentrate intensely on the smallest movement of his fingers. Thus, every moment of every rehearsal was absorbing. Ordinary existence ceased as the singers yielded their full concentration to J. Fred. They emerged from each rehearsal refreshed. Everyone was soon convinced, along with J. Fred., that John Bach was the greatest composer, and that the Mass in B Minor was his noblest composition. Singing the music was a deeply significant social and spiritual event. In addition, each individual was contributing his or her part to a momentous occasion.

After the choir had been in rehearsal for ten months, J. Fred. flamboyantly described the reaction of the singers to the rehearsals. He printed a public letter in the newspaper in which he wrote

> members of the choir . . . have braved the difficulties, and who, with keen artistic insight, doubtless ere this have had revealed to them unsuspected beauties in unlooked for places in this veritable masterpiece of unspeakable power and imperishable glory.[106]

J. Fred. expressed his belief that Bach was a composer for everyone, and that if anyone remained in the community who wanted to join the choir, there was still time to do so. He made an appeal for new members: The Bach Choir was to be "absolutely representative of the music resource of this community."[107] Yet, he reminded the readers, reaping the fruits of beauty came only with great effort. "Nothing short of complete surrender of the singers' time, industry and patience" was required.

J. Fred.'s confidence was obvious. He had designed a strategy for teaching nonprofessionals Bach's Mass and had a group that had been successfully rehearsing it for ten months. He had learned how to conduct using his hands alone and had convinced others that Bach's music was profoundly great and worth every effort required to make it sound beautiful.

The choir was ready, and on 27 March 1900 the American premiere of the complete Mass in B Minor took place in Central Moravian Church. The date, as planned, coincided as closely as possible with the anniversary of Bach's death. There were eighty-two in the chorus, five vocal soloists, with thirty-one in the orchestra. J. Fred. conducted from the organ. The Mass was performed in two sections: the "Kyrie" and "Credo" in the afternoon, the "Sanctus," "Benedictus," "Agnus Dei," and "Dona Nobis" in the evening. Each session was preceded by chorales played by the trombone choir.[108]

Programs from later Bach Festivals list the Novello edition as the one used in performances of the Mass. However, a full score published by Breitkopf and Härtel and signed by J. Fred. exists, which, according to tradition, was used in the premiere of the Mass. The score was given to the Bethlehem Bach Choir by J. Fred.'s daughter with other scores used in the early performances of The Bach Choir. Also, a set of instrumental parts published by Breitkopf and Härtel exists, again traditionally those used in the first performance of the Mass. Thus, it seems that the singers used vocal scores published by Novello, while J. Fred. and the orchestra played from music by the other publisher.[109]

The press prepared the public for the performance. Papers in Philadelphia carried a picture of J. Fred. with an article captioned "Bach Festival in Bethlehem." A Bethlehem paper included detailed, emotionally charged program notes drawn from Bach's first biography. Those who wanted to familiarize themselves with the music and who had already purchased tickets were invited to attend the Monday evening practice and a dress rehearsal at 9:00 A.M. the day of the performance.

Everyone involved with this premiere was aware of its importance. Though no one had heard the complete composition, all agreed that the Mass was a masterpiece. This performance was to be more than a local performance by a study group; it was the culmination of a series of performances of Bach's monumental works performed in Bethlehem and listed on the final page of the printed program. The local press assured the readers that this musical experience would be an extraordinary one.

> When we hear the mass performed under the conditions indispensable to our full comprehension of it we feel as though the genius of the last 2000 [200?] years were soaring over our heads. There is something unearthly in the solitary eminence which the B Minor Mass occupied in history.[110]

For a community with a history of outstanding musical achievements, the pastor called this one "the most notable musical event in the history of Bethlehem."[111]

Many people wanted to hear this performance, and an out-of-town critic informed his readers, "The seating capacity of the Moravian Church is fifteen hundred, and every seat was occupied."[112] The pastor continued his own report as he excitedly described the responses of both the audience and the press to the event.

> A great many persons were present from neighboring towns and from the large cities for the performance of this colossal master work created a real sensation. The city newspapers with scarcely an exception bestowed . . . enthusiastic praise on the splendid work of the big chorus which was made up of non-professional local talent.[113]

Beyond its historical importance, all the reporters agreed that the singing of the chorus was what made the event truly successful. The "voices are fresh, clear and vigorous . . . with variety of expression," showed "splendid training and spirit." In spite of the small size of the choir, it was "quite as effective as that of a much larger chorus."[114] The devotion of the members was singled out for praise. "The chorus singers, who for considerably more than a year have faithfully attended the rehearsals, braving every kind of weather. This shows a devotion to art of which any town may be proud."[115] While no writer attributed the competence of the choir directly to J. Fred., the choir's performance was an implicit compliment to him.

One critic felt the placement of the musicians at the back of the church with the audience seated in pews below them facing the front of the church contributed to the fact that everyone listened reverently throughout the performance. For the next festivals the pews were reversed so that they faced the choir. In the opinion of the church elders, the result was an irreverent spectacle, and the pews were never reversed again.

A local critic praised the performances of the local soloists. "It is very gratifying to say that an impartial estimate of the solo work must result in unreserved praise of our home talent." Others, praising those from out-of-town, wrote that the alto, Miss Katrin Hike from New York, "sang very beautifully," and the tenor, Mr. Nicholas Douty from Philadelphia, "was a delightful singer to listen to in sacred music."[116]

The response to the orchestra was mixed. Local reporters praised it, but one critic was not pleased at all with the way they played. "In the solo passages their shortcomings were very much in evidence," he wrote. As a result the vocal soloists were "greatly hampered by bad accompaniments." An anecdote told by a Lehigh University graduate verifies the musicians' wide range of capability.

> Such is his power of arousing enthusiasm among his friends that I know of one young man who started in just the Winter preceding that festival, on Mr. Wolle's urging, and without any previous instruction was able by the time the festival was held to play the 'cello in the orchestra, and to play it well, too.[117]

FIRST COMPLETE AMERICAN PRODUCTION.

# The Mass in B Minor,

COMPOSED BY

### John Sebastian Bach.

First public performance by

### The Bach Choir,

Mr. J. FRED. WOLLE, Organist and Conductor.

#### Soloists.

Miss KATHRIN HILKE, New York City, Soprano.
Miss LUCY A. BRICKENSTEIN, Bethlehem, Soprano.
Mrs. W. L. ESTES, South Bethlehem, Contralto.
Mr. NICHOLAS DOUTY, Philadelphia, Tenor.
Mr. ARTHUR BERESFORD, Boston, Bass.

Moravian Church,
Bethlehem, Pennsylvania,

TUESDAY, MARCH 27, 1900.

Afternoon, four o'clock.        Evening, eight o'clock.

Cover of the Mass in B Minor premiere program
(Archives of The Bach Choir of Bethlehem)

While there was no question that the chorus had received excellent training, one critic found J. Fred.'s conducting inadequate because of his "attempt... to play his instrument with one hand and conduct with the other." A local reporter found it admirable that J. Fred. conducted from the organ "as was customary in the good old days of Bach." While everyone agreed that the "successful rendition of Bach's Mass in B Minor is largely due to its conductor J. Frederic Wolle," one writer wrote exuberantly that J. Fred. "deserves the gratitude of his fellow townsmen for the aesthetic ideals and the National prominence he is giving to this community."[118]

The highest praise, especially from the local reviewers, was reserved for the Bethlehem community. The event was a local triumph, and the performance was clear evidence of the musical cultivation of the community – as it most certainly was. "There can be no doubt about the aesthetic and intellectual tone of a community where Bach's Mass in B Minor finds such enthusiastic appreciation and such artistic rendition." One reporter, reflecting that late nineteenth-century view that art was a more civilizing influence than industry, wrote that while Bethlehem's industrial achievements may be forgotten, "it will be remembered to the honor of Bethlehem that Bach's Mass in B Minor here received its first complete and successful American production."[119]

Every local report of the premiere described it as an important social occasion. Everyone who was important was at the performance, and each article listed the notables in attendance from out-of-town. Representatives of the New York Oratorio Society came, as well as Professor David Wood, J. Fred.'s organ teacher, and his wife. They were "guests of the festival" staying with the Wolles. Other visitors are mentioned from nearby communities.

A "side feature" of the festival was an exhibition of pictures by many famous artists displayed in the Chapel of the Young Ladies' Seminary near the Moravian Church.[120]

At a general meeting held soon after the first festival, the treasurer reported that the receipts were a bit over $1300. Since the expenses were only $800, the performance was indeed a financial success. The choir was also asked to perform the Mass in Philadelphia in the fall, but that performance never took place.

Of lasting importance was the desire of the members to continue rehearsing. Interestingly, future plans were "to produce other masterpieces of the world's best composers."[121] But performances by other composers remained the exception.[122]

The performance was not only the American premiere of the Mass, it was the first public performance by The Bach Choir. In addition, this was the beginning of many Bethlehem Bach Festivals that soon occupied complete weekends and which, with only three interruptions, continue to the present. Because it was the first of many performances by The Bach Choir, and the parent of numerous other national Bach choirs, this premiere played a major role in solidifying the Bach renaissance in America. It also thrust J. Fred. into a position of national musical prominence.

All the signs were right for J. Fred.'s next step. He had developed a stable group of singers willing to devote their time and energy to learn and to perform the monumental works of Bach. The singers had organized themselves to sing choral masterpieces and to give sharply defined festivals, not entertainments. The Bach Choir had Bach's most difficult composition nearly memorized, and the Mass in B Minor was a reliable centerpiece that could be revived each year. J. Fred. had perfected his conducting technique and had also learned that directing the ensemble and playing the organ at the same time did not work well. T. Edgar Shields, his assistant organist, was excellent, and J. Fred. decided to conduct the group from a podium in the future.

An announcement was placed in the local paper informing prospective singers of an application deadline for a continuing Bach Choir.[123] It is noteworthy that "studying the works of this great composer" is again given as the purpose of the choir. J. Fred. articulated a number of times that the only way to learn about music was by performing it.

# CREATING THE BACH CHOIR

The elders and members of the Moravian congregation had experienced the performance of the Mass as a religious service in their church with outsiders attending. Everyone had been reverent, and the elders believed a series of Bach Festivals could be religious occasions. In contrast to debates that were to occur in future years, the Board of Elders had no reason to refuse J. Fred.'s request for permission to use the church for another, longer, Bach Festival. J. Fred. and a choir from the Bethlehem community met all the necessary requirements for using the church for musical productions. The first Bach Festival was proof that everyone could successfully collaborate. There is not even a record of the elder's affirmative decision in the church diary.

The choir had made a profit selling tickets through the Moravian Bookstore and that did not offend the Moravian congregation. A longer festival would cost more, but apparently there was no great financial gamble. The premiere had made a profit. The community was now solidly behind J. Fred. They supported more Bach, because they felt such performances proved they were cultivated people. Bach performances, particularly when they were premieres, were a source of civic pride. They put Bethlehem on the map and reaffirmed a past that was rooted in musical excellence, a tradition many feared was disappearing until the festival proved otherwise.

In general, J. Fred. had earned the acclaim of music critics from Philadelphia and New York who encouraged people to travel to Bethlehem. Soon everyone realized that audiences of over a thousand people from beyond the Lehigh Valley would visit Bethlehem and remain for a number of days.

It is difficult to imagine a time when there were few opportunities to hear the large works of Bach. In 1900 a true Bach renaissance was in progress. Bach was new. Listening to his music made people feel cultivated. That Bethlehem was already the hub for the Lehigh Valley Rail Road, at that time one of the major railroads in the Northeast, was important. Bethlehem was easily accessible for people living in large metropolitan areas, and J. Fred. had the performance coincide with the train schedules. There were four fine hotels in town, and visitors to

Bethlehem agreed that the residents were friendly and provided many with places to stay in their homes.

The first Bethlehem Bach Festival was a success, and people eagerly awaited a chance to hear more Bach. With his new choir, The Bach Choir, J. Fred. began preparing for the Second Bach Festival.

## NOTES

1. From an unidentified clipping in a "Miscellaneous Scrapbook" in the Archives of the Bach Choir of Bethlehem.

2. The group is called The Bach Choir in the first program of the group's 1900 concert with the letter *t* capitalized. That is not necessarily the case in all documents, nor is the capitalization of the letter *t* consistent. This author used the original form of the title, except in quotations when it appears otherwise. Later, The Bach Choir was called the Bethlehem Bach Choir or The Bach Choir of Bethlehem.

3. "The Official Diary of the Congregation," 27 March 1900.

4. The Mass begins with a B minor chord, however, "A Mighty Fortress" normally ends on a D major chord. J. Fred. harmonized the final pitch of the chorale so that it would be the same as the one that begins the Mass.

5. "The Official Diary," 27 March 1900.

6. *Constitution and By-laws of the Bethlehem Choral Union Adopted September 1885* in the Archives of The Bach Choir of Bethlehem.

7. *The Daily Bethlehem Times*, 9 February 1886.

8. Ibid.

9. *Constitution and By-laws*, 8.

10. *The Daily Bethlehem Times*, 9 February 1886.

11. Ibid., 10 February 1886.

12. Ibid.

13. Ibid., 9 February 1886.

14. Ibid., 19 May 1886.

15. Ibid., 18 May 1886.

16. Ibid.

17. Ibid., 17 May 1886.

18. *The Daily Bethlehem Times*, 19 May 1886.

19. Ibid.

20. *The Moravian*, 18 May 1886.
21. Ibid., 30 June 1885.
22. Ibid., 8 September 1885.
23. "The Official Diary," 14 December 1886.
24. *The Daily Bethlehem Times*, 15 December 1886.
25. "The Official Diary ," 14 December 1886.
26. *The Daily Bethlehem Times*, 15 December 1886.
27. *The Moravian*, 22 December 1886.
28. Ibid.
29. *The Daily Bethlehem Times*, 2 May 1887.
30. Ibid.
31. *The Moravian*, 18 May 1887.
32. Ibid., 29 November 1887.
33. Ibid., 30 November 1887.
34. Ibid.
35. Ibid.
36. During J. Fred's lifetime, this work was called the "St. John Passion."
37. *The Moravian*, 30 May 1888.
38. Ibid.
39. *The Daily Bethlehem Times*, 1 June 1888.
40. Ibid., 6 June 1888.
41. Ibid.
42. Ibid., 4 June 1888.
43. Ibid.
44. Ibid.
45. Ibid.
46. Ibid.
47. Ibid.
48. "The Official Diary," 5 June 1888.
49. Program for "Messiah," in the Archives of The Bach Choir of Bethlehem..
50. *The Daily Bethlehem Times*, 19 December 1888.
51. *The Moravian*, 26 December 1888.
52. *The Daily Bethlehem Times*, 6 May 1889.
53. Ibid., 8 May 1889.
54. Ibid.
55. Ibid.
56. Ibid.

57. Ibid., 16 December 1889.
58. Ibid., 20 December 1889.
59. Ibid.
60. *The Moravian,* 19 February 1890.
61. *The Daily Bethlehem Times,* 8 April 1890.
62. Ibid.
63. "The Official Diary," 7 April 1890.
64. Ibid., 8 July 1890.
65. Ibid.
66. Ibid.
67. Raymond Walters, *The Bethlehem Bach Choir* (Boston: Houghton Mifflin Company, 1918), 42.
68. Ibid.
69. *The Daily Bethlehem Times,* 18 November 1890.
70. Ibid., 4 December 1891.
71. "The Official Diary," 4 April 1892.
72. Ibid., 8 April 1892.
73. *The Daily Bethlehem Times,* 8 April 1892.
74. Ibid.
75. Ibid.
76. Ibid.
77. Earl Johnson, ed., *First Performances in America to 1900* (Detroit, Michigan: College Music Society, 1979), 16–17.
78. James Robinson, "The Bach Choir in Bethlehem, Pa." n.d., pamphlet in the Archives of The Bach Choir of Bethlehem.
79. Raymond Walters, "Bach at Bethlehem, Pennsylvania," *The Musical Quarterly,* 21, no. 2 (April 1934): 185.
80. Francis Wolle, *A Moravian Heritage* (Boulder, Colo.: Empire Reproduction & Printing Company, 1972), 41.
81. Ibid.
82. Ibid.
83. *The North American,* 11 May 1903.
84. *The Daily Bethlehem Times,* 16 November 1892.
85. Ibid.
86. Ibid.
87. Ibid., 14 April 1893.
88. Ibid.
89. Ibid.

90. Ibid.
91. Ibid.
92. Walters, *Bach Choir*, 44.
93. "The Official Diary," 13 November 1893.
94. Ibid.
95. Ibid., 18 December 1894.
96. Ibid.
97. Ibid., 29 August 1894.
98. "The Official Diary," 18 December 1894.
99. *The Daily Bethlehem Times*, 18 December 1894.
100. Ibid.
101. Walters, *Bach Choir*, 45.
102. "Wolle Stands at Apex of the Bach Festival." Unidentified newspaper clipping written shortly after 26 May 1903. In the Archives of The Bach Choir of Bethlehem..
103. Copy of a photograph in the collection of the Archives of The Bach Choir of Bethlehem.
104. "The Official Diary," 1 and 9 January 1888.
105. Francis Wolle, *A Moravian Heritage*, 41.
106. Walters, *Bach Choir*, 47.
107. Ibid., 47.
108. Johnson, *First Performances*, 18–19.
109. The score and parts are in the Archives of The Bach Choir of Bethlehem.
110. "First Complete American Production." Printed program in the Archives of The Bach Choir of Bethlehem.
111. "The Official Diary," 27 March 1900.
112. "Bach's Mass in B Minor Sung at Bethlehem for the First Time In America. Special to the Ledger." Unidentified newspaper clipping in the Archives of The Bach Choir of Bethlehem.
113. Ibid.
114. All quotations from an unidentified newspaper clipping in the Archives of The Bach Choir of Bethlehem.
115. Ibid.
116. Ibid.
117. *The Daily Bethlehem Times*, 19 May 1902.
118. Ibid.
119. Each of these quotations is from an unidentified clipping in a "Miscellaneous Scrapbook" in the Archives of The Bach Choir of Bethlehem.

120. "The Official Diary," 9 May 1903.
121. Unidentified newspaper clipping in the Archives of The Bach Choir of Bethlehem.
122. Some of the exceptions are compact disks on which the choir sang a variety of Christmas carols and a concert celebrating the bicentennial of the founding of Bethlehem when they sang Haydn's *Creation*.
123. *The Daily Bethlehem Times,* 28 April 1900.

Chapter Nine

*Creating a Bach Festival*

Mr. Wolle is a genius. To think of undertaking such a great task in so small a town is wonderful.[1]

The only man in America who was able to give a Bach Festival, and that of three days.[2]

THERE WAS EVERY REASON for J. Fred. to think ambitiously again. The First Bach Festival had been a total success, and J. Fred. disclosed his plan for a Second Bach Festival to the choir. The festival would begin with the American premiere of Bach's complete *Christmas Oratorio* with one session in the afternoon and one in the evening. A premiere would attract Bach enthusiasts from many places, assuring a large audience. The many chorales in the work permitted the audience to sing along, and the first two parts of the oratorio were already known to many from the previous performance in Central Moravian Church. The *Passion According to St. Matthew* would be performed on the second day in two sessions. Much of the *Passion* was also familiar, though J. Fred. chose the soloists he had trained for the Mass to sing the recitatives. The Mass in B Minor would close the Second Bach Festival. It was already known to the musicians.

In addition to the practical considerations, the Second Bach Festival was to be a monumental musical celebration of the life of Christ beginning with His birth, describing His sacrifice and death, and concluding with the Mass, which continues His presence on earth. J. Fred.

left no doubt about his meaning. The souvenir program included a halftone drawing, "The Worship by the Magi," before the text of the *Christmas Oratorio*. A painting entitled "Crucifixion" preceded the text of the *St. Matthew Passion*, and the text of the Mass was introduced with a representation of Christ presenting the cup of wine to his disciples. This festival was music in the service of God, rooted in the deepest meaning and purpose of music in the Moravian Church. The dates selected were 23, 24, and 25 May 1901. After the festival the chorus gave J. Fred. a silver cup filled with roses, and he wrote in appreciation, "A cup was the symbol of the sacrifice of Him the story of Whose life the festival attempted to portray."[3]

The choir endorsed the plan, and rehearsals began in September of 1900. As the festival time approached, the pressure increased. "The Bach Choir is having frequent rehearsals in the church preparatory to the coming Festival," wrote the pastor.[4] These rehearsals generated so much excitement that people began attending them to listen. Two months before the festival the diarist recorded, "These practices are now attracting considerable audiences to the church each evening."[5] As the festival approached, "at intervals night and day," rehearsals were held simultaneously across the street in the Chapel of the Young Ladies' Seminary.[6] Ruth Doster assisted J. Fred. by "encouraging the singers and helping to drill them by sections & groups."[7] Finally, with a sense of excitement on the part of everyone "the great musical event long looked forward to was realized – the opening of the three day Bach Festival."[8]

The chorus had grown to one hundred and ten voices. One hundred boys' voices were added for the *Passion*. The boys led the congregation in the chorales. Their voices also set off the chorales from other movements of the composition. There were twelve vocal soloists; three times the number in the First Bach Festival. The women wore white for the oratorio and black for the *Passion* and the Mass. The men wore black suits and the boys white surplices.

The orchestra had doubled to include sixty musicians. The oboe d'amore, an "ancient" instrument called for by Bach, had been added.

Two instruments had been built for Frank Damrosch, conductor of the New York Oratorio Society, who used them in a performance of the *St. Matthew Passion* a few months before. However, the orchestra included English horns not called for by Bach and clarinets added by Franz, the nineteenth-century editor. J. Fred. had also rewritten Bach's trumpet parts because the range was too high for his players. Still, a critic complained that the first trumpet was flat and suggested that J. Fred. alter the part still further. Beginning with this festival J. Fred was no longer at the organ. It was played by T. Edgar Shields, his church assistant. J. Fred., standing free, conducted the chorus, the orchestra, and the soloists. He accompanied the recitatives at a Steinway piano.

The trombone choir played related chorales from the church steeple before each session. But they did not connect with the beginning of the Mass for this performance was played in "international pitch," and the trombones were tuned too high.[9]

Most of the pews in the center section of the sanctuary faced the gallery, putting the performers in view of the audience. The cost of these seats was $3.00 for each day, or $7.20 for the complete festival. While reversing the pews was not a problem for this festival, in later ones it became controversial. Chairs were placed on a special platform below the pulpit, also a later source of controversy.

The two most prominent East Coast music critics were seated side by side just below the pulpit. A member of the audience quipped, "There's Krehbiel, the critic of the New York Tribune, and Henderson, critic of the Times; Krehbiel is the greatest critic in the world, and Henderson is next to him."[10] Their presence indicated the festival had become national news. Krehbiel made that clear when he announced the event to his readers.

> The mere announcement that a Bach festival of three days' duration is to take place at Bethlehem, Penn. . . . had concentrated the interest of all lovers of choral music, East and West, upon the venturesome musical folk who projected the enterprise and the beautiful town they inhabit. . . . Bethlehem ignored by the writers of history hitherto, seems determined to write its name in the scrolls in letters so large

that even the wayfaring man who travels by railway express may read.[11]

For the moment the reality of such a festival in America was notable in itself and worthy of the highest praise.

There was another critic at the festival whose influence went far beyond New York and Philadelphia. His words were carried directly from Bethlehem to Leipzig where Bach had lived for many years. From there they were circulated to all interested Europeans. He was Professor Stanley, chairman of the Department of Music of the University of Michigan and the American reporter for the *Zeitschrift der International Musikgesellshrift Leipzig*. Stanley remarked on the spirit of goodwill that pervaded the festival. According to him those in attendance were relieved to find a situation free of a cult of personality. Bach's "masterpieces" were the focus. He wrote

> A pleasant feature of the festival was the sympathetic and appreciative manner in which all spoke of Mr. Wolle and the hesitation with which any such [negative] remarks were made. It was inspiring to see so many prominent musicians from all parts of the country gathered together to renew their fealty to the master and to revel in the sublime harmonies of his great masterpieces.[12]

On 23 May 1901 Krehbiel, Henderson, and Stanley waited with everyone else for the festival to begin. What were their reactions to Wolle and his Bach Choir? Their readers were eager to know.

Krehbiel saw J. Fred. as the moving force of the festival, but one who relied upon the work of others, and drew on the Bethlehem Moravian music tradition. Using the May season as a metaphor, he told his readers

> The zeal of Bach, which blossomed so beautifully this week, was the inspiration of Mr. Wolle, though the traditions of a century and a half underlie the last days' achievements. To Mr. Wolle in the first instance, therefore, is due the success of the festival; in the next it is due

to the zeal of the choir which he has nourished and stimulated till it had become akin to an artistic rapture, and finally, a share is due to the handsome encouragement given to the enterprise by the music loving people of Bethlehem.[13]

With great respect for the chorus, Krehbiel described how its performance of the *Passion* affected him so powerfully.

There were moments when the dramatic climaxes were reached when they struck like a thunderbolt, and always kept the critical listener amazed by the promptness of their attack, their easy mastery of the music and the wonderful clearness with which they presented the ... choral fabric. .... It is doubtful whether any previous performance in America was comparable with it – certainly none I have heard.[14]

Henderson expressed his reaction to J. Fred. in very personal terms, telling his readers, "he is a powerful and important musical force. His scholarship is solid, his skill as a leader admirable, and his magnetism unquestionable."[15] The critic spoke of J. Fred.'s achievement with the choir by describing the effect their singing of the Mass had upon the audience.

... what will dwell in the memory of every visitor is . . . the wonderful achievement of the chorus. .... Such choral singing is indeed rare, and to hear it is a privilege. Bach never wrote anything more glorious than the "Sanctus" of the Mass, and if he could have heard it sung as it was on Saturday, it would have brought tears to his eyes. It was a performance in which the sublimity of the music was perfectly disclosed. It is impossible to say more than that.[16]

Professor Stanley sent a long review titled "Aftermath of the Bach Festival" to Germany. He noted the deficient orchestra, the unschooled soloists, questioned J. Fred.'s practice of slowing down at every cadence, and his inconsistent and incorrect execution of musical ornaments. Stanley singled out the brass as particularly problematic. The trumpets and horn "failed to produce anything but a feeling of trepidation." He noted that J. Fred. had already rewritten these parts, but in a time when Bach interpretation was much more fluid than now, he suggested that "further revision would seem necessary if they [the brass] are to be efficient."[17] Most of the solo work was "in no sense adequate." How-ever, all these faults were excused because there was so little oppor-tunity in America to learn how to sing Bach. Stanley still wrote about J. Fred. in a reverential tone.

> Unlimited praise, and expressions of the highest respect and gratitude were heard on all sides for the man who by his sacrifice, enthusiasm and indomitable will brought this festival into being.[18]

Stanley continued

> The performances as a whole were so masterly, so full of reverence, so infused with the instinct of life, that these criticisms were offered with hesitation and would not have been made at all were it not for the fact that they sink into insignificance when compared with the trans-cendent merits of these productions.[19]

Other critics also felt the need to apologize for pointing out any nega-tive aspects of the festival.

The reaction of the audience and The Bach Choir to the festival was described by another critic writing of feeling exultant emotions.

> . . . the audience that had refrained from applause for three days, broke out into enthusiastic hand clapping just as the choir freed from all vocal labors, began to shower Mr. Wolle with flowers and the festival was over.[20]

The pastor concluded a lengthy diary entry with a practical com-ment, "A hired company of men and boys set to work immediately after the close of the final performance to get the church into readiness for Sunday. Everything was gotten into perfect order and the church locked at 3:30 A. M."[21]

In spite of all of the success, J. Fred.'s interpretation of Bach raised issues that were not readily dismissed. The critics concurred that the festival was not without flaws. The orchestra particularly was below standard. They questioned that a group of nonprofessionals was equal to the task of singing Bach solos.

Two interpretative practices were discussed that put J. Fred.'s scholarship into question. First, there was the excessive slowing of tempo at "every" cadence. Constant ritards were "monotonous" and "trying to modern sensibilities." What authority did J. Fred. have for this practice? The second issue had to do with improper use of musical ornaments.[22] Again, what was J. Fred.'s authority? Were these practices to become a "Bethlehem performance tradition?" If so, "Mr. Wolle may have to quarrel with other musicians," wrote Krehbiel.[23] They all found performing Bach with all of the repeats "exhausting." The critics had fulfilled their responsibility to their readers by defining the critical playing field. If J. Fred. intended to enter the game seriously on a national and international level, he would have to respond to their critiques. To develop an accurate performance practice, J. Fred. must rethink the prominence and persistence of musical ritards, inaccurate ornaments, and raise the standard of the orchestra and the soloists. While these issues were raised again with much greater insistence in future festivals, for the moment they were muted by success and novelty. After reflecting on his encounter with J. Fred.'s enterprise, Krehbiel wrote to his readers, "In dignity, beauty and seriousness of purpose and in devotion to a lofty ideal the project is without a follower in the history of music in this country."[24]

In the end the Bethlehem Bach Festivals were worth the attention of serious Bach lovers everywhere. J. Fred. was making a notable contribution to the Bach renaissance that was in full swing throughout the western world. Everyone awaited the next festival; a festival the three critics assured their readers would be worth attending.

Although spiritually elated by the success of the festival, J. Fred. was drained emotionally, and he and his family went to visit with his sister

Helen in Philadelphia. When the Wolles returned to Bethlehem, the choir made a spectacular gesture of love and thanks to their conductor. His house – now called Bach's Home – was filled with flowers and ferns, and a silver bowl filled with roses was placed on J. Fred.'s desk. He was overwhelmed. A letter expressing his appreciation was sent to every choir member. It survived as a rare devoted expression of J. Fred.'s effusive, poetic nature, always devoted to high purpose; these qualities endeared him to everyone. He began the letter like a parent.

June 15th, 1901

To My Bach Choir:

Can you adequately appreciate the overwhelming sensations of a man, who, after long years of waiting and many a heart-ache, finds himself on the threshold of unfolding plans; co-workers and friends upholding him with unexampled fortitude and enthusiasm, his every wish fulfilled, and finally crushed with inexpressible kindness?

Last Tuesday I returned to my home to find it fragrant with flowers and festooned with ferns. Huge bunches of American Beauties filled big vases. On my desk, your loving-cup. Language pales before the generous deeds of the past weeks. There are some deep emotions which words cannot convey. Your unprecedented adherence to the noble purpose during the years of drudgery, the triumphant results which your individuality and personality made possible, have received eloquent recognition and unstinted praise from the highest authorities in the land. In attempting to prove my unspeakable appreciation of all this, I can but go the more deeply into the study of our beloved Bach. The flowers are withering, but the cup conserves unfading memories. The sharp thorns of bitter disappointment are forgot in the bloom of the rose. A cup was the symbol of the sacrifice of Him the story of Whose life the festival attempted to portray. The loving-cup tells of the devotion, of the self-abnegation, of the sacrifices of heroic men and women to the highest ideal, and to an endeavor to express in substantial form their admiration and love for, not a weak interpreter, but a master genius before whose transcendent power we all must bow in reverence. In deep affection for my Bach Choir, I sign myself [signature] and in the years to come if from any cause we should be separated as fellow-students of a wondrous art, I still would sing, paraphrasing the words of Goldsmith,

*Where'er I roam, whatever realms to see,*
*My heart untravelled fondly turns to thee;*
*Still to my Bach Choir turns with ceaseless pain,*
*And drags of each remove a length'ning chain.*[25]

In September J. Fred. proposed his plan for a Third Bach Festival to the choir and rehearsals began. In October the Moravian Board of Elders discussed the choir's request to use the church.

The festival would last six days beginning on Monday evening and ending the following Saturday evening. The liturgical design of the Second Bach Festival would continue. "Director Wolle desires it to be understood that the object in view is to portray the three great events in the Life of Christ, His Birth, His Crucifixion and His Resurrection."[26] The festival would have two segments. The works sung in the Second Bach Festival would be repeated: *Christmas Oratorio* on Tuesday, the *Passion According to St. Matthew* on Thursday, and the Mass in B Minor on Saturday. They expressed the events in Christ's life. Performances of appropriate cantatas would precede these major works as a musical and spiritual preparation for the listeners. Monday "Sleepers wake, for night is flying," BWV 140 and "Magnificat" BWV 243 would be sung.[27] They prepare the listener for contemplating Christ's birth. "Sleepers wake" rouses everyone to a state of spiritual alertness, and "Magnificat" portrays the announcement to Mary that she would be the Mother of Christ. Both cantatas had been sung only once or twice before in America.[28] The *Passion According to St. Matthew* would be preceded by two solo cantatas contemplating the Crucifixion. J. Fred. planned "Strike, oh, strike," BWV 53 and "Gladly with my cross staff," BWV 29. In addition, the orchestra would play the Second Brandenburg Concerto, BWV 1047. The Friday evening before the Mass, the Easter cantatas, "The Heavens Laugh," BWV 31, and "God goeth up with shouting," BWV 43, composed by Bach for Ascension Day, would be sung. The cantatas were all sung in English with translations from the German by J. Fred. While the cantatas would be in the evening, the major works would be performed in two sessions during the day.

J. Fred. chose local soloists and instrumentalists from the newly formed Philadelphia Orchestra would supplement the local ensemble. The plan the Moravian Board of Elders received also included a request to turn most of the pews to face the choir gallery with permission to add seats below the pulpit on an extended platform. Tickets would not be sold at the church.

According to the pastor's account, there was "considerable discussion" by the elders. Some "opposed the use of the church for such purposes under any circumstances, others favored granting the request under certain stipulations."[29] The general board reached no agreement, an indication of the strength of the negative sentiment against the extended festival. A committee was appointed to settle the matter and to report back in two months. At the December meeting the elders gave permission for The Bach Choir to use the church for an extended festival "under very rigid conditions" not mentioned by the pastor in his diary entry.[30]

Probably because the elders did not grant permission for the use of the church until December, no festival was held in 1902. Six months was not enough time to rehearse all of the new music necessary for an extended festival. The new dates, 11 May to 16 May, were set, and they were announced in *The New York Sun* with the statement "the organist and the authorities of the church fell into dispute and other difficulties arose. Again this year [1903] it was doubtful there would be a festival."[31] Though the elders granted permission to use the church, they continued to discuss up until the festival whether or not to allow the pews to be moved. At the last moment they granted permission to have the first fifteen center pews face the choir gallery.

J. Fred. personally invited the leading music critics to attend, and Krehbiel of *The New York Tribune* and Henderson of *The New York Sun* accepted along with other notables. Dr. and Mrs. David Wood, J. Fred.'s organ teacher and his wife, were the Wolles' guests. A request was made for housing in private homes for four hundred out-of-town visitors, and local hotels were booked solid for the week.

As the festival approached, the number of rehearsals was increased to twice a week. Soon, everyone was rehearsing daily. In addition to the rehearsals in the church and the Women's Seminary, "there are private rehearsals of small groups of the Bach Singers at private homes."[32]

Too many conflicting expectations surrounded this festival. While it began with the most noble aims, and the participants were eager for its success, the conflicts that ensued were probably inevitable.

The Moravian congregation, represented by the Board of Elders and the pastor, thought they were permitting the church to be used for musical religious services, not for concerts or for musical spectacles. They viewed the festival as a part of the church's mission to outsiders. Those who attended were expected to act reverently and dress conservatively. It was assumed music lovers were coming to a church – not to a concert hall. The elders trusted The Bach Choir, particularly the choir's executive committee, to abide by the stipulations for the use of the church. Also, a service using local musicians was hoped for.

J. Fred.'s desire was for a festival to portray the three great events in Christ's life as expressed in the music of Bach, who in J. Fred.'s mind was the greatest universal composer and musician. Yet, he did have a goal that was not purely spiritual. J. Fred. was realizing a deep-seated desire to conduct Bach's works and to convey their spiritual message. But he was also working very hard to do so in a highly critical arena. He had invited the "best critics in the world" to the festival. He hoped for and probably expected their approval. At the very least, he was already assured they would express what they thought of his work. J. Fred. was a seasoned musician who had watched his father's reputation as a biologist develop based on the system of critique by other biologists.

The Bach Choir existed because the singers loved the experience of singing Bach under the direction of J. Fred. They loved their conductor unconditionally. It was probably not so much that they thought J. Fred. was beyond criticism, but that no one thought of criticizing him. "'The king can do no wrong,' is the song of the chorus – of the orchestra. And Mr. Wolle is king."[33] Also, the local press had told the choir they were doing an important civic duty by putting Bethlehem on the map. Thus, the choir members were proud to promote Bethlehem as a cultivated center of music.

Local music lovers wanted to hear Bach's music but they also felt a sense of pride. One citizen wrote to the editor of a local paper, "the general conclusion is that there is a taste for higher music in Bethlehem, more, perhaps, than in any other community for its size."[34] Like the members of the choir, music lovers from the Bethlehems were putting their community on the map by supporting the festivals.

Music lovers visiting Bethlehem were seeking a rare opportunity to join with others to listen to Bach in a religious setting. Approximately five hundred came to Bethlehem for the week to hear the performances they had been told about by the most prominent music critics in America.

Everyone at the festival was responding to an exciting new musical development, the Bach renaissance that had been launched by Felix Mendelssohn's 1829 performances in Berlin and Leipzig of Bach's *Passion According to St. Matthew*. Performances of other works followed, including the one J. Fred. heard in Munich when the 200th anniversary of Bach's birth was celebrated. In America Bach performances conducted by J. Fred. set the pace. He was the leader of the "Bach cult."

Because of the triumphs of J. Fred. and The Bach Choir, famous metropolitan music critics arrived in Bethlehem with a national agenda for the choir and with educated ears to critique the performances. H. E. Krehbiel's agenda was the most clearly defined and comprehensive. He articulated his idea in a lengthy piece written after he returned home and reflected on the events he had experienced in Bethlehem. Though he eloquently expressed his "dream" after the festival, Krehbiel arrived in Bethlehem with it already well in mind. This dream colored his responses to every musical and social event he experienced during the festival. He began his article, "Reflections on the Bach Festival," stating

> For three years past I have dreamed a beautiful dream whenever the thought of Bethlehem and its Bach festival presented itself to my mind. It was a dream of the establishment of a center of Bach culture in Bethlehem . . . which should set a standard for concert room and church, to which singers should repair to learn the correct manner of singing the old music, and musicians to hear authoritative readings. If Bach is to become a really living work for the people of today such a "Stylbildungschule" as Wagner wished to see established for his art is a necessity.[35]

Part of Krehbiel's grand plan was already possible as a result of the nature of Bethlehem and its tradition of Moravian music. He granted that Bethlehem was possibly already "set apart as the fountainhead of a cult, gentle, rare, elevated and pure, protected from the common place, selfishness, scant and pretense by the festival's gracious surroundings."[36] Yet, there was an additional musical requirement for Krehbiel's dream to become a reality. That was "such a measure of excellence in the performances as to set a standard for future readings of Bach's works."[37] While no other critic articulated this vision so dramatically and poetically, each held similar expectations. Furthermore, they shared their ideas in conversations with one another during the festival.

These critics had helped to promote the festival by approving the enterprise. They had also raised certain questions of quality and interpretation, and they were in Bethlehem partly to hear if J. Fred. had heeded their critiques as well as to inform their readers if the future Bach Festivals would be worth attending.

As each critic arrived, left the train, and walked across the covered bridge to the site of the festival, none knew the violent debate that would ensue. Each assumed everyone was eager to hear exactly what was required to make Bethlehem a Bach center. After all, each critic had received a special invitation to the festival and had been given a rail pass to Bethlehem. For them this festival was not a religious service offered to them by the Moravian Church, it was a series of concerts primarily for metropolitan music lovers who traveled to Bethlehem, possibly the national and international Bach school of American performances practice. That the festival was taking place in religious surroundings as Bach had intended was a wonderful bonus.

The question the visitors asked was "Would Bethlehem become the American Bayreuth?" This idea was first suggested by Henderson when he wrote

> As at Bayreuth, the interval for dinner refreshed the spirit as well as the body. The scenes around the church and in the street also reminded one of the shrine of Wagnerism. People came and went bare headed and stood in social groups to hear the trombones in the belfry play the chorale summon to the performance.[38]

Bethlehem was also called an American Oberammergau. Everyone in that town participated in a religious drama there like residents of Bethlehem were a part of the Bach festivals. Thus, both Bayreuth and Oberammergau became associated with Bethlehem. Along with these surface similarities was the deeper issue of The Bach Choir becoming a model of excellence by the effort of a whole community focused on performances of the music of Bach, the West's greatest composer.

### Monday Evening: Opening Night

Groups of festival-goers clustered around the Moravian Church listening to the trombone choir announce the beginning of the Third Bach Festival. When the chorales were ended, ticket holders moved into the church and took their seats. For those without tickets, a critic observed, "Tonight it seemed as if half of the young people of the town must have assembled around the church to hear the music without charge."[39]

"The long anticipated Bach Festival opened with the cantatas 'Sleepers, Wake! for Night is Flying,' and 'Magnificat'," wrote the pastor.⁴⁰ The music critics and other musically schooled listeners sat with their musical scores matching Bach's notes with the sounds J. Fred.'s ensemble produced.

Following the performance the critics telegraphed reviews to their newspapers. By the next morning their reactions to Monday evening's performances were public knowledge. It was clear to everyone that different groups had very different expectations, and those expectations were in conflict. By midweek Bethlehem was reeling. Angry debates became commonplace.

Krehbiel fired the first salvo. "There is only one thing wanting to make the Bethlehem Bach Festival ideally beautiful, and that is perfection of performance."⁴¹ Two years ago "it appeared reasonable to expect . . . that the period of preparation for the third festival would be devoted largely to making the performances as unique in character as the programs." Why had there been no improvement in the performances from the last festival? After all, The Bach Choir was willing to rehearse "twice, thrice, even six times a week," and most of the music at the festival was already known to the choir. Wasn't it reasonable to expect that they "might have had a little more distinctive character than has been disclosed up to the present time?" Visitors "who had come from distant places, attracted by the fame achieved by Mr. Wolle and his singers" had a right to expect a better performance than the one they had heard on opening night.

Many people came great distances on the recommendation of these critics. Now, contrary to what they were led to expect, the first performance was far from excellent. Everyone had a right to expect more than just a unique idea. It was Wolle's fault for not spending the rehearsal time wisely. In any case the devotion of the chorus could not be faulted, but was Wolle capable of making anything truly great from that devotion?

Henderson fired the second salvo. "It is not possible to indulge more than moderate praise of tonight's concert. The beauties of 'Sleepers Wake' were interpreted very imperfectly."⁴² The tenors made a "false entrance," attacks were generally uncertain and not together, and in several sections the full chorus "had bad moments." Henderson expressed openly what other critics sensed. "It seemed as if everyone were suffering from nervousness, the conductor most of all." He offered an excuse. Why not be nervous? The audience was filled with "musical prominence," with musicians holding scores in full view of the performers. However, to Henderson's ears, while there was not evident growth from the last festival, "This concert fairly maintained the singular excellence of the Bethlehem festivals." In the end he forgave Wolle, because he had provided the "musically elect" with an opportunity "to hear works of wonderful beauty;" an opportunity that was rare in America. "It was worth the longest journey by any visitor to hear the 'Misericordia' in the Magnificat."

Unlike Krehbiel, Henderson for the moment was willing to trade excellence for an opportunity to hear performances of Bach's choral music. Therefore, his readers received a more mild critique. They could take consolation in the realization that Bethlehem was no "less favored" than other towns in lacking tenors that were "sufficient," though the basses "have an immense vigor and energy."[43] Readers were informed that even though Wolle had rewritten the trumpet parts for performance on modern instruments, Bach's notes were too high, and the players still had difficulty playing them. However, every conductor had that problem with Bach. It was not Wolle's fault that modern instruments were not designed to play Bach's music.

The Moravian pastor also reacted to the first evening. He wrote that the attendance was "rather small" in comparison to other festivals. Because of the high cost involved in hiring outside musicians, the congregation worried that expenses would not be met. Should church money finance concerts? These thoughts expressed the official concerns regarding the "position of the regular service of the church." Also, "the chorale did not engage the effort of the audience to the degree that will doubtless be the case later."[44]

## Tuesday Afternoon and Evening: the Second Day

Everyone was talking. The critics defended their views among themselves and were busy saving face before members of the "musically elect." Some townspeople were already thinking, "If you don't like it here, then leave," although that sentiment was not directly expressed until Thursday. People assembled around Central Moravian Church in the afternoon and heard the trombone choir announce Bach's *Christmas Oratorio*. But, there was a difference. Everyone had read the reviews of Monday's performance. Bethlehem was no longer innocent. That had been destroyed by the metropolitan music critics, however inadvertently. Also, the Moravians noticed that some women were wearing high heels and fancy hats, and some were in evening dress. That was not the way Moravians dressed when they attended church. A sacred service was not a fashion show. To make matters worse, a number of the church ushers were sick, so young men from Moravian College were called in to seat the people. The seating did not go smoothly. The students did not show "adequate authority." Before the music began, people were noisy and talked as they did in a concert hall. No one was present with the authority to keep them silent. Finally, chairs had been placed in the pulpit area because of the demand for more seating. The elders had expressly forbidden seating there. Members of the congregation asked, "Who in The Bach Choir Executive Committee was going against the expressed desires of the Church?" When the audience faced the choir gallery, they thought about the performers and forgot about the music. The critics had turned services into concerts, and then, reversing the pews and the modish dress had turned concerts into spectacles.

After the oratorio was concluded, the critics telegraphed their reviews to their respective newspapers. Wednesday morning their readers were confronted with critical reactions that were more intensely negative than the ones they had read the previous day. Now no excuses were granted, and Henderson entered the fray. He spoke for all the critics when he informed his readers most emphatically, "Mr. Wolle has raised doubts among his admirers by some of his readings."[45]

In his Tuesday review, Henderson intensified his reaction. Now the choral tones were "often undeniably bad."[46] The tenors sounded "vulgar." The basses "groveled like beasts." Even though the sopranos and altos were acceptable, their singing was "too ragged." Unlike previous festivals, when the choir was "uplifting and vivifying," the group now sounded overtrained, and "every person in the church" felt that the "devotional spirits" that pervaded other festivals were gone. "Something has come over the spirit of the dream of Bach in this lovely town," Henderson continued. What has caused this change? he asked. "Two causes may be assigned for this in so far as the concerts themselves are concerned." The first cause was the orchestra and the second was "Mr. Wolle."

Already on Monday evening the "visitors" and a few members of the orchestra agreed that the orchestra should "have been placed under the ban of excommunication." It was "suggestive of the orchestra class in a suburban conservatory." Henderson lost all sense of turn-of-the-century decorum.

> The intonation of the orchestra is something not to be imagined. The man who has come here with music in his soul and expected to be moved by concords of sweet sounds suffers the pangs of bitter disillusionment when he hears this aggregation of instrumentalists discussing discord in almost as many tonalities as there are departments in the orchestra.

Seeking the cause for the failure of the first-day festival, Krehbiel had blamed J. Fred. Henderson was very specific. "He is decidedly overstrained, and his nerves are in no state to stand the trial of leading the uncertain footsteps of the little boat through the mass of Bach's polyphony." What had been an excellent choir in previous festivals was now a "little boat." The performances had become "uncertain footsteps."

There were faults with this festival that were more profound than J. Fred.'s momentary nervousness. They had to do with his musical scholarship. "Mr. Wolle adheres to ideas which give rise to disputes," Henderson stated. The ideas were regarding J. Fred.'s execution of Bach's musical ornaments, and the pace of the rhythm of Bach's music. Henderson was never more direct than in this critique of J. Fred.'s conducting.

> He excites the ire of some music lovers in his treatment of grace notes in vocal parts, and he persists in his heavy ritartandi on all cadences. But what is most serious of all is his omission of strict attention to matters of tempo and expression. An andante becomes a largo when the trumpet parts are difficult, and an adagio is shipwrecked in the allegro when it occurs in a chorale.

These were very harsh words, that J. Fred. made the music easier for the orchestra by slowing the tempo. That went beyond differences in scholarly views of interpretation.

Not only were there problems within the walls of the church; the actions of the townspeople offended Henderson. Some jokester had registered Bach as a guest in two of the hotels, and after the concert the critic was confronted by newsboys crying "Bethlehem paper – all about Bach." He thought he had left them behind in the city. What was happening to his dream of perfection? Still, "on the whole," Tuesday's "concert [was] emphatically better" than Monday's. There was hope things would get better.

Similar views were shared by each of the metropolitan critics. But, they asked, given the circumstances, how could they expect perfection? "In other words the general opinion is that Mr. Wolle has attempted too much with the forces he is able to muster."[47]

Reviewing the day's events, Krehbiel asked, "What had happened to the spirit of Bethlehem." Where was the sense of reverence that had set the Bach Festivals so apart from a city concert? First the performances had not improved, but at least the setting had been appropriate – now that had deteriorated as well. Even the critic noted that some people dressed as if they were attending a New York opening, and townspeople he had spoken with earlier in the day thought a musical critique was a personal attack on a performer, namely on "their" Mr. Wolle.

The pastor commented again upon the numbers attending and the singing of the chorales. All the seats were not taken, but there was "abounded response" when the "audience" sang. He expressed for the first time reactions that by Wednesday were frequently heard from other members of the congregations and residents of the town. The pastor regretted the loss of reverence. However, he held neither the orchestra nor "Mr. Wolle" responsible. The main causes were the critics and the visitors to the church. "The city papers have begun, through their representatives here, to make some pretty sharp criticisms."[48] These "technical criticisms" created the impression that the "Festival is a performance, and not a religious service." The critics caused the audience to take the sessions less seriously, particularly the playing of the trombone choir. Inside the church the "infusion of strangers" who were ignorant of the manner in which Moravians act in church had "swept away to a large extent the quiet demeanor we teach in connection with all the gatherings in God's house." The pastor admitted that there were too few sacristans, due to illness. "Certain observers" believed that turning the pews to face the choir gallery "touched [the sessions] with the idea of a 'spectacle'."

Few were happy as the festival approached midweek.

### Wednesday Evening: the Third Day

There was no afternoon performance, which caused one critic to note, "Today has been one of leisure for the visitors and one of hard work for the performers."[49] While festival-goers conversed or relaxed, J. Fred. drilled the orchestra and the singers. He made no published response to the debate that raged about him, however, these rehearsals were a clear indication that he was aware of what was going on, and that he was concerned.

Mr. Wolle and his orchestra spent the entire day in the church devoting the morning in rehearsing the concerto, and the two cantatas. . . . He was evidently striving for more contrast in tonal effect and made the players go over and over the passages in which he wanted shading to be especially effective.[50]

The piece played by the orchestra that evening, the Second Brandenburg Concerto, had been performed in New York earlier in the year by the Boston Symphony Orchestra. The critics came to Bethlehem with that performance in their ears. However, "nobody expected Bethlehem to furnish a rival to the Boston Symphony Orchestra and beyond a doubt they did not . . . but many who had bewailed the inadequate playing of the orchestra were doubtless agreeably surprised that it accomplished so much with the work."[51] At a time when all Bach instrumental works were edited, the critic wondered why "Mr. Wolle, who is a purist in all that is related to Bach's music" would have used an edition that bore so little resemblance to Bach's original. The keyboard was eliminated and the trumpet played an octave lower than Bach's original. However, the "beautiful performance" of the final chorale in the cantata was "profoundly impressive" so that "Mr. Wolle should be forgiven many things."

For the first time the Bethlehem community was addressed in the critiques.

> . . . the fact that Bethlehem two years ago was astonished to find the outside world taking such an interest in its musical doings, and it is lost in amazement at the presumption of that world in coming in and pretending to discover that all is not just as it should be.[52]

The critics resented the way their "technical criticism" was received. Comments like this in the national press ignited the final flame in the already heated debate that was taking place everywhere in town, and that evening in his diary the pastor responded with anger.

The metropolitan newspaper critics continue to be very severe, particularly upon the single performers. But an indignant reaction has begun to set in against this spirit of criticism, and many murmurings are heard against those who have been robbing the Festival of its devotional aspect and making it a bid for public musical approval.[53]

The "many murmurings" soon erupted in print. Bethlehem residents went to press themselves, and *The Bethlehem Times* printed a number of letters to the editor that were critical of the critics.

Thursday Afternoon and Evening: the Fourth Day

In the morning the newsboys shouted, "Bethlehem paper – all about Bach critics." Now the offended party, the Bethlehem community, had its say.

> To the Editor of the Times, Would it not be wise and courteous and eminently more judicious to call the attention of Mr. Wolle personally to any shortcomings, without rushing into print? . . . I thank God I am enabled to hear Bach in such placid historical surroundings and that Mr. Wolle will repeat the same program . . . when we will only be too glad to gratefully listen to his imperfect renditions again.[54]

Another reader attempted an impartial view and pointed out the positive results from the negative critiques. Here are a number of sentences from a letter that occupied a full column of print. After agreeing with the critic of the *New York Stats Zeitung* regarding the orchestra, the reader wrote

> The unfortunate conditions under which Mr. Wolle worked during the last few months are unknown to most people, and to those who know he is certainly considered a genius. However, the critics make no allowance. The lack of practice of the orchestra was probably more undesirable to Mr. Wolle than anyone else, and the nervous strain under the conditions to which he was subjected by the various acci-

# CREATING A BACH FESTIVAL 259

> dents which he must tolerate would render any other than a master of the art totally unfit for further work.

> Taken all in all, there is no question but that the criticisms have aroused the choir, orchestra and soloists to do their very best and instead of it being a secondary production, the severe criticisms have placed it unwillingly or unconsciously in the very first class.[55]

There was sarcastic praise for the critics in another letter. "Mr. Editor, we owe much to the critics, who have . . . made us proud of the great Bach choir."[56]

The debate in the press was not without humor. A professor cleverly made a wordplay on Bach's name, which means spring or steam in the German language.

> Sir. The bacteriologists have condemned the spring and also found microbes in the river. During the past week certain music bacteriologists have discovered that even the Bethlehem Musical Brooke "Bach in German" is polluted with the germ "Bacillius Prodigiosus Professor"[57]

### Thursday Afternoon and Evening: the Fourth Day

Thursday left little leisure for those who had come for the entire festival and many newcomers arrived for the *St. Matthew* performance. J. Fred. spent his time dealing with an emergency. The tenor engaged to sing the Evangelist was taken ill. The tenor soloist on Tuesday took his place. Even though it was the most difficult part in the work, he learned the role in two days. He and J. Fred. worked every moment between other performances rehearsing to save the *"Passion."* With the festival "nearing its climax," J. Fred.'s energy and concentration were surely taxed to the utmost. For the first time during the week, the church was full.

Krehbiel's critique indicated that the festival had taken a slightly different turn. He stated, "At two meetings to-day the 'Passion According to St. Matthew' was given, not in its absolute integrity, but with trifling and inconsequential excisions."[58] Each soloist was complimented with a "warm expression of praise," and Mr. Douty's achievement as the replacement for the indisposed tenor was congratulated. He "strove manfully and successfully with his cruel task." The choir was "letter perfect [rising] to climaxes marvelously. The spirit of Bach brooded over the performance." The religious feeling returned and was "vented in the swelling chorales by the congregation ('audience' seems out of place here)."

The second part of Krehbiel's review took on a different tone. "The conviction is written down with keen regret that Bethlehem cannot rise to its lovely mission." Expressing a point of view that musicians following the present-day quest for authentic performances would find compatible, Krehbiel's "lovely mission" required J. Fred. to make a study "of contemporary records and traditions which is essential to a truly artistic and historically correct performance of the music of Bach and his period." In Krehbiel's view J. Fred.'s conducting was uninformed and directed by "momentary notions," and even those were "open to questions." The choices were clear. "If the Bethlehem festivals are to remain only devotional functions," they are like the seasonal performances of the *Messiah* found in every city. "If the festival is to become a fetish," not open to criticism and directed by firm scholarship, then "it will soon lose all interest so far as musicians and music lovers – to whom Bach's music is neither novelty nor fit subject for sensational exploitation – are concerned." Krehbiel repeated the problems with ritards, musical ornaments, and the accompaniment of the recitatives. For the first time he identified authorities for an historic performance practice with specific applications of the ideas from historic sources as well as instances of J. Fred.'s noncompliance. Krehbiel knew what he demanded from J. Fred. Why did the results of his conducting not square with the known written information? Are there reasons why J. Fred. did what he did other than self-expression? If there were, what were they? The article was signed H. E. K. to make clear who was responsible for the critique.

Krehbiel was feeling the heat of the debate he had begun and needed to clarify his duty as a music critic, so his reactions could be correctly understood. This was not argument for the sake of argument. "It is the purpose of criticism, which aims not to . . . belittle or destroy, to say these things, for the purpose is kindly and constructive." He was asserting his dream of a national Bach school, and had been convinced by his past experiences that Bethlehem could be the site of such a school. But to do so lay in the hands of J. Fred. Krehbiel felt that the young conductor must enter the wider world of Bach scholarship, if he wanted to be taken seriously as a leader not just an innovator. The lesson for J. Fred. the musician was to expand his horizons beyond his musical parochialism and personal ego. Either he modified his interpretations, or he must devise new approaches that persuaded informed listeners that they were valid. After all, The Bach Choir was a scholarly pursuit. J. Fred. had said its purpose was to "study the music of Bach." Its roots were in Ruth Doster's study group. Of course, J. Fred. had a father who, although a botanist, had gone through the critical process Krehbiel proposed for J. Fred. Francis Wolle's international recognition was the result of entering into the worldwide debate about the characteristics of various algae. Observing his father, J. Fred. knew what was involved in national and international success. It was directly related to persuading others your ideas were the right ones. Acting as a responsible critic, Krehbiel was pointing the way to J. Fred.

The critic of *The New York Times* concisely expressed the desire for a performance in church. "What had been expected of the Bethlehem choir," he wrote in his report of Thursday's sessions, "had been a performance more closely approximating in spirit and in surroundings circumstances to those that prevail in Bach's time than could be offered by any concert performance."[59] Proper surroundings, however, were not enough. A performance had to approximate what prevailed in Bach's time. While this critic was also willing to grant that the soloists sang well, and "the singing of the chorus . . . showed it at its best, the orchestra was in its worst form." Finally, there were still questions of interpretation that J. Fred. had not addressed. They were the same ones Krehbiel had already pointed out.

For the pastor the performance of the *"Passion"* was reverent and Moravian. He wrote, "the singing of the chorus . . . was grand. Although the strain was very severe, there was no sign of weakening on the part of any." He was particularly pleased that "the recitations fortook of the simplicity, and yet the power, of our Passion book readings."[60]

The critics would not let those problems go away, regardless of how beautiful much of the singing was. The hounds were still at J. Fred.'s heels. He kept his public reserve, even though local reporters must have wanted him to respond. He had two more days until the conclusion of the festival, and he moved on to conduct a Friday evening of cantatas.

### Friday Evening: the Fifth Day

Only cantatas were sung in the evening. The critic from *The New York Times* wrote that many visitors used the free afternoon to attend an art exhibition displayed in the chapel of the Seminary for Young Ladies that included oils and watercolors primarily by local artists. The quality of the show was a surprise to many, for they were unaware of the Moravian tradition of excellence in the visual arts. "The collection has distinction and deepens the impression left by the festival itself of the taste and culture of the Lehigh Valley."[61]

Though H. E. K.'s report of the program was very brief, for the first time his comments went beyond those expected of a music critic.

> The performance presented many questions for the discussion of musicians (who, by the way, have been invited to leave the town, if they find themselves in disagreement with local opinion touching Bach's music, every Bethlehemite having received a gift of plenary inspiration in this matter).

He ended tersely, "Tomorrow the B minor Mass will be performed entire in two sessions, and so the meeting will end. H.E.K." We hear him thinking, "It will be as much a relief to me to leave as it will be for you to have me go." Another critic was also perturbed at Bethlehem's reaction to musical criticism. He reported

> indignation reached its climax today, when a prominent musician among the visitors was told by a person high in authority that if he did not like the performances he should go home and his railway fare would be paid.... They [Wolle and the Bach Festival] must improve, because they have attracted the attention of the country.... It is unfortunate that the conditions of the festival two years ago cannot longer satisfy, but they cannot.[62]

The pastor was impressed because the "church was now completely filled."[63] And to everyone's relief "this evening occupied not much more than an hour."

### Saturday Afternoon and Evening: the Final Day

This was the day of the Mass in B Minor, with "strangers pouring in all morning," according to the pastor.[64] Every seat was filled and the only space remaining was in the pulpit area. Apparently J. Fred. gave permission for chairs to be placed there and now even the pastor reacted with sarcasm.

> This created a little indignation and has taught the Board of Elders hereafter not to trust anything to the charge of those who cannot be held more definitely responsible than this shadowy Executive Committee which it now comes to light, had scarcely any existence or power at all.

The Mass was sung in two sessions. As soon as the second was concluded all traces of the festival were wiped from the sanctuary.

> Immediately upon the leaving of the audience the Head Sacristan, Bro. C. H. Eggert, had a corp of workers ready to restore the Church

The Bach Choir of Bethlehem on the Steps of Central Moravian Church, 1903. J. Fred Wolle, far right near the railing, has an "X" on his lapel. (Archives of The Bach Choir of Bethlehem)

to its usual conditions for Sunday, and at 10:15 pm. this had been accomplished and the lights went out.

Beyond the sanctuary, however, the aftermath of the festival could not be avoided.

### After the Festival

Bethlehem, like Nazareth, was founded as a closed Moravian community. Through its one hundred and fifty years up to the founding of The Bach Festivals, the outside world had slowly overwhelmed the community. Each time the Moravian congregation reacted by systematically divesting itself of its property, economic and political power, and its cultural influence. Throughout all the changes, Bethlehem remained largely culturally free of the outside critical music world and stayed strongly rooted in Moravian traditions. The flood of metropolitan critics and audiences that Bethlehem experienced in The Third Bach Festival was like a musical divestiture of what had begun as a closed religious community where God spoke through trombones.

Krehbiel wrote two long articles, "Reflections on the Bach Festival," in which he reiterated his dream of an American Bach School, his belief that Bethlehem could be its site, and his profound disappointment that it may not come about because J. Fred., in his wilfulness, persisted in ignoring Bach scholarship. He included lengthy quotations from sources that supported this view. What these sources stated was not what J. Fred. had done. J. Fred. could not ignore history and maintain a festival in the forefront of the Bach cult in America. Yet, Horatio Parker, one of the most prominent American composers of the time, defended J. Fred. against the critics. Parker's response was printed in *The Musical Courier*, a leading New York City music journal.

> A deserved tribute to the Bach Choir's rendition of the Mass in B Minor has been voiced by Prof. Horatio W. Parker, of Yale, who is one of the foremost composers of music in America. He states that during the past year he has heard the Mass rendered by the famous

Bach Chorus at Dusseldorf, Germany, and at Boston, by the Oratorio Society, assisted by the Boston Symphony Orchestra and again here [in Bethlehem] on Saturday and all in all, the Bach Choir of Bethlehem presented by far the most credible performance.[65]

While the pastor was willing to grant that he might "gain a truer perspective and larger view" with time, however, the "well nigh universal opinion" of those concerned with the "work of the Church itself" was that the musical success of the festival was "by no means an argument in favor of holding any others."[66] The influx of strangers, the lack of self-control of the audience, and the spirit of irreverence "all point strongly toward a rigid decision by the Board not again to allow the building to be used for anything similar. . . . It is not the kind of advertising of which an earnest congregation of Jesus Christ can be particularly proud."

J. Fred. reacted to all that transpired during the festival with characteristic controlled persistence, resilience, and ingenuity. In a press conference he apologized to his choir and restated that the purpose was the study of Bach's music. The reporter wrote, "Mr. Wolle regrets . . . that the choir had been held up as a model. His idea has been merely to meet and study the works of the master musician, Bach."[67] When asked for his assessment of the festival, " 'Considering the forces at his command,' said he, 'there has been accomplished a musical feat such as no other musical center has ever dared to attempt'." At the same time everyone was assured that he "is to take up the study of Bach's music again with the choir next Fall" selecting the next music from among the "500 or more available works for chorus." J. Fred. concluded the interview with a statement that there would be another Bach Festival, but it would be quite different from the one just past. "Mr. Wolle's idea is to hold the next one, perhaps next year, or possibly not until two years hence or later, on entirely different lines." Because the festival occurred in the Moravian Church, and J. Fred. directed the choir there, visitors had assumed the Bach Festivals were a Moravian enterprise. J. Fred. clarified the relationship when another reporter asked him about the connection between The Bach Choir and the Moravian Church. He told him directly

> No; there is no connection between Bach and the Moravians. I am a Moravian. I am also an admirer of Bach. It has been my ambition to impress the beauties of his compositions upon the public, and my position in the church choir offered the best means to that end.[68]

J. Fred. was well aware he had to modify his plans for future festivals. The festival was either a local event or it wasn't. The festival was either a concert or a sacred service. Since J. Fred. wanted festivals that were sacred services, he had to create another design. He would delve into the endless source of music by Bach with a different arrangement for the services.

By the fall of 1903, J. Fred. approached the Moravian Elders with a request to use the church for a series of services called a "Bach Cycle." He would retain the liturgical intent: the celebration of the Birth, Death, and Resurrection of Christ. He would divide the cycle into three festivals, "Christmas," "Lenten," and "Easter and Ascension." Cantatas and instrumental works expressing the meaning of each event were clustered around the large works. Some of the shorter compositions had been heard rarely, if ever, in America. By including a number of other works in the cycle, J. Fred. addressed a concern that had been expressed following the 1903 festival. He told a reporter

> When the third Bach Festival drew to its close the impression seemed to spread to a certain extent that the work of the Bach Choir was practically at an end. This, however, is not, and will not be, the case, for the field of the church cantatas of Bach is practically an unexplored one; the same is essentially true of the realm of orchestral works.[69]

J. Fred. continued, "it was decided to make the cycle program one essentially of the cantatas, but not exclusively so."[70] The works, except the Mass, would be sung in English using translations by J. Fred.

Central Moravian Church Trombone Choir, on the steps of the
Central Moravian Church.
This group played in the first Bach Festivals.
(Trombone Choir of Central Moravian Church)

In the hope of increasing the sense of reverence and promoting the view that The Bach Festivals were sacred services, J. Fred. proposed that the Bach Cycle take place within the church year. J. Fred. also included a historical dimension, for he desired "to perform the selected works as nearly as possible at the times for which they were written."[71] This format increased both the religious nature of the festival and the historical accuracy of each event. In addition, both ideas were unique. A problem mentioned by a Philadelphia critic was also addressed. "Six days of continuous Bach are too much for even the most strenuous musical digestion."[72] Each seasonal celebration would last three days.

# CREATING A BACH FESTIVAL

The Moravian Elders discussed J. Fred.'s request to use the church, but, according to the pastor, "The situation is a difficult one . . . the spirit of the musicians is everything that can be desired [while] the behavior of the audience from out of town is not by any means as reverent as is to be expected in God's House."[73] The elders did not "desire to obstruct in any degree the legitimate and worthy musical development of the choir [however] the loose arrangement in force at the last Festival could not be tolerated." What takes place in the sanctuary must further the mission of the church. Therefore, "the series of musical sessions, shall be regarded as a series of worshipful church services, in every sense." After a "long discussion," the elders "resolved to allow the use of the church on these occasions . . . The answer was accordingly sent to Bro. Wolle." The dates for the Bach Cycle were 28, 29, 30 December 1904; 12, 13, 14, April 1905; 1, 2, 3, June 1905. There would be two sessions each day, one at four and another at eight.

## The Christmas Festival

Instead of performing the *Christmas Oratorio* in two sections, J. Fred. cleverly interwove cantatas into the *Oratorio*. The cantatas prepared for the part of the *Oratorio* were sung each evening. On Wednesday afternoon, 28 December, the cantata "How Brightly Shines the Morning Star," BWV 1, and the *Magnificat* preceded parts 1 and 2 of the *Oratorio*. Thursday afternoon "O Jesus Christ, Light of My Life," BWV 116, and "The Lord is a Sun and Shield," BWV 79, were sung before parts 3 and 4. "The two interesting cantatas, neither having been heard before in this country," used the full trombone choir as an accompaniment.[74] A Saturday afternoon service Suite in B Minor, BWV 1067, and Second Brandenbrug Concerto, BWV 1047, encased the choral motet "Sing Ye to the Lord a New-Made Song," BWV 225, for double chorus. It was sung unaccompanied – another first for The Bach Choir. The two concluding sections of the *Oratorio* were sung that evening. J. Fred. had designed the cycle so that each group of musicians, including the trombone choir, was featured at least once during the festival.

The side pews were covered with Christmas decorations. Just before Christmas the pastor recorded that "every night during this week the large Bach chorus has been rehearsing for the Festival next week. The decorators are also at work in the church."[75] The first festival took place a few days after the Nativity was celebrated, but with no alterations to the church. At the insistence of the elders, the pews were not reversed, the traditional Moravian Christmas "putz" remained in the pulpit area, and the side pews were not used at all because they were covered with Christmas decorations.

The pastor, the elders, and the congregation were pleased with the Christmas Festival. Things went well. "The Festival partook of the character of true worship," the pastor wrote, and even though "many musical visitors were there from distant places [there was] little supercritical 'writing up' with hostile feelings which marred somewhat the Festival of 1903." The pastor drew an important analogy between the festival and the *Singstunde*, or Moravian song service. "It was more truly viewed as a rendition of worshipful song, rather than a concert performance of difficult music." Thus, he connected the festival with one of the most traditional Moravian worship services. J. Fred. was surely aware of this connection. By making the festival an extended *Singstunde*, he corrected the liturgical faults found with previous festivals. "The reverent spirit steadily deepened to the last chorale of the Christmas Oratorio on Friday evening." The church was not full, and with the decreased seating, the pastor was afraid there might be a financial loss. However, he was sure any loss would be made up in the spring.

The critical responses were noticeably different. First, many of the critics could not attend because of the Christmas season. One of the music magazines reported that "owing to the press of city engagements, not many critics from the metropolitan daily were in attendance, but Mr. Wolle received cordial letters from some of them."[76] A Philadelphia critic compared the Christmas Festival with the prior one with the result that

> there has been a remarkable smoothing out of the upper voices and the fatal shrillness of the sopranos which was noticed in previous festivals is not in evidence now, and they accentuated the devotional feature and eliminated much of what has heretofore smacked of the ordinary concert.[77]

Speaking of the orchestra, he observed, "the players to-day were not at their best, careful phrasing being absent at times, the winds too lacking in attack and tonation."

The *Musical Courier*'s critic also felt that the choir had improved. "Until more choirs take up this most difficult line of music the Bethlehem Bach Choir can hold the field unchallenged for great accomplishment."[78] Unlike the other critic, he was pleased with the orchestra for "all traces of crude playing were for the time lost."

Krehbiel summarized his experience much differently than his prior reactions.

> The attendance which was small the first day, seemed doubled at each succeeding session, and today, at both performances, the big, old white church was crowded. . . . This [the motet for double chorus] was performed with great success. The Christmas Oratorio was given in splendid style.[79]

The critics were no longer displeased with the treatment of the musical ornaments, and the problem of frequent ritards was not mentioned.

## The Lenten Festival

It was J. Fred.'s intention to have the choir study unfamiliar Bach cantatas and bring them to the public. Therefore, the programming for the three-day sequence was different from the Christmas Festival. Two cantatas comprised Wednesday afternoon. In the evening there were three. Thursday was devoted to the *Passion According to St. John*. Friday was again a day of cantatas.

The works were arranged to lead the listeners to an expression of deepest mourning, concluding, however, with a chorale "Christ has risen from the dead" that prepared them for the next Festival. To express the meaning of Easter further, the members of the choir wore black, and the pulpit recess was filled with palms and ferns.

There were many critics present, but again, praise was the critical response. The second cantata in the afternoon emotionally overwhelmed the congregation, and one of the critics described the scene, writing

> the crowning glory of the afternoon session was the chorale, "World Farewell" sung by the choir in lightest possible pianissimo. The voice of every instrument was hushed and from the choir loft there floated down the soft strains that fell like a benediction. The effect was almost magical. Many people in the audience were unable to restrain their tears. Its rendition flung an aureole of glory over the afternoon's session.[80]

In the evening the music evoked quite a different mood. The same critic described its effect.

"In the concluding chorale, 'All my days have I extolled Thee,' the audience contributed to the final outburst of harmony that for glorious volume of tone has never been surpassed in the old church."[81] The critic noted that "A Request" had been placed on each seat asking each person to approach the service in reverence and quietness.

People from everywhere arrived to fill the church and listen to the *St. John Passion*. Everyone was so moved that following the close of the festival "a large number of Dr. Wolle's friends and acquaintances called at his home on Church Street, where an impromptu reception was held, while they extended their congratulations."[82] The pastor ended his response to the festival writing

> an absence of self-sufficient musical critics from the great dailies of the cities was a marked relief, for while the music could stand criticism according to the highest standards, it could do more than merely seek

J.Fred. Wolle's birthplace (large building in center) and the meeting place for the Bach Choir Board, Church Street, Bethlehem
(The Moravian Archives, Bethlehem)

a standard, – it could be regarded as worship.[83]

To the relief of the congregation, the festival was a financial success.

### Easter and Ascension

The final festival began jubilantly. The opening cantata "The Heavens Laugh, the Earth Itself Rejoices," BWV 31, celebrated the Resurrection as symbolized in the awakening of spring. On Friday afternoon there were three works, two orchestral and one choral, with three cantatas in the evening concluding appropriately with "A Stronghold Sure is Our

God," BWV 80. The festival concluded with the Mass, which one critic described as

> a thrilling and inspiring ending. And as Dr. Wolle . . . released the last crashing chord with it came the joyous outburst of the choir, orchestra and soloists, who expressed their deep appreciation and admiration of Dr. Wolle by pelting him with showers of flowers.[84]

J. Fred. had triumphed over all obstacles.

As the press was preparing the public for the Bach Cycle, a local paper reported another of J. Fred.'s grand plans, that of constructing a Bach Shrine in Bethlehem. He envisioned it as a permanent temple used exclusively for performances of Bach by The Bach Choir. While the idea must have been discussed informally before the press release, it appeared in print in December 1904. The report was in appropriately formal language.

> With the approach of the cycle interest in one of Dr. Wolle's cherished ambitions has been revived. It is the erection of a temple patterned after the style of those of the ancient Gods, wherein to hold the recurring festivals. To surround it with environs similar to those of antiquity, he would locate it on a high promontory of an adjacent mountain, where, from its stately height, a most magnificent view of the surrounding country could be had and where the musical devotees may journey each year, there to be refreshed and receive renewed vigor at the musical shrine of the great John Sebastian Bach.
>
> Various plans are being considered for the creation of this temple, but probably the most prominent one is to make it a national affair, in which the entire musical world will be invited to share the expense. As yet the project is not ready to be launched.[85]

J. Fred. would make Bethlehem into a national center for Bach performances, and he would be the conductor. Wagner had a special opera house in Bayreuth for his works. There was a theater for performances of the Passion in Oberammergau. If Bethlehem in truth was both an American Bayreuth and an American Oberammergau, then it should have a Bach temple. There were mountain sites across the river in South Bethlehem that offered "a most magnificent view." Such a shrine freed J. Fred. from the restrictions of the Moravian Church. Considered more deeply, however, such a site removed Bach from Protestant Christianity. It placed him among the great thinkers of mankind. Bach was the universal musical expression of spirituality. The discussion of concert vs. service became a moot point. Every performance of Bach's music was a sacred service for all mankind – not only for Christians.

The idea of a special building in Bethlehem for Bach performances was expressed frequently. Finally, such a temple was offered to J. Fred. However, it was not in Bethlehem. It was in Berkeley, California in the mountains overlooking San Francisco Bay. He could not refuse it. At the beginning of the Bach Cycle no one could have known J. Fred. would be offered a position in California, accept it, and leave Bethlehem.

After his summer church obligations were concluded, the Wolles left for their cabin on the coast of northern Maine. J. Fred. received a letter there from the president of the University of California, Berkeley, asking if he would found a music department and begin a Bach Choir in the Bay area. He was offered a professional orchestra made up of symphony players whom he would select and a very large Greek amphitheater on the hillside overlooking the bay. All the performances of J. Fred.'s newly formed Bach Choir with symphony orchestra would take place there.

J. Fred. accepted on the condition that it be a year's trial and sent a letter to the Elders of the Moravian Church requesting a leave of absence. The pastor recorded the reaction of the community to the news of J. Fred.'s acceptance.

> Today our community was startled by the announcement from Bro. J. Fred. Wolle, organist of the church, that he had accepted a call to the Chair of Music in the University of California, and would leave for the West within a month. Having declined several other flattering

offers, this opening seems to be in direct line with the development of his work. The newspaper interview and the announcement have caused a great deal of discussion and regret among our people.[86]

The substitute organist, Frederick Rau, replaced J. Fred., and plans were made for The Bach Choir to disband and become the Bethlehem Oratorio Society. T. Edgar Shields, organist for The Bach Choir, assumed J. Fred.'s Lehigh University position as organist and choir director and became conductor of the Oratorio Society.

Quite suddenly, as J. Fred. left Bethlehem, The Bach Choir was gone, and with it The Bach Festivals. What had J. Fred. accomplished in those five years that were now past?

The Third Bach Festival must have been a great trial for J. Fred. Before that festival, he was considered locally a musical and organizational prodigy. He then gained fame because what he did was both groundbreaking and unique. These early achievements alone marked him as a significant innovator in the history of American music. He had become a mature musician and the recognized leader of the Bach movement in America. However, to become a mature musician he had to retain his uniqueness and personal expressiveness and at the same time mesh his views with what was known by others about the history of the performance of Bach's works.

The Bach Cycle was proof that J. Fred. survived these trials. After the Easter Festival, Krehbiel, J. Fred.'s greatest and most intense critic, informed his metropolitan readers that

> the recurrence of its annual Bach festival . . . will make Bethlehem, Pa., a sort of Mecca for serious minded musicians. The unvarying excellence of these cyclical performances of the Bach Choral works, given each year, has made them events worth going to hear.[87]

J. Fred. had made the necessary musical synthesis.

In addition to the musical demands made by the critics, there were those made by the Moravian Church. J. Fred. had to bring his own spiritual response to Bach's music in line with the views of the Bethlehem Moravian Congregation of which he was a devoted member. He had accomplished that, and the congregation was pleased. Spiritually, the success of the Bach Cycle, now considered as a series of religious services similar to extended *Singstunden* proved J. Fred. had made the transformation required of him by his spiritual community and by himself. The Bach Festivals had become truly Moravian services, and J. Fred. remained Brother Wolle.

However, J. Fred. and Krehbiel both knew Bethlehem could not become an American school for Bach, for J. Fred. lacked the money and the place necessary for a great and lasting international center for Bach performance. That is why J. Fred. accepted the position in California. The circumstance he required appeared to be in Berkeley.

Bethlehem's Bach Festivals were important beyond satisfying J. Fred.'s spiritual and musical growth. Hundreds of adults, children, and instrumentalists had sung and played thirty of Bach's greatest choral and orchestral compositions. Most of the pieces had never been heard in America at all, or if so only once or twice. Ten works were performed twice. The Mass had been sung four times in five years. No other choir in America had a comparable Bach repertoire. That such a record was achieved at all, let alone achieved in five years, astonished everyone and placed The Bach Choir in a prominent niche in the history of American music.

The intensity of the performance sequence of this Bach repertoire bears repeating, for it too was astonishing. The First Bach Festival was a one-day performance of one work, an American premiere. The Second Bach Festival was three days, with two pieces new to The Bach Choir, and one was an American premiere. The Third Bach Festival lasted six days, including ten compositions, seven of which were new to the choir and to the instrumentalists. Nearly half were American premieres or second performances in the United States. The Fourth Festival, the first segment of that nine-day Bach Cycle, lasted three days, included eight compositions: six were new. Eight new compositions were performed as part of The Fifth Bach Festival, which was also three days in length. Eight works made up The Sixth Bach Festival, seven works were new, the Mass was repeated, and the Festival lasted three days.

Not only had singers and instrumentalists studied through rehearsing and performing Bach's works, thousands of listeners had heard this music. They ranged from friends and relatives of the performers and residents of the Bethlehems to many of the most prominent musicians and music critics in America. The relatives and residents attended because they wanted to support their friends and relatives and hear Bach's music. The critics and famous musicians, listening with scores in hand, were most interested in the music. Many were avid members of the "Bach cult," and Bethlehem was the only place where an intense immersion in Bach's music was taking place. Everyone was associated with the Bach renaissance that was gaining ever greater force throughout the Western world.

Important musicians in audiences at The Bach Festivals had already performed or hoped to perform some of the same music with groups they conducted throughout the East and Middle West. Regarding the spread of Bach performances related to the work of J. Fred. and The Bach Choir, a Philadelphia critic wrote about The Fourth Bach Festival,

> What he has accomplished is shown by the way musical organizations all over the country have begun the study and production of Bach, and there are now a few which do not produce at least one of his big works during a season.[88]

Following Bethlehem other communities created Bach choirs. A local reporter informed area readers that the impact of The Bach Choir extended beyond Bethlehem when he wrote

> Mr. Wolle's missionary work is bearing fruit to a greater extent than realized here. Several Bach Choirs had been organized in large cities due to the wonderful impulse given the work of the old master by the younger one.[89]

To answer the question asked by his readers, "Why Bach Festivals in Bethlehem?" one critic answered, "In no other town than this, with this peculiar church, education, and social environment, and the absence of the rush . . . and great distractions of a large city, would such things be." These conditions were necessary but not sufficient. The critic had forgotten to mention the decisive element. Without J. Fred. Wolle there was no Bach Choir, and there were no Bach Festivals in Bethlehem. That was proven by his departure from Bethlehem.[90]

That departure was a very moving event. With his usual panache, J. Fred. gave a parting "gift" to the choir and its supporters. He played an organ recital in Packer Church where he had been the organist and choir director for nearly twenty years. The recital consisted of three pieces: one by Bach, an improvisation, and a chorale.

Each piece was extraordinary. The evening was the American premiere of one of Bach's most monumental works, which J. Fred. had transcribed for the organ. The Bach composition was "Art of the Fugue." The second piece was an extended improvisation based on themes from great compositions. One of the audience described the improvisation.

> Dr. Wolle displayed his inimitable originality and his great resources as an improvisor. Dr. Wolle interwove the most prominent themes of the great masters and his own composition into a life-picture. To his personal friends it appeared as if Dr. Wolle, in his improvisation, told, musically speaking, of his struggles in young manhood, his arduous labors to mount the steps of fame in the art of music and the zenith of his achievement, ending with the ever familiar strains of "Auld Lang Syne." The last number was rendered with exceptionally rare skill. The effect upon the audience cannot be accurately described.[91]

The concert concluded with a spiritual farewell when the audience rose and sang the "Doxology." Finally, J. Fred. made one more stunning and very telling musical gesture. The reporter recounted its effect on those in the church.

Dr. Wolle played the first two lines of the hymn to a gradual pianissimo and then ceased playing and quietly retired. At the close of the recital many remained to meet Dr. Wolle and say farewell, but he apparently did not trust himself to go through the ordeal of saying parting words to his friends. He had quietly returned home.[92]

The next day, 13 September 1905, he and his wife and daughter said farewell to many of their friends at "Bach's Home." J. Fred. spoke further to the large crowd at the train station. His speech was reported by the press. "Even the great Bach himself could have had no dearer friends no more loyal supporters. It is with the deepest pangs of regret that I cut loose from my friends, my family, my Church and my Bach Choir." Then, because "he had no more words of his own," J. Fred. read a poem, "Farewell." He and his family mounted the train and took their seats. The train pulled away from the Bethlehem station. The Wolles began their long journey west to California and the music lovers of the Bethlehems mourned the loss of their great Bach conductor.

## NOTES

1. *The Bethlehem Times*, 24 May 1901.
2. Raymond Walters, *The Bethlehem Bach Choir* (Boston: Houghton Mifflin Company, 1918), 187.
3. J. Fred. Wolle, unpublished letter, 18 June 1901. In the Archives of The Bach Choir of Bethlehem.
4. "The Official Diary," March 1901, n.p., 241.
5. Ibid., 13 March 1901.
6. Ibid.
7. Ibid., 25 March 1901.
8. Ibid., 20 May 1901.
9. "The Bach Festival at Bethlehem." Unidentified newspaper clipping in "Miscellaneous Scrapbook," in the Archives of The Bach Choir of Bethlehem.
10. Ibid.
11. *The New York Tribune*, 19 May 1901.

12. "Aftermath of the Bach Festival" in "Miscellaneous Scrapbook." A printed translation of Stanley's article for the *Zeitschrift der International Musikgesellshaft Leipzig*. Source and date unknown. In the Archives of The Bach Choir of Bethlehem.
13. *The Bethlehem Times,* 27 March 1901.
14. Ibid.
15. Reprinted in *The Bethlehem Times*, 27 May 1901.
16. Ibid., 27 May 1901.
17. Stanley translation, see note 12.
18. Ibid.
19. Ibid.
20. *The Philadelphia Press,* 25 May 1901.
21. "The Official Diary," March 1901, 246.
22. Krehbiel wrote, "I do not know Mr. Wolle's authority for . . . treating every appoggiatura in the instrumental parts as an acciatura [sic], he doubtless has one, but its validity ought to be tested." "Bach's The Passion According to St. Matthew." *The New York Tribune,* 24 May 1901.
23. Ibid.
24. Ibid., "Musical Notes," 12 June 1901.
25. Letter in the collection of the Archives of The Bach Choir of Bethlehem.
26. *The North American* [Philadelphia] 2 May 1903.
27. The letters BWV indicate the place a work occupies in the catalogue of Bach's compositions.
28. Earl Johnson, *First Performances in America to 1900* (Detroit, Michigan: College Music Society, 1979). Johnson mentions two performances of "Magnificat" before 1900: Cantata BWV 140 does not appear in his list of cantatas that received performances in American before 1900.
29. "The Official Diary," 7 October 1901.
30. Ibid., 4 December 1901.
31. "Music & Musicians," *New York Sun*, in "Photographs" album in the Archives of The Bach Choir of Bethlehem.
32. "The Great Bach Festival." Newspaper clipping with no source and no date in the Archives of The Bach Choir of Bethlehem.
33. "Wolle Stands at Apex of the Bach Festival," *The North American*, 1903. In the Archives of The Bach Choir of Bethlehem.
34. "Critical or Hypercritical," *The Bethlehem Times*, 1903. Clipping in the Archives of The Bach Choir of Bethlehem.

35. *The Bethlehem Times,* 3 June 1903.
36. Ibid.
37. Ibid.
38. *The Bethlehem Times,* 24 May 1901. Quoted from *The Philadelphia Times.*
39. Ibid.
40. "The Official Diary," May 1903, 363.
41. *The New York Tribune,* 12 May 1903. All statements by Krehbiel for the section "Opening Night" are from this source.
42. *The New York Sun,* 11 May 1903.
43. *The Public Ledger* [Philadelphia], 11 May 1903.
44. "The Official Diary," May 1903, 363. The source of all the pastor's comments on "Opening Night."
45. *The New York Times,* 12 May 1903.
46. *The New York Sun,* 12 May 1903. All quotes by Henderson are from this source.
47. *The New York Times,* 12 May 1903.
48. "The Official Diary," May 1903, 364. The source of the pastor's comments for the "Second Day."
49. "Bach Choir Shows a Great Success," 13 May 1903. Unidentified clipping in the Archives of The Bach Choir of Bethlehlem.
50. Ibid.
51. *The New York Times,* 13 May 1903. The source of all comments here by the New York music critic.
52. Ibid.
53. "The Official Diary," May 1903, 364–65.
54. *The Bethlehem Times,* 16 May 1903.
55. "Critical or Hypercritical," n.d. no sources. Clipping in the Archives of The Bach Choir of Bethlehem.
56. *The Bethlehem Times,* 16 May 1903.
57. Ibid.
58. *The New York Tribune*, 14 May 1903. The source for the comments by Krehbiel.
59. *The New York Times,* 14 May 1903. The source of the critic's comments.
60. "The Official Dairy," May 1903, 365.
61. *The New York Tribune*, 15 May 1903. The source for Krehbiel's comments on the Friday evening performances.

62. "Bach Festival Cantatas," 15 May 1903. Unidentified clipping in the Archives of The Bach Choir of Bethlehem.
63. "The Official Diary," May 1903, 365. The source of the pastor's comments.
64. Ibid.
65. "Mem.[orial] of the highly accomplished critics of New York and Philadelphia." Clipping with no source in the Archives of The Bach Choir of Bethlehem.
66. "The Official Diary," May 1903, 366–67. The source of the pastor's comments.
67. "Encouraged by the Past Week's Results, Mr. Wolle's Bethlehem Choir Will Begin Work on Music for Another Festival," 17 May 1903. Unidentified clipping in the Archives of The Bach Choir of Bethlehem.
68. *The North American* [Philadelphia], 11 May 1903.
69. *Musical Courier*, 21 December 1904. The source of J. Fred.'s comments.
70. Ibid.
71. Ibid.
72. *The Philadelphia Record*, 27 December 1904.
73. "The Official Diary," 5 October 1903. The source for the quotes pertaining to the Elders' meeting.
74. *The Philadelphia Inquirer*, 30 December 1904.
75. "The Official Diary," 21 and 28 December 1904. The sources of the pastor's comments about the Christmas Festival.
76. *Musical Courier*, 4 January 1905.
77. *The Philadelphia Record*, 27 December 1904.
78. *Musical Courier*, 4 January 1905.
79. *The New York Tribune,* 31 December 1904.
80. "Large Audience Greets Singers," Unidentified clipping in the Archives of The Bach Choir of Bethlehem.
81. Ibid.
82. "The Closing Day of the Lenten Festival of the Bach Cycle." Unidentified source in the Archives of The Bach Choir of Bethlehem.
83. "The Official Diary," 14 May 1904.
84. *The Globe* [Bethlehem], 5 June 1905.
85. Ibid., 25 December 1904.
86. "The Official Diary," 19 August 1905.
87. *The New York Herald*, 9 April 1905.

88. *The Evening Telegraph* [Philadelphia], 10 December 1904.
89. *The Bethlehem Times,* 3 June 1905.
90. *The Church Standard,* 7 January 1905.
91. *The Globe,* 12 September 1905.
92. Ibid.

Chapter Ten

# J. Fred. Wolle: Academic and Organ Virtuoso

"Our chapel organist, Mr. Wolle, whose playing makes morning prayers a delight."[1]

"the eloquent, deeply learned, deeply moving J. Fred. Wolle."[2]

"Great is Bach and Wolle is his Prophet."[3]

J. FRED. HAD GAINED a permanent position as a church musician and along with teaching piano lessons he could make a good living. He married, and he and his bride moved into a house that had been built for them on Church Street on a lot near his birthplace in the cluster of the prosperous new homes of his Moravian relatives and friends. From the back of the house, there was a panoramic view of the Lehigh River and South Bethlehem with its new university, railroad, and steel mills.

Settled in his new house, J. Fred. began planting a rose garden that would become one of the most beautiful in Bethlehem. It would also serve as a haven for the many spiders that J. Fred avidly collected throughout his life. While he was tending one of the rose bushes in the backyard one afternoon, a movement on the opposite bank of the river caught his eye. He looked up and gazed at the stone masons climbing up and down the massive scaffolding erected on the campus of the University. The masons were building a thirteenth-century French Gothic-style cathedral across from his new house. The appearance of such a structure almost in his backyard was completely unexpected. Even though he had looked at many similar churches in Europe, he had never seen one under construction. Watching a cathedral being built before his eyes was more than he could ever have imagined.

The site had been selected by Mary Packer Cummings and the Building Committee of Lehigh University. Mary Cummings was raising a memorial to her family, particularly to her father, Asa Packer, the University's founder. The president of the University broke ground on 28 May 1885 while J. Fred. was still in Europe. The scale and proportions of the building were monumental. The magnificence was in keeping with Asa Packer's dream of a great American education institution based on Christian beliefs. Packer had entrusted his University to trustees he knew well: ambitious, hard-working, farsighted capitalists who had helped him build the Lehigh Valley Rail Road into one of the great transportation enterprises of the East Coast. Carrying out Packer's vision, these men employed a faculty of prominent professors, and they planned a campus of grand buildings. The gift of Packer Memorial Church was the most recent addition defining the importance of religion at the University.

Mrs. Cummings had inherited a vast fortune from her father, and she made sure Packer Church was "richly appointed in every particular."[4] The building was described with pride in the *University Register*. "Packer Memorial Church is the munificent gift of Mrs. Mary Packer Cummings, daughter of the Founder of the University. It is one of the largest and most magnificent churches in the state."[5] A later description went further, "There is no more beautiful church edifice in the State and it is one of the noblest in the land."[6] The massive stone structure was completed in two years, and J. Fred. watched it rise as he planted his new rose garden. He had no idea of the importance that church would soon play in his life.

When J. Fred. returned from Munich to Bethlehem on 22 August 1885 to assume the organ position vacated by the death of Theodore, it was clear he would carry on the Wolle tradition of musical service to the church. His talent, training, and family background had prepared him to replace his deceased cousin, Theodore, and J. Fred. played his first service on 2 October 1885. As a sign of the importance Bach now held for him, he concluded with a Bach fugue. The following month he introduced himself to the Bethlehem community by giving an organ recital to benefit Foreign Missions.

For twenty years he held the demanding position of organist, choir master, and orchestra director at Central Moravian Church. When he began, there were two Sunday morning services and often one in the evening. They required a consistent standard of musical excellence and liturgical propriety. That high standard included the presence of classical sacred music in the services. At that time most Protestant churches were without choirs and orchestras. Vocal quartets were singing newly composed gospel music or transcriptions from operas with keyboard accompaniment. J. Fred. was responsible for a very different musical establishment. A detailed account gives an idea of the music required for special times during the church year.

> The first Sunday in Advent . . . In the evening the chorus sang at the beginning, "Lift up your ears," (Handel), and after the sermon, "He comes by not with regal splendor," (Crotch), both with instrumental accompaniment . . . 2nd Sunday . . . the opening choir piece was "Day of Vengeance," from Mozart's Requiem Mass with instrumental accompaniment.[7]

There were frequent *Singstunden* and love feasts during which J. Fred. used his excellent memory of the vast body of Moravian hymns and his ability to improvise. His continued success was commented on by the pastor in the church diary. "The music in the love-feast was especially fine. The choir being augmented by the singers from West Bethlehem and Laurel St."[8] Special services, particularly those during Lent, Easter, and Christmas, required great care and extensive preparation, for each involved more than the usual, weekly rehearsal with the choir and the orchestra. The pastor wrote, "Saturday evening the services of Holy Week opened. The church was entirely filled with a devout assembly. The choir and orchestra were full and strong, rendering the good old music of the occasion finely and the congregational singing was soul-stirring."[9] At another time the diarist recorded proudly, "On the whole the Passion Week & Easter music, which is such an attraction for many was well up to the standard."[10] J. Fred.'s niece, Hilda Doolittle, remembered the children's Christmas service when she received her candle as her Uncle Fred played the organ. ". . . the doors opened at the far end of the church and the trays of lighted beeswax candles were brought into the church by the Sisters in their caps and aprons, while Uncle Fred in the gallery, at the organ was playing very softly *Holy Night*."[11]

Each year the congregation expressed its appreciation for the music during the Easter season with special refreshments. The pastor recorded such an occasion in the year 1902.

> After the Easter Eve Vigils the choir and all the musicians were invited to the West rooms where a very agreeable surprise awaited them, in the place of refreshments furnished by a number of persons who appreciated their most faithful and excellent service through this entire busy season. A communication, expressing its appreciation in the form of a resolution, was also read from the Board of Elders, and was well deserved, for the musical part of the service has been most beautiful and effective.[12]

Funerals were frequent, often calling on the bilingual capability of the choir, for services were in either English or German. National holidays were still celebrated by the entire community with sacred services in the Moravian Church. For example, "July 4 there was fine music in the church morning & evening. After the morning service the orchestra played the Priest March from the Athalia as a Postlude."[13]

Four unique celebrations occurred while J. Fred. was Moravian's organist: the bicentennial of Count von Zinzendorf's birthday, the centennial of Washington's inauguration, Bethlehem's sesquicentennial, and the funeral of President McKinley. Each service required special music. For the birthday of Zinzendorf, the founder of the renewed Moravian Church, "very fine music was rendered by the choir at all of the services in the church."[14] *The Moravian* reported the event. "The Centennial of Washington's Inauguration was commemorated by a public service held in the large church on Tuesday, April 30, at 9 A.M. ... The opening anthem by the choir was Paine's Centennial Hymn."[15] The choice of music was an indication of how current the music often was, for Paine was one of the most prominent American composers at this time. He had composed this anthem for the opening of the Columbian Exposition. The musical centerpiece of the Bethlehem sesquicentennial was a grand chorus, "He Leads Us On," composed by J. Fred. for the commemoration of the founding of the city.

> The Music of the large choir and orchestra, for which careful preparations had been made, fully met the expectation of the people, and its character was sustained throughout in the subsequent services. One of the selections, rendered with impressive effect, was a composition by the choir-master, J. Fred Wolle, produced for the first time on that occasion. The text in three stanzas, opened with the words: "He leads us on by paths we do not know."[16]

The memorial service for President McKinley was recorded in detail by the Moravian pastor. That service included The Bach Choir on one of the rare occasions the choir sang a piece not composed by Bach.

> ... there was a prelude of the trombonists followed by a march on the organ. The former was the tune of the words "Remote we pray the country's good," and the latter by Chopin. Then a portion of the Bach choir sang "My Jesus as thou wilt."
> ... The Bach choir then sang "Lead, Kindly Light." ... while Prof. Wolle played the Beethoven funeral march the vast congregation ... silently withdrew from the sanctuary.[17]

J. Fred. not only sustained the high musical quality of worship at Central Moravian Church, he incorporated Bach's music into Moravian devotions. Under his direction Bach's music became an expressive part of the worship service. In a diary entry the pastor discussed how close the relationship between Bach's music and the Moravian service became. The entry was written only a few weeks after the premiere performance of Bach's B Minor Mass and speaks of the interchangeability of the music sung by The Bach Choir and the choir of the Moravian Church.

> The music of all these services [Lenten] was of a high order. The singing of the "Crucifixus" [ from the "B Minor Mass"] at the close of the afternoon service was particularly excellent because of its very thorough practice in the recent rehearsals of the Mass in B Minor. These services so single in their rationale, and yet so solemn and stately again made a profound impression and revealed the doctrinal and liturgical genius of the Moravian Church at its best.[18]

Five years before the premiere of the B Minor Mass, "Crucifixus" was sung during the Good Friday services by the Moravian Church Choir. It was sung again at a love feast the following August. In the year 1904 the pastor wrote that this Bach chorus had become a "traditional" part of the Lenten celebration.

> . . . the order of the service was as usual [Good Friday], except that after the close of the service, after a moment's pause, during which the congregation was again quietly seated, the choir sang the "Crucifixus" from Bach's Mass, which has been sung now in connection with this service for a number of years. The entire congregation remained seated in meditation during the singing, then quietly dispersed.[19]

The "Crucifixus" was not the only Bach choral composition J. Fred. introduced into Moravian sacred services. Finding Bach and the Moravian Holy Week particularly compatible, J. Fred. began to add choruses from the *St. Matthew Passion* to Lenten services in 1896. Performances of the Bach cantata "Bide with us" BWV 6, the motet "I wrestle and pray, till bless'd by Thee" were part of love feast services. These and other works were probably sung more frequently than the records indicate. The titles of the anthems sung in regular sacred services were not usually recorded.[20] Thus, the Moravian Church expanded its musical leadership in American church music. Though Bach's music became more and more a part of public concerts, few churches in America at the turn of the nineteenth century were capable of integrating Bach's music into their sacred services even if they had wished to do so.

• • •

When the construction of Packer Memorial Church was complete, an organist/choir master was needed. J. Fred. was offered the position. He accepted, and served the University for nearly twenty years at the organ console from when Packer Memorial Church was consecrated on 13 October 1887. At Lehigh University the position of organist/choir master was a faculty appointment, so J. Fred.'s name appeared in the University catalogue with the names of thirty-eight other faculty. Four hundred students were enrolled the year he began.

From the time of its founding by Asa Packer, Lehigh University was an Episcopal parish. As a result, Packer Church was not a conventional college chapel. It was a fully functioning Episcopal Church in which "Divine Service is held on every Sunday morning . . . according to the form of the Protestant Episcopal Church, under the auspices the University was placed by its Founder."[21] As late as 1902, it was the regulation that "Attendance, either at the Packer Memorial Church or at the church of his selection, is required of every student."[22] Thus, in addition to the daily chapel service, J. Fred. played an Episcopal liturgy every Sunday at the University and the Moravian service at Central Moravian Church.

The University Chapel Choir was organized in the English boy choir tradition. Young boys sang the soprano and alto parts, and the students sang tenor and bass. The editor of *The Lehigh Burr,* the student journal, described the new chapel choir. "The fifteen young boys who have been practicing for some time past, under the instruction of Prof. Wolle, appeared for the first time in connection with the former choir at Chapel services on Sunday, February 19 [1888]. The entire choir of thirty voices made a very favorable impression.[23] Some choir boys came from workers' homes directly above The Steel, for the Chapel Choir was a "balance of twenty men and twenty to thirty boys from the Bethlehems and 'Shanty Hill,' shock-headed freckle-faced boys full of the joy of living, but orderly and attentive under the baton of the Maestro."[24] Thus, J. Fred.'s influence extended into the working-class neighborhood beyond his patrician Moravian family or those of wealthy industrialists. That must have endeared him to many blue-collar families. These were the boys who participated in the performance of *St. Matthew Passion* at Central Moravian Church. The choir remained a source of college pride. In soliciting members at the beginning of a spring term, the editor of the college newspaper wrote

> We should think that every man in the college, who has any ability whatever, would hasten to try for a place in the college choir and secure the advantages of Mr. Wolle's training. There are quite a number of men in the college with excellent voices who have in no way displayed the slightest desire to avail themselves of this exceptional opportunity. Especially is this true of Freshmen.[25]

The exceptional singing of the choir was praised frequently, for "Mr. Wolle, besides having enjoyed the instruction of the best musicians of America and Europe, is a teacher of rare ability, and we know that those who will make the sacrifices necessary to attend [rehearsals] will never regret it."[26] A choir member remembered that "Dr. Wolle's facility of expression was unsurpassed."[27]

Besides the weekly Sunday liturgy, there were daily chapel services at the University. These were fifteen minutes long, and included prayer, singing of hymns, scripture readings, short announcements, "declamations by students, faculty, and invited guests," and an organ postlude.[28] The music at the chapel service was taken very seriously by many students and quite early in his tenure, they requested that the name of each postlude be printed the week before in the college newspaper. J. Fred. responded immediately, and the editor of *The Brown and White* prepared the readers for what they could expect to read in print. "Mr. Wolle has very kindly consented to announce the postludes a week in advance. For the interval between now & Christmas, Mr. Wolle will favor those who attend chapel with many selections for pastoral and Christmas music so appropriate to this season of the year."[29] Thus, many editions of the student paper contained the titles and composers' names of the postludes. In addition, the editors encouraged the students to remain for the postlude as a part of their musical education. "Mr. Wolle is always at his best when seated at the organ, and his short selections after the morning service afford a keen pleasure to the true lovers of music. . . . There is a keen pleasure in this musical enjoyment, as well as in a mathematical formula."[30] Because of his concern for the students' musical education, the pieces he played were far more than music appropriate for a specific season, and J. Fred. clarified his long-range educational plan. "For the time between commencement Mr. Wolle intends to have a very comprehensive program laid out, which will include music from all the great composers."[31]

While he could have easily improvised a postlude each day, J. Fred. played the full range of organ repertoire. His choices were not only timely but of high quality. The composers included: Bach, Faulkes, Shelly, Elgar, Jonas, Thiele, Rheinberger, Schumann, Whitter, Mendelssohn, Handel, Gabriel-Marie, Beethoven, Widor, Kroger, Merkel, Lemines, Guilmant, Wagner, Chopin, Schubert, Baren, Morandi, Gounod, Hoffman, Smith, Vogt, Capoccio, Oatkin, Verdi, Wolkmann, Liszt, Spohr, Mascagni, Smart, Haydn, and Archadelt. Many of these composers are still played.

This list shows that while J. Fred. was playing organ recitals of Bach's music for national audiences, at the University he did not stress Bach. Because his obligation was to the students' broad education, he played music by English and French composers along with pieces by German composers Mendelssohn, Schumann, and by his teacher, Rheinberger. In fact, until his American premiere of Bach's "Art of Fugue" in Packer Memorial Church in 1928, J. Fred. never played an all-Bach organ concert in Bethlehem.

While he was busy preparing premieres of Bach's choral music in Central Church, the organ repertoire printed in the student newspaper emphasized that at Lehigh J. Fred. played Wagner's music frequently. Selections were performed from *Rienzi, Tannhauser, Siegfried, Götterdämmerung, Parsifal,* and a complete scene from *Lohengrin,* with soloists and chorus. He performed music from *Tristan and Isolde* in recitals elsewhere.

The pervasive presence of Wagner was evidence of J. Fred.'s mastery of the orchestral organ. This broad repertoire also indicated J. Fred. accepted the organist as a virtuoso soloist. In Packer Memorial Church music was to be as impressive as the building. That view was the reverse of the Moravians', where the organ remained an accompanying instrument, and the organist should not engage in technical display. J. Fred. adhered to the Moravian expectation when he played in Central Moravian Church. Thus, J. Fred. functioned in two musical worlds, apparently moving between them with ease.

J. Fred.'s organ-playing at Lehigh University was described by a graduate who left a very personal account, which is at the same time a rare description of J. Fred.'s approach to the organ.

> I have been able to hear many organists with far greater reputations than his, but never in my humble opinion, one who could compare with him. At his occasional recitals (alas! they were like angels' visits!) he always played without notes and without assistance; [many organists had others change stops for them as they played] yet with never the tiniest break or hitch in the smooth, even volume of his tone and perfect accuracy of his touch. I had the pleasure of knowing him personally, and many were the hours I spent in the dim, cool church where he practiced of an afternoon – frequently I fear, to the detriment of my mechanics and calculus, but it was worth more than that. Bach was his idol and hobby, but he was not above Wagner (his transcription of Siegfried's Death March from 'Die Götterdammerung' is magnificent), nor even Widor and his former master and teacher, Rheinberger of München.[32]

Students attending chapel services not only heard J. Fred. play the most recent organ music daily, they heard performances that were unsurpassed in quality. Many students were aware of this and wanted to hear him more frequently. The editors of the student paper asked why it was that Professor J. Fred. Wolle played so many recitals elsewhere, yet limited his playing at Lehigh University to chapel and Sunday services.

> It seems a shame that with our fine organ and the expert musician who plays it we should reap such little benefit therefrom. With the exception of a hymn every morning, and several of them on Sunday, the instrument is silent to us. . . . Would it be inconsistent with the purposes for which our chapel was built should Mr. Wolle once in a while give us the rare treat of a sacred concert? I think not, for there are many Episcopal Churches in our land that do this very thing.[33]

Was the organ in Packer Memorial Church simply a church decoration? Why wasn't the music in the service as grand as the chapel itself asked "Musicus" in a letter to the editor?

> Our chapel is noted through the land as the finest college church in the Union, and naturally its organ is a center of interest. "What sort of a tone has it?" we have been asked by many, and forced to acknowledge that we did not know. Let us then hear it at times, for now it appears more as a handsome ornament than anything else. Surely the exquisite chords of Mendelssohn or the grand harmonies of Mozart could find no fitter instrument for their rendering than that which graces our fair church. Musicus.[34]

Always sensitive to students' requests, J. Fred. responded by giving an organ recital the next month at Lehigh. It was a full virtuoso recital with music by J. Fred.'s contemporaries: Thiele, Guilmant, Thomas, Lemmens, and Selby. J. Fred. played only one piece by Bach.[35] In a review of the concert, the paper reported, "A large audience was present, and altogether the affair was a most successful one. To Mr. Wolle and the choir are due the thanks of the University for their kindness in affording such a rare treat."[36]

The program also provided a glimpse into the choral repertoire of the University Chapel Choir. The choir sang Stainer's "Te Deum," and

"Jubilate Deo, in D" by J. T. Field. These were typical pieces sung in the nineteenth-century English cathedral tradition. J. Fred. was fully aware of what was current and appropriate in an English-style liturgy. A later article mentions rehearsals of "Te Deum" and "Jubilate Deo" by Mendelssohn, perhaps the most cherished composer of the day. Speaking of the rehearsal for the Mendelssohn choruses, the student editor commented

> Mr. Wolle was pleased with the attendance [at the rehearsal] of last Friday, and is confident that the music on this occasion [Baccalaureate] cannot be other than first class, provided the men continue to manifest their interest by regular and prompt attendance at the rehearsals.[37]

Yet, J. Fred. still did not consider Lehigh University as a place for regular organ recitals. Evoking the Episcopal tradition of organ concerts, in 1890 the editors of *The Burr* graciously complained again that Professor Wolle was not playing frequently enough at Lehigh.

> The recent announcement in Chapel of the choir festival at the Church of the Nativity [South Bethlehem] reminds us of the fact that we have a choir and an organ and an organist. Except for the service on Sundays and a hymn at the morning Chapel, we never have the pleasure of hearing them. An organ recital, with music by the Choir, is perfectly practicable, and, judging from the large audience with which the one held two years ago was favored, would be well received and furnish a delightful musical treat.[38]

J. Fred. reacted by playing a full recital the following term with a vocal soloist replacing the chapel choir. "The following program was exquisitely rendered," wrote the editor of *The Lehigh Burr*.[39] While the major work was by Rheinberger, a composition by J. S. Bach, "phrased by Liszt," and one by Widor, a great nineteenth-century composer for the organ, were performed. The soprano sang arias by Haydn and Beethoven.[40] These organ recitals never became annual events, though J. Fred. did perform "one of his delightful recitals,"[41] in 1898,[42] and one in 1899. "This recital surpassed the one Mr. Wolle gave last year, and further demonstrated his exceptional ability as an organist."[43] In 1903, "A good audience was present and thoroughly enjoyed Mr. Wolle's able rendition."[44] The program included the prelude to Wagner's opera *Parsifal*.

J. Fred.'s tenure as a Moravian/Episcopal organist was not without complications. When J. Fred. accepted the Lehigh University position, he was unable to play a second Sunday morning service at Central Moravian. The trustees agreed to hire a substitute with an adjustment in J. Fred.'s salary.

> The committee of the Board of Trustees arranged with Bro. J. Fred. Wolle, the organist in the church, that in view of the engagement at Packer Memorial Church every Sunday at 10:30 o'clock, besides every morning during the week, $50 of his present salary be surrendered by him, reducing it to the figure before the recent increase, the substitute in the Church Sunday mornings be paid at the rate of $1.00 for each service by the trustees.[45]

This adjustment slightly offset the $80.00 he received at Lehigh.[46] However, there was no choir for that service. The Board of Elders lived uneasily with this condition for many years, but in 1901 they demanded a resolution. The pastor delineated the difficulties in his diary entry. While it is clear the J. Fred.'s Lehigh appointment was at the center of the problem, there were political complications as well.

> The Board of Elders met in the evening. At the meeting one of the periodical discussions of the church-music, organist and choir was introduced and the dissatisfaction with existing arrangements, particularly with the fact that an agreement entered into a number of years ago by the Board of Trustees without consulting the Board of Elders, to have a substitute play on regular Sunday mornings is yet continued and with the fact that there is no choir on ordinary Sunday mornings. . . . It was eventually decided to ask the Trustees to meet the Elders

in joint session on July 15 to consider the whole matter & all factors involved.[47]

A committee was appointed to find a solution; however, J. Fred. was never available for the meetings. No one wanted to confront him directly so the problem was solved behind the scenes, and, "a new departure was made, the Church Choir having consented to be on duty at both services hereafter. An anthem was rendered, and the chants of the Litany were all sung."[48] This solution was in effect until the assistant organist, T. Edgar Shields, resigned to accept another position. Committees met, but J. Fred. was unavailable again. Finally, "At 3 p.m., another meeting of the Committee on church music took place in the Vestry, Bro. J. Fred. Wolle, the organist, being present this time."[49] There is no record of the resolution, but J. Fred. continued playing one Sunday morning service in Central Moravian Church, and when the service was finished, he rushed through the covered wooden bridge that crossed the Lehigh River to Packer Memorial Church and played the Episcopal service.

As with other professors who were making nationally recognized contributions in their disciplines, the momentous Bach revivals accomplished by J. Fred. were promoted and reviewed by Lehigh's student editors in a spirit of comraderie. After a general description of the music of Bach's *St. Matthew Passion*, the editor wrote warmly about J. Fred.'s American premiere. At the same time he made clear the extent the university contributed to the performance of the Passion music.

> Among Mr. Wolle's most difficult undertakings he may undoubtedly count one of his greatest successes. There were a number of University men in the choruses, and a generous sprinkling of them throughout the audience, in addition to which the boys of the chapel choir participated as a chorus and did remarkably well. Thus we feel that we have even greater college interest in the Passion Music than if we were not represented by the voices of the college men and the choir boys. *The Burr* believes that it voices its most hearty congratulations to Mr. Wolle and those whom he led through the Passion Music.[50]

Appropriately, the performance of Bach's Mass in B Minor was front-page news in *The Brown and White*. Naturally, the university association was stressed, "The rendition of Bach's Mass in B Minor given Tuesday in the Moravian Church, Bethlehem, was a magnificent success and reflects great credit on its promoter and conductor, Mr. J. Fred. Wolle, organist of Packer Memorial Chapel."[51] The other festivals were regularly promoted in the Lehigh paper, with the account of the Festival in 1903 including the names of five Lehigh professors and three students who sang in the festival chorus.[52]

Filled with pride, *The Brown and White* also reported the notable and important organ recitals Professor Wolle played at the World's Columbian Exposition in Chicago in 1893 and the 1904 St. Louis Exposition.

Two organs with capabilities that must have thrilled J. Fred. were built for the Chicago and St. Louis exhibitions. Like everything at both fairs, they were to impress the world with America's technical progress and to provide Americans with the finest examples of musical culture. They did impress, and many people who heard them played by the finest organists of the day were introduced to music they had never heard before. Even familiar music was a new experience played on such fine organs by the best organists in the world. Both instruments were important enough to be removed when the fair was over. They still survive at least in part: the Chicago Exposition organ is at the University of Michigan Ann Arbor, and the St. Louis organ, purchased by John Wanamaker, was placed in his department store in Central Philadelphia.

Theodore Thomas, the most prominent symphonic conductor of the time, planned the musical performance at "The World's Columbian Exposition" in Chicago. The organ was part of a concert scheme he designed "to make a complete showing to the world of the musical progress of America, both executive and creative, in all departments." He also wanted to provide Americans with the best music "as exemplified by the most enlightened nations of Europe."[53] The grandeur of the exposition was also expressed musically by an exposition orchestra of 114 men, two large military bands, an adult chorus of 1000 voices, and a chorus of 1200 children. For some performances even these large groups were expanded. For example, Bach's *St. Matthew Passion* and the cantata "Eine feste Burg" were performed by a chorus of 600 and an orchestra of 150. Even more grand was Joseph Haydn's *The Creation*, which was performed with 1250 voices in the chorus.

J. Fred. Wolle at the organ console, St. Louis World's Fair
(Archives of The Bach Choir of Bethlehem)

The grand orchestral organ of sixty stops was in the central Festival Hall. For six months, from May to October 1893, there were nearly sixty organ recitals; all were free to the public.

J. Fred., one of the twenty organ recitalists, played two programs: "#43" on 13 October at 5:00, and "#52" at noon on 22 October. The 13 October program was traditional with a variety of works by well-known composers of the day, Rheinberger, Widor, Shelly, and Thiele. That recital did not suggest what was to come, for it included only two short pieces by Bach. J. Fred. did leave his stamp on the first program by playing an extended piece by Handel, Concert in G Minor. Handel's instrumental works were seldom performed at the time. He also played his Wagner transcription of "Siegfried's Death March," a piece he played often on other organs.

Recital #52 was the most unique organ program played at the exposition. That recital was the record-making, all-Bach program, probably the first of its kind in America. J. Fred., at a time before the works of Bach were numbered, played Fantasia and Fugue in G Minor, Passacaglia and Fugue in C Minor, Chorale in G, "Alle Menschen muessen sterben," Prelude and Fugue in G, Aria in F, Toccata and Fugue in G, Fugue in G Minor, and Fugue in D.[54] Because this recital took place before Bach's works were numbered, compositions were known by the form and the key. Wolle's program was intended for serious listening, not as light entertainment. By providing Americans with "the best music exemplified by the most enlightened nations of Europe," J. Fred.'s Bach recital expressed Thomas' musical ideals for the exposition. J. Fred. had constructed a performance of the greatest music, which he played on one of the greatest American organs.

J. Fred.'s Chicago Exposition recital was also unique because it contained works by a single composer.[55] This recital was a unified concert; one of J. Fred.'s most persistent ideas. A single theme shaped it, i.e., the music of Bach, it presented the "best" music by the West's greatest composer, and it contained music by a single individual. His "Bach Program" was one of the first times he realized his ideal. While the unified concert was one of J. Fred.'s contributions to modern concert programming, the idea was firmly rooted in the Moravian view of a musical program as a spiritual experience. The Chicago Bach recital resembled a Moravian *Singstunde* in intent, for both celebrated a single sacred theme experienced through music. Everyone at the time accepted the view that all Bach's music was spiritually edifying. An all-Bach performance was the most spiritual concert possible.

Eleven years later J. Fred. played the next landmark recitals at the St. Louis Exposition. The first recital was more audacious than the

Chicago Bach recital, for it was not only an all-Bach program, it consisted of a single piece, the *Goldberg Variations*. Bach composed the variations for the harpsichord, but J. Fred. transcribed them for organ. The performance was another American premiere. The second recital explored some of Bach's intimate organ works, the choral preludes composed for specific church services. J. Fred. played few of the monumental organ pieces. Thus, the second St. Louis recital was even more like a Moravian *Singstunde* than the Bach program in Chicago had been.

When J. Fred. proposed his plan to play two Bach recitals to Ernest R. Kroeger, "Master of Programs," he was told, "he would drive the people from Festival Hall."[56] Although Kroeger finally consented to the performance of the *Goldberg Variations*, he "was still in doubt as to whether an audience at one hearing could stand thirty movements of Bach."[57] As had been the case in Chicago, again, no other organist played such singular programs. "Dr. Wolle is the only organist who would presume to render two entire Bach programs on the grand organ in Festival Hall. These consecutive recitals will be the finest interpretations of Bach by any organist who has played at the Exposition, with the possible exception of Guilmant."[58]

Kroeger's fears were unfounded. For both recitals, "The audiences were enormous."[59] The first recital attracted one of the exhibition's largest audiences. J. Fred. wanted to do more than give another Bach premiere; he wanted to exhibit the capabilities of the exhibition's "grand organ." He "was careful to select from Bach's compositions one of the multiple movements which would illustrate to the best advantage the majority of the 140 speaking stops."[60] Compared with the organ in Chicago, the St. Louis organ possessed more than twice the number of stops. J. Fred. mastered the organ in two weeks, practicing after midnight when the fairgrounds were deserted. As always he was intensely involved in devising the best way to project Bach's emotions, and at the fair he was using the latest technology to do so. Thus, he was doing more than making a transcription, J. Fred. was rewriting the *Goldberg Variations*. He was orchestrating a harpsichord piece for an organ that offered 140 individual instruments that could be coupled into almost an endless number of combinations. Then, there were pedals added to the four keyboards. In addition, the loud and soft of the instrument could be increased or decreased from second to second. Thus, J. Fred. not only left his stamp on the exhibition, he placed his stamp on the performance of Bach's keyboard music, as he was doing with Bach's choral works in the Bach Festivals.

While a detailed account of J. Fred.'s orchestration of the *Goldberg Variations* in 1904 is lacking, there is a description of an organ recital in 1921 when he played sections that provide clues to his approach. On that program were pieces by Johann Sebastian Bach titled "Serenade for Flute, Gigue for Oboe, "Music Box," "Medley on Two Jolly Folksongs," and "Trumpet Fanfare." Bach never wrote pieces with these titles. They were titles J. Fred. added to works that existed in pure form. The program identifies the pieces. "The above five numbers were written to amuse the insomnia which afflicted Baron on his sleepless nights."[61] Bach composed his variations for such a Baron. J. Fred. reconceptualized each variation, viewing it as a characteristic piece, a favorite form of Romantic composers. Such pieces were short and self-contained, expressed a single mood, and usually painted a picture in sound. J. Fred. gave each variation a different character by using a unique combination of organ stops. Each variation had its own sound. Thus, there was constant variety for the audience. His transcription "completely captivated the audience."[62] He performed single variations in other recitals.

J. Fred.'s *Goldberg Variations* for the St. Louis organ brought together his genius and skill by creating a perfect melding of Bach's music with a musical instrument that resembled an orchestra. He brought Bethlehem to St. Louis, for his recitals were Bach Festivals of keyboard music. He performed the complete composition on one other occasion in Ann Arbor, Michigan, on the organ from the World's Colombian Exposition on which he had played his first all-Bach concert.

In Bethlehem papers J. Fred.'s reception in St. Louis was eagerly reported, including mentioning the Bethlehem visitors to the Exposition who attended his recital. A number of reviews of J. Fred.'s concerts taken from a St. Louis paper were quoted in the student newspaper. One review emphasized the daring of J. Fred.'s programming only works by Bach.

> Dr. Wolle's first entire Bach program, rendered yesterday on the great organ in Festival Hall, attracted one of the greatest audiences of the season. Many of those who attended the recital were attracted merely to hear a man who was brave enough to give nothing but Bach during the recital. They were wonderfully gratified.[63]

On his way back to Bethlehem, J. Fred., now recognized as one of America's finest organists, played recitals in Indianapolis and Niagara Falls. For many years he played in every major city on the East Coast, always receiving rave reviews.

After his return from St. Louis with his reputation greatly enhanced by the daring of his Bach programming, *The Brown and White* ran a feature article describing J. Fred.'s success.

> It is a sense of gratification to the student body that Dr. J. Fred. Wolle is again presiding at the chapel organ during morning prayers. The following are among the notices given by the St. Louis press concerning the recital given by Dr. Wolle in the Festival Hall at the St. Louis Exposition last month. They will be read with interest and pride by all Lehigh men: A remarkable organist gave two extraordinary recitals at Festival Hall today at 11:30 a.m. Dr. J. Fred. Wolle, of Bethlehem, is the high disciple of Bach in America. He is the only musician who has dared to make the music of that master the subject of a popular festival in this country every year. . . . Dr. Wolle is the only organist who would presume to render two entire Bach programs on the grand organ in the Festival.[64]

Like other great organists in the nineteenth century, J. Fred. was an accomplished improvisator. In addition, his Moravian organ background stressed improvisation. He must have improvised frequently, but accounts are rare. A Lehigh University graduate wrote of one of J. Fred.'s improvisations in Packer Memorial Church.

> Just after the Spanish War, "Hot Time in the Old Town Tonight" was a popular lilting tune. During the chapel one Sunday morning he improvised on this tune, making it one moment a lively hymn and the next the largo movement of a dirge.[65]

When J. Fred. played his farewell recital for members of The Bach Choir, he created a serious autobiographical improvisation. A news reporter described that very moving experience.

> Dr. Wolle displayed his inimitable originality and his great resources as an improviser. Dr. Wolle interwove the most prominent themes of the great masters and his own compositions into a life picture . . . of his struggles in manhood, his arduous labors to mount the steps of fame in the art of music and zenith of his achievements, ending with the ever familiar strains of "Auld Lang Syne." . . . the effect upon the audience can not be accurately described.[66]

When J. Fred. returned from California, he played an organ recital in Packer Memorial Church dedicated "to the Bach Choir and its friends." The program closed with an improvisation that must have been equally moving as the one he had played on his departure from Bethlehem. The subject of the improvisation was a hymn describing a soul's homesickness. In the spirit of a Moravian *Singstunde*, blessing J. Fred.'s return the audience stood and sang "Doxology," "Praise God from whom all blessings flow . . . Praise Father, Son and Holy Ghost."

J. Fred.'s stature as an Episcopal organist was summed up by Elwood Worcester, a prominent turn-of-the-century Episcopalian cleric. Worcester had been chaplain at Lehigh University for several years while J. Fred. was the chapel organist. Comparing organists he had known, Worcester began, "Among such men, who all possessed perfect technique, one can discriminate only according to the temperamental idiosyncrasies which appeal most to one's nature."[67] Worcester went on to compare J. Fred. with other organists he had worked with as a minister, including David Wood, J. Fred.'s blind Philadelphia teacher.

> I imagine that, in the course of my ministry, I have been as fortunate as any clergyman who ever lived, in the organists with whom I have been associated. First came the eloquent, deeply learned, deeply moving J. Fred. Wolle, a true musician in every sense of the word and a great interpreter of Bach.... Of them all, Mr. W. Lynwood Farnam ... enjoyed the widest fame. He was pronounced by good judges the greatest organist living, and by some, the greatest organist of all time. ... Having heard the best organists of our day, I must say that David Wood's interpretations have made the most indelible impression on my ... mind. During the Communion office, Mr. Wood always extemporized reverently, unobtrusively, airs and chords not of this earth. During all these years, whenever I have celebrated the Sacrament, these melodies have fallen on my ear like voices from another world.[68]

Worcester's statements make clear why J. Fred. held David Wood in a position of the highest respect as long as he lived. Sometime after 1911, J. Fred. printed a booklet of press releases. The following are two typical statements referring to his organ recitals. "NEW YORK TIMES. The apparent freedom of effort with which he managed his pedaling was grateful to the eye. MUSICAL COURIER, New York. Wolle is an organ genius."

J. Fred. had played the organ locally before he went to Munich, but when he returned to Bethlehem, at age twenty-one, he began to build a career in earnest. Two decades later, at age forty, he was known nationally as one the greatest organists in America. He had given recitals at two world exhibitions, performed in most major East Coast cities, and Andrew Carnegie offered him the post of organist in his Pittsburgh Carnegie Hall. J. Fred. refused the offer, preferring Bethlehem to another steel town. On the Lehigh Valley Rail Road, he traveled easily, where he wished, playing organ dedications, sharing programs with other organists, performing solo recitals, accompanying singers, and in at least one instance collaborating with a pianist by playing the orchestral part of Anton Rubenstein's Concerto for Piano in D Minor on the organ.

Moravians like J. Fred. were always concerned that music might be trivialized and become popular entertainment. Concerts should be elevating, hopefully religious, experiences. J. Fred. consistently maintained his Moravian musical background by playing programs that were entirely "serious." A music critic noted J. Fred.'s musical purpose when he reviewed J. Fred.'s New York organ debut. "His selection of pieces was serious, making no concession to the tastes of the flippant or careless. Yet, it proved, through the skill of the player, to be extremely entertaining."[69] This critic's comment that J. Fred. used his skill to be entertaining would have surely distressed him. But later in the review the critic wrote, "Mr. Wolle is an organist of excellent parts; his scholarship is sound, *his aim dignified*, [the author's italics] his technical skill is ample."[70] His attitude set him apart from other organists who included virtuoso crowd-pleasers along with serious pieces by Bach and Handel. J. Fred. believed with his ancestors that the organ was neither an instrument for entertainment nor for the display of virtuosity. The only concession to entertainment J. Fred. ever made was as the coach of the Lehigh Glee Club.

Not that he rejected the capability of the organs he played. On the contrary, for a critic wrote, "he plays Bach with a rich coloring of registration and delicate finesse of phrase."[71] After hearing J. Fred. play the sumptuous "Love's Death" from *Tristan* by Wagner, another reviewer commented "that the organ touched with the coloring suggested orchestral scoring can be a satisfactory substitute for orchestra."[72] Noting the modern taste for varied orchestral sounds on the organ used by J. Fred., a California critic wrote that the "Use of stops is original and shows the modern tendency for highly colored tonal effects."[73] However, a New York critic felt J. Fred. was excessive in this regard. "He believes in varied registration, and practices it perhaps a little too much, but his playing is smooth, and reposeful."[74]

This critic's comment was significant in another way. He remarked that J. Fred. played smoothly even though he changed registration frequently. According to the Lehigh student who spent many hours listening to him practice, J. Fred. always performed alone. For an organist that means he changed his own registration rather than having someone assist him. J. Fred. made his own changes by pulling or pushing the knobs on both sides of the keyboard so rapidly that his hands were not off the keyboard for long. This was an art in itself. The result was smooth playing without interruptions.

While the organ was not an instrument for entertainment, J. Fred. did not view it as an unemotional machine. For him registration enhanced and intensified emotion. J. Fred. had complained that European organists – he probably included Rheinberger – played Bach without emotion. They played without dynamic changes and with few changes in registration. These players argued that Bach wrote few dynamic markings and made no indications of registration, because he did not want these changes. If he had wanted more emotion, he would have written the necessary indications. J. Fred. took the position that all music was emotional and spiritual, especially the music of Bach. In a paper he delivered called "The Orchestra of Bach," J. Fred. criticized the way other organists played Bach ". . . it seemed that the purpose of nearly every organist is to make him sound as dry and ugly as possible," he wrote. "Even if it had been the custom in former days to play Bach in a stiff and dry manner, it was not common sense to do so today, but he would give his work natural expressiveness and human interpretation."

While J. Fred. was speaking of playing Bach, his idea went much further. Again, J. Fred. was firmly rooted in the Moravian tradition. Moravianism was called "the religion of the heart." Christian faith was an emotional experience, expressed through music, the language of the heart. Therefore, J. Fred. often changed the dynamics and the registration when he played and gave the music *natural* expressiveness, human [not mechanical] interpretation, and spiritual significance. Other reviews show his extensive emotional power and artistic insight into the possibilities of expression on the organ.

THE PHILADELPHIA PRESS. A musician of rare genius. THE PITTSBURGH POST . . . the large audience attested appreciation of Mr. Wolle's playing by frequent encores. THE PITTSBURGH PRESS. Exquisite playing at Carnegie Music Hall. Master of the organ. CHICAGO TRIBUNE . . . his conception of the Toccata [Bach] was a revelation even to the famous musicians with whom he was associated. SAN JOSE MORNING TIMES. Manages the pedals with utmost ease . . . and trills with them as unconcernedly as with his fingers. ERIE DAILY TIMES, Erie, Pa. . . . Wagner's 'Liebestod' held the audience spellbound. NEWS, Salt Lake City. He has awakened a great deal of interest in musical circles throughout the country. MUSICAL AMERICA. Great is Bach and Wolle is his prophet."[75]

For some reason J. Fred. reserved his most consistent Bach performances for the choral works. Except for the Ann Arbor recital and the American premiere of *The Art of the Fugue* in Bethlehem, strangely none of the recitals he played after the Expositions was an all-Bach program. What is more puzzling is why J. Fred. never played Bach's organ works at the Bach Festivals. The fact that he played *The Art of the Fugue* on the Lehigh University organ indicates the Lehigh instrument was adequate. Possibly a reason was that concerts were not part of J. Fred.'s Bach Festivals. Saturday morning concerts and recitals were added long after his death.

J. Fred. became so well-known as an organist that a reader of a musical magazine was prompted to ask the editor's opinion. He counted J. Fred. among the eight most prominent organists in America, giving a sense of J. Fred.'s stature as ranked by his contemporaries.

Sir: will you kindly tell me . . . if possible the best four organ players now residing in America. In my opinion, I will consider Clarence Eddy of Chicago and Mr. J. Fred. Wolle of Bethlehem, two of the best. The editor responded, ". . . beside those you mention, we might add Charles Heinroth, of the Carnegie Institute, Pittsburgh; Will C. MacFarlane, Portland, Me.; William C. Carl of New York; T. Teticus Noble, St. Thomas Church, New York City; Samuel P. Learner, New York; Arthur S. Hyde, New York."[76]

J. Fred. springs to life when reading the University documents describing his activities as a coach of the glee club. For these singers J. Fred. was not a public figure who was any more famous than other members of the faculty they heard lecture daily. They were often surrounded by famous men, so they saw no need to mythologize him.

Male glee clubs – Lehigh was not coeducational during Wolle's time – were the rage during the late nineteenth century, and there was almost as much concern that Lehigh have an excellent glee club as an outstanding football team. Mr. J. Fred. Wolle was the "coach" of the club. His name appeared frequently in the student newspaper and always with a sense of respect and pride. The following description of Professor Wolle is typical.

> In him the Club has a rare musician and an efficient coach, who is intensely interested in this organization and will devote a great deal of valuable time to the development of a Club worthy of the university. The musical education received at these rehearsals is alone worthy of your attendance.[77]

The glee club was newly formed each year, because seniors had graduated and there was always a new group of freshmen. Also, the glee club was a student-run organization, and the men chose a "coach" each year. Some years the students coached themselves, or there was no glee club due to lack of committed singers. After a period when there was no glee club, J. Fred. was asked to coach the group, and the newspaper reported "Professor Wolle was interviewed by the committee appointed at the last meeting, and very willingly agreed to act as director provided the students showed the proper interest in the success of the club."[78] In the same edition the editor expressed both J. Fred.'s enthusiasm and his concern for excellence.

> Mr. Wolle was, as he usually is over such matters, very enthusiastic and is anxious to do everything he possibly can to help the club along

> ... but let them remember that some sacrifices are necessary on the part of Mr. Wolle, and that he cannot afford to and will not spend his time with the club unless the members are in earnest and willing to attend the rehearsal promptly and regularly and give strict attention to business.[79]

These accounts of J. Fred.'s personality do not reveal a musician dominated every moment by the works of Bach, but a person who also actively performed and arranged popular music. As J. Fred. was creating record-setting performances of Bach masterpieces in Central Moravian Church, across the Lehigh River he was rehearsing the university glee club of sixteen or eighteen singers in "Massa's in the Cold, Cold Ground," "Old Jim Crow," and "Cottage Wee."[80]

The Glee Club performed in local concerts and on tours with the Lehigh Banjo Club, the University orchestra, and small groups of male singers. While the Glee Club never sang music that was "serious," several years after J. Fred. began conducting the group, *The Lehigh Burr* commented

> There seems to be a growing tendency on the part of the Glee Club to lighter music . . . than before. This is quite commendable and opens a field for originality. A committee of the Glee Club has been approached to draw up an arrangement under Mr. Wolle's instruction, a new medley of the latest and best songs of the day.[81]

As a result the Glee Club began singing among other songs "Lehigh Medley arr. Wolle," and "Brown and White, arr. Wolle." *The Brown and White* reported, "For the first time the Glee Club rendered Mr. Wolle's new Lehigh song, 'The Brown and White,' which of course was enthusiastically and deservedly encored." Clearly, J. Fred. was knowledgeable of the popular music for, "Among the favorites were 'Breezes of the Night,' and 'They Kissed, I saw them Do it.'"[82] Salon songs were included in the programs also. "The concert ended with a rendition of 'When the Snow Flakes Flutter Low,' which in its beauty and artistic finish showed the excellent training given to the club by Prof. Wolle [for they were all encored]."[83] J. Fred. was clearly a musician attuned to every facet of the music of his day, and a person who applied the same standards to all the music he performed regardless of musical style or depth.

Therefore, the Glee Club was a great success, and the student newspaper contained many accounts of which this was typical. "Lehigh will undoubtedly have a glee club that will rank among the college organizations and will meet with the hearty reception, with which the clubs of former years were invariably greeted."[84]

Judging from the description of an alumnus, while J. Fred. insisted on a high performance standard, at the same time he associated with his singers in a fraternal way.

> It was necessary that humorous songs [in the glee club] be rendered with the same musical finish as the more serious ones. It is recalled that in "Little Johnny Had a Mirror" there occurred a low D flat for second basses. The Doctor was always worried about it in rehearsal, but when Jim Budd and Bill Whilden would hit it on the nail, the Doctor would beam and pat these husky singers on the back.[85]

From the many times J. Fred.'s name was mentioned in the student journal and newspaper, it was clear he was an active, highly respected member of the faculty. A Lehigh University alumnus spoke of the feeling the students had for J. Fred., and gave a rare, detailed description of his appearance. While other accounts mentioned J. Fred.'s kindness and quietness, this account is unique in pointing out a nervous quality expressed in his speech and hands.

> In person, Mr. Wolle is tall and big boned, with the stoop of much leaning over the keyboard. His hands are firm and powerful, and never still; his face is strong and kindly, his soft voice, but rather high pitched, and his speech is rapid and nervous. He is singularly modest and lovable, and comes from an old Moravian family. He was well known to all the students at Lehigh in my time, and was not above directing and leading our glee club – a task that did little to add to his

laurels, I fear. Though it made him ever more popular with the boys, if such a thing were possible.[86]

J. Fred.'s niece, Hilda Doolittle, remembered seeing him walk rapidly "past the house and wave his music at us (when we shouted at him to come in) and say, 'I'm late for choir practice.'"[87]

. . .

In the year 1904, Moravian College and Theological Seminary conferred an honorary Doctor of Music degree upon J. Fred. The degree was in recognition "of your eminent ability as a musical director and performer of your excellent services given to the Moravian Church in the masterful accompaniment of congregational singing and the choir anthem and of the services you have rendered to the musical world at large in your interpretation of Bach and of the other great masters."[88]

The musical priorities for an organist in the Moravian Church were clearly outlined by the president conferring the degree. Accompanying congregational singing and the choir were of the most importance. Interpretation of Bach was secondary. In fact The Bach Choir was not mentioned at all, even though by 1904 it had an international reputation.

The degree was in recognition of his "musical and liturgical service to the Church."[89] The press report of the ceremony concluded with the statement, "As far as is known Mr. Wolle is the only Moravian in the world who has had so marked a distinction conferred upon him."[90] At a time when there were no graduate degrees in music in America, the honorary doctorate from Moravian College was a mark of high academic distinction everywhere. From then on Professor Wolle was Dr. Wolle. At a later date J. Fred.'s broader musical achievements were again recognized academically with honorary doctorates from the University of Pennsylvania and Princeton University.

Thus, J. Fred. was fully credentialed. He had received the highest recognition for his service to the Moravian Church and established his reputation as one of America's greatest organists. His choir was notable for its performances of Bach's choral works, and he was fluent in every style of music. An active national leader in two professional musical organizations, J. Fred. possessed boundless musical intelligence and energy.

All these attributes were duly considered by the president and trustees of the University of California, when they offered J. Fred. an opportunity that appeared to provide unlimited potential for him as a conductor of Bach's choral music. Music departments were rare in America, and with few models to follow, J. Fred. was to "use his own ideas in developing the music department."[91]

In an interview J. Fred. discussed his new appointment with a newspaper reporter who wrote, "The university exerts a dominant influence in educational matters, and Dr. Wolle feels there is an excellent opportunity for an awakening in the Bach cult."[92] J. Fred. told the editor of *The Moravian* that President Wheller assured him the people in the immediate vicinity of the university "are highly cultivated, and greatly appreciative of the very best in music. Renewed interest is shown in higher education and the development of the fine arts in the West."[93]

In the same interview he gave his reason for accepting President Wheller's offer, "Owing to the unfolding of this higher refinement of human society, this seems to be the time for an awakening in the liberal support of art tendencies."[94] He expressed the excitement that pervaded his time when there was the shared belief that cultivation of the arts would result in a more refined society. J. Fred. not only held that belief, but felt he was an artist who could create this "more refined society."[95] J. Fred.'s contemporaries also were convinced that he was one of the leading practitioners of their philosophy. The musical medium for this social agenda was the music of the greatest composer of Western music, J. S. Bach, followed closely by Wagner, Handel, Beethoven, Mendelssohn, and Mozart.

By extending opportunities to experience the arts to the citizens of California, the University of California – J. Fred. called it "a liberal and enterprising educational institution" – offered J. Fred. the opportunity

## ACADEMIC AND ORGAN VIRTUOSO

to expand his musical social mission beyond what he could do in Bethlehem.

Like the residents of Bethlehem, everyone at Lehigh University was shocked at the news of J. Fred.'s departure. Although the college term began after he left Bethlehem, the first fall issue of *The Brown and White* reported the sense of loss students felt.

> Dr. Wolle, for many years the University organist, and well known for his Bach festivals, has accepted the newly created chair of Music at the University of California. He left for California last week after he had given a farewell recital to the members of the Bach Choir in the University Chapel. The students from Lehigh will miss Dr. Wolle from morning chapel very much, nevertheless they wish him success in his new field of work.[96]

J. Fred.'s acceptance of President Wheller's offer was national news. But the press also made public that J. Fred. had been President Wheller's second choice. Walter Damrosch, conductor of the New York Symphony Orchestra, had informed a reporter that

> About three months ago I got a letter from him [Wheller] asking me whether, in case a chair of music were established in the university, and a suitable permanent orchestra organized in San Francisco, I will consider an offer of a professorship and a position of director of the orchestra... I promptly replied... it would be impossible for me to consider the proposition suggested, as all my future interests were bound up in the New York Symphony Orchestra.[97]

Typically, J. Fred. made no press response and requested a leave of absence from Central Moravian Church. Already described in the previous chapter, his request was granted and the family left Bethlehem for Berkeley. There he found himself a VIP. The reception he received was reported in *The Bethlehem Globe* immediately.

> Prof. Wolle dined with President Wheller yesterday, after which they went around the city together. President and Mrs. Wheller have

planned a reception for Dr. Wolle for next Thursday evening, when a large number of musical people around the bay will be given the opportunity of meeting the distinguished arrival.[98]

Immediately, J. Fred. organized a university chorus and a professional orchestra. To prepare for Bach performances, he expanded the chorus, including singers from local church choirs and children from Berkeley public schools. The orchestra grew to 104 instrumentalists. Dr. J. Fred., Professor of Music, began giving lectures in music history and composition. The San Francisco earthquake in 1906, his mother's death in the same year, and his daughter's serious illness caused J. Fred. to wonder if leaving Bethlehem had been a good idea. However, he decided to remain in California and permanently resigned his positions in Bethlehem.

The earthquake delayed the development of a "great Pacific Coast Bach Chorus," and the Mass in B Minor was not performed until 1909. About 10,000 people attended the performance in the University's Greek Theater. "With a touch of musical reverence and custom, Dr. Wolle brought the atmosphere of Bethlehem when he opened his festival with four trumpets who stood upon the hill tops and gave three German chorales . . . the greatest he [J. Fred.] ever saw."[99] The Second Bach Festival was held in May 1909. The festivals were immensely successful and a proposal to erect a "permanent chapel for Dr. Wolle's Bach choir" was made to the members of the Berkeley Chamber of Commerce. "A permanent home here for the choir would do much to make Berkeley famous all over the world . . . the festival would continue through a week, and would bring to Berkeley music lovers from every part of the globe, just as pilgrims flock to the festivals at Beyreuth [sic] and Oberammergau."[100]

J. Fred. was a professor of music at the University of California, three thousand miles from Bethlehem, Pennsylvania, because he was an expert Bach interpreter who could create choirs that sang Bach's monumental choral works. Yet, he was hardly conducting Bach. In reality J. Fred.'s contribution to the "cultivation" of the people in the San Francisco Bay area was not as a choral conductor. It was as an orchestral conductor. He gave them "the opportunity to listen to the classics interpreted by an ideal orchestra under the leadership of a master, cultivating, at last a musical taste in California second to none in the world."[101] Though that was not what J. Fred. had expected, it was undoubtedly as a symphony conductor that J. Fred. experienced his greatest growth as a musician while he was in California.

Almost overnight he became one of America's leading orchestral conductors. Each spring and fall, he gave a series of symphonic concerts in The Greek Theater. The extent of the repertoire he conducted was astonishing even for a seasoned orchestral conductor, which J. Fred. was not. Except for pieces by Wagner, he knew none of the works before he went to Berkeley. Yet, in the six years he lived there, J. Fred. conducted a professional orchestra that played most of the significant orchestral literature of his time. He conducted symphonies by Haydn, Mozart, Beethoven, Brahms, Schubert, Schumann, Tchaikowsky, Mendelssohn, and Dvořák; piano and violin concertos by Chopin, Liszt, Beethoven, and Tchaikowsky; a concert entirely devoted to Wagner; descriptive music by Richard Strauss, Wolf, Berlioz, Dvořák, Chabrier, Debussy, Goldmark, MacDowell, and Rimsky-Korsakov; and other works by Bach, Beethoven, Elgar, Glazounoff, Gluck, Grieg, Rameau, Rubinstein, Suk, Weber, Saint-Saëns, Massenet, and Nicolai. The only area he did not venture into was opera, though J. Fred. did collaborate in dramatic performances in The Greek Theater by conducting incidental orchestral music for a number of plays.

While J. Fred. received only rave reviews in response to his musical performances, according to his nephew Francis, "Yet at the end of six years, when his sabbatical leave came up, he and his family returned without hesitation to Bethlehem."[102] J. Fred. discovered he was a practical musician. He did not want to talk about music and had not done so at Lehigh University. He called the ladies of the town who came to his lectures "the pelicans." They were in his classes to absorb culture by hearing him give lectures and play the music on the piano. "Working in and with music – in this way only does one get to the heart of what music is all about," he told his nephew.[103] In addition, the family did not like the climate. They missed the family and the Moravian community. In spite of the musical resources at his disposal, his nephew wrote "the university atmosphere was alien to him and on the whole he did not care for it."[104]

Quite unexpectedly, The Bethlehem Steel Company gave him an opportunity to return to Bethlehem. Charles Schwab, the President, was visiting San Francisco, and he attended one of J. Fred.'s concerts. A devoted music lover, Schwab was very familiar with J. Fred.'s work, though he had not attended any Bethlehem Bach Festivals. Schwab was eager to develop Bethlehem into an ideal industrial community, full of opportunity and culture and for that reason he wanted J. Fred. to return to Bethlehem. If he reestablished The Bach Choir and the annual festivals, Schwab would underwrite any deficit.

Charles Schwab, president of Bethlehem Steel
(Special Collections, Lehigh University)

Initially, he placed no limit on his support either financial or political. Since Schwab was the president of one of the great steel companies of the world, his financial and political attributes seemed limitless. The idea of a permanent home for The Bach Choir may have been discussed also. J. Fred. accepted Schwab's offer, and the Wolles left California for Pennsylvania with trunks of Oriental objects Jennie had purchased in Chinatown. In a rare reference to J. Fred.'s wife, his nephew wrote that "she [Jennie] reveled in the Chinese-made rugs, china, pottery and furniture, and after the return to Bethlehem their home reflected the exquisite taste of her Chinatown purchases."[105]

J. Fred. returned to Bethlehem a consummate musician. With his talent, musical skill, and reputation, he was prepared to confront the most daunting musical situations and turn them into triumphs. He was the equal of the finest organists, choir masters, and orchestral conductors in America. His return to Bethlehem would cap the musical achievements of the Wolle dynasty.

## NOTES

1. *The Brown and White*, 26 January 1905. This is the Lehigh University student newspaper. Bound volumes are in Special Collections at Lehigh University.
2. Elwood Worcester, *Life's Adventure* (New York: Charles Scribner's Sons, 1932), 140.
3. "Organ Recitals by J. Fred. Wolle." [n.d.], 8. Pamphlet in the Archives of The Bach Choir of Bethlehem.
4. *Register of Lehigh University*, 1898–99, 17.
5. Ibid., 1904–05, 11.
6. Ibid., 1894–95, 35.
7. *The Moravian,* 11 December 1899.
8. "The Official Diary of the Congregation," 17 November 1901.
9. Ibid., 28 April 1896.
10. Ibid., 7 April 1901.
11. H. D., *The Gift* (New York: A New Directions Book, 1982), 10.
12. "Official Diary," 29 March 1902.
13. Ibid., 4 July 1897.
14. Ibid., 27 May 1900.
15. *The Moravian*, 8 May 1889, 294.
16. Levering. *A History of Bethlehem, Pennsylvania*, 770.
17. "Official Dairy," 19 September 1901.
18. Ibid., 13 April 1900.
19. Ibid., April 1904.
20. In addition to entries in the church diary, there is a handwritten document in the Archives of The Bach Choir of Bethlehem containing the

titles of Bach works performed in Central Moravian Church. The performances are listed chronologically. Since the manuscript does not contain all the Bach references found in the church diary, this list may represent information from another unidentified source(s).

21. *The Lehigh Burr*, 1889–90, 30.
22. Ibid., 1901–02, 14.
23. Ibid., 20 February 1888, 107–8.
24. "Class of 1891 Henry C. Quigley, Correspondent," *Lehigh Alumni Bulletin,* February 1933, 13.
25. *The Brown and White,* 14 February 1898.
26. Ibid., 22 February 1900.
27. *Lehigh Alumni Bulletin,* see note 24.
28. Yates, Ross, *Sermon in Stone: Packer Memorial Church* (Lehigh University, Bethlehem, Pennsylvania: 1988), 8.
29. *The Brown and White,* 7 December 1898.
30. Ibid.
31. Ibid.
32. *The Bethlehem Times,* 19 May 1902. In scrap "Book 6" in the Archives of The Bach Choir of Bethlehem.
33. *The Lehigh Burr,* 8 February 1889, 90.
34. Ibid.
35. *The Lehigh Burr,* 20 March 1889, 124–25. The full program was Fantasia and Fugue in G Minor, J. S. Bach; Minuet in B flat, Handel, arranged by W. T. Best; "Spring Song in A," Harry Rowe Shelly; "Prayer and Cradle Song in A flat," Felix Alexander Guilmant; Melody in A, Ambroise Thomas; Fanfare in D, Nicolas Jacques Lammen; Theme and Variations in A flat, Louis Thiele.
36. Ibid.
37. Ibid., 2 June 1898.
38. Ibid., 15 November 1890, 37. J. Fred.'s previous organ recital was not two years before, but two terms before, in 1889.
39. Ibid., 6 June 1891.
40. Ibid., for the complete program.
41. *The Brown and White,* 8 March 1897.
42. Not reviewed.
43. *The Brown and White,* 10 March 1899.
44. Ibid., 24 April 1903.
45. "The Official Diary," 12 September 1887.

46. "Pay Roll 1893–1898." Manuscript in Special Collections at Lehigh University.
47. "The Official Diary," 8 July 1901.
48. Ibid., 20 October 1901.
49. Ibid., 26 October 1901.
50. *The Lehigh Burr*, 22 April 1892.
51. *The Brown and White*, 29 March 1900.
52. Ibid., 15 May 1903.
53. Rose Fay Thomas, *Memoirs of Theodore Thomas* (New York: Moffat, Yard and Company, 1911), 386–387 both quotes.
54. *Official Programme of Exposition Concerts, Chicago May–October, 1893*. Organ Concert No. 52 Organist, J. Frederick Wolle Bach Program. In the special collection of the Chicago Public Library.
55. The chief organist at the Exposition, Clarence Eddy, performed more works by Bach than J. Fred. played. Eddy played a total of thirteen Bach pieces. J. Fred. had played ten. Eddy, however, distributed Bach among the twenty-one concerts he gave.
56. "Bach at St. Louis." Unidentified clipping with handwritten date, "Nov. 5, 1904." Archives of The Bach Choir of Bethlehem.
57. Ibid.
58. "Dr. Wolle at Exhibition," *St. Louis Republic*, 28 October 1904. Loose clipping in the Archives of The Bach Choir of Bethlehem.
59. Unidentified and undated newspaper clipping in the archives of The Bach Choir.
60. "Bach at St. Louis"; see note 56.
61. "Organ Recital March 17, 1921." A loose program in the Archives of The Bach Choir of Bethlehem.
62. Ibid.
63. *The Brown and White*, 15 November 1904.
64. Ibid., 15 November 1904.
65. Yates. *Sermon in Stone*, 11.
66. *The Bethlehem Globe*, 12 September 1905.
67. Worcester, *Life's Adventure*, 140.
68. Ibid., 141–43.
69. *The Lehigh Burr*, 6 December 1897. Quoted from the *New York Tribune*.
70. Ibid.
71. Loose newspaper item in Book 6. Archives of The Bach Choir of Bethlehlem.

72. Ibid.
73. "Organ Recitals . . ." in Book 8. Archives of The Bach Choir of Bethlehem.
74. Ibid.
75. "Organ Recitals by J. Fred. Wolle." See note 73.
76. Scrapbook 6. Archives of The Bach Choir of Bethlehem. Loose news item. [n. d.].
77. *The Lehigh Burr*, 19 October 1900.
78. Ibid., 14 March 1898.
79. Ibid.
80. Ibid., March 1889.
81. Ibid., 11 April 1894.
82. *The Brown and White*, 14 February 1893.
83. Ibid., 16 February 1901.
84. Ibid., 12 November 1900.
85. Henry C. Quigley, Class of 1891, Correspondent, *Lehigh Alumni Bulletin,* February 1933, 13.
86. *The Bethlehem Times,* 19 May 1902.
87. H. D. *The Gift*, 102.
88. "Bach Choir Leader Honored with Degree." Unidentified newspaper clipping in the Archives of The Bach Choir of Bethlehem.
89. *The Moravian,* 18 January 1933.
90. Ibid.
91. *The North American Sunday,* no date. Archives of The Bach Choir of Bethlehem.
92. Ibid.
93. *The Moravian,* 20 September 1905.
94. Ibid.
95. Ibid.
96. *The Brown and White,* 21 September 1898.
97. *Public Ledger,* [Philadelphia], Undated clipping in the Archives of The Bach Choir of Bethlehem.
98. *The Bethlehem Globe,* 28 September 1905.
99. Unidentified newspaper clipping in the Archives of The Bach Choir of Bethlehem.
100. *The Bethlehem Globe,* 23 June 1909.
101. "Dr. Wolle to Conduct Symphony Concerts," 7 Feburary 1906. Unidentified newspaper clipping in the Archives of The Bach Choir of Bethlehem.

102. Francis Wolle, *A Moravian Heritage*, 44.
103. Ibid., 43.
104. Ibid., 43.
105. Ibid., 43.

Chapter Eleven

## *Church Composer*

J. Fred. Wolle. . . . composer.
—Central Moravian Church Bulletin[1]

FOLLOWING THE PRACTICE of his ancestors, J. Fred. composed almost entirely for the Moravian Church. Although he achieved international fame as a conductor of Bach, and national fame as an organist in the high Romantic style, "to us of the Moravian Church he is particularly endeared because of what he did to enrich the musical and liturgical services of our own Church."[2] Similarly, it was "in recognition of his musical and liturgical services to the Church" that Moravian College granted J. Fred. an honorary degree in 1904.[3] Two Wolle chorales were printed and remain in the repertoire of the Moravian Church, "these have become great favorites in Moravian circles; the former being sung regularly on Palm Sunday, ["Ride On!" Ride On in Majesty"] and the latter repeatedly during the Advent season ["Once He Came in Blessing"]."[4]

Generally, the chorales are firmly in the musical style of the nineteenth century. They possess melodies that are mostly scale-wise, and the rhythms are simple and direct. J. Fred. employed harmonizations in four parts using keys and chords associated with the harmonic language of sacred music in the Victorian hymn tradition. Each chorale shows J. Fred.'s complete mastery of this musical style. At the same time these chorales embody the theology of the Moravian Church as expressed by J. Fred. He deviated enough from the Victorian style to make each chorale stand out from the thousands that were composed during that century, an era known for its pious Christianity.

"Once He Came in Blessing" was composed in the year 1888. This is an Advent hymn in which J. Fred. expressed the belief that within the blessing of the lowly birth of Christ was his sacrifice.

*1. Once He came in blessing*
*All our ills redressing,*
*Came in likeness lowly,*
*Son of God most holy;*
*Bore the Cross to save us, Hope and freedom gave us.*
*. . . . . . . . . .*

*4. He, who well endureth,*
*Bright reward secureth;*
*Come Thee, O Lord Jesus,*
*From our sins release us;*
*Let us here confess Thee,*
*Till in heaven we bless Thee.*[5]

The chorale is in the key of G Major with modulation to the parallel key E Minor. J. Fred. used these keys symbolically and used them to harmonize the words expressing the birth and its qualities of sacrifice. Because the ideas are closely related so are the keys. The phrases "Once He came," "in likeness lowly," and "Son of God most holy," are in G Major, a confident key. However, he expressed Christ's coming sacrifice, "All our ills redressing," "Bore the Cross to save us," and "From our foolish errors," in the key of E Minor. Though the chorale is strophic, i.e., the same melody for a number of different verses, the key symbolism present in the first verse continues through the other verses as well. J. Fred. composed this setting very thoughtfully, imbuing the words with rich musical and spiritual meaning. This type of harmonic treatment is not at all conventional in the nineteenth century. Melodies were composed and harmonized with little concern for such subtle treatment of the theological meaning of the text.

J. Fred. composed "Ride On! Ride On in Majesty" in the year 1888. It is a hymn for Palm Sunday. This hymn is the partner of "Once He Came in Blessing." "Ride On! Ride On in Majesty" describes the beginning of Christ's sacrifice.

> 1. Ride on! ride on in majesty!
> In lowly pomp ride on to die;
> O Christ Thy triumphs now begin
> O'er captive death and conquered sin.
> . . . . . . . . . .
> 5. Ride on! ride on in majesty!
> In lowly pomp ride on to die;
> Bow They meek head to mortal pain,
> Then take, O God, Thy power, and reign.[6]

True to his key symbolism, J. Fred. composed this chorale in E Minor with modulations to the closely related key of G Major. The order of keys in this hymn is exactly opposite from the order J. Fred. used in the companion hymn. The phrases "in lowly pomp ride on to die" "to see the approaching sacrifice" are in the key of E Minor, while "majesty!" and "Hosanna cry!" are in the key of G Major. In this hymn the triumph of Christ and the pain of the coming crucifixion are intimately related and, as in the other hymn, so are the keys.

Comparing these two Moravian chorales reveals a remarkable similarity between them. In both J. Fred. exercised great care in setting the hymns. He did much more that compose generally appropriate tunes harmonized in conventional ways. For both hymns he chose the key of G Major to express the redemptive Christ and the key of E minor to express the pain of Christ's sacrifice. Even the choice of these two texts was certainly not coincidental. They encapsulate for Moravians the two most important events in Christ's life. It is interesting that in the collection of his manuscripts at Lehigh University, these two chorales were copied on the same sheet of music paper by J. Fred. – one tune on the front and the other on the back. This manuscript may indicate that J.

# CHURCH COMPOSER 327

Fred. composed the hymns together not just in the same year. This creative sensitivity to the musical expression of Moravian theology was a remarkable quality of J. Fred.'s musical thinking that was lifelong. It made no difference whether he used the works of Bach to create complete festivals or composed a "simple" hymn setting. As evidence of the vitality and validity of J. Fred.'s expression of these beliefs, these hymns remained part of Moravian hymnody for more than one hundred years. Since they were included in the most recent revision of the American Moravian hymnal, they are a testimony to the contribution of J. Fred. to the religious and music life of Bethlehem.

J. Fred.'s third contribution to Moravian hymnody was composed in the years 1889 and 1890. It is a chorale setting of a poem from the Middle Ages, "Day of wrath, that day of mourning," describing the final day of judgement. J. Fred. chose a contemporary translation of this Latin hymn, a version made in 1848 in Elizabethan English, which sounded "ancient" to Victorians.

> *1. Days of wrath, that day of mourning!*
> *See fulfilled the prophet's warning,*
> *Heaven and earth in ashes burning!*
> . . . . . . . . . .
> *8. Kind of majesty tremendous,*
> *Who dost free salvation send us,*
> *Fount of pity, then befriend us!*
> *9. Think, kind Jesus! my salvation*
> *Caused Thy wondrous incarnation,*
> *Leave me not to reprobation.*
> . . . . . . . . . .
> *19. Spare, O God, in mercy spare him!* [mankind]
> *Lord all-pitying, Jesus blest,*
> *Grant him Thine eternal rest.*[7]

J. Fred. brought his usual penetrating reading of this text to the chorale. The key is D Minor. He chose that key because D Minor was "of a heavy and dark cast . . . soulful, solemn and grand."[8] D Minor was also the key of choice for musical setting of the Requiem Mass of which the "Dies Irae" is a major part. In addition to the musical key symbolism, this chorale contains many instances of skillful word painting, however, one was particularly inspired. Verse one concludes with the phrase "Heaven and earth in ashes burning." J. Fred. set this phrase with a melody that is a D Minor scale that descends a full octave. Thus, Heaven and earth collapse musically and arrive at the bottom of the scale in dust. There are few hymn settings as highly charged symbolically and as dramatic in the whole chorale literature as J. Fred.'s "Dies Irae," composed in 1889.

The following year J. Fred. surpassed his original conception by recomposing the "Dies Irae." J. Fred. realized that the text actually could be divided into two parts. The first eight verses described God, the final Judge, and His wrath. Verses ten through nineteen asked if the birth and death of Christ might act as a protection against God's wrath on that day of judgement. After he divided the text into these two sections, J. Fred. expressed the two meanings by composing a new chorale, which he added to the original one. Thus, he turned his 1889 setting into an absolutely unique double chorale. While his solution to express a theological belief so directly within a hymn was without precedent, the desire to express religious hymns dramatically and at the same time very personally was part of the spirit of the time. J. Fred. applied this Victorian musical and Christian spirit to a hymn setting.

While J. Fred. chose keys for these two "Dies Irae" chorales that are directly related, the keys are not related in the same way as they are in the two earlier chorales. There the sections are in major and minor keys that share the same key signature, the same number of sharps. For the two "Dies Irae" chorales, J. Fred. exploited the other major/minor relationships existing in the tonal system that governs most Western music. The first chorale is in D Minor, and the second is in D Major, what is called the parallel major key. J. Fred. uses the juxtaposition of minor/major to express the two ideas of the text, the fatal judgement in minor, and the optimism of Christ's intercession in major. D Major is "ample, grand, noble. It is suited to the loftiest purposes."[9] In his choice of keys, J. Fred. was tapping into deep musical associations in the same way he did in his use of minor and major. Just as the change from minor to major is stunning, in the same way the change of key from D Minor to D Major is highly expressive to an informed musician.

When J. Fred. used a double chorale for the "Dies Irae," he solved a generic problem in composing music for hymns in which different emotions were expressed in separate verses. Normally, the hymn tune was not intended to express specific emotions at all. The meaning of individual words was not reflected in the music. Music's function was to convey the text "to the heart." The significance of J. Fred.'s "Dies Irae" is that not only was he sensitive to changes in the poetry, he reflected the changes within the chorale. The effect of singing eight verses in minor and then changing to major at the mention of Christ's intercession must have been stunning in its time.

Like the first "Dies Irae" chorale, the second contained musical word painting. The most dramatic occurred in the ninth verse, which concluded with the phrase "Leave me not to reprobations!" At this point J. Fred. composed a melody that drops a full octave with no intervening pitches. Again, such a setting is perhaps unique in Christian hymnody. The norm was melodies that remained fundamentally scalewise. Further, to enhance the meaning of "reprobations," J. Fred. added a B flat to the harmony. That pitch is not in the key of D Major, but it is in the key of D Minor from which J. Fred. borrowed it. In this subtle but striking detail, J. Fred. ingeniously reminded the singers of the day of judgement. While the "Dies Irae" is no longer in the Moravian hymnal, J. Fred.'s setting makes him a master of American hymnody.

J. Fred. composed four liturgical chants for the Moravian Church. Three were printed in the Moravian Hymnal published in 1923. The other chant, "Gloria in Excelsis" was not printed and was believed lost until it was recently found in the collection of The Moravian Museum of Bethlehem.

"Gloria in Excelsis" was probably the first chant J. Fred. composed. The church diary contains a reference to its performance on Christmas, 25 December 1895. "In the English liturgy the Gloria in Excelsis was chanted for the first time instead of being read in concerts as hitherto. The chant was composed by our organist, J. Fred. Wolle."[10]

*Glory to God in the highest,*
*And on earth peace, good will*
*Toward men.*
*We praise Thee,*
*We bless Thee,*
*We glorify Thee,*
*We give thanks to Thee,*
*For Thy great glory.*
*Lord God, Lamb of God,*
*That takest away the sins of the world,*
*Have mercy upon us.*[11]

Wolle composed this chant with the same care and spiritual sensitivity as is evidenced in the chorales. The first section, expressing praise and adoration, is in the key of G. The final section, asking for forgiveness of sins, Wolle sets in the related key of E Minor. These are exactly the same key relationships Wolle used in the two printed chorales. The melodies for both verses descend as if the singers are bowing. The rhythm is identical for each section, because God's glory is the source of forgiveness.

In 1923 a revised Moravian hymnal was published. J. Fred. was very involved in preparing this edition. *The Moravian* reported that, "From 1920 to 1923 he rendered invaluable service to the Moravian Church at large as a member of the Hymn-book Committee, which produced our present hymnal. He went over each chant, tune, melody and chorale with meticulous care. He was thoroughly imbued with the spirit of the ancient chorales."[12] Chants were composed for the new hymnal to replace those from the early nineteenth century.

Though these chants are more modest in length than the chorales, they also display J. Fred.'s sensitivity to the musical expression of Moravian beliefs. "The Canticle of Praise" is eight short chants that are part of a long spoken liturgy. Two other chants were for rites of ordination: one for a deacon and one for a presbyter.

J. Fred.'s chants for the "Canticle of Praise" replaced a litany by the great Moravian liturgical composer, Christian Gregor. Gregor's canticle was an extended piece for three-part choir with string accompaniment. For the 1923 Hymnal, Gregor's choir piece was revised to include spoken sections and vocal responses. Though J. Fred. eliminated the string accompaniment and composed chants harmonized in four parts, he retained the flavor of Gregor's choral canticle. J. Fred.'s chants are a bit too difficult for gracious congregational singing and could be sung more easily by trained voices. This chant began with the statement "Magnify Him forever." Both the rhythms and the arrangements of voice parts were similar to music for a choir. Interestingly, this phrase was the only instance in J. Fred.'s compositions that resembled the music of Bach or Handel. The sound was decidedly that of baroque music. Other sections of the canticle contained unusual intervals or rhythms more suited for choir singing. Though some sections resembled baroque musical gestures, others were more in the classical style, and the final chant was very modern because of its chromatic harmonies. It was as if J. Fred. were transporting the congregation through an abbreviated history of church music to emphasize the idea of "forever" that occurred frequently in the canticle. The final chant was the one richest in musical symbolism. He set the final section, "His mercy endureth forever," using chords that were very modern in sacred music in the 1920s. The chords wander over a vast tonal area, as if they investigate all musical space, thus "forever." Not only were the chords modern and full of theological meaning, the melody was totally symbolic as well. J. Fred. had the soprano part sing only the pitch B flat – another way of stating "forever." Both the text and the chants for the "canticle" have been eliminated from the most recent hymnal.

Two other chants are for the ordination of a deacon and a presbyter. Though the rites are different, J. Fred. composed two "Doxologies" in the same key. Appropriate to the occasion of high elevation, J. Fred. chose the key of B Major, a key with five sharps. Again, J. Fred. showed his mastery of innovation. B Major is not used for any other chorale or chant in the entire hymnal. Both chants are further heightened in their expressiveness by the use of unexpected chromatic chords that resolve in unusual ways. Both chants conclude with the same "Amen, Hallelujah." In this case J. Fred.'s chants were replaced in the most recent hymnal with ones that Moravian composers associate with an earlier tradition. They verify the recognition given to J. Fred. in his Moravian obituary. "He was thoroughly imbued with the spirit of the ancient chorales."[13] Using the fully developed Romantic harmony, J. Fred. recast that "ancient" spirit in the spirit of the early twentieth century in a way to make him revered by his Moravian contemporaries.

When the sacred song "Ueber den Sternen" was composed is not known. Though J. Fred. used very simple rhythms associated with the chorale style, this song was probably written for the choir, for J. Fred.'s harmonies and individual voice lines are more difficult to sing than those found in the usual hymn. Though there is a manuscript score of "Ueber den Sternen" in the Lehigh University collection, copies of the individual voice parts are also in the folder indicating the song was probably sung by a choir or small group of trained voices. The song is pleasing, competent, and typical of the time, but it is not as distinguished as J. Fred.'s other hymns and chants. The reason for its composition is unknown, and there are no records of its performance. The song remains unpublished.

Manuscripts of three extended sacred compositions for chorus composed by J. Fred. exist. They are titled "Bonum est," "Ambassadors of Christ!," and "He Leads Us On." These pieces are early works, composed between 1884 and 1888.

"He Leads Us On" is the most notable. This is a his last large-scale choral work. At the end of the manuscript there was a notation in J.

Fred.'s hand, "Aug. 25th 1888." While this anthem was not as complex or innovative harmonically as the two earlier anthems, it was more complex in its form, the use of soloists, and in the orchestral accompaniment. Unlike the two earlier choruses however, "He Leads Us On" had another important characteristic of Romantic music, grandeur. The nineteenth-century musical style was grand, solemn, dramatic, rich in the use of harmony, and in the interaction between soloists, chorus, and orchestra. "He Leads Us On" had all these characteristics. Though it was less innovative harmonically, this anthem was no regression. Because of its grandeur and length, J. Fred.'s anthem was the finest composed by a Moravian composer in the nineteenth century. Though other non-Moravian Americans had composed large-scale cantatas and oratorios following the Civil War, "He Leads Us On" may be among the finest single anthem composed by an American before 1890.

While this anthem also was never published and had no influence beyond Bethlehem, "He Leads Us On" was valued in the Bethlehem Moravian community. The work was first performed in 1894, four years after it was composed. The premiere was an important occasion, the sesquicentennial of the founding of Bethlehem. A detailed description of the celebration was written by Bethlehem historian, Bishop Levering.

> The music of the large choir and orchestra, for which careful preparation had been made, fully met the expectation of the people, and its character was sustained throughout in the subsequent services. One of the selections, rendered with impressive effect, was a composition by the choir-master, J. Fred Wolle, for the first time on that occasion. The text, in three stanzas, opened with the words: "He leads us on by paths we do not know."[14]

A year later the piece was performed again for the Festival of the Married Brothers. That performance was notable enough to appear in the church diary account. "The composition of our organist Br. J. Fred. Wolle to the words "He leads us on" sung for the first time at the Festal Evening service of the 150th Anniversary of the Beth. Congregation last year, was given in this service and thus brought into regular use."[15] The anthem was apparently sung annually for the Festival of the Married Brothers. J. Fred. felt his anthem, "He Leads Us On," was good enough to be the musical centerpiece of a number of important public celebrations, including the sesquicentennial of Bethlehem in 1892 and the twenty-fifth anniversary of The Bach Choir in 1925. The anthem was revived in 1956 as part of the service celebrating the sesquicentennial of the completion of Central Moravian Church. The published text for this *Singstunde* contained this note on "He Leads Us On":

> This anthem is a setting of Hiram O. Wiley's hymn which is an elaboration on Zinzendorf's hymn "Jesus still lead on." Composed in August 1888, when Dr. Wolle was organist and choir master of this church, it has become the composer's best known anthem. This afternoon it is being performed in Central Church for the first time in fifty years. Like most of Dr. Wolle's compositions, this anthem has never been published. Copies for use in this service have been made available through the courtesy of Lehigh University Library which is the repository of the Wolle manuscript.[16]

The anthem was a spacious work; 10 minutes is penciled in on the autograph. It is scored for four-part chorus with solos for a soprano and bass, the string orchestra with the addition of two horns, three trombones, and organ. This orchestration is highly unusual for the period, for there are no winds and J. Fred. used the trombones in solo passages throughout the anthem. From the presence of the trombones, it is clear that J. Fred. planned the piece for Moravian services where trombones figure so prominently. The composition contains another very Moravian quality. The organ is never used soloistically. It accompanies the voices and instruments by playing sustained chords exactly as it did in the anthems of Peter Wolle and his predecessors. "He Leads Us On" was a composition by one of the great organists of the time, and yet J. Fred. continued a tradition of Moravian use of the organ by composing a part that dutifully and modestly called no attention to the organist. Such a restrained use of the organ, the grand Romantic instrument, was extraordinary. It could only have been written by a Moravian with a very strong sense of tradition. Finally, again in the Moravian tradition, this was a concerted anthem at a time when very few churches had orchestras. If J. Fred. had composed this anthem for another church, it would have been accompanied only by the organ. When other churches did use an orchestra to accompany the choir, it would have been for Christmas or Easter, not for an ordinary church festival like that for the Married Brothers.

"He Leads Us On" is squarely in the Romantic style of the New German School – but not the conservative polyphonic style of Rheinberger. Even though J. Fred admired his teacher enough to play organ works by him and conduct his sacred compositions on a number of occasions, he did not copy his compositions. There is no counterpoint anywhere in the anthem. This music is much more Wagnerian in that broad melodies are accompanied by a rich orchestration over slow moving harmonies giving the piece an expansive feeling.

"He Leads Us On" is a setting of the poem by the same name in the high Victorian style.

> *He leads us on*
> *By paths we do not know;*
> *Upward He leads us*
> *Though our steps be slow;*
> *Though oft we faint and falter by the ways,*
> *Though storms and darkness oft obscure the day,*
> *Yet, when the clouds are gone,*
> *We know He leads us on.*
> *He leads us on*
> *Through all the unquiet years;*
> *Past all our dreamland hopes and doubts and fears*
> *He guides our steps;*
> *Through all the tangled maze of sin,*
> *Of sorrow, and o'erclouded days,*

*We know His will is done,*
*And still He leads us on.*
*And He, at last,*
*After the weary strife,*
*After the restless fever we call life,*
*After the dreariness, the aching pain,*
*The wayward struggles, which have been in vain,*
*After our toils are paid,*
*Will give us rest at last.*

— Hiram O. Wiley

J. Fred. wrote an extended musical introduction in which the two arch-Romantic instruments, the horn and the cello, play solos. Violins and violas accompanied them with a moving figure, while the cellos, basses, and organ play very long chords. The key is G flat Major, the same key Theodore chose for "Asleep in Jesus." It is the key for profound, otherworldly expression.

When the chorus enters, J. Fred. creates a melody that emphasizes the words "Though our steps be slow." The altos sing the first part of the phrase and the sopranos complete it. The men enter with the same melody in unison. They break off at the word "faint," the rhythm becomes irregular for "falter," and the orchestra becomes agitated when the basses sing about storms and darkness, and the harmonies become ambiguous and dissonant expressing "Oft obscure the day."

J. Fred. repeats the first seven lines of the poem using the same melody, but the choral voices are arranged differently and the accompaniment is enriched by more active and wide-ranging figures in the strings. For the conclusion of the verse, the chorus breaks into parts and reaches a climax with the first use of rich, chromatic harmonies. A rather ecstatic interlude follows.

For the second verse, J. Fred. returns to the quiet opening, but now the key is even more distant, E-flat Minor. The chorus disappears, and a soprano solo emerges. "Unquiet years," "dreamland hopes and fears" are all set expressively, building to a very dramatic section in which J.

Fred. expresses the "tangled maze of sin" by having the cello play erratic, rapid chromatic passages while the harmonies constantly change and the rhythm in the upper strings is all off the beat.

The key changes and we arrive triumphantly and optimistically in C Major. For the first time the chorus sings in four parts, the violins play the opening melody and, of the greatest importance, the trombones sound. There is hope! This repetition of the text allows J. Fred. to extend the piece, as well as provides him an opportunity to give the work symphonic proportions. The section is like the development of a symphony. This anthem is not just operatic, it is also in the grand symphonic tradition.

The first section of the final verse is a bass solo, balancing the soprano solo earlier. Every dramatic word finds its reflection in the orchestration and harmony. The chorus enters with a variation of the original melody, and the verse comes to a peaceful conclusion in the original key of G-flat Major.

Probably the most beautiful part of the piece is the coda J. Fred. composed to separate lines he took from various verses. Again the feelings of faltering, darkness, obscure ways, and clouds are expressed, but everything is transformed, because of the assurance that now God finally gives rest. (Again, the resemblance in key to his Uncle Theodore's "Asleep in Jesus," which expressed the same thoughts, is remarkable.) The organ is silent, strings pluck harp-like, a solo violin plays the opening melody in a high register, and the trombones sound God's word.

This section is not only the most beautiful, it is the most inspired musically. As the violin plays the opening of the anthem, the motive associated with the text "He leads us on," the choir sings the end of the final stanza of the set to the chorale "Old Hundred." The text of that hymn is "Praise God from whom all blessings flow." By combining these two pieces of music, each with its own meaning, J. Fred. achieves a richer combined meaning, Christ's leadership is a blessing of God. In any context, this level of musical composition is rare. For J. Fred. to have composed such a section that expresses Moravian belief so effectively is an act of genius.

To conclude the anthem, J. Fred. has the chorus repeat "He will give us rest" three times – sacred number symbolism; first with the choir *a capella*, like the voices of angels, then with full orchestra including the trombones, and finally by the chorus again singing *a capella*. The strings enter muted, the chorus sings "At last," and the anthem concludes with the motive "He leads us on" played very low by the organ, then higher by the violas, the second violins, and finally, the first violins play the motive ending on the pitch G flat. The piece ends in the same key as it began.

J. Fred.'s hymns, liturgies, and church anthems are all of such high quality in musical invention and sacred expression that they are reasons to forge him a rightful place as a Moravian composer of note. At the same time his music is evidence not only that the Wolle musical dynasty of composers remained intact through three generations, but that each composer added to and shaped that tradition.

J. Fred. did not only compose sacred music, he wrote three solo songs and a duet for two sopranos. J. Fred. composed an *Alma Mater* for Lehigh University, and arranged two medleys of popular songs for the University men's chorus he coached. Nothing was published.

As might be expected each of the songs contains telling musical gestures. "Aunt Jane's Moon Song" contains a number of these gestures. It is a cradle song with a folklike melody. Each of the four verses begins the same but ends differently. While the melody is in triple meter, the piano accompaniment is in duple meter. This opposition of rhythmic patterns is unusual. The effect is one of frequent rhythmic dissonance between the voice and the piano. In addition, the left hand of the piano remains unchanged throughout, creating the repeated motion of a lullaby. To add harmony, J. Fred. wrote a right-hand accompaniment based on an ascending scale of triads that are rolled. For verses three and four, the right-hand pattern is repeated, but now it descends. Like the bass, the harmony reflects the repeated motion of a lullaby. Also, as with the bass rhythms, the harmonies are not always in sync with the melody. Many subtle dissonances occur between the song and the accompaniment. The song is carefully crafted and captures the various moods of the poem. There is no date on the unpublished manuscript.

"The Daisy" is dated August '92. Again, the melody is somewhat ballad-like in character, however, the piano accompaniment is technically demanding and harmonically rich. Unfortunately, the manuscript of the third art song, "Cloudland," is only a sketch with an incomplete text. However, of his three songs, J. Fred. preferred this one, for he selected it for the concert that celebrated the twenty-fifth anniversary of The Bach Choir. Nicholas Douty, J. Fred.'s soloist of many years in the Bach Festivals, sang "Cloudland" followed by an aria from Richard Wagner's opera *The Valkyre*.

In 1922 J. Fred. wrote a poem "To Bethlehem's Town." He set the text with a simple melody almost like a song for children. The accompaniment is for piano, which supports the melody like a hymn. J. Fred. copyrighted the text, which seems to have been circulated in typed form. The song, however, survives only as a manuscript not in J. Fred.'s hand, in the Archives of The Bach Choir of Bethlehem.

"Concert of Witches," a rather strange duet for two sopranos, was finished in September 1915. It contains some word painting and has an accompaniment that is somewhat mysterious. The most interesting feature of the duet is that the melody is in triple meter and the accompaniment is in duple, a device he had used earlier in "Aunt Jane's Moon Song."

J. Fred.'s five extant art songs are proof he could write very satisfactorily when the occasion arose.

The Lehigh University *Alma Mater* J. Fred. composed for male quartet is stately and stirring. The two medleys, also for male quartet, are four-part harmonizations of turn-of-the-century popular songs. They are light and entertaining in a rather restrained, barbershop quartet style.

While the body of work J. Fred. left is very modest, much of it is excellent and innovative. It is unfortunate that he did not take himself more seriously as a composer. He could have been a fine one, and often was. According to Francis Wolle, J. Fred.'s nephew, his uncle Fred. composed so little because he was humbled by his study of Bach's music. Francis recounted, "after he [J. Fred.] became immersed in Bach he was too modest to compose any further. Bach was too great to emulate, he said, and besides that, Bach had said all there was to say musically."[17]

## NOTES

1. "Sesquicentennial Service 1806." Sheet inserted into the score of "He Leads Us On," Lehigh University Special Collections, Bethlehem, Pa.
2. *The Moravian,* 18 January 1933.
3. Ibid.
4. Ibid.
5. *Hymnal and Liturgies of the Moravian Church* (Bethlehem, Pa.: Globe-Times Printery, 1923), 104.
6. Ibid., 152.
7. Ibid., 636.
8. John R. Parker, *A Musician's Biography: or Sketches of the Lives and Writing of Eminent Musical Characters* (Boston: Stone and Fovel, 1824), 42.
9. Ibid.
10. "The Official Diary of the Congregation," 25 December 1895.
11. Manuscript in the collection of the Moravian Museum of Bethlehem, Pa.
12. *The Moravian,* 18 January 1933.
13. Joseph Levering, *A History of Bethlehem, Pennsylvania, 1741–1892,* (Bethlehem, Pa.: Times Publishing Company, 1903), 45.
14. "The Official Diary ," September 1893, 375.
15. "Sesquicentennial Service 1806." See note 1. [September 1893, 375 Official Diary of the Moravian Church of Bethlehem Pa., 1888–95]
16. Francis Wolle, *A Moravian Heritage* (Boulder, Colo.: Empire Reproduction & Printing Co., 1972), 45.
17. Ibid.

Chapter Twelve

## *Permanently in Bethlehem*

Dr. Wolle is the full accomplishment of a century or more.[1]

He knows the vastly complicated scores of Bach as perhaps no one else in the world knows them. And with this erudition he is able to give you the contagious rapture of his own inextinguishable rapture.[2]

As the old Moravian "Sister" was heard to say last week – "He's a very fine musicion [sic], but he's yet a finer man."[3]

J. FRED.'S RETURN TO BETHLEHEM from California seemed almost secretive. It was as if a stranger had left the train station and had checked into a hotel somewhere in South Bethlehem. In a community where the arrival of every guest was reported in *The Globe*, J. Fred.'s arrival was never mentioned. What a marked contrast to his departure, when his admiring choir members gathered at "Bach's Home" and crowds bid his family farewell on the platform of the train at that same train station. Was he unable to face Bethlehem, as he had been unable to leave it when he finished his final recital in 1905 and disappeared unnoticed through the back door and walked home alone? Where were the reporters? Where were his friends? Where was the family of brothers and close relatives? Surely, someone must have known he was coming. He must not have arrived unexpectedly. A trip across the United States by rail was not an overnight jaunt. Yet, there is no record of his arrival.

Even when his presence in Bethlehem did become newsworthy, it was only briefly noted. A single paragraph in *The Globe* mentioned that Dr. Wolle "has a year's leave of absence from the University of California [and] had consented to lead part of the work [Mendelssohn's oratorio "St. Paul"]."[4]

In six years J. Fred. had been nearly forgotten by the media. In a report of a "special rehearsal" held a few days later the reporter did not even get J. Fred.'s name right. "Bethlehemites will be pleased to learn that Prof. Fred C. Wolle will be present at the concert, and has been invited to lead a portion of the concert, and it is hoped that he may be persuaded to do so."[5] If J. Fred. did assist, there was no report of it, for the concert was not reviewed. A reception was later reported in which T. Edgar Shields, the conductor, was honored, and Dr. Henry Drinker, the president of the Bethlehem Oratorio Society, "referred to Mr. Shields recognized ability as a musician and a conductor."[6] The chorus J. Fred. had left had thrived during his absence. Schwab's invitation to reinstate the Bach Festivals entailed much more than was apparent when he discussed his plan with J. Fred. in California.

There was no position for J. Fred. as a conductor, so he began working to secure a position as organist. To that end, he gave an organ recital in grand style on the Packer Memorial Church organ. That made the news. Dr. J. Fred. Wolle, the famous virtuoso organist, was back in Bethlehem as a visitor, and *The Globe* reported, "Dr. Wolle Gave Brilliant Recital. Fine program in Packer Church by Master Organist, Dr. J. Fred. Wolle of the University of California Delighted An Audience of His Old Home Friends . . . Last Evening."[7] The recital began with a number of major Bach works followed by standard pieces by Romantic organ composers including Wolle's arrangement of Wagner's "Siegfried's Death March." The conclusion was calculated to arouse old memories, and it did. The musical symbolism of the final pieces was not lost on a "well-known organist," who had been "asked to comment upon the recital."

> Dr. Wolle followed it [the final piece] with two chorales, "Now Thank We All Our God," and "Sing Hallelujah, Praise the Lord," both quite familiar to Bethlehem audiences and evidently musical bonds between himself and his hearers. It is this ability to see and feel the musical sympathies of his hearers that gives Dr. Wolle his greatest strength.[8]

This recital was meant to be a thankful celebration of J. Fred.'s return. He had come back to his roots with "Sing Hallelujah, Praise the Lord" one of the best-known Moravian hymns that was composed by Bechler, Bishop Wolle's teacher in Nazareth.

However, J. Fred. still walked a delicate balance between convention and controversy. Two comments stand out.

> Dr. Wolle took the fugue faster than he did six years ago when he last played it here. In many respects he had acquired in the interim idiosyncrasies that give a new flavor to his work. The fugue gained in brilliance, even though it may somewhat have lost in sympathetic appeal.

and

> In the latter ["Aria in the style of a flute solo"] there was perhaps, a freedom of tempo that might cause comment if it had not been so well adapted to this purpose.[9]

Still, the review abounded in phrases performers want their public to read: "wonderful impressive and appealing," "a rare treat," "delightful effect produced by the handling of his registers," "tossed off with apparent ease." Dr. Wolle's organ playing was a delight. At least as an organist, J. Fred. was assured an appreciative audience in the Bethlehems, "at the close there came a spontaneous burst of applause that didn't seem out of place even though it was in a church. The audience liked Dr. Wolle's recital."[10] J. Fred. was again front-page news.

However, T. Edgar Shields' post at Packer Memorial Church was not offered to J. Fred., and if he expected to resume the Central Moravian Church position, he soon realized there had been great changes there also. There was no reason why Albert Rau, who replaced J. Fred., should relinquish the position and apparently no one pressed him to do so. Initially, many doubted that Rau could follow in J. Fred.'s footsteps. Yet, within a few months after J. Fred.'s departure, Rau proved he was equal to the task. The pastor noted in the congregation diary that the Christmas services had gone extremely well.

> Many fears had also been entertained concerning the music, now that Bro. Wolle is no longer here. Under the direction of Bro. Albert Rau, however, a fine large choir has been gathered, very few of the old singers being absent. With this was a strong orchestra which had volunteered for service. So that the very brightest prospects are before us, musically.[11]

By Easter, the most demanding time for a Moravian Church organist, the pastor noted that Rau's acceptance by the congregation was complete. Just a few weeks before J. Fred. returned to Bethlehem, Rau dedicated a new organ in the Moravian Church in South Bethlehem, which was an example of the quality of his playing and the level of appreciation it generated.

> Prof. Albert G. Rau, who presided at the organ during the day, opened this service with a greatly enjoyed recital, consisting of Prelude in G (Bach): Chorale, "Herr Jesus Christ dich zu uns wend;" Chorale, "Herzlich tut mich dich verlangen (Bach);" "Andante Cantabile" (Ch. Widor), and Guilmant's "Prayer and Cradle Song." Mr. Rau was heard at his best on the new instrument.[12]

In marked contrast to J. Fred., Rau had a great love for Moravian history in general and for music history specifically. For many years he served as vice president of the Moravian Historical Society, a group in which J. Fred. had a life membership but was not active in any notable way. While J. Fred. had shown little interest in the musical manuscripts piled in the church attic, Rau viewed them as evidence of a great musical past. He became convinced they constituted a tradition that must be revived, and began such a revival just a few months before J. Fred.'s return, when the *Passion* by Karl Henrich Graun was sung, probably using a manuscript from the church attic.

The resemblance of that performance to the first Bethlehem Bach Festivals was striking, including the presence of the trombones, the congregation's singing, and the American premiere. More important was the fact that the service was free of the problems associated with the Bach Festivals: ticket sales, disrespectful listeners, critical disputes, and rearranging the church. The sacred service, with a collection to cover the performance costs, received a spirited report in *The Moravian*, similar to Fred.'s early Bach performances.

> The rendition was a success in every way, the attack by the chorus being prompt and full and the varying shades of expression being well delivered. The attendance on the part of the members of the congregation and of others residing in Bethlehem and neighboring towns was very large, every seat of the large auditorium being taken. As it was intended that this rendition should take the place of the regular Lenten service, the session was opened with the playing of Tune 165a by the trombones and after the opening chorale, Tune 151a, Bro. F. W. Stengle read the Scripture lesson. . . . Near the close of the cantata there was a brief intermission, during which a collection was taken; the total was nearly enough to cover the very heavy expenses of the service. While the collection was taken the trombones played Tune 519. Just before the last chorus, Bro. Thale [the head pastor] offered the closing prayer. The congregation joined in singing the chorales printed on the programs. This is the first time that this work has been rendered in this country. It was sung annually during Passion Week in the Domkirche of Berlin.[13]

It was not necessary to seek in the works of Bach for great music to make Bethlehem an important center for sacred music. Bethlehem would resume its rightful place in American music by reviving music Moravians had created and performed in their communities. Rau's recognition and revival of Moravian music did place Bethlehem solidly as an important American musical center. His contribution was as important and lasting in the American Colonial Revival as J. Fred.'s contribution was to the Bach revival in America.

Not only was Moravian music being revived, performances of Bach's choral music continued after J. Fred.'s departure. The Moravian pastor summarized the situation in his diary.

> In place of the former Bach Choir there are now a number of smaller amateur organizations which are studying music, and if these are rightly led they will perhaps accomplish as much in their way as was the more finished choir of singers which has gone to pieces since Prof. Wolle left for the University of California.[14]

Later in 1907 a "Bach Chorus" was actually formed that performed "a delightful evening, using altogether the works of Bach."[15] The performance was in the chapel of the Moravian Sunday School. In the same year the Oratorio Society of the Bethlehems was formed with T. Edgar Shields conducting. The Society was endorsed by Lehigh University. This was the group J. Fred. had attended soon after he returned to Bethlehem. There is no record of how this group ceased and became the nucleus of the renewed Bach Choir. However, that did occur, and Shields withdrew as the conductor and became the organist for the new group.

Though J. Fred. did not yet have a church music position, he could be confident of his drawing power as an organ recitalist, he had the beginnings of a choir, and he was assured a patron in Charles Schwab. The next move was to begin planning the revival of The Bach Festivals.

In early October J. Fred. made a request to the Moravian Elders to hold a Bach Festival in Central Moravian Church. The board secretary reported that "after careful and full consideration [the Elders resolved] the church shall not be used for any concert or festival to which admission is charged."[16] According to J. Fred.'s nephew, members of the Moravian Church "were not at all pleased to see J. Fred. back again and gave him anything but a pleasant welcome. . . . Fred was deeply hurt by the Moravian repudiation of him and his work."[17]

Had Schwab been a Moravian he might have been able to press the elders to allow a Bach Festival in Central Church. However, he was not, and while he would underwrite any deficit, he had made clear he was not giving the festivals to Bethlehem. The community had to share in the cost. Thus, without ticket sales, the festivals were doomed.

Dr. Henry Drinker, president of Lehigh, and Dr. Clewell, principal of Moravian College for Women, suggested a place where the festival could be held and where the choir could rehearse. Dr. Clewell offered the college chapel free of charge for the weekly rehearsals of the choir, which would be the Moravian offering to the festival, and Dr. Drinker proposed that The Bach Choir could perform in Packer Memorial Church without charge. The solution was ideal. The Moravians would continue to support the festival, and Lehigh University would support the arts. The University trustees accepted the plan immediately. There were clear advantages to the University that were reported in *The Brown and White*.

> Aside from the duty of the University to encourage and stand behind a movement of this kind for the promotion of the study of classical music, it is unquestionably a distinct advantage to the University to be known as the home of the study of Bach in this country and of a Music Festival known and celebrated throughout the world . . . a Mecca for the gathering of the lovers of Music from the north, the south, the east and west.[18]

Visitors, like the music critic who wrote for the *Musical Courier*, also felt Lehigh University was an ideal site for Bach.

> And none of the splendid concert halls of Europe can vie with the Packer Memorial Church on the Pennsylvania hillside as a temple for the music of Bach. There, with the open windows framed in the green [ivy] and the breeze fresh from the mountains, we leave the dust and noise of the city far behind us and are transplanted into a slower young and poetic world which seems more in accordance with the age in which Bach lived.[19]

Henry S. Drinker, President of Lehigh University
(Special Collections, Lehigh University)

Another reporter examined his synthesis of industry, history, and Lehigh University more profoundly.

> In the Bethlehems, where the new and the old of American thought are strangely commingled, both extremes are met. In the [Lehigh] valley, which has welcomed the growth of manufacturing industry, the Bethlehem Steel Company, with its millions of money and thousands of men; on the hill above it, amidst the warm welcome of a great and hospitable university, and idealist institution and a choir producing the sublimest music of a magic composer – there are the extremes. And Bethlehemites are proud of both.[20]

The planning for a Bach Festival could proceed, and a new board met in the Moravian College for Women at the invitation of Dr. Clewell. The purpose of the meeting was to formally reestablish The Bach Choir and reinstate The Bethlehem Bach Festivals. The new board members left a very clear record of this crucial moment in their minutes when all the necessary players met in person or in spirit, and Dr. J. Fred. Wolle was asked to come to the double parlors at the Moravian Seminary.

J. Fred. stood for a moment in front of the grand brick college building before he went inside. He was truly returning home. This was where he had been born and raised. He walked up the front porch steps, turned left, opened the broad, heavy door, and stepped across the large stone threshold into an impressive hallway with a high ceiling. As a child, he had often played in this hall. In the rooms in the floors above, he had listened to the music classes taught by Sr. Brown. This was where his family had taught him to be unassuming, to be a quiet Moravian.

Passing the room that had been his father's office, he walked toward the doors of the double parlors, "the blue parlors," at the end of the entrance hall. He had met an endless number of young ladies with their parents in these parlors and had been trained to be courteous and genteel, qualities that served him well throughout his life.

His parents would first introduce him as "our son Freddy." As he grew older, Freddy became "our son Fred." When he joined the Seminary faculty, he was "Professor Wolle" and after his Moravian College honorary doctorate, people greeted him as, "Dr. Wolle." Officially, he preferred, "J. Fred. Wolle," but his friends always called him simply "Fred."

It was early evening when he entered the blue parlors to greet the people who had come there to help him rebuild The Bach Choir and begin the festivals. The parlors, which still exist, were opulently furnished. On the walls were frescos by Gustavus Grunewald, a fine artist who taught painting at the Seminary. Pastoral scenes of eighteenth-century Bethlehem enclosed the people assembled with a vision of a perfect past evoking the quiet force of Moravian faith and industry.

Through the large windows at the end of the rooms the gigantic blast furnaces of the steel company could be seen on the other side of the river. Their glow continued throughout the night – long after the Lehigh University students had ceased studying and had turned off their recently installed electric lamps. In contrast to the frescos on the walls, beyond the parlors moved a dynamic present: the result of a very wealthy association between the Lehigh Valley Rail Road, a powerful steel industry, and a proud university. The people invited to the Seminary that evening were its progeny. In various ways they were actively engaged in making that present.

According to the minutes of the Board of The Bach Choir, thirteen distinguished individuals greeted each other in "the parlor of the Moravian Seminary." Everyone was perfectly dressed. All were prominent, most were wealthy, and each person was accustomed to making things happen. Both men and women were present. That was unusual, for this was not a social gathering. Business was to be enacted; the important business of creating a choir to sing Bach. However, men and women had always worked as equals in the Bach enterprise in Bethlehem.

Dr. J. H. Clewell, the president of the College and Seminary for Women, greeted Dr. W. L. Estes, a local surgeon and medical lecturer at the University. Both of them had supported J. Fred.'s choral enterprises before he left Bethlehem, and Dr. Estes' wife, Jeanne, had been one of J. Fred.'s devoted soloists. Mr. and Mrs. Albert Cleaver, civic leaders and philanthropists, were also present. Mr. Cleaver owned and managed large mining and manufacturing interests in the Lehigh Valley. He was also a Lehigh University trustee and a member of the board of the hospital where Dr. Estes practiced. These men and their wives had been close associates for many years. The Cleavers were most enthusiastic when they heard that Mr. Charles Schwab had invited J. Fred. to return to Bethlehem. The couple had worked diligently to arrange this meeting. Some historians give the Cleavers credit for organizing the new choir.[21]

In the room was Mr. Frank Hoch, treasurer and general manager of the Industrial Limestone Company. Cement production was another very prosperous area industry. Mr. Hoch was also the secretary and treasurer of the Globe Printing Company, printers of the local newspaper. A devoted music lover, he was the treasurer of the Oratorio Society of the Bethlehems. Joining the group were Councilman and local businessman Asa C. Huff and the conductor of the Oratorio Society of the Bethlehems, T. Edgar Shields. He was the University chapel organist, organist and choir director of the Episcopal Cathedral of the Church of the Nativity in South Bethlehem, professor of music at the Seminary, and much admired by all for his musicianship and his diplomacy.

Acting as the host, Dr. Clewell called the meeting to order and asked everyone to be seated. He said their purpose was to form "an organization for the rendering of Bach music under the direction of Prof. J. Fred. Wolle."[22] Mr. Hoch, acting as the secretary, wrote, "On motion, properly recorded, Dr. H. S. Drinker was unanimously elected President of the Organization."[23] In a letter written later to J. Fred., Drinker states, "I was the person mainly responsible for the re-institution of the choir (with Mr. and Mrs. Cleaver, who suggested it to me)."[24] Dr. Drinker was not present, but his Packer Memorial

Packer Memorial Church, Lehigh University
(Special Collections, Lehigh University)

Church election as president fused the group, making it possible for them to achieve their purpose, for he united industrial, professional and business wealth, and political power with university tradition and cultural influence.

Mr. Huff recorded in the Minutes ". . . the name of the Organization was decided upon as The Bach Choir." The work had been accomplished. The meeting adjourned. The Bach Choir and The Bach Festivals would begin again in Bethlehem. It was 19 October 1911. Their business completed, the members of the new Board of the Bach Choir left the blue parlors. An annual salary of $3,000 was proposed for his work with The Bach Choir. J. Fred. accepted the offer and also assumed the post of organist at a Lutheran Church in nearby Allentown. Dr. J. Fred. Wolle was home. He was 48 years old. Secure in Bethlehem at last, J. Fred. resigned his Berkeley professorship and asked his family to return to "Bach's Home." Jennie, J. Fred.'s wife, and their daughter were soon unpacking trunks filled with Oriental objects and placing them throughout the house. In a rare reference to Jennie, J. Fred.'s nephew wrote that "she reveled in the Chinese-made rugs, china, pottery and furniture, and after the return to Bethlehem their home reflected the exquisite taste of the Chinatown purchases."[25] After six years, the Wolles were permanently in Bethlehem.

At the next meeting of The Bach Choir Board the dates for the Bach Festival were set and soon $4,085 were pledged by guarantors. J. Fred. had six or seven months to prepare the choir for the revival of the festival in May. The program would consist of four cantatas; two had been performed at earlier festivals and the Mass would again be the concluding work.

Writing a number of years after these events, a music critic described perfectly what had transpired. He asked, "What is a Bach festival doing in such a place?" Then, he answered

> The Moravian tradition of religious music; a modern university reluctant to be identified with the scientific training for what the Lehigh degree is best known, and able to offer in its spacious "Packer Memorial Church" an ideal background for choral music; the fruits of

modern industry, in the form of financial resources . . . and indisputedly the fortunate existence in Bethlehem of Dr. J. Fred. Wolle.[26]

To be back in the Women's Seminary chapel for rehearsals brought J. Fred. great satisfaction. The chapel adjoined his birthplace and, except for the addition of electric lighting, was unchanged from his boyhood. He had listened to innumerable fine concerts by faculty and students in that hall. In his youth he was the chapel organist, and the organ he played each morning was still to his right as he faced "his" Bach Choir.

At the height of his powers J. Fred. began the first choir rehearsal. As he greeted the group, he was well aware that it was very different from the one he had left in 1905. This first rehearsal was not a renewal; it was a true beginning. The group was twice as large. Nearly all of the singers were new, for just thirty-one from 1905 had returned; twenty-two from the Central Moravian Church Choir. This new choir was the kind J. Fred. had always wanted for The Bach Festivals with the majority of the singers from the Bethlehems. He described that choir enthusiastically to a reporter.

> Dr. Wolle has said about his singers "We have asked all ages, and we want them all ages. The young inexperienced, unreliable, but fresh flexible voice. The 'not so young' but routined, dependable voice, indispensable even though it shows the traces of a twang. This delicious mixture it is that gives the singing of the Choir the buoyancy of youth with the response of maturity. The singers are wonderful in their exhibition of loyalty, patience, responsiveness and endurance. Nothing is too difficult for them. They respond to every demand. Many are the sacrifices they must make to attend rehearsals. All honor to the individual, unpraised, unhonored and unsung chorus member.[27]

J. Fred. extended his expressive hands and began the first of hundreds of rehearsals that were to take place in that chapel over the next twenty-two years. Now he must teach the group three cantatas and the Mass.

J. Fred. Wolle conducting The Bach Choir in
Packer Memorial Church, 1917
(Archives of The Bach Choir of Bethlehem)

Two women remembered the rehearsals well and eagerly described their weekly experiences under Dr. Wolle. When they were interviewed, they were both in their nineties. Both have since died.

> I joined the choir in 1923 loving Bach as I did through piano lessons. . . . Monday was Bach night. Who would have imagined doing anything else. As I recall we were allowed three absences not consecutive for sickness or some good reason. Secretaries of each section kept strict account of each member's record and there better be a good reason for absence.[28]

Later in the interview, Miss S. verified that J. Fred. consistently used his technique of rehearsing new pieces beginning with the ending.

> Dr. Wolle's method of attacking a new cantata was unique. All measures were numbered by fives. Dr. Wolle would announce, "Cantata 78 the last five measures from the end." Diligently complying with his request, we repeated these five measures until he was satisfied. Then, the request for the last ten measures, continuing in reverse until we arrived at the beginning. Then, the beginning was a bit weak, but what a glorious feeling of accomplishment as we neared the end. And we had more and more confidence.

Only after the whole movement had been learned were specific trouble spots isolated and measures rehearsed individually. This elderly person recalled such an instance. "Then, of course there were definite trouble spots like measure 24 in the "Qui Tolis" of the Mass in B Minor. Certain attacks needed more emphasis. . . . Dr. Wolle was pleased with what we had done, and he usually was, he gave us that welcome message." In the course of the interview, a favorite expression of J. Fred.'s came to light, and he emerged as a model of propriety.

> He had certain expressions that he liked to use on occasion. One of them was "sittery," which is Pennsylvania German for shakey. He loved to say that and so do I. He had another expression that he used quite often. He would never say darn or anything like that. He got me away from saying it too! But he would say "Hunky dory" if something pleased him or just in general and then once in a while he made it a little longer. "Hunky dory, and the goose hangs high." Those were expressions of his.

When the interviewer asked, "So The Bach Choir was a big part of your life wasn't it?" Miss S. responded immediately "It was one of the best parts. I'm so glad that it happened."

Another woman who had been a member of the new Bach Choir had many memories of J. Fred. She called him Fred Wolle, then Dr. Wolle, for he had been a close friend of her family. She was born and raised in Bethlehem in a Moravian family with an ancestor who had founded the town. "When we had rehearsal at seven-thirty, he'd be there at seven o'clock at the door. And he stood at the door and shook hands with every person as they came in and mentioned them by name " 'cause he knew them all."[29]

Knowing the names of all the singers was helpful, for "If anyone tried to do something at a rehearsal, like knit, or have a book, or something, you know, he'd call them out by name. This was a big family affair." A quality that bound The Bach Choir together like a family was the loyalty Fred Wolle had for his singers.

> [H]e never put anyone out. One of the – now what was her name – she was one that took attendance for many years. She sang alto, Annie Rhinehart . . . her voice began to go flat. And she would sing out. It was hard not to hear her. But, anyway he would never put anybody out. And if anybody complained to him about someone, he would say, "Well they are members of The Bach Choir, you know." Once you were in, you were in the family, and that was it. This was something. This endeared him to us.

When asked to describe Fred Wolle's appearance, Miss L. said

> He was more or less slender. . . . He was a thin wiry kind of a person, and swayed just like a tree in the wind. He was very graceful. Very enthusiastic. He wasn't six foot tall. His hair was very bushy. I think he had a moustache. He never had a beard.

J. Fred.'s nephew described him as an individual in a constant state of intense concentration with a sense of hurrying

> that was accented by his short, fast steps and by the shoulders thrown forward and head bent down . . . when he was called or spoken to, he gave a slight start, looked up, and upon recognition was instantly all affability. . . . This quality of ready sympathy made him much loved by many people. Of course he could be stubborn too.[30]

Miss L. had vivid recollections of J. Fred.'s conducting during rehearsals. Like many others, she commented on the extraordinary control he had of the choir, in part due to his mastery of the music but also because of his efficient conducting using only modest gestures.

As a rule when he was directing, he wasn't using his music.

> It was there, but he didn't use it. He knew it. . . . His fingers, when he was directing, and we were sitting on this side, his little finger was for the first altos. His fingers were perfectly – well – they spoke. You could tell just exactly what he wanted you to express. And he didn't swing himself around on the podium. He did a little more of it in the beginning, but toward the end he wasn't well, and he didn't have to do that. He looked at different ones, you know, key people in the choir, certain ones who led each part.

As J. Fred. became ill near the end of his life, Miss L. said though he moved less, his grace remained.

> The two years he was sick, he had some kind of mobile trouble. His hands were stiff. He kept on going, and then he sat on his stool during the whole rehearsal. And as I said, he would just motion his head and his fingers, his hand you know. By that time there were always enough people who had been there from the beginning, and it didn't take long for the new people to catch on. There wasn't any problem knowing what he wanted. He could make that known somehow to each instrument. He'd just nod his head. It was easy. It looked easy from our stand point.

Miss L. was one of J. Fred.'s strongest singers. There is a story that a tenor new to the choir asked Miss L. where her vocal score to the Mass was. "Young man, I don't need a score," she replied.

Miss L. always remembered Fred's spiritual character and his charismatic effect on the choir.

> [H]e could organize anybody if he wanted to, that was willing to sing. He had that physical ability, and well that spiritual ability really that he could just get people to do what he wanted. And our choir was composed of people who were people who had no musical ability

to sing the Mass in B Minor. It was the way he taught, you see. They wanted to do something for him as well as for themselves.

Both Miss S. and Miss L. spoke of the presence of Mrs. Wolle and Gretchen, their daughter, at the rehearsals. "Mrs. Wolle sat in the last seat. And she was just as loyal as anybody else," related Miss L. Later in the interview Miss L. said,

> Gretchen didn't sing either, and she could have sung in the choir of course, but she wasn't interested in music either. But, she always came to rehearsals, like they were always together you know. This was nice. . . . When I think of it, now that I'm older, I think that was nice that they would give up one whole evening every week to go to something they weren't interested in. Because they loved him. That's the way people were with him.[31]

Two of the most penetrating descriptions of J. Fred.'s conducting were written by music critics who covered the 1914 Bach Festival. Both writers deepen the personal accounts of Miss L. and Miss S.

The first writer asked a very specific question, "What makes this singing so remarkable and gives it the cogent power to bring thousands of persons from 'all over to the four sessions, of an hour and a half each, to hear one hundred and ninety-one performers with organ and (nowadays) full-fledged professional orchestra?"[32] He answered his question. "It is the absolute devotion of The Bach Choir to the genius of Dr. J. Frederick Wolle and the music of Bach." But this music critic knew devotion to a conductor and the music of Bach was not enough. J. Fred. "did" things as a conductor that brought about this devotion. To identify what J. Fred. did, the critic left the audience and watched J. Fred. from the angle of the choir. The reviewer described in detail what he saw.

> I snuggled into a corner by the organ for a few minutes, on the side away from the audience, that I might see him in the full swing and fervor of unconscious action as the choir sees him, taking its guidance

Central Moravian Trombone Choir in the belfry of
Central Moravian Church
(Trombone Choir of Central Moravian Church)

from his face as well as from his hands – and indeed, from his shoulders, his genuflecting body, his whole being. He uses no baton. His fingers are as lively as a deaf-mute's. What it means for a conductor to have the musicians "in his grasp" is literally exemplified. Now the digits expand like a water-lily's petals, now they are clenched like a miser's; even the corrugations of the arteries seem to mean some delicate mutation of a phrase, some dynamic shading too subtle for the tongue to tell of. The singers breathe and feel, relax or agonize, with him; they would sing their very lives away rather than disappoint his impassioned pleading for his climaxes.[33]

The second observer responded even more ecstatically and expressed those feelings that set the spiritual experience above the material one.

When to such intensely self-forgetful enthusiasm is added a profound searching of the scripture of Bach, it is a leadership men and women are bound to follow with all their might, if they had an interest in life superior to the material phases. Each singer makes it his breath, of mentality, of nervous energy to the performances; and with this blazing zeal on the part of conductor and conducted, is there room for wonder that a light shines upon the green hills of Bethlehem, and that pilgrims are led thither by the starry sign in the heavens that guided the world to another Bethlehem centuries ago?[34]

Count Ludwig von Zinzendorf, the Moravian leader who named Bethlehem, would have been pleased to have heard that this dimension of the spiritual mission of his settlement led by Christ was sustained.

Perhaps the best summary of J. Fred.'s personal and spiritual leadership beyond Bach's music was delivered by the Executive Committee of The Bach Choir to Mrs. Wolle and Gretchen at his death.

Through his love of fun, his drollery, his gentleness, his delight in all things lovely, his devotion to strict artistic honesty and moral standard, his social geniality, and humanity, one looked into far depths of clear faith and spirituality.[35]

Still one musical problem plagued the festivals: that was the relatively poor quality of the mainly amateur orchestra. The Choir Board addressed it directly. With the assurance that financial deficits would be taken care of by Charles Schwab, J. Fred. was directed to hire members of the Philadelphia Orchestra to accompany the choir at a cost of $725, with $2.00 "per man" for rehearsals. One of J. Fred.'s wealthy neighbors, Mrs. Ruth Linderman, who later became the president of The Bach Choir, agreed to pay for the rehearsals. The critics would finally be silenced, and The Bach Festivals could move to achieve international status.

The choir board also decided to "procure the trombone choir of Central Moravian Church to announce the several sessions from the tower of Packer Memorial Church."[36] Every commentator on the festivals mentioned the profound effect the trombone choir had on the audience. "At once a hush spread over the campus and all stood reverently listening. It was an impressive sight. In the belfry tower the trombonists held the vast audience spellbound as if by some magical power."[37]

The musical success of one of the cantatas sung on Friday set the tone for the entire festival. The chorale in *It is Enough* was performed by "the seated chorus, singing without accompaniment, electrified the audience with a chant of the most ethereal and delicate pianissimo, so exquisite and pure."[38] Before the evening performance, many people requested that J. Fred. perform that chorale again, and he did so that evening. "Exquisite pianissimo" is a phrase encountered frequently in the musical critiques, and a choir member recounted how it was achieved. The chorales were frequently rehearsed without text with each singer humming through a comb covered with tissue.[39] Another critic noted that the intimate tone quality was so pervasive that "it was in these more intimate choruses that the choral body did its finest work."[40]

J. Fred. had gained the admiration of everyone for reestablishing The Bach Choir and The Bach Festivals. Both Drinker and Schwab expressed their support and thanks to the choir at a rehearsal before the

Festival of 1915. They had been invited to speak by J. Fred. Their comments were reported the next day in the local paper.

> Dr. Drinker spoke of the important position that the choir had attained in the musical organizations of America, and of the fact that wherever he traveled on university business he heard the Bach Choir praised far and wide for its work, giving the Bethlehems an unique reputation which has grown as year by year the peculiar excellence of this classic musical festival becomes more and more appreciated through the country.[41]

While Drinker spoke of the choir's national reputation, Schwab stressed its international prestige. He also noted his role in providing the highest level of critical coverage of the festival.

> [N]othing that has been done, in this community, as far as I can learn from travels throughout the world, has reflected so much credit upon it as the Bach Choir and especially is that true, I think, from these last few years' performances. . . . Dr. Drinker and our friends have been anxious to have Mr. Hendersen, Mr. Fink, and other musical critics here, and they are all coming to this concert on Friday and therefore I think the choir ought to feel proud.[42]

Schwab transported the critics from New York to Bethlehem regularly in his private rail car and probably had them as guests at his Bethlehem mansion. He concluded his speech with a flourish.

> I want to let you know, not from what I have said, but from my presence here, that I am intensely interested in this choir, intensely interested in its work, intensely interested in its success, and I take this opportunity to thank the ladies and gentlemen personally, who are members of this choir, for all the work they had done, and wish them the success they so richly deserve.[43]

By 1914 the fame of J. Fred.'s Bach Festival reached the highest levels of the Federal government, with the assistance of Schwab's Washington influence. "Several officials of President Wilson's Cabinet and other Washington officials are included in the number of those who have secured tickets and accommodations."[44] The connections in Washington bore fruit in subsequent years as The Bach Choir assumed a position as the "unofficial" Bach Choir of the United States. In 1916 ex-President Theodore Roosevelt and his wife attended the festival, and Mrs. Roosevelt, as a widow, continued coming to Bethlehem each spring, often as the guest of Dr. Drinker and his wife. In May Bethlehem became a place to meet the rich and famous in sylvan surroundings. Many made the pilgrimage to Bethlehem not only to hear Bach, but to participate in a prestigious national social event. This elevated social importance was the final element necessary for the annual Bach Festivals to succeed permanently in Bethlehem.

Confident in the future of his choir and The Bach Festivals, J. Fred. sent each choir member a poem he had written in gratitude for a gift they gave him following the 1915 Festival. His thank-you combined his love of Bach and "his" choir with his literary nature and his scientific interest, each one emblematic of God's universal system in which J. Fred. was an active agent.

### TO MY BACH CHOIR

*A spider, omen of good luck,*
*Has built her web upon my wall,*
*Unthinking eyes see but a horrid spider;*
*That is all.*
*But he who looks beneath, beyond*
*The spider, in her geometric orb*
*Can almost see the God of nature and of man*
*Display in miniature a corner of His universal plan.*
*Now, sitting there, within that chair*
*(And it and I will often have been sat upon)*
*I see a picture of familiar faces*
*Whose song ascends of familiar faces*

*Whose song ascends to heavenly places.*
*There are some duties you and I must do from day to day*
*For which good money pays, and people say:*
*There are some debts which you and I contract*
*Which only love cay pay.*
*You owe me naught: I owe you much*
*For all I am and have.*
*You gave me both your lungs and throat;*
*This swelled my little head.*
*Ah! Dear Bach Choir, you are my child;*
*And though at times you drive me wild*
*Disdaining up-beats, bars and notes,*
*Your father fondly on your notes,*
*Your father fondly on you dotes.*
*Nor notes nor bars did e'er great music make:*
*Who thinketh thus, hath made a grave mistake.*
*Unless the lines are sung with heart and soul*
*All music fails to play its most important role.*
*Real singing takes more heart than voice,*
*More soul, by far, than lung;*
*And if our singing ere had been good*
*It is because this fact is understood.*
*So, like lowly spider which weaves from day to day*
*Her well-nigh perfect pattern, but how, she cannot say,*
*May you go on, unconscious of the wondrous work you do*
*In unfolding all the patterns St. Sebastian wove for you.*
*And some day, when my right arm fails, my eyes*
*grow dim, my ears grow dull,*
*And you, too, are quite out of joint, your voices*
*cracked, your breath comes hard,*
*Perhaps the melding melodies of the music of the Mass*
*Will be accepted by St. Peter as a genuine heaven-ward pass.*
*And then, indeed, she'll without an earthly leader*
*When she has aeroplaned to live beyond the stars,*

*– My old Bach Choir, – with nothing to impede her,*
*Her troubles o-er with up-beats, notes and bars.*
*Postscript. –*
*Do not be disappointed if you find that it is so*
*That they sing a little better than you ever did below.*
*N.B. –*
*I wonder if they sometimes have rehearsals in the fall*
*And how high is the percentage that resists the Halliwell call.*

Bethlehem, Pennsylvania, 3 July 1916.[45]

With the advent of World War I, J. Fred. said he would halt the festivals if people felt they compromised the "Allied cause" in the slightest. One New York critic wrote, "Bethlehem's Bach Festival takes place as usual without a twitter of opposition."[46] Another New York critic went further in defending festival performances of music that is German, but German not corrupted by Prussian forces.

> The Bach Festivals are important not only to art in America but to our humanity. At the present moment they provide an overwhelming reminder of the sublimity and the sublime humility which a German whom Prussia had not corrupted could express in tone.[47]

A Christian theologian discussed the subject directly in an article "Bach in War-Time." He attacked the idea that Bethlehem was the American Bayreuth, again elevating Bethlehem closer to the position envisioned by its founder, Count Zinzendorf.

> We want no Bayreuth in America any more than we want the things for which Bayreuth stands. But we do want the things of which Bach sang. And those of us who heard the great choir under Dr. Wolle's dynamic leadership believe that Bethlehem will increasingly become a shrine for America, not only musically, though that is much, but for the higher things whose hand-maidens the great arts have ever been.[48]

Not only did Bethlehem become an icon of humanity and civility, J. Fred. became its standard-bearer. A music critic eloquently expressed this attitude, directing his words to future historians.

> In imagination one can fancy the musical historian of the future writing about old Bethlehem and the remembered J. Fred. Wolle, who made his native city famous for the study of Bach's music in an uncouth age in which he lived, and so kept a glimmering lamp of art trimmed and burning during the dark and stormy days of the great World War.[49]

J. Fred.'s musical response to the war was as dramatic and romantic in spirit as one could imagine. The Mass in B Minor concludes with the words "Dona nobis pacem" "Give us peace." J. Fred. held out the final word, "pacem," for fifty seconds. The audience dissolved in tears. "A few started to applaud, but were quickly silenced by others: the choir themselves were overcome by their own performances, and silently the church emptied."[50]

The "Star-Spangled Banner" was sung by everyone before each session of the festival on Fridays, "its familiar measures punctuated by dramatic pauses and by high notes prolonged."[51] On Saturdays the anthem was sung outside to the accompaniment of the trombone choir before the two sessions of the Mass. The American, British, and French flags hung above the choir.

The Bach Festivals continued annually with only one interruption. In the year 1924 the festival was canceled just ten days before the event because J. Fred. was incapacitated by a severe illness.

In addition to singing the annual festivals in Bethlehem, the "new" Bach Choir was soon performing at events that were in no way associated with the annual festivals. As long as The Bach Choir was tied to The Bach Festivals, they only sang in the spring and in Bethlehem. Freeing the choir from the festivals was an important step. There could be performances at other times during the year and in other places.

The first concert outside the festival and outside Bethlehem was in New York's Carnegie Hall, January 1917, at the invitation of the Philharmonic Society of New York during the celebration of the seventy-fifth anniversary of its founding. J. Fred. conducted a number of chorales and four choruses from the Mass in B Minor. There were eight curtain calls. One critic echoed others by stating, "It is safe to say that, while Saturday's performance was not flawless, it was by far the best Bach singing ever heard in New York."[52] All expenses were paid by Charles Schwab.

The following year The Bach Choir returned to Carnegie Hall, and again the costs were underwritten by Schwab. Bach selections were programmed with excerpts from Wagner's most religious music-drama *Parsifal*. "The placing together in the same program of the religious music of Bach and the mystic sacred music of *Parsifal* was a stroke of genius."[53] The pairing was probably suggested by J. Fred. In a way, it summarized his musical life. Further, J. Fred. dramatically connected Bach and the Moravians with the United States. Following the "Star-Spangled Banner," sung by everyone and conducted by J. Fred., the Bethlehem Trombone Choir softly intoned a Moravian chorale. The choir followed immediately with the "Kyrie" from the Mass as J. Fred. had done in 1900 and in 1912. Chorales harmonized by Bach were sung between major choruses of the "Mass" in the spirit of a Moravian *singstunde*. The audience was again "rapturous" in response to great choral literature "presented in a manner which can be attained by no other body of singers."[54]

The Bach Choir portion of the concert was repeated a month later in Allentown before two thousand soldiers of the United States Army Ambulance Service. National anthems of Britain and France followed the "Star-Spangled Banner." The program was underwritten by Schwab.

In 1920 J. Fred. and The Bach Choir joined Walter Damrosch in New York as part of a week-long Festival of Music. Damrosch, an annual visitor to Bethlehem, had the highest respect for J. Fred. The concert was held in the Regiment Armory Auditorium. Music by the three German "B's," Bach, Beethoven, and Brahms, comprised the program. Transporting the long tradition of the Trombone Choir to New York City, the trombones played from one of the towers of the armory as the guests entered. Again, New Yorkers were astonished at the singing of the choir. "Such virtuosity . . . awakens in the music lover of New York a feeling of helpless envy and the keen pain of the unattainable."[55] Schwab paid all of the bills.

The choir was asked to return for the second Festival of Music held the next year. Chorales and sections from the Mass again were performed, and uniting J. Fred.'s two favorite composers – Bach and Wagner – the choir joined the New York Oratorio Society in two opera choruses by Wagner.

William Hendersen called a truce in his review of the concert. He wrote, "About their manner of singing chorales there will always be differences of opinion, but Dr. Wolle stands bravely by his own faith."[56] That truce held for the remainder of J. Fred.'s life.

The players of the Philadelphia Orchestra asked The Bach Choir to join them in the Philadelphia Academy of Music for a concert conducted by J. Fred. In addition to many sections from the Mass, J. Fred. conducted the Second Brandenburg Concerto. There were only rave reviews, but now the "high art of the interpretation" was praised above the "marvelous singing."[57] At last J. Fred.'s interpretation of Bach's music had triumphed.

The following year the choir returned to Philadelphia. The concert was apparently not up to the usual level, and the critics did not hesitate to register their disappointment. However, J. Fred. solidified a lasting friendship with Leopold Stokowski who offered him his baton. J. Fred. said this was as intimate as offering to use someone else's toothbrush.

Other concerts outside The Bach Festivals continued during J. Fred.'s life. There were two in Washington, D.C. The first was in 1925 when the choir sang the "Mass" as part of the International Conference on World Peace Through Music. The second was in 1926, when the Coolidges gave a reception for the choir in the White House. In 1930 a concert was given in Hershey, Pennsylvania for the Pennsylvania

German Society and another in Harrisburg. Two concerts were performed in Liberty High School in Bethlehem, the first for the Pennsylvania Education Association, and the second in celebration of the twenty-fifth anniversary of The Bach Choir, sponsored by the Bethlehem community.

Typically, as J. Fred. led The Bach Choir to a position of international prominence, he was actively involved in many other aspects of his musical career. In 1921 he accepted a position as organist and choir director in a large church in Allentown. He gave many organ recitals, particularly in the first years after he returned to Bethlehem. He conducted a choral society in Harrisburg, where a reviewer wrote, "Last night's rendition [*Elijah*] exceeds those heretofore given. The chorus never sang with more spirit and spontaneity."[58] J. Fred. added a similar choral society in York, Pennsylvania. Both groups sang the standard Romantic choral concert literature, including works by Rheinberger rather than compositions by Bach.

J. Fred. lived that same gratifying balance of work, pleasure in work, and refined comfort offered in a Moravian community that Bishop Wolle had described so consistently in his diary. J. Fred. expressed his feelings in an interview he gave in transit from Bethlehem to Harrisburg by rail. The reporter "asked it he was not pretty done up" as a result of all of the activity. J. Fred. responded, " 'No I like it. It is not work, it is pleasure. It helps me work. I am resting.' And he was enjoying a dining car dinner to the fullest extent."[59] A Bethlehem Moravian craftsman a century earlier would have given a similar response to the question.

For many years the Moravian Trombone Choir had ascended the circular steps in the stone tower of Packer Memorial Church to announce the beginning of The Bach Festivals. Those announcements each spring were joyous ones.

Now it was midwinter in the year 1933. The Moravian Brothers unpacked their trombones, lined up, and climbed the stairs to the belfry of Central Moravian Church. When they all stood in the open air, each player faced inward toward the bell. As always when they began their first chorale, everyone within hearing stopped to listen.

The first chorale was a death announcement. The second chorale followed. It announced the death of a married Brother.

Many drew in their breath. "Fred. Wolle has gone home," they thought. "Bro. J. Fred. Wolle was called from his home on Church Street to his eternal home in the 70th year of his earthly life."[60] It was the 12th of January.

As it had been for generations of Moravians, the third chorale reminded them that their time on earth was a passage to eternal life. Death was J. Fred.'s gain.

The loss was great to those who remained. Jennie, his widow and "his best critic, just because she was not musical," never recovered.[61] She died a year later.

The question in everyone's thoughts was would The Bach Choir and The Bach Festivals survive his passing? Were J. Fred. Wolle's life and the life of The Bach Choir so intertwined that, like the life of Jennie, one could not survive without the other? Possibly the Bach enterprise in Bethlehem was already finished. J. Fred. had been too ill in the fall to resume the rehearsals after the festival in 1932. "A Festival in 1933 is out of the question," the secretary of the choir had already told the guarantors in a letter he sent out on December 5. "For the last two years the health of the Conductor made it necessary for him to cease all activity but directing the Bach Choir. We all hope he will recover and resume his activities so that the festivals can be continued for many years."[62]

J. Fred. had not recovered and now that the trombones had announced his death, the choir prepared for the memorial service in Packer Memorial Church. The members assembled where they had sung Bach's spiritual messages so often, uplifting themselves and so many others. But there was no one to conduct "My Bach Choir." The church "was filled with his multitude of friends. . . . At his own prior request, and at the request of his family, there was no music of any kind. It can be readily understood that the emotional strain would have been almost unbearable, if there had been."[63] The service was brief. After the Moravian Bishop J. Taylor Hamilton read the poem "He Leads Us On" from J. Fred.'s anthem, the Bishop recited the text of Bach's "World Farewell." The Bethlehem Episcopal Bishop represented the Packer Memorial Church congregation and "read the concluding prayers of the Episcopal Service." "There was not a dry eye," Miss L. remembered.[64]

At the graveside, sixteen members of the trombone choir played. They were the first to break the musical silence. Now music might be possible, and

> after the family had withdrawn, a small group of the Bach Choir, possibly fifteen or twenty, gathered at the grave and attempted to hum "World Farewell," but most understandably were overcome with emotion.[65]

Paul de Schweinitz, the boyhood friend Freddy had played church with, concluded the obituary he wrote for *The Moravian*, "Thus, one of the most notable figures in all Moravian musical history has been taken from us."[66]

There was music in Central Moravian Church the following Sunday. The prelude was a transcription for organ by J. Fred., a piece he had played in many organ recitals, "Siegfried's Funeral March," from Wagner's opera *Twilight of the Gods*. There was no music by Bach at the service. The life of Dr. Wolle that was so intertwined with Bach's music had been remembered earlier in Packer Church. It was the life of the Moravian Brother Wolle that was celebrated in Central Church. The Moravian Choir sang "as a tribute to Dr. Wolle, his composition 'Once He Came in Blessing,' our favorite Advent hymn."[67] The two services reverently recognized Dr. J. Fred. Wolle's greatest musical achievements.

In Nisky Hill Cemetery, a plain gravestone lays flat in the Moravian way, beside it an identical stone for Jennie. When you stand just behind the two grave markers, Packer Memorial Church becomes visible across the Lehigh River beyond the furnaces of Bethlehem Steel. Only a few blocks from the cemetery "Bach's Home" is still a private residence. There J. Fred. and Jennie Wolle lived most of their life together, graciously welcoming guests "with a beautiful garden and house full of treasures."[68]

For the thousands who attend The Bach Festivals in Bethlehem each spring, the memory of these two Wolles touches the world again. Remembering her father, Gretchen Wolle told a reporter, "Bethlehem is a wonderful place . . . and I am proud that my father had a part in making it so."[69] Behind his achievement stands the legacy of two generations of musicians, the philanthropy of Charles Schwab and his capitalist empire, the Packer Memorial Church at Lehigh University, and the spiritual beliefs of the Moravian Church.

## NOTES

1. Albert Rau, "Development of Music in Bethlehem, Pennsylvania," *Transactions of the Moravian Historical Society* 13 (1944): 59.
2. *The Public Ledger* (Philadelphia), 2 June 1914.
3. *The Boston Evening Transcript*, 2 June 1915.
4. *The Globe*, 22 May 1911.
5. Ibid., 25 May 1911.
6. Ibid., 15 June 1911.
7. Ibid., 23 June 1911.
8. Ibid.
9. Ibid. for both quotations.
10. Ibid.
11. "The Official Diary of the Congregation," 3 December 1905.
12. Ibid., 7 June 1911.
13. Ibid.
14. "The Official Diary," 2 April 1907.
15. Ibid., 23 November 1907.
16. Minutes of the Board of Elders of the Congregation of Bethlehem, Pa. Volume 4 opened 1877, 9 October. Insert at page 281.

17. Francis Wolle, *A Moravian Heritage* (Boulder, Colorado: Empire Reproduction & Printing Company, 1972), 44.

18. *The Brown and White*, 11 June 1912.

19. Ibid.

20. *Musical Courier,* 3 June 1914.

21. Raymond Walters, "Bach at Bethlehem, Pennsylvania," *The Musical Quarterly*, April 1935, and in *The Bethlehem Bach Choir* (Boston: Houghton Mifflin Company, 1918).

22. Board Minutes of the Bach Choir of Bethlehem, 19 October 1911, Archives of The Bach Choir of Bethlehem.

23. Ibid.

24. Francis Wolle, *A Moravian Heritage*, 44.

25. "My Dear Dr. Wolle, Oct. 22, 24," letter in the Archives of The Bach Choir of Bethlehem.

26. *The Boston Evening Transcript,* 2 June 1915.

27. Typescript in the file "Photographs," Archives of The Bach Choir of Bethlehem.

28. The subsequent references are from a taped interview with Bertha-Mae Starner, 14 June 1995. The audio tape and typescript are in the Archives of The Bach Choir of Bethlehem.

29. Typescript of a taped interview with Martha Luckenbach, 11 October 1993, Archives of The Bach Choir of Bethlehem.

30. Francis Wolle, *A Moravian Heritage*, 40.

31. Luckenbach interview. Actually, Gretchen did sing in the first Bach Choir as a young woman. She is listed among the sopranos in the program of the first Festival.

32. *The New York Outlook*, 20 June 1914.

33. Ibid.

34. Untitled and unidentified newspaper clipping. Filed in the folder Photographs, 1914, Archives of The Bach Choir of Bethlehem.

35. "Resolution Adopted by the Executive Committee February 18 1933" in the program of the memorial service in memory of Dr. J. Fred. Wolle, Archives of The Bach Choir of Bethlehem.

36. Minutes of the Bach Choir of Bethlehem, 2 May 1912, Archives of the Bach Choir of Bethlehem.

37. "Ninth Bach Festival Opens in the Chapel at Lehigh University," 29 May 1914. Unidentified newspaper clipping in the Archives of The Bach Choir of Bethlehem.

38. Raymond Walters, "Bach at Bethlehem, Pennsylvania," 97. This cantata in present editions does not have a chorale. J. Fred. must have added one for these performances.

39. Related to the author by Richard Schantz of Bethlehem, who was told the story by an elderly member of The Bach Choir.

40. Raymond Walters, op. cit., 101.

41. *The Globe,* 26 May 1915.

42. Ibid.

43. Ibid.

44. Typescript filed in the folder Photographs, Archives of The Bach Choir of Bethlehem.

45. Unpublished manuscript, Archives of The Bach Choir of Bethlehem. Bess Halliwell took attendance and recruited choir members.

46. Raymond Walters, "Bach at Bethlehem, Pennsylvania," 134.

47. Ibid.

48. Ibid., 144.

49. *Musical Courier,* 2 June 1915.

50. Francis Wolle, *A Moravian Heritage,* 45.

51. Raymond Walters, "Bach at Bethlehem, Pennsylvania," 143.

52. Ibid., 173.

53. Ibid., 185.

54. Ibid., 187.

55. Ibid., 191.

56. Ibid., 195.

57. Ibid., 202.

58. *Musical Courier,* 24 June 1914.

59. *The Easton Free Press,* 27 May 1915.

60. *The Moravian,* 18 January 1933.

61. *The Globe-Times,* 18 May 1962.

62. Board Minutes of the Bach Choir of Bethlehem, 5 December 1933, Archives of the Bach Choir of Bethlehem.

63. Ibid.

64. Interview with Martha Luckenbach.

65. Ibid.

66. *The Moravian,* 18 January 1933.

67. Ibid.

68. *The Globe-Times,* 19 May 1962.

69. Ibid.

*Appendices*
*Bibliography*
*Index*

# Appendix A

## *Compositions by Peter Wolle*

### Anthem and Liturgies

A1. "Bringt her dem Herrn Lob" [fragment]

VOICE PARTS: s., a., t., b.
INSTRUMENTAL PARTS: vln. I, II: vla.; bass; trpt. I, II.
AUTHOR OF TEXT: Cyriacus Guenther (1650–1704)
MORAVIAN SOURCE OF TEXT: probably *Gesangbuch zum Gebrauch der Evangelischer* . . . , #1615.
DEDICATION: none.
DATE OF COMPOSITION: before January 1816.[1]
PLACE OF COMPOSITION: probably Salem, N.C.
DATE AND PLACE OF PREMIERE: unknown.
SUBSEQUENT PERFORMANCES: Nazareth, Pa., 24 January 1816.[2]
MANUSCRIPT SOURCE: Moravian Music Foundation N [s44.2] Beth. ms. and Sto {1} Beth. ms.

A2a. "Come Joyful Hallelujahs Raise"

VOICE PARTS: s, I, II, a., b.
INSTRUMENTAL PARTS: vln. I, II; vla.; vcl.; bass.; fl. I, II; clarino I; organ. Trombones were added for performances in Lititz.

AUTHOR OF TEXT: possibly Peter Wolle.
DEDICATION: composed for the celebration of 4th of July 1815.[3]
DATE OF COMPOSITION: July 1815.
PLACE OF COMPOSITION: Salem, N.C.
DATE AND PLACE OF PREMIERE: 4 July 1815, N.C.
SUBSEQUENT PERFORMANCES: Nazareth, Pa., 27 October 1816;[4] Lititz, Pa., 4 July 1843, 2 July 1876, 1st and 4th July 1889.
MANUSCRIPT SOURCE: Moravian Music Foundation S 237 Salem ms.
PUBLISHED SOURCE: unpublished.

*also*

A2b.

VOICE PARTS: s. and b.
INSTRUMENTAL PARTS: keyboard.
DATE OF ARRANGEMENT: unknown.
PLACE OF COMPOSITION: unknown.
DATE AND PLACE OF PREMIERE: unknown.
SUBSEQUENT PERFORMANCES: there must have been many, for the collection in which this appears was popular.
MANUSCRIPT SOURCE: Moravian Music Foundation La [44.28] Beth ms.
PUBLISHED SOURCE: *Collection of Anthems, Ariettas and Chorales.*

*also*

A2c.

VOICE PARTS: s. I, II, a., t., b.
INSTRUMENTAL PARTS: vln. I, II; vla.; vcl.; fl. I, II; clar. I, II; hn. I, II; clarini I, II; organ.
DATE OF ARRANGEMENT: unknown.

PLACE OF COMPOSITION: unknown.
DATE AND PLACE OF PREMIERE: unknown.
SUBSEQUENT PERFORMANCES: unknown.
MANUSCRIPT SOURCES: Moravian Music Foundation Beth. ms. and B [439] Beth. ms.
PUBLISHED SOURCE: unpublished.

A2d. Arrangment by Barbara Jo Strauss.[5]

A2e. Arrangement by Jean Doherty, 1992.

MANUSCRIPT SOURCE: Moravian Historical Society, Lititz, Pa.
PUBLISHED SOURCE: unpublished.

A3. "Der Herr ist Gross"

VOICE PARTS: s. I, II, t., b.
INSTRUMENTAL PARTS: vln. I, II; vla.: vcl.: fl. I, II; clar. I, II; hn. I, II; organ.
AUTHOR OF TEXT: after J. A. P. Schultz (1747–1800) "Herr unser Gott sey hoch gepriest."
SOURCE OF TEXT: unknown.
DEDICATION: none.
DATE OF COMPOSITION: 6 September 1814.
PLACE OF COMPOSITION: Nazareth, Pa.
DATE AND PLACE OF PREMIERE: probably September 1814 in Nazareth, Pa.
SUBSEQUENT PERFORMANCES: 13 April 1815 in Salem, N.C. *Zum Friedens-Dank-Fest.*
MANUSCRIPT SOURCE: Moravian Music Foundation N [s48] Beth. ms. and N [342].1 Beth. ms.
PUBLISHED SOURCE: [?]

A4. "Es ist Ein Koestlich Ding, Dem Herren Danken"

VOICE PARTS: s., a., t., b.
INSTRUMENTAL PARTS: vln. I, I; vla.; vcl.; fl. I, II; hn. I, II; organ.
AUTHOR OF TEXT: unknown.
SOURCE OF TEXT: earliest Moravian use by J. F. Peter (1746–1813).
DEDICATION: none.
DATE OF COMPOSITION: unknown.
PLACE OF COMPOSITION: unknown.
DATE AND PLACE OF PREMIERE: unknown.
SUBSEQUENT PERFORMANCES: unknown.
MANUSCRIPT SOURCE: Moravian Music Foundation B 424 Beth. ms. and N [342].1 Beth. ms.
PUBLISHED SOURCE: unpublished.


A5a. "Fuer mich, O Herr mein Gott und Heiland"

VOICE PARTS: chorus I s., a., t., b.; chorus II, s., s., t., b.
INSTRUMENTAL PARTS: vln. I, II; vla.; vlc.; organ.
AUTHOR OF TEXT: unknown.
SOURCE OF TEXT: unknown.
DEDICATION: none.
DATE OF COMPOSITION: spring 1815.
PLACE OF COMPOSITION: Salem, N.C.
DATE AND PLACE OF PREMIERE: 1815, Holy Saturday before Easter, Salem, N.C.
SUBSEQUENT PERFORMANCES: unknown.
MANUSCRIPT SOURCE: Moravian Music Foundation S 233 Salem ms. and B 422 ms.
PUBLISHED SOURCE: unpublished.

A5b. "For me, O Lord My God"

VOICE PARTS: chorus I, s., a., t., b.; chorus II. s., a., t., b.
INSTRUMENTAL PARTS: vln. I. II; vla.; vlc.; bass; organ.
ARRANGER OF THE MUSIC: Clarence Dickinson.
TRANSLATOR OF THE TEXT: Helen A. Dickinson.
PUBLISHED SOURCE: New York: H. W. Gray Co., Inc., 1954.


A6. "Glory be to the Most Meritorious Ministry"

VOICE PARTS: s., a., t., b.
INSTRUMENTAL PARTS: keyboard.
AUTHOR OF TEXT: C. I. Latrobe (1758–1936)
SOURCE OF TEXT: English Moravian Tune Book, 1790.
DATE OF TEXT: 1790.
DEDICATION: none.
DATE OF COMPOSITION: March 1854.
PLACE OF COMPOSITION: Canal Dover, Ohio.
DATE AND PLACE OF PREMIERE: March 1854, Canal Dover, Ohio.
SUBSEQUENT PERFORMANCES: many for this Doxology is still used at the Ordination of Deacons.
MANUSCRIPT SOURCE: Moravian Music Foundation B [51C.7] Beth. ms.
PUBLISHED SOURCE: unpublished.


A7. "Happy Soul Thy Days Are Ended"

VOICE PARTS: s., a., t., b.
INSTRUMENTAL PARTS: vln. I, II; vla.; vlc.; organ.
AUTHOR OF TEXT: Charles Wesley (1708–1788).
Moravian source of the text. *Liturgy and Hymns for the Use of the Protestant Church . . . ,* 1843, #1155.

DEDICATION: none.
DATE OF COMPOSITION: possibly 1849.
PLACE OF COMPOSITION: unknown.
DATE AND PLACE OF PREMIERE: 6 November 1862, Bethlehem, Pa.
SUBSEQUENT PERFORMANCES: unknown.
MANUSCRIPT SOURCE: Moravian Music Foundation B [951] Beth. ms. and N [212] 2 Beth ms.
PUBLISHED SOURCE: unpublished.


A8a. "Ich bin in meinem Geiste so gern"

VOICE PARTS: s. I, II; a., b.
INSTRUMENTAL PARTS: vln., I. II; vla.; vlc. English version is incomplete, with no instrumental parts.
MORAVIAN SOURCE OF TEXT: *Gesangbuch zum Gebrauch der Evangelischen . . .*, 1778, #1615.
DEDICATION: none.
DATE AND PLACE OF PREMIERE: unknown.
SUBSEQUENT PERFORMANCES: unknown.
MANUSCRIPT SOURCE: Moravian Music Foundation La [42a] Beth ms. and La [44.24] incomplete version with English translation, and SMB [73.64].
PUBLISHED SOURCE: unpublished.


A8b. "Behold My Soul Thy Saviour"

VOICE PARTS: incomplete [what does this mean?].
INSTRUMENTAL PARTS: missing.
MANUSCRIPT SOURCE: La [42b] Beth ms. and La [44.24] Beth. ms. and SMB [73.64] Salem ms.
PUBLISHED SOURCE: unpublished.

A9. "Now rest in peace; our pray'rs when dying"

VOICE PARTS: s. I, II; a.; b.
INSTRUMENTAL PARTS: vln. I, II; vla.; vlc.; organ.
AUTHOR OF TEXT: unknown.
SOURCE OF TEXT: A Collection of Hymns for the Use . . . , London, 1843, #843.
DEDICATION: none.
DATE OF COMPOSITION: 19 October 1817.
PLACE OF COMPOSITION: Salem, N.C.
DATE AND PLACE OF PREMIERE: probably in late October 1817, Salem, N.C.
SUBSEQUENT PERFORMANCES: unknown.
MANUSCRIPT SOURCE: Moravian Music Foundation S 248 Salem ms. and SS 136 Salem ms.
PUBLISHED SOURCE: unpublished.


A10. "Schmecke, und erfahre, Gnadenwolk"

VOICE PARTS: s. I, II; a.; b.
INSTRUMENTAL PARTS: vln. I, II; vla.; vlc.; basso; organ.
AUTHOR OF TEXT: unknown.
SOURCE of text: unknown.
DEDICATION: none.
DATE OF COMPOSITION: 19 January 1816.
PLACE OF COMPOSITION: Salem, N.C.
DATE AND PLACE OF PREMIERE: 4 May 1816 in Salem, N.C.
SUBSEQUENT PERFORMANCES: unknown, but probably later performances in Lititz and Bethlehem.
MANUSCRIPT SOURCE: Moravian Music Foundation S 242 Salem ms. and B 437[a] Beth ms.
PUBLISHED SOURCES: unpublished.

A11. "Sing Hallelujah, Christ Doth Live"

VOICE PARTS s. I, II; bass.
INSTRUMENTAL PARTS: keyboard.
AUTHOR OF TEXT: Christian Gregor (1723–1801).
SOURCE OF TEXT: Anon. Moravian English translation, 1801.
DEDICATION: none.
DATE OF COMPOSITION: unknown.
PLACE OF COMPOSITION: probably Philadelphia, Pa.
DATE AND PLACE OF PREMIERE: probably Philadelphia, Pa.
SUBSEQUENT PERFORMANCES: unknown.
MANUSCRIPT SOURCE: unknown.
PUBLISHED SOURCE: *Hymn Tunes, Used in the Church of the United Brethren*, 1872, 115–122.

A12. "Wiederholts mit frohen Toenen"

VOICE PARTS: chorus I; s., a., t., b. and chorus II; s. I, II; a.; bass.
INSTRUMENTAL PARTS: vln. I, II; vls.; vlc.; fl. I. II; hn. I, II; clarini I, II; organ.
AUTHOR OF TEXT: unknown.
MORAVIAN SOURCE OF TEXT: *Nachtrag zu dem Gesangecbuche . . .* , Gnadau, 1812.
DEDICATION: none.
DATE OF COMPOSITION: probably 1816.
PLACE OF COMPOSITION: Salem, N.C.
DATE AND LOCATION OF PREMIERE: 24 December 1816 in Salem, N.C.
SUBSEQUENT PERFORMANCES: probably many, for the anthem appears in a number of collections.
MANUSCRIPT SOURCE: Moravian Music Foundation S 247.1 Salem ms.0, La [14] Beth. ms., La [44.37] Beth. ms., SMB [75.86] Salem ms., SS 131 Salem ms., and B 374 Beth. ms.
PUBLISHED SOURCE: unpublished.

## Instrumental Pieces

### A13. March

INSTRUMENTAL PARTS: clar., hn., bassoon.
DEDICATION: probably none.
DATE OF COMPOSITION: 22 August 1816.
PLACE OF COMPOSITION: Salem, N.C.
DATE AND PLACE OF PREMIERE: unknown but probably in Salem.
SUBSEQUENT PERFORMANCES: unknown.
MANUSCRIPT SOURCE: no copy found. This march is mentioned in Peter Wolle's Diary.
PUBLISHED SOURCE: unpublished.

### A14. Minuet and Trio

INSTRUMENTAL PARTS: clarinet I and II; hn. I, II.
DEDICATION: probably none.
DATE OF COMPOSITION: 10 December 1814.
PLACE OF COMPOSITION: Salem, N.C.
DATE AND PLACE OF PREMIERE: unknown, but probably played in Salem, N.C.
SUBSEQUENT PERFORMANCES: unknown.
MANUSCRIPT SOURCE: no manuscript found. This composition is mentioned by Peter Wolle in his Diary.
PUBLISHED SOURCE: unpublished.

## Tune Books

### A15. *A Collection of Moravian Hymn Tunes*

VOICE PARTS: single-line melodies.

INSTRUMENTAL PARTS: none.
SOURCE OF TEXTS: no texts.
DEDICATION: none.
DATE OF COMPILATION: ca. 1856.
PLACE OF COMPILATION: possibly Bethlehem.
MANUSCRIPT SOURCE: unknown.
PUBLISHED SOURCE: New York, 1856. [full citation, pagination?]

A16. *Hymn Tunes, Used in the Church of the United Brethren, Arranged for Four Voices and the Organ or Piano-forte; to which are added Chants for the Litany of that Church, and a Number of Approved Anthems for Various Occasions.*

VOICE PARTS: s., s., t., b.
INSTRUMENTAL PARTS: organ or piano.
DATE OF COMPILATION: ca. 1835.
PLACE OF COMPILATION: Bethlehem.
MANUSCRIPT SOURCE: unknown.
PUBLISHED SOURCE: Bethlehem, PA.: Moravian Publication Office, 1836, with numerous editions after this publication.

## Vocal Solos and Duets

17. "Am Fenster bey Mondschein"

VOICE PARTS: single voice.
INSTRUMENTAL PARTS: keyboard accompaniment.
AUTHOR OF TEXT: unknown.
SOURCE OF TEXT: unknown.
DATE OF COMPOSITION: unknown.
PLACE OF COMPOSITION: unknown.
DATE AND PLACE OF PREMIERE: unknown.

SUBSEQUENT PERFORMANCES: unknown.
MANUSCRIPT SOURCE: Brown University, Providence, R.I., Harris Collection, copybook of Susan Miller.
PUBLISHED SOURCE: unpublished.


A18. "An mein Clavier"

VOICE PARTS: solo song.
INSTRUMENTAL PARTS: piano accompaniment.
AUTHOR OF TEXT: unknown.
SOURCE OF TEXT: unknown.
DATE AND PLACE OF PREMIERE: unknown.
SUBSEQUENT PERFORMANCES: unknown.
MANUSCRIPT SOURCE: Moravian Music Foundation SMB [73.24] Salem ms. and SMB [81.9] Salem ms.
PUBLISHED SOURCE: unpublished.


A19. "The Cottager's Morning"

VOICE PARTS: duet.
INSTRUMENTAL PARTS: piano accompaniment.
AUTHOR OF TEXT: unknown.
SOURCE OF TEXT: unknown.
DEDICATION: none.
DATE OF COMPOSITION: unknown.
PLACE OF COMPOSITION: possibly Philadelphia.
DATE AND PLACE OF PREMIERE: unknown.
SUBSEQUENT PERFORMANCES: unknown.
MANUSCRIPT SOURCE: unknown.
PUBLISHED SOURCE: Philadelphia: J. C. Klemm, n.d.

A20. "If That High World"

VOICE PARTS: duet.
INSTRUMENTAL PARTS: piano accompaniment.
AUTHOR OF TEXT: Lord Byron.
DEDICATION: none.
DATE OF COMPOSITION: unknown.
PLACE OF COMPOSITION: possibly Philadelphia.
DATE AND PLACE OF PREMIERE: unknown.
SUBSEQUENT PERFORMANCES: unknown.
MANUSCRIPT SOURCE: unknown.
PUBLISHED SOURCE: Philadelphia: J. G. Klemm, n.d.


A21. "Jesus Makes My Heart Rejoice" and "Jesus unser Hort ist Treu."

VOICE PARTS: solo voice.
INSTRUMENTAL PARTS: vln. I, I; vla.; vlc.; organ.
AUTHOR OF TEXT: H. Louis von Hayn.
DATE OF TEXT: 1776.
ENGLISH TRANSLATOR: Bishop F. W. Foster.
DATE OF ENGLISH TRANSLATION: 1789.
DEDICATION: none.
DATE OF COMPOSITION: 24 June 1812.
PLACE OF COMPOSITION: probably Nazareth, Pa.
DATE AND PLACE OF PREMIERE: unknown.
SUBSEQUENT PERFORMANCES: unknown.
MANUSCRIPT SOURCE: Moravian Music Foundation B [881].26 ms.
PUBLISHED SOURCE: unpublished.

## A22. "Mein Tod"

VOICE PARTS: single voice.
INSTRUMENTAL PARTS: piano accompaniment.
AUTHOR OF TEXT: unknown.
SOURCE OF TEXT: unknown.
DEDICATION: none.
DATE OF COMPOSITION: 12 April 1811.
PLACE OF COMPOSITION: Nazareth.
DATE AND PLACE OF PREMIERE: unknown.
SUBSEQUENT PERFORMANCES: unknown.
MANUSCRIPT SOURCE: Moravian Music Foundation SMB [53.30] Salem ms.
PUBLISHED SOURCE: unpublished.


## A23. "To The Eolian Harp"

VOICE PARTS: solo song.
INSTRUMENTAL PARTS: piano accompaniment.
AUTHOR OF TEXT: unknown.
SOURCE OF TEXT: unknown.
DEDICATION: none.
DATE OF COMPOSITION: unknown.
PLACE OF COMPOSITION: possibly in Philadelphia.
DATE AND PLACE OF PREMIERE: unknown.
SUBSEQUENT PERFORMANCES: unknown.
MANUSCRIPT SOURCE: Moravian Music Foundation LMB [5.1] Beth ms.
PUBLISHED SOURCE: unpublished.

A24. Vocal Anthology

DATE OF COMPOSITION: finished 9 January 1815.
PLACE OF COMPOSITION: Salem. NC.
MANUSCRIPT SOURCE: unknown but assembled in Salem and mentioned by Peter Wolle in his diary.
PUBLISHED SOURCE: unpublished.


A25. "As Slow Our Ship"

VOICE PARTS: solo song.
INSTRUMENTAL PARTS: piano accompaniment.

This song was part of a concert at Moravian College in 1976. A tape of the concert is in the music library of Moravian College, Bethlehem, Pa. It is said to be in the *Philadelphia Music Journal and Review,* date unknown.


A26. "Herr mein Gott" is mentioned by Wolle in his dairy as it appears in the translation by Seadle, et. al., 25.

"Ich bin in meinem Geiste," a hymn mentioned by Wolle in his diary as translated by Seadle, et. al., 24.


## NOTES

1. Barbara Jo Strauss. "A Register of Music Performed in Concert, Nazareth, Pennsylvania from 1796–1845: an Annotated Edition of an American Moravian Document." Master's thesis, University of Arizona, 1976. p. 99.
2. Ibid.
3. Ibid., 229

4. Ibid., 200.
5. Ibid., Appendix 8.

Appendix B

# Compositions by Theodore Wolle

## Anthems

B1. "Asleep in Jesus"

VOICE PARTS: s.; a. I, II; t.; b.
INSTRUMENTAL PARTS: organ.
AUTHOR OF TEXT: Margaret Mackay, Scottish poet and writer.
ORIGINAL SOURCE OF TEXT: *The Amethyst*, Edinburgh annual. Date not known.
MORAVIAN SOURCE OF TEXT: *The Moravian Hymn Book,* "Funeral Anthem," #870.
DATE OF TEXT: 1832.
DEDICATION: Robert Rau, tenor soloist and trombone choir member, Central Moravian Church.
DATE OF COMPOSITION: March 1877.
PLACE OF COMPOSITION: Bethlehem.
DATE AND PLACE OF PREMIERE: 27 August 1877, Central Moravian Church, Bethlehem, Pa.
SUBSEQUENT PERFORMANCES: Theodore Wolle's funeral; Memorial service for President Garfield, September 1881; Memorial service for General Grant, August 1885.
MANUSCRIPT SOURCE: Moravian Music Foundation; individual

voice parts in Bethlehem Collection, B [921].
PUBLISHED SOURCE: individual sheet-music format, Bethlehem, Pa.: Comenius Press, 1897; *Moravian Hymnal*, 1920, No. 936. B2.

"Blessed Are the Dead"

VOICE PARTS: adult "choir piece," probably s., a., t., b.
INSTRUMENTAL PARTS: probably organ.
AUTHOR OF TEXT: Latin hymn.
ORIGINAL SOURCE OF THE TEXT: Roman Catholic Requiem Mass
Theodore Francis Wolle (1832–1885).
DATE OF COMPOSITION: possibly 1866 or 1867.
PLACE OF COMPOSITION: Bethlehem, Pa.
DATE AND LOCATION OF PREMIERE: date unknown, but the premiere probably took place in Central Moravian Church.
MANUSCRIPT SOURCE: unknown.
PUBLISHED SOURCE: unknown.

This anthem is mentioned by Peter Wolle in his dairy, 14 January 1867.

## Song

B3. "English Farewell Song"

VOICE PARTS: female voices.
INSTRUMENTAL PARTS: probably piano accompaniment.
AUTHOR OF TEXT: original by student of the Moravian Female Academy.
DATE OF COMPOSITION: early July 1872.
PLACE OF COMPOSITION: Bethlehem, Pa.
DATE AND LOCATION OF PREMIERE: July 1872, chapel of the Moravian Female Seminary.
SUBSEQUENT PERFORMANCES: unknown.

MANUSCRIPT SOURCE: unknown.
PUBLISHED SOURCE: unknown.

The song is mentioned in *The Moravian*, 11 July 1872. It was included in a list of compositions performed by seminary students.

# Appendix C

## *Compositions by J. Fred. Wolle*

### Anthems

C1. "The Ambassador of Christ"

VOICE PARTS: s., a., t., b., with soprano solo.
INSTRUMENTAL PARTS: string orchestra with organ.
AUTHOR OF TEXT: Ludwig von Zinzendorf.
MORAVIAN SOURCE OF THE TEXT: *The Liturgy and Hymns of the American Province* . . . , 1880, #725.
DATE OF COMPOSITION: 5 June 1886 is on the mauscript in Wolle's hand.
PLACE OF COMPOSITION: probably Bethlehem, Pa.
DATE AND LOCATION OF PREMIERE: unknown, but probably Central Moravian Church.
SUBSEQUENT PERFORMANCES: unknown.
MANUSCRIPT SOURCE: Lehigh University 784.2 W864a T Vault.
PUBLISHED SOURCE: unpublished.

C2. "Bonum Est"

VOICE PARTS: s. I, II;  a.; t. I, II; b.; with soprano and tenor solos.
INSTRUMENTAL PARTS: organ.
ORIGINAL SOURCE OF TEXT: The Bible, Psalm XCII.
MORAVIAN SOURCE OF TEXT: The Bible, King James Version.
DEDICATION: to the 1884 class of Moravian Parochial School.
DATE OF COMPOSITION: probably 1884.
PLACE OF COMPOSITION: probably Bethlehem.
DATE AND LOCATION OF PREMIERE: probably Bethlehem.
SUBSEQUENT PERFORMANCES: unknown.
MANUSCRIPT SOURCE: Lehigh University, 784.2 W864b T Vault.
PUBLISHED SOURCE: unpublished.


C3. "He Leads Us On"

VOICE PARTS: s., a., t., b., with soprano and bass solos.
INSTRUMENTAL PARTS: vln. I, II; vla.; vlc.; bass; hrn. I, II; alto, tenor, bass, trombones; organ.
AUTHOR OF TEXT: setting by Hiram O. Wiley of Ludwig von Zinzendorf's hymn "Jesus still lead on."
ORIGINAL SOURCE OF TEXT: Zinzendorf's hymns.1721.
MORAVIAN SOURCE OF TEXT: Wiley text unknown.
DEDICATION: none.
DATE OF COMPOSITION: 25 August 1888 on the manuscript in Wolle's hand.
PLACE OF COMPOSITION: probably Bethlehem, Pa.
DATE AND LOCATION OF PREMIERE: June 1892, Central Moravian Church.
SUBSEQUENT PERFORMANCES: 19 September 1893. "Brought into regular use."[1]
MANUSCRIPT SOURCE: Lehigh University 784.2 W862h T Vault.

Full score in Wolle's hand with additional set of instrument parts dated 1904.
PUBLISHED SOURCE: unpublished, but there are two sets of choir parts in the Lehigh University collection that are printed.

## Songs and Arrangement for Chorus

### C4. "The Four Maries"

VOICE PARTS: t. I, II; b, I, II.
INSTRUMENTAL PARTS; none.
SOURCE OF TEXT: traditional.
DEDICATION: none.
DATE OF ARRANGEMENT: 1891.
PLACE OF ARRANGEMENT: Bethlehem.
DATE AND PLACE OF PREMIERE: unknown.
SUBSEQUENT PERFORMANCES: H. D. mentions the song a number of times in *The Gift*, 19, 79–80.
MANUSCRIPT SOURCE: Lehigh University 784.2 W864 T Vault.
PUBLISHED SOURCE: unpublished.

### C5. "Lehigh University Alma Mater Song"

VOICE PARTS: t. I, II; b. I, II.
INSTRUMENTAL PARTS: unaccompanied.
AUTHOR OF TEXT: unknown.
DEDICATION: none.
DATE OF COMPOSITION: 12 March 1901.
PLACE OF COMPOSITION: probably Bethlehem.
DATE AND LOCATION OF PREMIERE: unknown.
SUBSEQUENT PERFORMANCES: unknown.
MANUSCRIPT SOURCE: Lehigh University 784.2 W864 T Vault.

Vocal score in Wolle's hand.
PUBLISHED SOURCE: probably unpublished.

C6. "Medley '91"

VOICE PARTS: t. I, II; b. I, II.
INSTRUMENTAL PARTS; none, probably unaccompanied.
TITLES OF SONGS: "Long May She Live Our Lehigh Fair"; "O Ain't You Coming To De Old Plantation"; "My Bonnie Lies Over the Ocean," "Polly Wolly Doodle All the Day"; "She Said at the Chinese Theatre"; "The Monkeys There Got Over This Morning Prayer"; "Comrades, Comrades"; "New Coon in Town."
DEDICATION: none.
DATE OF COMPOSITION: 1891.
PLACE OF COMPOSITION: probably Bethlehem, Pa.
DATE AND LOCATION OF PREMIERE: unknown.
SUBSEQUENT PERFORMANCES: unknown.
MANUSCRIPT SOURCE: Lehigh University 784.2 W894g T Vault.
Vocal score in Wolle's hand.
PUBLISHED SOURCE: unknown.

C7. "Medley"

VOICE PARTS: t. I, II; b. I, II.
INSTRUMENTAL PARTS: unaccompanied.
TITLES OF THE SONGS: "We Meet Tonight Boys with Mirth and Song," "Oh the Bulldog On the Banks," "Rock-a-bye Baby On the Tree Top," "Johnnie Jones and His Sister Sue," "Here's to Good Old Lehigh," "Jingle Bells," "Little Annie Rooney," "Long Come a Pelican," "I Like to Cheer for the Brown and White."
DEDICATION: none.

DATE OF COMPOSITION: unknown.
PLACE OF COMPOSITION: probably Bethlehem, Pa.
DATE AND LOCATION OF PREMIERE: unknown.
SUBSEQUENT PERFORMANCES: unknown.
MANUSCRIPT SOURCE: Lehigh University 784.2 W894g T Vault. Not in Wolle's hand.
PUBLISHED SOURCE: unpublished.

Liturgical Chants

C8. "Dies Irae"

VOICE PARTS: s., a., t., b.
INSTRUMENTAL PARTS: none.
AUTHOR OF TEXT: Thomas of Celano, in Latin.
DATE OF TEXT: c. 1250.
ENGLISH TRANSLATOR: William Josiah Irons.
DATE OF ENGLISH TRANSLATION: 1848.
DEDICATION: none.
DATE OF COMPOSTION: Chant I, 1889; Chant II, 1890.
PLACE OF COMPOSITION: probably Bethlehem.
DATE AND LOCATION OF PREMIERE: unknown date, but the location was probably Central Moravian Church.
SUBSEQUENT PERFORMANCES: many, for the chants were a part of the regular liturgy until recently.
MANUSCRIPT SOURCE: Chant I, unknown; Chant II, Lehigh University 784.2 W894 T Vault.
PUBLISHED SOURCE: *Hymnal and Liturgies of the Moravian Church*, 1923, #929.

C9. "Doxology at the Ordination of a Deacon"

VOICE PARTS: s., a., t., b.
INSTRUMENTAL PARTS: none.
AUTHOR OF TEXT: C. I. Latrobe (1758–1836).
MORAVIAN SOURCE OF TEXT: English Moravian Tune Book, 1790.
DATE OF THE TEXT: 1790.
DEDICATION: none.
DATE OF COMPOSITION: 1923.
PLACE OF COMPOSITION: probably Bethlehem.
DATE AND LOCATION OF PREMIERE: unknown.
SUBSEQUENT PERFORMANCES: many, for the chant was used in The Rite of Ordination.
MANUSCRIPT SOURCE: unknown.
PUBLISHED SOURCE: *Hymnal and Liturgies of the Moravian Church,* 1923, 161.

C10. "Doxology at the Ordination of a Presbyter"

VOICE PARTS: s., a., t., b.
INSTRUMENTAL PARTS: none.
AUTHOR OF TEXT: C. I. Latrobe (1758–1790)
MORAVIAN SOURCE OF TEXT: English Moravian Tune Book, 1790.
DATE OF HYMN: 1790.
DEDICATION: none.
DATE OF COMPOSITION: 1923.
PLACE OF COMPOSITION: probably Bethlehem, Pa.
DATE AND LOCATION OF PREMIERE: unknown, but the location was probably Central Moravian Church.
SUBSEQUENT PERFORMANCES: many, for this chant was used for The Rite of Ordination.
MANUSCRIPT SOURCE: unknown.
PUBLISHED SOURCE: *Hymnal and Liturgies of the Moravian Church,* 1923, 162.

## C11. "Glory be to God on High"

VOICE PARTS: s., a., t., b.
INSTRUMENTAL PARTS: none.
AUTHOR OF TEXT: 7th century Latin from 4th century Greek.
SOURCE OF TEXT: English translation *Book of Common Prayer*.
DATE OF TEXT: 1549.
MORAVIAN SOURCE OF TEXT: probably *The Liturgy and Hymns of the American Province of the Unitas Fratrum, or the Moravian Church*, (Bethlehem: Moravian Publication Office, 1891).
DEDICATION: none.
DATE OF COMPOSITION: probably 1895.
PLACE OF COMPOSITION: probably Bethlehem, Pa.
DATE OF PLACE OF PREMIERE: 25 December 1895, Central Moravian Church.
SUBSEQUENT PERFORMANCES: unknown.
MANUSCRIPT SOURCE: Moravian Museum in Bethlehem, Pa.
PUBLISHED SOURCE: unpublished.

### Hymns

## C12. "Once He Came in Blessing"

VOICE PARTS: s., a., t., b.
INSTRUMENTAL PARTS: none.
AUTHOR OF TEXT: Jan Roh.
DATE OF TEXT: 1547.
MORAVIAN SOURCE OF TEXT: English translation by Catherine Winkworth in an American Moravian hymnal in 1876.
DATE OF TRANSLATION: 1863.
DEDICATION: none.
DATE OF COMPOSITION: 1888.
PLACE OF COMPOSITION: probably Bethlehem.

DATE AND LOCATION OF PREMIERE: unknown, but the location was probably Central Moravian Church.
SUBSEQUENT PERFORMANCES: many, for this hymn is still a part of Moravian hymnody.
MANUSCRIPT SOURCE: unknown.
PUBLISHED SOURCE: *Hymnal and Liturgies of the Moravian Church*, 1923, #154.

C13. "Ride On! Ride On in Majesty"

VOICE PARTS: s., a., t., b.
INSTRUMENTAL PARTS: none.
AUTHOR OF TEXT: Henry Hart Milman.
DATE OF TEXT: 1827.
DEDICATION: none.
DATE OF COMPOSITION: possibly 1888.
PLACE OF COMPOSITION: probably Bethlehem, Pa.
DATE AND LOCATION OF PREMIERE: unknown.
SUBSEQUENT PERFORMANCES: many for this hymn is still part of Moravian hymnody.
MANUSCRIPT SOURCE: unknown.
PUBLISHED SOURCE: Hymnal and Liturgies of the Moravian Church, 1923, #219.

C14. "Ueber den Sternen"

VOICE PARTS: s., a., t., b.
INSTRUMENTAL PARTS: none.
AUTHOR OF TEXT: unknown.
ORIGINAL SOURCE OF TEXT: unknown.
MORAVIAN SOURCE OF TEXT: unknown.
DATE OF HYMN: unknown.

DEDICATION: none.
DATE OF COMPOSITION: unknown.
PLACE OF COMPOSITION: probably Bethlehem.
DATE AND LOCATION OF PREMIERE: unknown.
SUBSEQUENT PERFORMANCE: unknown.
MANUSCRIPT SOURCE: Lehigh University 784.2 W 864 T Vault.
PUBLISHED SOURCE: unpublished.

## Instrumental Pieces

C15. "Sketch Book"

INSTRUMENTAL PARTS: keyboard.
DEDICATION: none.
DATE OF COMPOSITION: 1884–85.
PLACE OF COMPOSITION: Munich.
DATE AND LOCATION OF PREMIERE: not applicable.
SUBSEQUENT PERFORMANCES: not applicable.
MANUSCRIPT SOURCE: Moravian Music Foundation.
PUBLISHED SOURCE: unpublished.

C16. "Three Keys Musical Nonsense"

INSTRUMENTAL PARTS: probably string quartet.
DEDICATION: none.
DATE OF COMPOSITION: unknown.
PLACE OF COMPOSITION: unknown.
DATE AND LOCATION OF PREMIERE: unknown.
SUBSEQUENT PERFORMANCES: unknown.
MANUSCRIPT SOURCE: Lehigh University 784.2 W864 T Vault. Score in Wolle's hand.
PUBLISHED SOURCE: unpublished.

C17. A keyboard piece attributed to Wolle.

All other information unknown.
MANUSCRIPT SOURCE: Moravian Music Foundation Lmisc [21.1b] Beth. ms. with a "caption": J. Fred. Wolle.

## Organ Transcriptions

C18. *Die Meistersinger von Nuernberg* [Overture]

INSTRUMENTAL PARTS: organ.
COMPOSER OF THE ORIGINAL: Richard Wagner.
MANUSCRIPT SOURCE: Lehigh University 784.2 W 864g T Vault.
PUBLISHED SOURCE: unpublished.
All other information unknown.

## Songs and Vocal Duets

C19. "Aunt Jane's Moon Song" ©1893

VOICE PARTS: soprano.
INSTRUMENTAL PARTS: piano accompaniment.
AUTHOR OF POEM: unknown.
ORIGINAL SOURCE OF THE POEM: an unidentified printed pamphlet is attached to the manuscript.
DATE OF POEM: unknown.
DEDICATION: none.
DATE OF COMPOSITION: unknown.
PLACE OF COMPOSITION: probably Bethlehem.
DATE AND LOCATION OF PREMIERE: unknown.
SUBSEQUENT PERFORMANCES: unknown.
MANUSCRIPT SOURCE: Lehigh University 784.2 W864 T Vault.
PUBLISHED SOURCE: unpublished.

C20. "Cloudland" ©1893

VOICE PARTS: soprano or tenor.
INSTRUMENTAL PARTS: piano accompaniment.
AUTHOR OF POEM: unknown.
ORIGINAL SOURCE OF POEM: unknown.
DATE OF POEM: unknown.
DATE OF COMPOSITION: unknown.
PLACE OF COMPOSITION: probably Bethlehem.
DATE AND LOCATION OF PREMIERE: unknown.
EARLY PERFORMANCE: 1893.
MANUSCRIPT SOURCE: Lehigh University 784.2 W864 T. Vault.
PUBLISHED SOURCE: unpublished.

Manuscript is incomplete.


C21. "The Daisy" ©1892

VOICE PARTS: soprano or tenor.
INSTRUMENTAL PARTS: piano accompaniment.
AUTHOR OF POEM: Gilford Howard.
ORIGINAL SOURCE OF THE POEM: Evening Star [place and date unknown].
DATE OF POEM: 20 February 1892.
DEDICATION: NONE.
DATE OF COMPOSITION: 1892.
PLACE OF COMPOSITION: Bethlehem, Pa.
DATE AND LOCATION OF PREMIERE: unknown.
SUBSEQUENT PERFORMANCES: unknown.
MANUSCRIPT SOURCE: Lehigh Univerity 784.2 W864 T Vault.
PUBLISHED SOURCE: unpublished.

C22. "Concert of Witches"

VOICE PARTS: soprano and alto.
INSTRUMENTAL PARTS: piano accompaniment.
AUTHOR OF POEM: unknown.
DATE OF THE POEM: unknown.
DATE OF COMPOSITION: 1915.
PLACE OF COMPOSITION: Bethlehem, Pa.
DATE AND LOCATION OF PREMIERE: unknown.
SUBSEQUENT PERFORMANCES: unknown.
MANUSCRIPT SOURCE: Lehigh University 784.2 W864 T Vault.
PUBLISHED SOURCE: unpublished.


C23. "To Bethlehem Town"

VOICE PARTS: soprano.
INSTRUMENTAL PARTS: piano accompaniment.
AUTHOR OF THE POEM: J. Fred. Wolle.
DATE OF THE POEM: possibly 1922.
DEDICATION: William E. Brooks, D.D.
DATE OF COMPOSITION: 1922.
PLACE OF COMPOSITION: Bethlehem, Pa.
DATE AND LOCATION OF PREMIERE: unknown.
DATE OF SUBSEQUENT PERFORMANCES: unknown.
MANUSCRIPT SOURCE: Archives of The Bach Choir. Manuscript not in Wolle's hand.
PUBLISHED SOURCE: unpublished.

Appendix D

# *Glossary*

*Aeltester Conferenz*: "Elders Conference" handled moral and spiritual matters and secular problems as they affected the community.

*Aufsehere Collegium*: "board of overseers" handled mundane questions as they affected the community.

*Bruedergemeine*: the German title for the Moravian Church. Comprised of three parts theologically: 1. the *Urgemeine*, the "original congregation," which is the model of unity of the Christian Church; 2. *Gemeine*, the "congregation" or "assembly," contains the children of God, living and in heaven; 3. *Religionen*, "denominations," the varied groups of Christian believers and non-believers on earth.

*Chor* system: ordering the community by gender, age, and marital status into groups of children from weaning to age 6, girls and boys ages 6 to12, older girls and older boys ages 12 to 17, single women, single men, married women, married men, widows, and widowers.

*Chorhaus*: "choir house," the building where members of a choir lived communally.

*Chorsaal*: the hall for devotions in the choir house.

*Collegium Musicum*: "musical groups" providing music for the church.

*Daily Text*: Old and New Testament passages, hymn verses, and prayers selected by *lot* and arranged by day throughout the year to serve as guides to personal conduct. There was a special version for children.

*Gemeine*: "community" or "congregation." They were synonymous because theologically a Moravian community was a community of believers (i.e., a congregation).

*Gemeinhaus*: a house for the activities of the congregation.

*Gottesacker*: "God's acre," a garden "or a dormitory where the departed members of the congregation sleep until the coming of their Lord." Vogt, *Shaker*, 92.

*Herzensreligion*: "religion of the heart," the shared experience of a personal relationship with Christ.

*Lebenslauf*: a spiritual "memoir" recounting an individual's spiritual journey on earth.

*Liturgish Leben*: "to live liturgically," the practice of regarding all activities as service to God.

*Lot*: a method by which Christ, their chief elder, communicated directly with an *Aeltester Conferenz*.

*Lovefeast*: sharing a simple meal during a service or a service in itself.

*Ortsgemeine*: "settlement congregation," an isolated, self-contained Moravian village.

*Pfleger*: the spiritual leader of a choir.

*Platz*: "center square," the center of the settlement. The settlement was "regarded as a sanctuary in which god is present," Vogt, *Shaker*, 84.

*Saal*: the "hall" where the congregation gathered for religious devotions. Theologically, the presence of the divine was associated with a community of believers gathered for worship, not with a building.

*Singstunde*: "hour of singing," when the pastor and congregation sang hymn verses with a unified theme.

*Vorsteher*: the "economic administrator" of a congregation.

Appendix E

# *Positions Held by Peter, Theodore, and J. Fred.Wolle*

## Peter Wolle

1810–1814: teacher at Nazareth Hall, Nazareth, Pa.
1814–1817: teacher at boys' school, Salem, N.C.
1815–1819: music supervisor of Salem, N.C.
1817–1819: leader of Single Brothers in Salem, N.C.
1819–1822: Pastor at Bethania, N.C.
1823–1826: Pastor at Lancaster, Pa.
1826–1836: Pastor at Philadelphia, Pa.
1836–1838: Principal of Linden Hall, Lititz, Pa.
1838–1853: Pastor at Lititz, Pa.
1845: consecrated a Bishop of the Moravian Church.
1853–1855: Pastor Dover First Moravian Church, Dover, Ohio.
1855–1861: member of the Provincial Board of the Moravian Church.
1861–1862: temporary pastor at Sharon, Ohio.

## Theodore Wolle

1853–1860: Professor of Music at Greensborough Female College, Greensboro, N.C.
1860–1864: Professor of Music at Edgeworth Female Seminary,

Greensboro, N.C.
1864–1865: Professor of Music at School for the Deaf and Dumb, Raleigh, N.C.
1865–1885: Professor of Music at Female Seminary, Bethlehem, Pa.
1865–1872: organist in Old Moravian Chapel, Bethlehem, Pa.
1872–1885: organist and choirmaster at Central Moravian Church, Bethlehem, Pa.

### J. Fred. Wolle

1881–1884: organist at Trinity Episcopal Church, South Bethlehem, Pa.
1882–[ ? ]: teacher of mathematics, Moravian Parochial School, Bethlehem, Pa.
1882–1884 and 1885–1892: conductor of Bethlehem Choral Union.
1883–1884: conductor of Concordia Glee Club, Bethlehem, Pa.
1892: conductor of Oratorio Society of the Bethlehems.
1885–1905: organist and choirmaster, Central Moravian Church, Bethlehem, Pa.
1887–1905: organist and choirmaster Packer Memorial Church, Bethlehem, PA.
1887–1905: Professor of Music, Lehigh University, Bethlehem, Pa.
1889–1905 and 1912–1933: conductor of The Bach Choir of Bethlehem.
1905–1912: Chair of the Department of Music, University of California at Berkeley.
1914: conductor of the Harrisburg Choral Society, Harrisburg, Pa.
1914: conductor of the Oratorio Society of York, York, Pa.
[?]–1932: organist and choirmaster Lutheran Church, Allentown, Pa.

# GENEALOGICAL TABLE  *411*

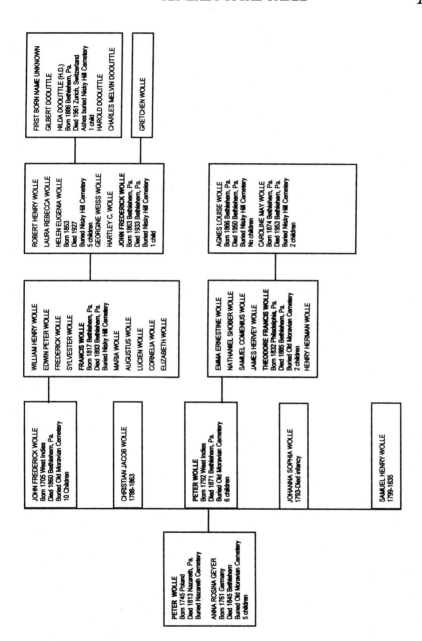

Appendix F: Genealogical Table of the Musical Wolles

# *Bibliography*

## Primary Unpublished Sources

A. Account Books 1890–1904, Lehigh University, Bethlehem, Pennsylvania.

B. Archives of The Bach Choir of Bethlehem [housed in Moravian Archives, Bethlehem, Pennsylvania].

    1. Letter from Robert S. Taylor to Mr. Robert B. Hampson, 23 September 1977.
    2. Luckenbach, Martha. Interview: audio tape and transcript, 11 October 1993.
    3. Starner, Bertha-Mae. Interview: audio tape and transcript, 14 June 1995.

C. Board Minutes of The Bach Choir of Bethlehem, Office of The Bach Choir of Bethlehem, Pennsylvania.

D. Moravian Archives, Bethlehem, Pennsylvania.

    1. Minutes of the Board of Elders of the Congregation of Bethlehem, Pa. Volume IV opened 1877.
    2. Official Diary of the Congregation of the Moravian Church of Bethlehem, Pennsylvania 1896.
    3. Philharmonic Society Inventory and Programs.
    4. Francis Wolle. Correspondence.
    5. James Wolle. Letters.

# BIBLIOGRAPHY

6. Peter Wolle. Letters. P. U. C. 1827–1840.
7. Philip W. Wolle. Francis Wolle's Library List, Part II.

E. Nazareth Diary [translation from the German], Moravian Historical Society, Nazareth,Pennsylvania.

F. Wolle Genealogy, Reeves Library, Moravian College, Bethlehem, Pennsylvania.

## Published Books and Music

Buck, Dudley. *The Centennial Meditation of Columbia*. New York, N.Y.: Edwin K. Kalmus, n.d.
_____. *Second Motette Collection, Composed, Selected and Adapted by Dudley Buck*. Boston: Oliver Ditson Company, 1871.
*A Collection of Hymns for the Use of the Protestant Church of the United Brethren*. London, 1790.
Colling, E. S. and F. W. Wilson. *Songs of Lehigh University*. New York City: Hinds, Noble & Eldridge, 1911.
*English Moravian Tune Book*. London: 1790.
*Gesangbuch der Evangelisher Bruedergemeine*. Herrnhut und Bad Boll: 1967.
*Gesangbuch zum Gebrauch der Evangelishen Bruedergemeinen*. Barby: 1778.
Gregor, Christian. K. Koepe, ed. and trans. *Canticle of Praise*. Winston-Salem, N.C.: The Moravian Music Foundation, 1985.
_____. *Choral-Buch 1784*. Winston-Salem, N.C.: The Moravian Music Foundation Press, 1984.
Homman, Charles. *Chamber Music for Strings*. John Graziano and Joanne Swenson-Eldridge, eds. Madison: A-R Editions, Inc., 1998.
H[ueffel], C[hristian] G[ottlieb]. *Auzug aus bisher in den evangelishen Brueder-Gemeinen gebraechlichen Choral-Buch mit ausgeschrieben Stimmen der Choral Melodin*. n.p., n.d.
*Hymnal and Liturgies of the Moravian Church*. Bethlehem, Pa.: Provincial Synod, 1920.
Latrobe, Christian Ignatius. *Anthems for One, Two or more voices performed in*

the Church of the United Brethren, Collected, and the Instrumental parts adapted for the Organ or Piano Forte. London, 1811.

_____. Hymn-Tunes, Sung in the Church of the United Brethren, Collected by Chr. Ign. LaTrobe. London: n.d.

The Liturgy and Hymns of the American Province of the Unitas Fratrum or the Moravian Church. Bethlehem. Pa.: Moravian Publishing Office, 1890.

Lonas, Henrich. *Choralbuch der Evangelische Brueder Kircke. Auszug aus Chr. Gregors Choralbuch vom Jahr 1784.* Gnadau, 1842.

Nitschke, A. *Choral-Buch der Evangelischen Bruedergemeine vier stimmig arrangirt von A. Nitschke.* Koenigsfeld, 1868.

Wolle, J. Fred. "Dies Irae." *Hymnal and Liturgies of the Moravian Church.* Bethlehem, Pa.: Provincial Synod, 1920.

_____. "Doxology at the Ordination of a Deacon." *Hymnal and Liturgies of the Moravian Church.* Bethlehem, Pa.: Provincial Synod, 1920.

_____. "Doxology at the Ordination of a Presbyter." *Hymnal and Liturgies of the Moravian Church.* Bethlehem, Pa.: Provincial Synod, 1920.

_____. "Once He Came In Blessing." *Hymnal and Liturgies of the Moravian Church.* Bethlehem, Pa.: Provincial Synod, 1920.

_____. "Ride On! Ride On in Majesty." *Hymnal and Liturgies of the Moravian Church.* Bethlehem, Pa.: Provincial Synod, 1920.

Wolle, Peter. *A Collection of Moravian Hymn-Tunes.* New York: 1856.

_____. *Hymn Tunes, Used in the Church of the United Brethren, arranged for Four Voices and the Organ or Piano-forte: to which are added Chants for the Litany of that Church and a Number of Approved Anthems for Various Occasions.* Bethlehem, Pa.: Moravian Publication Office, 1836.

_____. "The Cottager's Morning." Philadelphia; J. G. Klemm, n.d.

_____. "If That High World." Philadelphia: J. G. Klemm, n.d.

Wolle, Theodore. *Asleep in Jesus.* Bethlehem, Pa.: Comenius Press, 1897.

## Newspapers

*Allentown Morning Call*, 1937.
*Bethlehem Daily Times* [also *Bethlehem Times*], 1873–1905.
*Bethlehem Globe* [also *The Globe*], 1882–1962.
*Boston Evening Transcript*, 1915.
*The Brown and White*, 1896–1914.

*Church Standard*, 1905.
*Easton Weekly Press*, 1915.
*Evening Telegraph*, 1904.
*The Greensborough Patriot* [also *The Patriot and Flag*], 1850–1865.
*The Lehigh Burr*, 1889–1901.
*The Moravian*, 1857–1933.
*Musical Courier*, 1904–1915.
*New York Herald,* 1905.
*New York Outlook,* 1914.
*New York Sun*, 1903.
*New York Times* 1903.
*New York Tribune*, 1901–1904.
*North American*, 1903.
*Philadelphia Inquirer*, 1904.
*Philadelphia Press*, 1901–1904.
*Philadelphia Record*, 1904.
*Public Ledger*, 1903–1914.
*St. Louis Republic*, 1904.
*Times Star*, 1905.
*Zeitschrift der International Musikgesellshaft Leipzig*, 1903–1904.

## Secondary Sources: Books

Asti, Martha Secrest. "The Moravian Music of Christian Gregor (1723–1801): His Anthems, Arias, Duets, and Chorales." Ph.D. diss., University of Miami, 1983.
Baker, Mary Taylor. "Wolle Genealogy." n.d.
Blume, Fredrick., ed. *Die Musik in Geschishte und Geganwart*. Band 13. Kassel: Bärenreiter, 1966.
Bowen, Catherine Drinker. *History of Lehigh University*. Bethlehem, Pa.: Times Publishing Company, 1924.
Caldwell, Alice May. "Music of the Moravian 'Liturgishe Gesange' (1791–1823): From Oral to Written Tradition." Ph.D. diss., New York University, 1987.
Cerson, Robert A. *Music In Philadelphia*. Westport, Conn.: Greenwood Press, 1970.

_____. *Constitution of* [sic] *By-Laws of the Bethlehem Choral Union Adopted September 1885.* Bethlehem, Pa.: The Comenius Press, 1885.

Cumnock, Francis. *Catalogue of the Salem Congregation Music.* Chapel Hill: The University of North Carolina Press, 1980.

David, Hans T. *Musical Life in the Pennsylvania Settlements of the Unitas Fratrum.* Winston-Salem, N.C.: The Moravian Music Foundation, 1959.

_____. Albert Rau [coauthors]. *A Catalogue of American Moravian Music 1742–1842.* Bethlehem, Pa.: The Moravian Seminary and College for Women, 1938.

Duffiled, Samuel Willoughby. *English Hymns: Their Authors and History.* New York; Funk & Wagnalls, 1886.

Edmunds, Mary Lewis Rucker. *Letters From Edgeworth.* Greensboro, N.C.: 1988.

Freise, Adelaide, L. *Records of the Moravians in North Carolina.* Vol. 7. Raleigh: State Department of Archives and History, 1974.

Gatens, William J. Victorian Cathedral Music in Theory and Practice. Cambridge University Press, 1986.

Grider, Rufus J. *Historical Notes on Music in Bethlehem, Pa.* Winston-Salem: The Moravian Music Foundation, 1957.

Guion, David M. *The Trombone Its History and Music.* New York: Gordon and Breach, 1988.

Hacker, H. H. *Nazareth Hall an Historical Sketch and Roster of Principals, Teachers and Pupils.* Bethlehem, Pa.: Times Publishing Co., 1910.

Hall, Harry Horbart. "The Moravian Wind Ensemble: Distinctive Chapter in America's Music Volumes I and II." Unpublished Ph.D. diss., George Peabody College for Teachers (1967).

Haller, Mabel. *Early Moravian Education in Pennsylvania.* Nazareth, Pa.: Moravian Historical Society, 1963.

Hartsell, Lawrence W. *Ohio Moravian Music.* Winston-Salem, N.C.: The Moravian Music Foundation Press, 1988.

H[ilda] D[oolittle]. *The Gift.* New York, New York: A New Direction Book, 1982.

Heintze, James R. ed. *American Musical Life in Context and Practice.* New York: Garland, 1994.

Henry, James. *Sketches of Moravian Life and Character.* Philadelphia: J.B.

Lippincott, 1859.

Hessen, Robert. *Steel Titan the Life of Charles M. Schwab.* New York, New York: Oxford University Press, 1975.

Hitchcock, H. Wiley and Stanley Sadie, eds. *The New Groves Dictionary of American Music.* London: Macmillian, 1986.

Johnson, Earl. ed. *First Performances in America to 1900.* Detroit: College Music Society, 1979.

Jordan, John W. *Encyclopedia of Pennsylvania Biography.* Vol. III. New York: Lewis Historical Publication Co., 1914.

_____. *Historic Homes and Institutions and Genealogical & Personal Memoirs of the Lehigh Valley Penna.* Vol. 1. N.Y.: The Lewis Publishing Corp., 1905.

LaTrobe, John Antes. *The Music of the Church.* London: R.B. Seeley and W. Burnside, 1831.

Levering, Joseph Mortimore. *A History of Bethlehem, Pennsylvania, 1741–1892.* Bethlehem, Pa.: Times Publishing Co., 1903.

Mack, Elmer L. *Why a Bach Choir in Bethlehem.* Bethlehem, Pa.: Printed privately, 1973.

Malone, Dumas. ed. *The Dictionary of American Biography.* XX. New York: Charles Scribner's Sons, 1936.

Martin, Alfred. *Historical Sketch of Bethlehem in Pennsylvania with some Account of the Moravian Church.* Philadelphia: John L. Pile, 1873.

Moore, William J., ed. *Greensboro.* Woodland Hills, Ca.: Windsor Publishers, n.d.

Morris, Harry T., ed. *50 Year Book.* Bethlehem, Pa.: Times Publishing Co., 1941.

Morrison, Ernest. *Sing, Harrisburg, Sing.* Mechanicsburg, Pa.: W & M Printing, 1987.

Mussulman, Joseph A. *Music in the Cultured Generation.* Evanston: Northwestern University Press, 1971.

_____. *Nachrichten aus der Brueder-Gemeine 1842.* Gnadau: 1842.

_____. *Official Programme of Exposition Concerts Chicago May–October, 1893.* n.p.

Ogden, John C. *Excursion Into Bethlehem & Nazareth in Pennsylvania in the Year 1799: With a Succinct History of the Society of the United Brethren, Community Called Moravians.* Philadelphia: Charles Cist, 1800.

Parker, John R. *A Musician's Biography: or Sketches of the Lives and Writing of Eminent Musical Characters.* Boston: Stone and Fovel, 1824

Pfatteicher, Philip H. *Commentary on the Lutheran Book of Worship.* Minneapolis: Augsburg Fortress, 1990.

_____. *Program of the Memorial Service in Memory of Dr. J. Fred. Wolle.* n.p., n.d.

_____. *Register of Lehigh University,* 1894–1895, 1898–1899, 1904–1905.

Reichel, William C. *Historical Sketch of Nazareth Hall from 1755 to 1869.* Philadelphia: J.B.Lippincott & Co., 1869.

_____, and Wm. Digler. *A History of the Moravian Seminary for Young Ladies at Bethlehem, Pa.* Lancaster, Pa.: The New Ear Printing Company, 1901.

_____. *A History of the Rise, Progress, and Present Condition of the Moravian Seminary for Young Ladies at Bethlehem, Pa.* J.B. Lippincott & Co., 1881.

Robinson, James. *The Bach Choir in Bethlehem, Pa.* n.p., n.d.

Rocker, Mary Lewis. *Letters From Edgeworth.* Greensboro, N.C., n.p., 1988.

Rohrer, Gertrude, Martin. *Music and Musicians of Pennsylvania.* Port Washington, N.Y.: Kennikat Press, 1940.

Sadie, Stanley, ed. *The New Grove Dictionary of Music and Musicians.* London: Macmillan, 1980.

Seadle, Peter S. and Irene P. "The Diaries of Peter Wolle." *The Three Forks of Muddy Creek,* 10. Winston-Salem: Old Salem, Inc., 1984.

Steelman, Robert. *Catalogue of the Lititz Congregation Collection.* Chapel Hill:University of North Carolina, 1981.

Stevenson, Robert. *Protestant Church Music in America.* New York: W.W. Norton, 1966.

Strauss, Barbara Jo. "A Register of Music Performed in Concert, Nazareth, Pennsylvania from 1796–1845: an Annotated Edition of An American Moravian Document." Master's thesis, University of Arizona, 1976.

Surratt, Jey L. *Gottlieb Schober of Salem.* Macon, Ga.: Mercer University Press, 1983.

Thomas, Rose Fay. *Memoirs of Theodore Thomas.* New York: Moffat, Yard and Co., 1911.

_____. *Two Centuries of Nazareth 1740–1940.* Nazareth, Pa.: Nazareth Pennsylvania Bicentennial, Inc., 1940.

Walters, Raymond. *The Bethlehem Bach Choir.* Boston, Houghton Mifflin, 1918.

Wienandt, Elwyn A. *Choral Music of the Church.* New York: Free Press, 1965.

Wolle, Francis [Rec.], *Desmoids of the United States and List of American Pediastrums with Eleven Hundred Illustrations of Fifty-Three Colored Plates.* Bethlehem, Pa.: Moravian Publications Office, 1884.

Wolle, Francis. *A Moravian Heritage.* Boulder, Colorado; Empire Reproduction & Printing Co., 1972.

Worcester, Elwood. *Life's Adventure.* New York: Charles Scribner's Sons, 1923.

Yates, Ross. *Bethlehem of Pennsylvania the Golden Years.* Bethlehem, Pa.: Lehigh Litho, 1976.

———. *Lehigh University A History of Education in Engineering, Business, and the Human Condition.* Bethlehem, Pa.: Lehigh University Press, 1992.

———. *Sermon in Stone Packer Memorial Church.* Bethlehem, Pa.: Lehigh University, 1988.

## Articles

Gibson, Linda S., "Toward a Description of Teacher-Child Dispute Process in a Mainstream Nursery-Age Classroom; Negotiating Rules and Relationships," unpublished paper presented at the 15th Annual Ethnography in Education Research Forum, Feb. 1994, Philadelphia: University of Pennsylvania.

Hark, Ann. "The American Renaissance of Johann Sebastian Bach," *The Etude,* August 1935.

Jones, Perry. "The Bach Choir Approaches its Centennial," *Choral Journal,* 34/9, 1994.

Kroeger, Karl. "A David Mortiz Michael's Psalm 103. *Moravian Music Foundation Bulletin,* 21, 2, 1976.

Leaver, Robin. "New Light on the Pre-History of the Bach Choir of Bethlehem," *Journal of Riemenschneider Bach Institute,* 22, 2, 1991.

———. "The Revival of the St. John Passion: History and Performance Practice," *American Choral Review,* 31/1, 1989.

———. "Two Pupils of Rheinberger and Their Use of the Organ in Performance of Bach's *St. John Passion.*" *The Tracker,* 33.

Mann, Alfred. "*Zur maehrischen Bachpflege in Amerika,*" *Bachiana Ed Alia Musicologia,* 1983.

McCorkle, Donald M. "Prelude to a History of American Moravian Organs." *American Guild of Organists,* October (1958), reprints.

Nelson, Vernon H. "J. Fred Wolle's Hymns." Unpublished paper read at the Third Annual Moravian Music Conference, Moravian College, Bethlehem, Pa., 1998.

Nolte, Ewald V. "Christian Ignatius Latrobe on The Practice of Sacred Music" *The Moravian Music Foundation Bulletin,* 11, Fall 1966.

Rau, Albert. "Development of Music in Bethlehem, Pennsylvania." *Transactions of the Moravian Historical Society,* 13, 1944.

Summerville, Suzanne. "Johann Ludwig Freydt: Music Teacher to the Congregations." *The Moravian Music Foundation Bulletin,* 22, 2.

# Index

Alberti bass, 74
Alexanderia, Virginia, 49
Anders, John D., 83
*Arietta*, 72, 73
"Asleep in Jesus," 153–58, 160
Augmented sixth chords, 78

Bach, Johann, S., 152, 171, 175, 184–88, 192–94, 207, 210–17, 219–32, 237, 247–50, 296, 298–304, 306–9, 313–14, 317, 331
Baltimore, Md., 49
Barby, Germany, 38
Bechler, John, 38–39, 41–43, 84
Beck, Charlotte, 179
Beethoven, Lugwig van, 59, 100, 134, 136, 139, 171, 186, 297, 314, 317
Bellini, Giovanni, 134
Bethania, N.C., 49, 67, 98
Bethlehem: Choral Union, 183, 196–99, 222–24; Iron Company, 131, 184; Oratorical Society, 217–19, 276, 346, 350; Steel Company, 318
Bishop, Henry, 139
Bible, 27, 28, 31, 42
"Blandwood," 114, 119
Boys' Choir, 32

Brahms, Johannes, 185
Brown, Caroline, 174, 175
Bruch, Max, 209
*Bruedergemeine*, 22
Buelow, Hans von, 185
Bull, Ole, 174

Carnegie, Andrew, 307, 367
Carnegie Hall, 309, 367
Central Moravian Church [Bethlehem], 112, 133, 146, 147, 171, 187, 196, 199, 202–4, 226, 229, 253, 288–90, 294, 297, 297–98, 313–14, 346, 353, 361, 369, 371
Chabrier, Emmanuel, 317
Chapel Hill, N.C., 49
Chicago World's Fair. *See* World's Columbian Exposition
Childrens' choir, 111
Choir system, 32
Chopin, Frederic, 134, 136, 139, 293, 317
Civil War, 97–99, 120, 121, 125, 130, 132, 133, 139–40
"Come, Joyful Hallelujahs Raise," 74, 75, 110
Comenius, Johan Amos, 56
Coppola, Pietro A., 118
Cleaver, Albert, 351

*421*

Clewell, J. H., 348–49, 351–52
*Collegium musicum*, 29, 36, 37, 39, 41, 60, 65, 66, 100, 110–11, 135
Cummings, Mary Packer, 286

Daily text, 28
Darmosch, Franck, 240
Damrosch, Walter, 315, 367
Debussy, Claude, 317
Doles, Johann F., 37
Doolittle, Hilda, 175, 178–79, 288, 313
Doster, Ruth, 216, 218, 222–23
Dressler, Madame, 133, 138
Drinker, Henry, 342, 347, 351, 361, 362, 363
Dvořák, Antonin, 218, 317

Edgeworth Female Seminary, 114, 116–19, 122–23, 134
Eichner, Ernst, 37
Elgar, Edward, 293, 317
Entertainments, 100, 101, 134, 137, 230
Estes, William L., 350

Field, J. T., 296
Figured bass, 40–41, 80, 84–85
Fortepiano, 49, 55, 67, 80, 89, 101, 109, 114, 119, 176
"*Fuer Mich, O Herr,*" 76, 79

*Gemeinhaus*, Nazareth, Pa., 23
Genlick, Joseph, 59
Girls' Boarding School, Salem, N.C., 49
Glazounov, Alexander, 317

Globe Printing Company, 350
Gluck, Christoph, 317
God's Acre: Bethlehem, 171; Nazareth, Pa., 23, 25
Goldmark, Karl, 317
Gounod, Charles, 293
Graun, Karl H., 345
Greensborough Female Seminary, 113, 114, 116, 120
Greensborough, N.C., 113, 114, 120, 121, 122, 123, 130, 153
Gregor, Christian, 69, 72, 79, 84, 158, 331
Grider, Rufus, 140, 141
Grieg, Edvard, 317
Guilmant, Alexander, 293, 295, 302
Gyronwetz, A., 37

Hagen, Francis, 135
Handel, George F., 199, 204, 207, 287, 293, 301, 307, 314, 331
Harrisburg, 369
Haydn, Joseph, 38, 60, 71, 100, 115, 150, 170, 172, 176, 183, 194, 293, 297, 300, 317
"He Leads Us On," 335–38
Henderson, William, 239–41, 246, 250–55
Herman, Johann G., 56, 57
Hoch, Frank, 350
Hoffmeister, Franz Anton, 37
Hueffel, L., 84, 86
Huff, Asa, 350–52

Idealism, 140–41
Industrial Limestone Company,

350
Institute for the Deaf & Dumb, and Blind, Raleigh, N.C., 123–24

Jardine & Sons, 148

Klose, Edwin G., 206
Kotzeluch, Leopold, 59
Krehbiel, H. E., 239–41, 243, 246, 248–49, 251–52, 254–265, 271, 276–77

Lancaster, Pa., 48
Latrobe, Christian Ignatius, 39–40, 69–70, 75–76
Lehigh: Banjo Club, 311; Chapel Choir: 291–92, 296; River, 95, 298, 372; University, 96, 103, 118, 213, 227, 276, 291, 293–99, 304-5, 312, 332, 347, 348, 349–53; Valley Rail Road, 96, 131, 217, 286, 350
Lemines, Jaak Nickolas [?], 293
Lincoln, Abraham, 98
Lincolntown Female Seminary, 123
Linden Hall, 110
Linderman, Ruth, 361
Liszt, Franz, 134, 186, 187, 293, 317
Lititz, Pa., 86, 87, 110–13
Little Boys' Choir, 32, 33
Lot(s), 34
Love feast, 60, 62, 65, 287, 290

MacDowell, Edward, 317
Mackay, Margaret, 155

Mascagni, Peitro, 293
Massenet, Jules, 317
Melodeon, 99–100, 115, 118, 119, 171, 173
Mendelssohn, Felix, 100, 134, 136, 139, 172, 175, 187, 196, 202, 209, 293, 295, 296, 314
Mendelssohn Quintette Club, 136, 174
Merkel, Gustaf Adolf, 293
Michael, David Moritz, 33, 34, 36–38, 41–43, 48, 84
Moravian: College, 253, 313, 349; College for Women, 347–48; Historical Society, 344; Music Foundation 89; Parochial School, 142, 173, 177, 182, 183, 202, 207, 213, 218; Seminary for Girls, 110, 125, 132, 133, 134, 138, 139, 171, 172, 175, 177, 179, 180, 229, 353; Theological Seminary, 38, 43, 47, 111
Moehring, John, 21, 22, 25, 27, 102
Morandi, Rosa, 293
Morehead, John Motley, 114, 117, 121, 124
Morgan, G. W., 149, 151
Mozart, Wolfgang A., 37, 59, 71, 97, 134, 139, 172, 176, 187, 314, 317

Nazareth: Day School, 21, 22, 27, 29; Hall, 21, 22, 29, 32–33, 36–38, 42–44, 47, 71, 110, 111, 176; Theological Seminary, 43

Neapolitan sixth, 78
Neisky, Germany, 34
New York Oratorio Society, 229, 239, 346
Nicolai, Otto, 317
Nisky Hill Cemetery, 171

Organ, 30, 31, 39, 41, 52, 80, 11, 118, 135, 146–52, 161, 172, 175, 184, 187–89, 294–98, 299–304, 307–9

Packer, Asa, 286
Packer Memorial Church, 103, 279, 286, 293–96, 297–99, 305, 343, 347, 351, 352, 354, 369, 370, 371, 372
Paganini, Niccolo, 175
Parker, Horatio, 265
Pennsylvania and Lehigh Zinc Works, 95, 131
Peter, Johann Friedrick, 66
Philadelphia Academy of Music, 368
Philadelphia Orchestra, 246, 361, 368
Philharmonic Society, 100, 103, 112, 135, 136, 137, 140–45, 170, 173
Phiharmonic Society of New York, 367
Princeton University, 314
Pleyel, Ignatz, 37
Public examinations 31, 55
Pyrlaeus, John C., 179

Quarter hour, 27

Raff, Joachim, 136
Raleigh, N.C., 49, 130
Rameau, Jean P., 317
Rau, Albert, 344, 345
Rau, Robert, 155, 181-82
Rheinberger, Joseph, 186–89, 197–99, 202, 294
Richmond, Virginia, 121, 122
Richsecker, Flora, 182
Rimsky-Korsakov, Nicholai, 317
Rolling Mill and Foundry, 95, 96
Roosevelt, President and Mrs., 363
Root, George F., 182
Rossini, Gioacchino, 100, 151
Rubenstein, Anton, 307, 317
"Rules for Interludes," 41

Salem diary, 50
Salem, North Carolina, 49
Saint-Saëns, Camille, 317
Salisbury Band, 121
Sayre, William, 216–17
Schober, Charles, 121
Schober, Maria Theresa, 67
Schubert, Franz, 71, 134, 174, 293, 317
Schumann, Robert, 101, 139, 214, 293, 317
Schwab, Charles, 318, 346–47, 350, 362, 367–69, 372
Seidel, Elizabeth, [Wolle], 177–80
Seidel, Henry, 179–180
Selby, William, 295
Shelly, Howard, 293
Shields, T. Edgar, 239, 276, 298, 342, 346, 350

## INDEX

Shober, Henrietta R., 89
Single Brothers' Choir, 33, 34, 36–38, 42, 47, 56, 57, 67, 74
Single Sisters' Choir, 175
*Singstunde,* 28, 61, 62, 270, 287, 301, 305
Spohr, Louis, 100, 103, 293
Stainer, John, 296
St. Louis Exposition, 302–4

Stokowski, Leopold, 369
Strauss, Richard, 317
Suk, Josef, 317
Susedorff, Adelide Francesca, 125

Tannenberg, David, 39, 148
Tchaikovsky, Peter I., 317
Thalberg, Sigismond, 139
Thomas, Ambroise, 295
Thiele, Siegfried, 295
Trombone choir, 23, 25–26, 41, 60, 64, 67, 102, 133, 155, 160, 167–71, 173, 192, 250, 268, 269, 368, 369

Union Paper Bag Machine Co., 177
University of California, Berkeley, 275, 314–19, 346
University Chapel Choir [Lehigh], 291, 292, 296
University of Pennsylvania, 314

Wachovia, 49, 67
Wagner, Richard, 103, 187–88, 293, 294, 297, 301, 307, 314, 317, 342, 367, 371

Washington, D.C., 49, 368
Washington, George, 65
Weber, Karl M., 317
Weiss, Jedidiah, 68, 159, 167–70, 173–74
Weiss, Timothy, 174
Whitefield, James, 22
Widor, Charles-Marie, 293, 294, 296, 344
Wolle, Agnes, 192
Wolle, Augustus, 95–96, 102, 104, 136
Wolle, Christian J., 21
Wolle, Comenius, 95, 97
Wolle, Emma, 110
Wolle, Francis, 133, 141, 168, 171, 176–79
Wolle, Gretchen, 358, 360, 372
Wolle, Hartley, 185
Wolle, Helen [Doolittle], 172
Wolle, James, 68, 95, 99, 111–13, 133, 136
Wolle, Jennie, 319, 352, 370–72
Wolle, J. Samuel, 192
Wolle Sylvester, 133
Wolf, Hugo, 317
Wood, David, 149–52, 184–86, 229
Worcester, Elwood, 306
World's Columbian Exposition, 299–302, 304–5

York, Pa., 369
Young Boys' Choir, 111

Zinzendorf, Ludwig von, 21, 28, 56, 71, 360